T0328931

High-Performance Coaching for Managers

"In a world that has become increasingly complex, organizations are looking to their managers to set higher standards of performance for their employees. William Rothwell and Behnam Bakhshandeh do a stellar job of explaining how to do this through performance coaching by describing what it is and how it can be used to achieve results. This book provides practical and research-based guidance on coaching employees regarding what they should do, how they should behave, and how best to measure success. This will be a great resource to any organization attempting to increase overall productivity and performance on the job".

Marsha G. King, PhD
Director, Leadership Coaching Certification Program
Center for Leadership and Organization Effectiveness
School of Management, University at Buffalo

"In today's world, there has been an unprecedented influx and demand for coaching, where self-proclaimed professional and personal coaches can be found in every other corner. Even without an official title most managers and leaders, need to play the role of coach to fully unleash their people's performance and potential. Whatever your role may be, many coaches lack a structured approach and practical tools to deliver effective coaching. *High-Performance Coaching for Managers* gives managers and coaches alike a unique practical step by step paradigm to unleashing high performance from their employees and is a must read for anyone looking to take their coaching to new heights."

Rani Salman
Managing Partner at Caliber Consulting

"I am excited for this book to be published and to be shared with the full spectrum of managers, clients, and talent development professionals.

Rothwell and Bakhshandeh focus on a very specific use of performance coaching, and I believe the profession will benefit and come to understand a facet of coaching in a much more concrete way".

Ethan S. Sanders
President and CEO
Sundial Learning Systems, Inc.

"If you think of someone you've worked with or for that you consider to be a great leader, they were also likely a great coach. Great leaders are great coaches. *High-Performance Coaching for Managers* provides a comprehensive and practical approach to building a culture of coaching in order to unleash the full potential of today's workforce."

Steve King
VP, Chief Learning & Talent Officer
Rich Products Corporation

As a person who operates in the various states of coaching outlined in this book, I found each chapter insightful and intuitive. The text will serve as an excellent fundamental foundation for new and experienced coaches. Rothwell and Bakhshandeh have provided a roadmap for those walking on the coaching path!

Jamie Campbell
Assistant Dean, Diversity Enhancement Programs
Smeal College of Business
CEO Action for Racial Equity Fellow

High-Performance Coaching for Managers

A Step-by-Step Approach to Increase Employees' Performance and Productivity

William J. Rothwell

647 Berkshire Drive
State College, PA 16803
Phone: 814–441–4087
Email: williamjrothwell@rothwellandassociates.com
or wjr9@psu.edu

Behnam Bakhshandeh

195 Crystal Park Blvd.
Greenfield Township, PA 18407
Phone: 760–518–9804
Emails: Behnam@PrimecoEducation.com
or bzb9@psu.edu

With a Foreword by
Ethan Sanders

President and CEO
Sundial Learning Systems, Inc.

Routledge
Taylor & Francis Group

NEW YORK AND LONDON
ROUTLEDGE/ A PRODUCTIVITY PRESS BOOK

First published 2023
by Routledge
605 Third Avenue, New York, NY 10158

and by Routledge
4 Park Square, Milton Park, Abingdon, Oxon, OX14 4RN

Routledge is an imprint of the Taylor & Francis Group, an informa business

ISBN: 978-0-367-74060-3 (hbk)
ISBN: 978-0-367-74058-0 (pbk)
ISBN: 978-1-003-15592-8 (ebk)

DOI: 10.4324/9781003155928

Typeset in Garamond
by Apex CoVantage, LLC

William J. Rothwell dedicates this book to his wife *Marcelina*, his daughter *Candice*, his son *Froilan*, his grandsons *Aden* and *Gabriel*, and his granddaughters *Freya* and *Lina*.

Behnam Bakhshandeh dedicates this book to his three children: his daughters *Poneh (Renee)* and *Shima* and his son *Behzad*, and his two beautiful grandchildren: grandson *Gabriel (Behrouz)* and granddaughter *Darya*.

Contents

PHASE THREE—ANALYZING THE SOLUTION

PHASE FOUR—IMPLEMENTATION AND EVALUATION

SUPPORT, MAINTENANCE, SELF-EVALUATION, AND SELF-RATING

Foreword

I have spent a large portion of my career trying to convince clients that they should keep three important concepts in mind: (1) Training is not a panacea to all performance issues; (2) Classroom training is a small part of the learning universe; and (3) If you put a good performer in a bad system, the system wins every time (credit to Dr. Geary Rummler for this most appropriate of sayings). While I cannot trace these concepts to any particular event in my career, I know that they crystalized in my mind when I had the extraordinary opportunity to work on two ASTD Competency studies with Bill Rothwell (*ASTD Models for Human Performance Improvement* in 1996 and *ASTD Models for Workplace Learning and Performance* in 1999). Bill and I were literally trying to redefine the profession which was rapidly changing and growing more complex by the moment. Without question, it was my years working at ASTD and conversing with Bill that launched me into a meandering journey to better understand how organizational systems work, how leaders effect these systems, what the role of a consultant truly is, and how do we affect change in organizations that are often entrenched in counterproductive practices.

I have often wondered about the true success rate of performance consultants. I have dreamt about a study that calculated the batting average of all performance consulting projects in the past 50 years. The closest I got to this answer was when I was fortunate enough to work for the US Navy's Human Performance center, where we attempted Performance Consulting on a historic scale. While I witnessed a great number of successes, I also saw countless interventions that were well conceived, well designed, and utterly ignored when it came to implementation. For most of my career, I've believed that success in consulting is primarily predicated on the skill and the influence of the consultant themselves. However, in recent years, I have begun to see that a lot of what dictates success is the temperament of the client, the willingness of the stakeholders to change, and the availability of data to answer fundamental questions about the goal and the root causes.

When I was asked to review this book, I assumed it would be a fresh view of what makes coaches successful. As I reviewed the manuscript, I was immediately struck by the discussion of "performance consultant versus performance coach." In my mind, coaching has always been one of those "other learning interventions" beyond formal training, but it wasn't necessarily related to the practice of performance consulting. What I didn't expect was this idea that directive coaching is a specific technique that managers (and consultants) can use to help their employees improve performance and learn from the manager's expertise. I should disclose that part of my mindset about coaching is influenced by the fact that I am married to a psychotherapist. Prior to this book I believed that like a great therapist, coaches should not provide answers or insights; instead, they should lead people to their own conclusions and discoveries. Essentially that should act as a mirror by helping people reflect on their own mindsets and belief, until they reach new insights. The more I delved into this book, the more brilliant I realized it was. Perhaps, one of the reasons we struggle at times as performance consultants is because we aren't doing enough to help the client learn and grow. The mere fact that performance consultant call their counterparts "clients" and not "coachees" might indicate that we see our job as serving their needs and interests, rather than helping them become smarter.

I've always been a huge proponent of Action Learning, and I believe strongly that teams only get better when they get smarter. It is the reflective nature of Action Learning (through the Socratic method) that helps the team get smarter and ultimately to gain better insights and make better decisions. Rothwell and Bakhshandeh have taken a similar idea and applied it in a revolutionary way. As they point out in the opening chapters of this book, it is the idea of one-on-one work between a coach and a coachee that truly holds the promise of improving performance. Layered onto this idea is the notion that the supervisor can act in this directive coaching capacity. On the very day that I read Chapters 1 and 2 of this book, I was working on a manager's course for one of my clients, and we were discussing how realistic it is to suggest that every manager could be a coach to their subordinates. Years ago I had read some very interesting research that indicated that coaching was highly dependent on "chemistry" between the coach and the coachee. In fact, it was suggested that most people would need to try out multiple coaches before they found one that they truly connected with (again, similar to the advice we give people when seeking out a therapist). If this is true, then it is not realistic to think most managers will be the right fit to be an employee's coach, and in fact, a manager's positional authority (in particular that they have the right to judge the employee on their performance) might actually preclude them from acting in a coaching capacity.

By introducing the notion of "directive coaching" versus "non-directive coaching," I believe that the authors have cracked the code on how coaching can be appropriate in a variety of circumstances. When I think of my own relationships with my team and how much of my effort is involved in coaching versus "managing," it all seems to make sense. For most of my employees, I am (and I hope they are) quite comfortable acting in this directive coaching mode. I do have thirty years of experience in the field, I've seen our profession from a variety of vantage points, and I enjoy seeing people benefit from my experience. However, I also have a few employees who I feel responsible for helping them figure out their career goals and aspirations. One in particular began as my graduate student and then worked for me in several organizations. In this relationship, we are comfortable in both the directive and nondirective modes; with me offering my experience around specific tasks and outcomes, and at times helping them reflect on their career and their future. Of course, I would offer this same opportunity to any employee who asked for my help, but it seems to have just grown organically in this circumstance.

I am excited for this book to be published and to be shared with the full spectrum of managers, clients, and talent development professionals. By focusing on a very specific use of performance coaching, I believe the profession will benefit and come to understand a facet of coaching in a much more concrete way. I hope that many talent development professionals will weave these concepts into their courses and other learning experiences.

I feel fortunate to have known Bill Rothwell for so many years and I have enjoyed getting to know Behnam as we collaborated on this foreword.

Ethan Sanders
President and CEO
Sundial Learning Systems, Inc

Preface

Coaching has grown to be highly popular. Many people find themselves needing a helping hand or find themselves thrust in the role of offering advice to others. That is especially true of managers who, while conducting performance reviews, may find a need to provide specific feedback and advice about what to do to improve job performance to those employees reporting to them.

The Purpose of the Book

This book offers a step-by-step, systematic approach to high-performance coaching. While many approaches to coaching could help to facilitate performance improvement, the authors of this book favor a planned approach to coaching that is geared to helping others identify what they need to do to improve their job performance.

An effective high-performance coaching effort meets the needs of the organization and its people. It relies on a positive view of people and a strong effort to encourage participation and inclusion in all aspects of the coaching experience.

The Target Audience for the Book

This book provides a comprehensive, step-by-step approach to implement a high-performance coaching effort for human resource practitioners, consultants, managers, and others who are interested in managing and improving human performance.

This book is thus written for anyone who seeks to improve human performance for themselves or others.

The Organization of the Book

This book is organized in a step-by-step approach. It is meant to track what a high-performance coach or a manager-as-coach must do to facilitate coaching.

Examined in more detail, the book consists of a **Preface** to summarize the book, an **Acknowledgments** to thank contributors, an **Advance Organizer** to help readers assess chapters they may wish to focus, and a summary of the **Authors' Biosketches**.

The book is organized in six major parts. The first part sets the context and is entitled "**Building a Strong Foundation for High-Performance Coaching Journey**." It consists of three chapters. **Chapter 1** describes the general concept of coaching; **Chapter 2** defines and describes performance coaching; and **Chapter 3** describes the mindset, attitude, behavior, and performance of a performance coach.

The second part is called "**Phase One—Building Relationship and Recognizing the Situation**." It is composed of three chapters. **Chapter 4** describes the first step in performance coaching: How to establish relatedness and building rapport? **Chapter 5** describes the second step: What is the issue at hand? **Chapter 6** reviews the third step: What should be happening?

The third part is called "**Phase Two—Analyzing the Gap**." In the three chapters of this part, **Chapter 7** (step 4 of performance coaching) poses this question: What is the measurable gap? **Chapter 8** poses this question: How important is the gap? **Chapter 9** poses this question: What are the root causes of the gap?

The fourth part, called "**Phase Three—Analyzing the Solution**," has three chapters. **Chapter 10** poses the question guiding step 7 of performance coaching: How many ways can the gap be closed? **Chapter 11** poses the question guiding step 8: What is the most effective way to close the gap? **Chapter 12** poses the question guiding step 9: What are the consequences of closing the gap?

The fifth part is "**Phase Four—Implementation and Evaluation**." **Chapter 13**, which reviews step 10 of performance coaching, examines this question" What are the damages of inaction? **Chapter 14** looks at step 11: How to implement the solution? And, finally, **Chapter 15** addresses step 12 of performance coaching: How to evaluate the successful implementation?

The sixth and final part of the book is called "**Support, Maintenance, and Self-Evaluation**." **Chapter 16**, the last chapter of the book, examines such questions as these: How effective are you? How do you know if you are effective and productive? Maintaining and implementing learned disciplines and providing opportunities for high-performance coaches self-evaluations and self-ratings. An **Appendix** reviews sources for education and implementations that will take readers to additional places that can broaden and deepen their understanding of performance coaching.

Acknowledgments

William J. Rothwell would like to express his special thanks to Behnam Bakhshandeh for establishing the project plan, setting up our deadlines, and successfully managing the project to its completion.

Behnam Bakhshandeh would like to express his gratitude to William J. Rothwell for his vast knowledge of organization development and all related fields and his contributions to his growth advancement. Thank you for all of your contributions to academia and all related field of Workforce Education and Development.

Both authors like to express their special gratitude to Mr. Farhan Sadique for his masterful work in compiling the Appendix of Resources at the end of this book.

William J. Rothwell
State College, Pennsylvania
November 2021

Behnam Bakhshandeh
Greenfield Township, Pennsylvania
November 2021

Authors

William J. Rothwell, PhD, SPHR, SHRM-SCP, RODC, CPLP Fellow

William J. Rothwell is a professor in the Masters of Professional Studies in Organization Development and Change program and also in the PhD program of Workforce Education and Development at The Pennsylvania State University. He has authored, coauthored, edited, or coedited 127 books since 1987.

His recent books since 2017 include *Organization Development (OD) Interventions: Executing Effective Organizational Change* (Routledge, 2021); *Virtual Coaching to Improve Group Relationships: Process Consultation Reimagined* (Routledge, 2021); *The Essential HR Guide for Small Business and Start Ups* (Society for Human Resource Management, 2020); *Increasing Learning and Development's Impact Through Accreditation* (Palgrave, 2020); *Workforce Development: Guidelines for Community College Professionals*, 2nd ed. (Rowman-Littlefield, 2020); *Human Performance Improvement: Building Practitioner Performance*, 3rd ed. (Routledge, 2018); *Innovation Leadership* (Routledge, 2018); *Evaluating Organization Development: How to Ensure and Sustain the Successful Transformation* (CRC Press, 2017); *Marketing Organization Development Consulting: A How-To Guide for OD Consultants* (CRC Press, 2017); and *Assessment and Diagnosis for Organization Development: Powerful Tools and Perspectives for the OD practitioner* (CRC Press, 2017).

He can be reached by email at WjRothwell@yahoo.com or by phone at 814–863–2581. He is at 310B Keller Building, University Park, PA 16803. See his website at www.rothwellandassociates.com, his videos on YouTube, and his wiki site at https://en.wikipedia.org/wiki/William_J._Rothwell

Behnam Bakhshandeh, PhD, MPS

Behnam's formal education includes a PhD in the Workforce Education and Development (WFED) with concentration on Organization Development (OD) and Human Resources Development (HRD) from the Pennsylvania State University, a master's degree in Professional Studies in Organization Development and Change (OD&C) from the Pennsylvania State University, World Campus, and a bachelor's degree in Psychology from the University of Phoenix.

He is also the founder and president of Primeco Education, Inc. (www. PrimecoEducation.com) a coaching and consulting company working with individuals, teams, and organizations on their personal and professional development since 1993. He has authored and published three books in the personal and professional development industry. His last book is *Organization Development Intervention* (Routledge, Taylor & Francis Group, 2021). The other two titles are *Anatomy of Upset; Restoring Harmony* (Primeco Education, 2015) and *Conspiracy for Greatness; Mastery of Love Within* (Primeco Education, 2009). Besides these books, he has designed and facilitated seventeen coaching modules for individuals, couples, public, teams, and organizations; 9 audio/video workshops; sixteen Articles on personal and professional development topics, and twenty one seminars and workshops.

He is an accomplished business manager, known widely as a dynamic writer, speaker, personal, and professional development coach and trainer. Implementing his skills as a passionate, visionary leader, he produces extraordinary results in record time. Behnam brings his broad experience and successful track record to each project, whether it involves personal development, implementing customer-focused programs, integrating technologies, redesigning operational core processes, or delivering strategic initiatives.

Before designing Primeco Education technology, Behnam led educational programs and later managed operations for a global education organization based in two major US cities. During these seven years, Behnam worked personally with tens of thousands of participants. He was accountable for expanding customer participation, training program leaders, increasing sales, and improving the finance department's efficiency and management of the overall operations for the staff and their team of over 400 volunteers, who together served an annual client base of over 10,000.

Behnam designed the Primeco Education technology in 2001. Since then, he and his team members have helped countless businesses and individuals not only to achieve their goals but also to transform their thinking. His proven methodology and approach are based on his extensive experience in business and human relations. Behnam enjoyed expanding into psychology as an addition to his already strong background in philosophy and ontology. He particularly enjoyed and was inspired by Applicative Inquiry, Positive Psychology and the work of many psychologists who used the Humanistic Psychology approach for empowering and treating their patients. Behnam finds these two psychological approaches very similar to his own work, methodology, and approaches.

He can be reached by email at Behnam@PrimecoEducation.com and by phone at 760–518–9804. He is at his office at 27 N. Main Street—Suite 202, Carbondale, PA 18407.

Advance Organizer

Complete the following Organizer before you read the book. Use it as a diagnostic tool to help you assess what you most want to know about performance coaching—and where you can find it in this book *fast*.

The Organizer

Directions

Read each item in the Organizer in the following. Spend about 10 minutes on the Organizer. Be honest! Think of performance coaching as you would like to practice it to help others improve their job performance. Then indicate what topics related to performance coaching you would like to learn more about so as to develop yourself professionally. For each item listed in the center column, indicate with a **Y (for Yes), N/A (for Not Applicable), or N (for No)** in the left column whether you would like to develop yourself in that area. When you finish, score and interpret the results using the instructions appearing at the end of the Organizer. Then be prepared to share your responses with others you know to help you think about what you most want to learn about performance coaching. If you would like to learn more about an item, refer to the number in the right column to find the chapter in this book in which the subject is discussed.

The Questions

Circle Your Response for Each Item Below	I Would Like to Develop Myself to:	Chapter in the Book in Which the Topic is Covered:
Y N/A N 1.	Know more about the general concept of coaching.	1
Y N/A N 2.	Know about *performance coaching* specifically.	2
Y N/A N 3.	Know more about the mindset, attitude, behavior and performance to do performance coaching effectively.	3
Y N/A N 4.	Address this question: *How to establish relatedness and build rapport at the outset of performance coaching?*	4
Y N/A N 5.	Address this question: *What is the issue at hand?*	5
Y N/A N 6.	Address this question: *What should be happening?*	6
Y N/A N 7.	Address this question: *What is the measurable gap?* 7	7
Y N/A N 8.	Address this question: *How important is the gap?*	8
Y N/A N 5.	Address this question: *What are the root causes of the gap?*	9
Y N/A N 10.	Address this question: *How many ways can the gap be closed?*	10
Y N/A N 11.	Address this question: *What is the most effective way to close the gap?*	11
Y N/A N 12.	Address this question: *What are the consequences of closing the gap?*	12
Y N/A N 13.	Address this question: *What are the damages of inaction?*	13
Y N/A N 14.	Address this question: *How can the solution be implemented?*	14

Y N/A N 15.	Address this question: How can the success of the *implementation be evaluated?*	15
Y N/A N 16.	Address this question: *How effective are you as a performance coach?*	16
Total		

Scoring and Interpreting the Organizer

Give yourself *1 point for each* Y and a *0 for each N or N/A* listed above. Total the points from the *Y* column and place the sum in the line opposite to the word **TOTAL** above. Then interpret your score as follows:

Score		
16–14	=	Congratulations! This book is just what you need.
Points		Read the chapters you marked *Y.*
13–11	=	You have great skills in performance coaching already,
Points		but you also have areas where you could develop
		professionally. Read those chapters marked *Y.*
10–8	=	You have some skills in performance coaching, but you could
Points		still benefit to build skills in selected areas.
7–0	=	You believe you do not need much development in
Points		performance coaching. Ask others—such as mentors—to see if they agree.

BUILDING A STRONG FOUNDATION FOR HIGH-PERFORMANCE COACHING JOURNEY

It is an honor and a privilege for coaches to provide coaching for individuals, teams, organizations, and organizations' leadership. In whatever capacity, these individuals or organizations are placing their trust in the coaches, as internal managers-as-coaches or as external coaches such as Organization Development (OD), Human Resources Development (HRD), Workplace Learning & Performance (WLP), Training and Development (T&D) trainers, facilitators, or consultants. In all these cases, coaches' skills and competencies make a difference in developing the intent of coaching undertaken. The primary purpose of this book is to:

(1) educate a performance coach or a manager-as-coach in the concept of Performance Coaching and
(2) provide models, methods, and tools on how to conduct High-Performance Coaching.

The following three chapters provide a coaching background and what high-performance coaches need to know, develop, and deliver for their subordinates and coachees during the high-performance coaching journey.

DOI: 10.4324/9781003155928-1

Chapter 1—The General Concept of Coaching

What Is Coaching and Its Influence and Presence of Coaching on
Organizations?

Chapter 2—Performance Coaching

What Is Performance, Performance Coaching, and Performance
Management?

Chapter 3—Mindset, Attitude, Behavior, and Performance

How Individual's Mindset, Attitude, and Behavior Impact Individual and
Team Performance

Chapter 1

The General Concept of Coaching

Behnam Bakhshandeh

Understanding coaching—what it is, how it works, and what is at work during coaching—will help you convince executives how coaching will contribute to their professional growth. Coaching should interest any manager or to anyone in the human resource fields.

This chapter offers you a summary of what coaching is and what place it occupies in organizations. In this chapter, we define key terms and some general information about how coaching contributes to organizational productivity. This chapter shows how coaching can empower individuals, teams, and organizations to be more productive. It will lead into Chapter 2, which distinguishes performance coaching from other coaching categories. Chapter 1 addresses:

- What is coaching?
- Performance Coaching versus Performance Consultant
- What are different types of coaching?
- What is a coaching culture?
- How should coaching be used?
- What role does coaching play in talent development?
- How is coaching used in talent development?
- What do selected survey results reveal about coaching effectiveness?

DOI: 10.4324/9781003155928-2

What Is Coaching?

During the last few years, coaching has become popular. Despite coaching's popularity, few research publications have appeared about it—or about performance coaching. Still, many business writers tout coaching for how much it can help to increase organizational productivity and improve individual job performance.

General Definitions of Coaching

There are many definitions of coaching offered by varied professional associations. For example:

- The Association for Talent Development (ATD) defines coaching as "applying a systematic process to improve others' ability to set goals, take action, and maximize strengths" (ATD 2014a, 4).
- The International Coaching Federation (ICF) defines coaching as "using an interactive process to help individuals develop rapidly and produce results; improving others' ability to set goals, take action, make better decisions, and make full use of their natural strengths" (Arneson, Rothwell, and Naughton 2013, 5).
- Whitmore (2017) defined coaching as "unlocking people's potential to maximize their performance. It is helping them to learn rather than teaching them" (13).
- Cox, Bachkirova, and Clutterbuck (2014) described coaching as "a human development process that involves structured, focused interaction and the use of appropriate strategies, tools, and techniques to promote desirable and sustainable change for the benefit of the coachee and potentially for other stakeholders" (1).
- Berg and Karlsen (2007) described coaching as "the process of challenging and supporting a person or a team to develop ways of thinking, ways of being and ways of learning. The purpose is to achieve personal and/or organizational goals" (4).
- Saporito (1996) stated that "[c]oaching can help the leader to better understand and optimize her impact on the organizational transformation. Coaching can also facilitate leaders' commitment to the process and help to connect all development activities—individual and organizational— back to core business issues and needs" (96).

■ Bakhshandeh (2009) described and defined coaching as "a highly effective tool for individuals and organizations who choose to have their future realized now instead of someday. It is a systematic but non-linear inquiry into one's authenticity; it is for healthy, ambitious, brave, and open-minded people who strive for excellence" (35).

While specific definitions vary somewhat, it should be clear that coaching can be a powerful way to improve productivity. This book emphasizes the value of coaching.

The Prevalence of Coaching

Coaching has emerged as an important area of expertise for managers and human resource professionals. In 2004, while creating a competency context as a foundation for certification, the American Society for Training and Development (ASTD DBA Association for Talent Development 2014)—now called the Association for Talent Development (ATD)—designated coaching as a specialization area. Coaching remained one of ten elements of expertise in the 2013 version of the competency model of ASTD (Ellinger and Kim 2014). Coaching is widely used by business consultants, performance consultants, and OD practitioners to assist organizations in shaping their vision, achieving their missions, setting goals, carrying out staffing efforts, and improving job performance. Since the 1980s, many studies have been conducted on coaching in organizations. The findings of these studies have refined the concept of coaching, and it is now widely understood to mean a process in which a coach (personal or professional) and a coachee (an individual, a team, a business, or an organization) work in partnership to formulate goals and establish plans for improvement (Vidal-Salazar, Ferrón-Vílchez, and Cordón-Pozo 2012).

According to Arneson et al. (2013):

■ Over 27% of organizations have effectively integrated professional business coaching in their talent development portfolios.
■ By implementing coaching practices, 47% of organizations have recognized the skills of productive and successful managers.
■ Fewer than 46% of organizations have ignored coaching.

Establishing coaching cultures in organizations is one effective way to engage employees. A coaching approach to productivity improvement will enhance an organization's ability to leverage the abilities of the workforce. According to Downs (2017) and ATD (2014b), these statistics are worthy of note:

■ Eighty percent of employees engaged with coaching improved their communication, productivity, performance, and business management strategies.
■ Sixty-five percent of employees in organizations with a robust coaching environment grew more engaged with their work and other employees.
■ Organizations that focus on building coaching cultures reported higher revenue and employee engagement than those not focused on coaching.

The *ICF Global Coaching Client Study* published by iPEC (2020) reported that "[c]oaching is profoundly beneficial in the eyes of companies and individuals who hire a coach, with 99% viewing it as 'satisfied' or 'very satisfied' and 96% stating they'd repeat the process." In addition, *ICF Global Coaching Client Study* reported:

■ Over 33% of Fortune 500 companies employ Executive Coaching as their standard leadership development method (Source: The Hay Group).
■ When combining coaching with training, average individual productivity increased by 86%, when contrasted to 22% when only provided training (Source: The Personnel Management Association).
■ Nearly 86% of organizations who have utilized coaching favorably rated it for their investment in coaching, and their return on investment (ROI), by affirming that at the minimum, at least the coaching investment has paid for itself.

Many studies and reports are available for backing the use and benefit of coaching and its positive impact on individuals, teams, and organizations. Given the purpose of this book, we are just mentioning some of such reports that are related to productivity and performance.

On a special research and report conducted by Zhou (2020) on ROI of coaching, she provides the following summary:

■ Over 95% of coaching clients have rated their coaches' quality as "good" or "excellent." (Source: 2009 ICF Global Coaching Study).
■ Nearly 51% of organizations who established a robust coaching culture reported noticeably greater productivity and revenue compared to their industry peer businesses (Source: Human Capital Institute).

■ According to a study conducted by the *International Society for Performance Improvement,* coaching has a 221% return on investment (Source: International Society for Performance Improvement).

According to Coetzee (2018), a coaching survey conducted by *Clear Coaching Limited* in 2007 reported the following tangible benefits and increases in different areas from using coaching programs by a large range of organizations:

■ developed new skills or improved existing skills   by 50%
■ teams working relationships and connection   by 50%
■ noticed and considered others' perspectives   by 47%
■ clarity and improvement in work life   by 43%
■ increased individual motivation   by 43%
■ improved work environment   by 40%
■ increased sales and revenue   by 23%
■ attained their goals   by 20%

Furthermore, regarding the general benefits of coaching and the positive influence of coaching on individuals, Coetzee (2018) reported some statistics from a survey conducted by *The International Coaching Federation (ICF)* with 210 coaching clients about the use of coaching and values they have received from participating in coaching programs.

In this study, 197 out of 210 participants were employed professionals. All participants had at least nine months of an ongoing formal professional coaching relationship with a coach. Over 80% of the participants had undergraduate degrees, and over 33% had Master's degrees or higher advanced degrees. The study results:

■ reported business coaching as "very valuable"   70%
■ revealed sensitive information in their coach that had not been confined to their spouses, best friend, or even their therapist   50%
■ opened up to their coach more than anyone else at that time   12%

According to Coetzee (2018) and the study's findings, and according to the participants sharing information, some of the notable results of coaching were as follows:

■ designed smarter goal setting   62.4%
■ established more balance in their lives   60.5%

- brought down their stress levels   57.1%
- developed more self-confidence   52.4%
- improved their lives' quality   43.3%
- had more income   25.7%

Public Perceptions of Coaching

Coaching is often a term in search of a meaning. Many definitions exist of coaching. It bears many similarities to other efforts to develop workers. Coaching means working with individuals, teams, and organizations to create new practices while retiring unworkable behaviors.

Research conducted by the International Coaching Federation (ICF) has revealed that most people know coaching and have shaped impressions about it (ICF 2011). Based on many studies' findings, managerial coaching is defined as an effective supervisory practice that enhances workforce learning and performance.

Performance Coaching versus Performance Consulting

Given the close proximity and similar characteristics between coaching and consulting, there is some confusion among the public, businesses, and organizations about what Performance Coaching and Performance Consultants are or do. This distinction lies in the overall concept and differences between the terminologies of coaching and consulting. "Most dictionaries will not offer any great distinctions between the terms consulting and coaching. They are defined as the giving of advice, professional or otherwise, or instruction to those practicing in a profession" (Strosinski 2003, n.p.). However, both a consultant and a coach concentrate on assisting and helping their clients to resolve their business problems; the distinction, however, is their approach. Often, the lines between consulting and coaching get blurry and therefore create ineffective situations that do not serve the client and do not provide solutions for clients' needs (Forbes 2018).

Here are some differences between coaching and consulting by several professionals:

- "coaching is 'done with you' and consulting is 'done for you'" (ValuProp 2021, n.p.).
- Coaching usually consists of the coaches working directly with one or several individuals in an organization, but on a one-on-one basis while

consulting mostly consists of the consultants working with many people in the form of teams, groups, departments, or organizations (Indeed 2021).

■ Coaching involves developing the coachees' competencies and abilities by using tools and techniques to work out and resolve any issues by themselves. However, consulting includes assisting the clients getting to the bottom of their issues by providing consulting, training, and other form of workshops and exercises (Indeed 2021).

■ "Coaching can help turn an entrepreneur into a great leader. Consulting, on the other hand, provides that much-needed expertise and assistance" (Forbes 2018, n.p.).

■ The distinction between a coach and a consultant is the means by which they are informing and advising their clients. "As a consultant, your role is to enhance leadership and organizational capacity. A coach helps individual leaders develop clarity on what he or she needs to focus on and create action plans to achieve those goals" (Jordyn 2020, n.p.).

The following are some distinctions between performance coaching and performance consulting:

Performance Coaching

■ *Performance coaches* work with individuals. They focus on the individuals' future potential and maximize the coachees' performance with the main goal of maintaining the coachees' learning and retention instead of teaching them. Usually, performance coaching is practiced and delivered by managers-as-coaches, as an important tool or approach for enhancing the coachees' and employees' capacity and job/work performance (Strosinski 2003).

■ *Performance coaching* and training programs will advance job performance by "(1) improving individual abilities, (2) stimulating motivation, (3) matching individual ability to activity requirements, and/or (4) matching the individual to contextual requirements" (Rothwell and Kazanas 2003, 402).

■ In the context of managers/supervisors and employees/workforce relationship, *performance coaching* can be characterized simply as the support which managers/supervisors provide to their subordinates in appraising their job performance, including their behavior and attitude in order to increase their productivity and improve their performance effectiveness at their jobs and related tasks (Pfeiffer 1990).

- *Performance coaching* as a form of coaching and mentoring is increasingly becoming more attractive to organizations and businesses, showing more interest in developing their workforce in KSAs (knowledge, skills, and abilities) and competencies (Mcleod 2004).

Performance Consulting

- A *performance consultant* analyzes and assesses an organization's performance inconsistencies and work environment discrepancies regarding production outcomes and results. The performance consultants assist the organization's management to come up with a plan, or design the applicable procedures, techniques, and tools for enhancing teams, groups, and the departments' performance for that entire organization or workplace (Strosinski 2003). "The intended result often results in increased productivity, decreased costs, efficient and effective work practices and a safer working environment" (Strosinski 2003, 1).
- *Performance consulting* comprises recognizing and clarifying an organization's needs and offering training strategies and models that potentially would meet that specific need. However, not all organizational issues can or will be resolved by training. That being said, recognizing if training would be a solution is a critical process in conducting a performance consult (Training Industry 2018).
- *Performance consulting* is a form of assessing and evaluating an organization's current performance status of their operations, and it can offer some new approaches, practices, and procedures that the organization can implement in order to increase its productivity and become more effective (Berg and Karlsen 2012).
- The objective of *performance consulting* is to examine, analyze, and explain the process of the "how" and identifying the "what" that an organization needs or wants to undertake or achieve, that eventually would improve or increase the organizations' overall productivity and performance (Mcleod 2004).

Coaching Types

Coaching is based on trust. It can be targeted to individuals, teams, work groups, departments, and even organizations. Coaching is often categorized into two areas: (1) personal coaching and (2) professional coaching.

Personal Coaching

Some examples of personal coaching are: (1) life coaching, (2) couples coaching, (3) relationship coaching, (4) health and velocity coaching, (5) wealth and finance coaching, (6) spirituality coaching, and (7) mentorship.

Professional Coaching

Some examples of professional coaching are: (1) business coaching, (2) managers coaching, (3) executive coaching, (4) career coaching, (5) leadership development coaching, (6) team building, (7) performance coaching, (8) communication coaching, (9) vision, mission, and values coaching, (10) strategy and goal setting coaching, (11) feedback coaching, and (11) performance coaching.

In the professional coaching category, content can be delivered by one-on-one or group coaching. While sometimes called *peer coaching*, it is associated where managers or experienced coworkers offer advice to other workers. Coaching can also be offered to groups in so-called *team coaching*

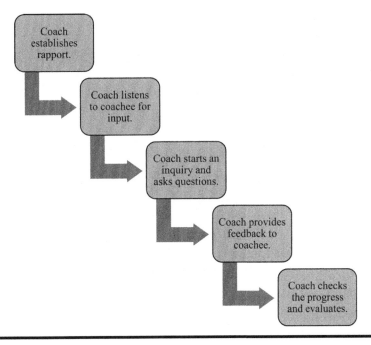

Figure 1.1   Context and Process of Coaching between the High-Performance Coach and Coachees.

Source: Copyright 2021 by Behnam Bakhshandeh.

in which a manager or experienced coworker offers guidance to others. Team coaching is sometimes delivered as a seminar to many people at once (Berg and Karlsen 2012). One-to-many coaching can be delivered by an internal or external coach.

Executive Coaching

This approach to coaching has become an essential tool for talent development professionals as a practical strategy for leadership and team development. Executive coaching finds its place in leadership development programs within diverse industries around the world (Gan and Chong 2015).

Team Building and Team Coaching

This coaching is an increasingly common approach for modern organizations using teams to achieve a competitive advantage in highly competitive global markets (Hagen and Aguilar 2012).

Managerial Coaching

Among organizations, this approach to professional coaching is considered a forward motion leadership creativity that can enhance the relationship between managers and workers (Hsieh and Huang 2018).

High-Performance Coaching

As a general concept, this specialized coaching approach is an effective team learning process to improve training and develop leaders for specific projects and implement HPWTs (high-performance work teams) that differ from other work teams. HPWTs are teams that can perform at the highest level of effectiveness over long periods, accomplishing many difficult and complex organizational goals (Hagen and Aguilar 2012). We need to note here that as much as the topic of our book is similar to the topic of this concept of coaching for high-performance teams, the approach and direction focus on high-performance coaching for managers, such as high-performance coaches' or managers-as-coaches' positions, both internally and externally.

Feedback Coaching

This coaching is used for performance feedback, which is vital to performance management. It is also used as an important communication vehicle by providing workers with feedback on their performance (Hsieh and Huang 2018). One popular technique for feedback coaching is multisource feedback or 360-degree feedback. In this method, the feedback comes from the managers and subordinates, senior managers, peers, and even people from outside of the organization.

Use of Coaching in Management and Leadership Development

Coaching could develop managerial skills among managers in organizations. When used in this way, coaching can directly affect individuals and team productivity.

Managerial Skills

Coaching could develop leadership in teams and positively influence management behaviors and attitudes. In many organizations, the concept of coaching became a natural approach to management skills training (Berg and Karlsen 2012). This book sheds light on accepted among industry management and HR departments as reasons for poor worker performance and reveals how coaching can be used for corrective action.

Developmental Skills

Coaching can inspire, motivate, and encourage personal development among workers while indirectly nurturing the financial sustainability of the organization. The coaching process is defined as a direct, interactive, collaborative, and confidential process in which the coach and participants engage in effective ways to achieve personal and organizational objectives (Vidal-Salazar et al. 2012).

Acquiring, developing, engaging, and retaining talent is growing more complex. Workplaces are also accelerating, posing challenges for finding suitable ways to speed up talent acquisition, development, engagement, and retention. This harsh reality demands more creative approaches. Coaching provides one such approach (Maltbia, Marsick, and Ghosh 2014).

Coaching and Talent Development

Coaching is becoming one useful tool for Talent Development profession-als. Vidal-Salazar et al. (2012) expressed their views of coaching as a tal-ent development tool as "a particularly useful tool in the field of human resources for small and medium enterprises (SME), as the work of many of these companies depends on the learning of a job" (426).

Talent Development and Retention

Many organizations are shifting responsibilities that are traditionally connected to talent development professionals' work, such as coaching practices and develop-ment activities, to operating managers. This is an apparent shift in responsibili-ties of an organization's leaders and managers from monitoring, managing, and administrating accountabilities and control to acting as identifying talent and developing human capital with coaching and mentoring to work toward an organization's strategy for managing and developing its workforce (Kim 2014).

Managerial Coaching Skills and Competencies

Given the option of using internal coaches, organizational leaders should develop the skills of HR practitioners' coaching skills and competencies. Coaching competencies and skills can be developed through systematic training by professional coaches or skillful managers (McLean et al. 2005).

Use of Coaching by Workforce Education and HRD Professionals

Executive coaching, managerial coaching, performance coaching, and team coaching are becoming new ways to empower managers and workers to increase their productivity. Managers and aspiring talent development practi-tioners should grow more familiar with effective coaching.

Coaching Culture

A coaching culture means a work environment in which organizational members readily apply coaching with each other. A coaching culture, when it exists, is not an isolated effort; rather, it is a central theme that runs throughout the organization. Coaching culture shapes how workers interact with each other. And using coaching in interactions is not regarded as merely a dyadic (one-on-one) interaction. Instead, it is viewed as the pervasive use of a coaching approach in employee engagement efforts and a way that shapes relationships among individuals and teams (Milner, Milner, and McCarthy 2020). Vesso (2014) claims,

> in a coaching culture, coaching flows in all directions from all parties, making a networked web across the organization consisting of many connections between people in the same departments, across departments, between teams, and up and down and across the hierarchy
>
> *(112).*

Some Definitions of Coaching Culture

According to research done by Milner et al. (2020), these definitions can help to understand coaching culture:

■ Clutterbuck, Megginson, and Bajer (2016), "[t]he principles, beliefs, and mindsets driving people's behavior in the workplace are deeply rooted in the discipline of coaching" (9).
■ Vesso and Alas (2016), "[It is] an organizational development model that provides the structure that defines how the organization's members can best interact with their working environment, and how the best results are obtained and measured" (308).
■ Jones and Gorell (2014), "[w]here [Coaching culture] people are empowered and where coaching happens at every level. And not only does it happen at every level, but it adds to bottom-line performance. It is the recognized development tool that touches every part of the employee lifecycle" (16).
■ Hawkins (2012), "[w]hen a [This] coaching approach is a key aspect of how the leaders, managers, and staff engage and develop all their people and engage their stakeholders in ways that create increased individual, team and organizational performance and share value for all stakeholders" (21).
■ Lindbom (2007), "[a] coaching culture is one in which the regular review of performance and just-in-time feedback is expected" (102).

- Clutterbuck and Megginson (2005), "[c]oaching is the predominant style of managing and working together, and where a commitment to grow the organization is embedded in a parallel commitment to grow the people in the organization" (19).
- Hart (2003), "[a]n organizational setting in which not only formal coaching occurs, but also, most or a large segment of individuals in the organization practice coaching behaviors as a means of relating to, supporting and influencing each other" (2). (Milner et al. 2020, 239).

Coaching cultures occur when individuals and groups adopt coaching to make changes to improve individual mindsets, attitudes, and behaviors within their work environments by implementing an official or unofficial coaching relationship and collaboration (Milner et al. 2020; Bakhshandeh 2009).

What Key Elements Exist in Establishing a Coaching Culture?

Gormley and Nieuwerburgh (2014), after reviewing many publications, suggest that these elements are essential to create coaching cultures:

- Senior managers must support and promote a coaching culture throughout the organization.
- A coaching structure should target attempts by the senior managers in all departments.
- Managers and workers should speak and act to support coaching.
- Organization leaders must express robust personal commitment by conducting role-playing and developing their skills as an example of coaching workability.

(Gormley and Nieuwerburgh 2014)

To create a strong foundation for a coaching culture, Hawkins (2012) suggested that leaders concentrate on developing "a sustainable and meaningful coaching strategy and culture" (Gormley and Nieuwerburgh 2014, 90). This effort should incorporate a coaching strategy formed by collaborating with the employees and stated in the organization's vision, mission, and strategy (Gormley and Nieuwerburgh 2014).

Figure 1.2 represents the relationship between creating an organization's coaching culture (on the background of the organizations' visions, missions, and values) and creating a high-performance organization that would increase the value of the organization. Coaching culture could be a foundation for

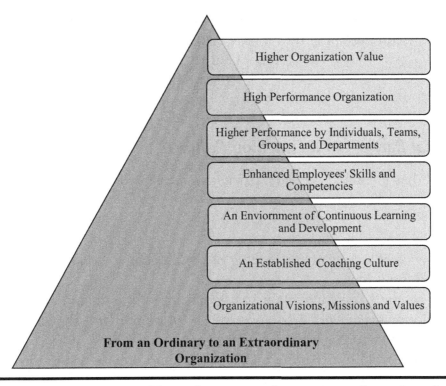

Figure 1.2   How to Use a Coaching Culture to Develop an Extraordinary Organization.

Source: Copyright 2021 by Behnam Bakhshandeh.

establishing an extraordinary corporate culture as a new norm (Bakhshandeh 2009). We will have more to say on this issue in Chapter 2.

Effectiveness of Coaching Culture

Research on coaching effectiveness has pointed to these benefits:

- increased interest in goal setting, commitment, and achievement attitude
- enhanced individual and team performance and productivity
- created deeper critical thinking and solution-focused behavior
- the increased positive environment of creativity and innovation
- enhanced optimism and hope for a better life through resilience and self-effectiveness
- increased individuals' cognitive endurance, mental and physical well-being
- created less resistance and more flexibility with workload and schedule
- reduced workplace anxiety, stress, burnout, and overall turnover

- increased abilities for accepting change and conversions
- advanced developing transformational leadership among managers

(Milner et al. 2020; Whitmore 2017; Gormley and
Nieuwerburgh 2014; Bakhshandeh 2009)

Potential Barriers to a Coaching Culture

Research has identified potential barriers to establishing and sustaining coaching cultures. Among them:

- the organization's current culture
- absence of a clear understanding of how coaching works and the coaching values
- not seeing a coaching culture as significant for the organization
- senior management's resistance and a viewpoint that establishing such a coaching culture is costly or unnecessary
- overall low-level experience, skills, and competencies within the organization's managers
- a perception that insufficient time, money, or other resources exist to support the effort

(Rothwell, Stavros, and Sullivan 2016;
Whitmore 2009; Bakhshandeh 2009)

Coaching Delivery Approaches

There are two general approaches to coaching delivery: (1) Directive Coaching and (2) Nondirective Coaching. The matter of which one is better or more effective than the other is not the topic of this segment, but just to compare the two delivery approaches side by side and then underline the delivery approach that would fit for use by a high-performance coach or manager-as-coach.

Nondirective Coaching

In this approach to coaching, the coaches encourage the clients to form their views of the issue at hand and come up with their own conclusions in order to nurture the coaching relationship. On the other hand, this approach involves coaches listening to clients' stories, experiences and what they are facing, along with all their challenges while at the same time conducting inquires to provide openings and awareness for the clients to make their own decisions through their inner growth journey (Wilson 2020; Whitmore 2017; Bakhshandeh 2009).

It is apparent that with a nondirective approach, the coachees recognize solution that match their personal or professional desires and needs. Therefore, given their own direct involvement, there is a higher probability for the coachees to take on their actions to implement the recognized changes in their personal or professional environment. With this approach, the coach does not need to be a subject matter expert, given the coach's job is to ask practical and relevant questions and to provide space of thinking and inquire and keep reminding the coachees to remain nonjudgmental, open-minded, and nonresistant (see Figure 1.3). Nondirective coaching is one of the popular methods that would work very well for nontechnical and nonperformance applications (2020, 2017, 2009).

The downside of non-directive coaching is the fact that this approach can take a long time to produce the outcome and for the coachees to come to their conclusions. In some cases, they may not reach any conclusions by themselves.

Directive Coaching

In the directive coaching approach, the coaches are more directly involved with coaching by providing their knowledge, experience, and professional advice because they are a subject matter expert. The coaches and coachees' relationship in this approach is very similar to athletic coaching where the coaches ask some questions to understand the mindset of the coachees or to see what they are resisting, or stopped by, after which the coaches provide their input and even show the coachees a "how-to" (2020, 2017, 2009). Because of this, directive coaching is popular among technical and performance-related professionals (see Figure 1.3).

One of the biggest benefits of the directive coaching approach is to be used when the coachees cannot recognize the issue at hand or simply do not know what else to do! This deficit might be caused by a lack of experience, knowledge, or simply an unmatched performance level required for that particular job, work, or position.

The downside of directive coaching is that the coachees may not understand the concept or techniques independently and might take a little more time than usual to practice and build their experience. However, with their effort on

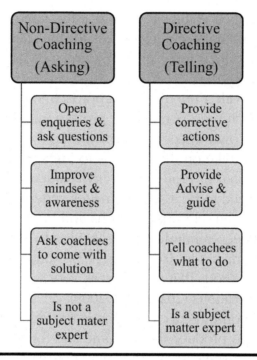

Figure 1.3   Side-by-Side Comparison of Directive and Nondirective Coaching Approaches.
Source: Copyright 2021 by Behnam Bakhshandeh.

learning, their manager or supervisor's support, their application of examinations, and their evaluation for effectiveness and performance, the knowledge will saddle in, and the coachees will be able to repeat what they have learned.

While reading this book and applying its tools and techniques, remember that all coaching conversations and approaches are based on directive coaching. We attempt to develop you as a high-performance coach and an effective manager-as-coach to provide professional and relevant performance coaching for your employees.

Survey About Coaching Effectiveness

In 2020, one of this book's authors surveyed several organizations' executives about their perceptions regarding coaching in their organizations. The survey helped to learn more about coaching and its models for affecting productivity and professional growth. The details, methodology, and results of this research on coaching follow.

Research Main Questions and Survey Statements

To achieve the purpose of this survey, five main questions were selected as primary research questions for this survey. Each main question (RQ) had three survey statements (SS) that would enable the survey to allow to expand its findings. Please note that, on the following questions, when we use the term *Coaching Programs*, this includes different forms of coaching—such as organization coaching, team coaching, executive coaching, managerial coaching, performance coaching, individual coaching, and group coaching.

Criteria for Selecting Participants

All survey participants were executives, senior managers, department managers, or business owners/operators.

Criteria and Approach

Participants had to (1) have at least ten employees, (2) have been in business for at least five years, and (3) have participated in coaching programs with Primeco Education. For this survey, this author uses "Coaching Programs" to mean executive coaching, managers' training, performance coaching team training and development, OD, and personal and professional development seminars and workshops. The research survey (including fifteen statements: 5 RQ and 3 SS for each) went to 70 potential participants by email invitation. Eighty percent (fifty six out of seventy) of participants responded within the designated 18-day survey period.

Likert Five-Level Response

To conduct a short study, this author selected the survey and questionnaire methods. According to Trochim and Donnelly (2008), survey research is one of the most valuable parts of measurement in many applied social types of research. One of the most popular interval-level response formats is the *Likert Five-Level Response* format, which was used on our survey. The following is an example of such a format used by our research survey:

1	2	3	4	5
Strongly Disagree	*Disagree*	*Neutral*	*Agree*	*Strongly Agree*

Results

The following are the results of this short survey:

RQ#1: ***Is coaching an effective approach to an organization's productivity?*** 86.31% of responses to the three supportive *survey statements* resulted in a combination of *54.76%* who chose *Strongly Agree* and *31.55%* who chose *Agree* with a *Mean* of 4.39 out of a *Maximum* of 5 (see Tables 1.1 and 1.6).

Table 1.1   Results of Survey for the Research Question #1.

	Research Questions and Statements		
RQ#1	**Is Coaching an Effective Approach to an Organization's Productivity?**	*Strongly Agree*	*Agree*
SS#1	Coaching programs had a positive impact on increasing our productivity.	71.43%	23.21%
SS#2	Coaching programs increased our employees' attention to detail.	46.43%	37.50%
SS#3	Coaching programs positively affected product quality and speed of production.	46.43%	33.93%
Survey Statements (SS) Average		54.76%	31.55%
Research Question #1 (RQ#1) Total of Strongly Agree and Agree		**86.31%**	

RQ#2: ***Could coaching be used for developing leadership among managers?*** 93.69% of responses to the three supportive *survey statements* resulted in a combination of *59.17%* who chose *Strongly Agree* and *34.52%* who chose *Agree*, with a *Mean* of 4.50 out of a *Maximum* of 5 (see Tables 1.2 and 1.6):

Table 1.2   Results of Survey for the Research Question #2.

	Research Questions and Statements		
RQ#2	**Can Coaching Be Used for Developing Leadership Among Managers?**	*Strongly Agree*	*Agree*
SS#4	Coaching programs increased the level of leadership in our business.	64.29%	32.14%
SS#5	Coaching programs increased our manager's involvement with our employees.	55.36%	37.50%

SS#6	Coaching programs increased our manager's initiating of a team approach more often.	53.57%	33.93%
Survey Statements (SS) Average		59.17%	34.52%
Research Question #2 (RQ#2) Total of Strongly Agree and Agree		**93.69%**	

RQ#3: *Is coaching influencing workforce attitude and behavior positively?* 80.69% of responses to the three supportive *survey statements* resulted in a combination of *44.98%* who chose *Strongly Agree* and *35.71%* who chose *Agree*, with a *Mean* of 4.23 out of a *Maximum* of 5 (see Tables 1.3 and 1.6):

Table 1.3   Results of Survey for the Research Question #3.

	Research Questions and Statements		
RQ#3	**Is Coaching Positively Influencing Workforce Attitude and Behavior?**	*Strongly Agree*	*Agree*
SS#7	Coaching programs brought our workforce closer together.	53.57%	35.71%
SS#8	Coaching programs caused a decrease in our employees' absences and lateness.	28.57%	33.93%
SS#9	Coaching programs increased the level of respect and camaraderie among our employees.	52.79%	37.50%
Survey Statements (SS) Average		44.98%	35.71%
Research Question #3 (RQ#3) Total of Strongly Agree and Agree		**80.69%**	

RQ#4: *Does coaching organize a competitive edge?* 82.73% of responses to the three supportive *survey statements* resulted in a combination of *45.83%* who chose *Strongly Agree* and *36.90%* who chose *Agree*, with a *Mean* of 4.27 out of a *Maximum* of 5 (see Tables 1.4 and 1.6):

Table 1.4   Results of Survey for the Research Question #4.

	Research Questions and Statements		
RQ#4	**Does Coaching Organize a Competitive Edge?**	*Strongly Agree*	*Agree*
SS#10	Coaching programs had a positive impact on our teams, producing fewer errors.	42.86%	37.50%

(Continued)

Table 1.4 (Continued)

	Research Questions and Statements	Strongly Agree	Agree
RQ#4	**Does Coaching Organize a Competitive Edge?**		
SS#11	Coaching programs increased our customer satisfaction and customer retention.	48.21%	41.07%
SS#12	Coaching programs expedited and increased our business expansion.	46.43%	32.14%
Survey Statements (SS) Average		45.83%	36.90%
Research Question #4 (RQ#4) Total of Strongly Agree and Agree		**82.73%**	

RQ#5: *Does coaching have a positive influence on employee performance?* 80.36% of responses to the three supportive *survey statements* resulted in a combination of *44.05%* who chose *Strongly Agree* and *36.31%* who chose *Agree*, with a *Mean* of 4.22 out of a *Maximum* of 5 (see Tables 1.5 and 1.6):

Table 1.5   Results of Survey for the Research Question #5.

	Research Questions and Statements	Strongly Agree	Agree
RQ#5	**Does Coaching Have a Positive Influence on Employee Performance?**		
SS#13	Coaching programs increased our employees' retention.	33.93%	35.71%
SS#14	Coaching programs increased ownership attitude among our employees.	46.43%	42.86%
SS#15	Coaching programs created an environment of partnership among our employees.	51.79%	30.36%
Survey Statements (SS) Average		44.05%	36.31%
Research Question #5 (RQ#5) Total of Strongly Agree and Agree		**80.36%**	

Table 1.6   Summary and Distribution of the Survey Results (Measures of Center and Measures of Spread).

Field	Minimum	Maximum	Mean	Std. Deviation	Variance	Count
RQ#1	Is coaching an effective approach to an organization's productivity?					
SS#1	1	5	4.63	0.72	0.52	56
SS#2	1	5	4.27	0.83	0.70	56

SS#3	3	5	4.27	0.77	0.59	56
	Average Mean		4.39			
RQ#2	Can coaching be used for developing leadership among managers?					
SS#4	3	5	4.61	0.56	0.31	56
SS#5	3	5	4.48	0.63	0.39	56
SS#6	3	5	4.41	0.70	0.49	56
	Average Mean		4.50			
RQ#3	Is coaching positively influencing workforce attitude and behavior?					
SS#7	3	5	4.43	0.68	0.46	56
SS#8	1	5	3.86	0.91	0.84	56
SS#9	3	5	4.41	0.68	0.46	56
	Average Mean		4.23			
RQ#4	Does coaching organize a competitive edge?					
SS#10	3	5	4.23	0.76	0.57	56
SS#11	3	5	4.38	0.67	0.45	56
SS#12	2	5	4.21	0.86	0.74	56
	Average Mean		4.27			
RQ#5	Does coaching have a positive influence on employee performance?					
SS#13	2	5	4.00	0.87	0.75	56
SS#14	2	5	4.34	0.71	0.51	56
SS#15	2	5	4.32	0.80	0.65	56
	Average Mean		4.22			

Overall, in all five research questions and categories, the survey results showed strong support and agreement on the positive impact and effect of coaching programs on OD and employees' performance, productivity, and positive attitude. Table 1.6 represents the summary results of the survey:

The overall results of this survey indicated how business and organizational professional coaching have a positive impact on workforces (including management) increasing productivity, performance at a higher level, having a positive attitude and productive behavior, and providing leadership at all levels of management.

Tips for Successful Coaching

We have found these tips to be helpful in guiding successful coaching of any kind:

- **Remember that coaching is a relationship**
  - As a coach, you are always in a two-way relationship with your coachee. Building a background of relatedness and establishing rapport is a key to starting mutual trust and a workable coaching environment (Bakhshandeh 2009). We will discuss the concept of building rapport on a much deeper level in Chapter 4.
- **Don't take over**
  - It is natural for a coach to take over and tell the coachee what to do during coaching because the coach knows what is needed. This approach will create resistance to the coaching process and will negatively influence the coaching relationship and damage the coachee's trust (Worley 2012; Bakhshandeh 2009).
- **Select the best coaching method**
  - Coaching is not a "one size fits all" approach. As a skilled and developed coach, you need to select the coaching type based on the apparent needs for change in an individual or the issues relating to team performance (Bakhshandeh 2009).
- **Coaching is an inquiry**
  - As much as individuals or teams express their desires or attention to get to a certain point during the coaching or by the end of the coaching structure, there are no pinpoint ends to a change approach. Coaching magic arises from the journey.

Coaching and Developmental Questions for Managers

We ask you to answer the following discussion questions and express your perspectives on what coaching is, how the coaching process works, and some best practices you can implement to lead to practical coaching approach with your team members, individually or as a team:

(1) How do you rate yourself from 1 to 10 (1 being the lowest and 10 being the highest) on clearly understanding what coaching is and how it works?

(2) How do you rate yourself from 1 to 10 (1 being the lowest and 10 being the highest) about your ability to conduct an effective coaching structure?

(3) What area of coaching do you think you need to develop or experience more?

References

Arneson, Justin, William J. Rothwell, and Jennifer Naughton. 2013. "Training and Development Competencies Redefined to Create Competitive Advantage." *T + D* 6, no. 1: 42–47.

ASTD DBA Association for Talent Development. 2014. "The Coaching Approach: A Key Tool for Successful Managers." *Whitepaper. PDF*, e-ISBN: 978-1-60728-514-4 (digital only).

ATD-Association for Talent Development. 2014a. www.td.org/newsletters/atd-links/what-is-coaching.

ATD-Association for Talent Development. 2014b. "ATD Competency Model: Talent Development Redefined." *ATD Competency Model Graphic and AOE.pdf*. www.tdcascadia.org/assets/2014/12/ATD-Competency-Model-Graphic-and-AOE.pdf.

Bakhshandeh, Behnam. 2009. *Conspiracy for Greatness: Mastery of Love Within.* San Diego, CA: Primeco Education, Inc.

Berg, Morten Emil, and Jan Terje Karlsen. 2007. "Mental Models in Project Management Coaching." *Engineering Management Journal* 19, no. 3: 3–13.

Berg, Morten Emil, and Jan Terje Karlsen. 2012. "An Evaluation of Management Training and Coaching." *Journal of Workplace Learning* 24, no. 3: 177–99.

Clutterbuck, David, and David Megginson. 2005. *Making Coaching Work: Creating a Coaching Culture.* Wimbledon: CIPD Publishing.

Clutterbuck, David, David Megginson, and Agnieszka Bajer. 2016. *Building and Sustaining a Coaching Culture.* London: Kogan Page Publishers.

Coetzee, Francois. 2018. "Coaching, Leadership. NLP with Purpose." https://nlpwithpurpose.com/blog/coaching-statistics/.

Cox, Elaine, Tatiana Bachkirova, and David Clutterbuck. 2014. "Theoretical Traditions and Coaching Genres: Mapping the Territory." *Advances in Developing Human Resources* 16, no. 2: 139–60.

Downs, L. 2017. "Why You Need a Coaching Culture. ATD-Association for Talent Development." www.td.org/insights/why-you-need-a-coaching-culture.

Ellinger, Andrea D., and Sewon Kim. 2014. "Coaching and Human Resource Development: Examining Relevant Theories, Coaching Genres, and Scales to

Advance Research and Practice." *Advances in Developing Human Resources* 16, no. 2: 127–38. https://doi.org/10.1177/1523422313520472.

Forbes. 2018. "Forbes Coaches Council. Key Differences Between Coaching and Consulting (And How to Decide What Your Business Needs)." www.forbes.com/sites/forbescoachescouncil/2018/06/14/key-differences-between-coaching-and-consulting-and-how-to-decide-what-your-business-needs/?sh=51e9cd13d712

Gan, G. C., and C. W. Chong. 2015. "Coaching Relationship in Executive Coaching: A Malaysian Study." *The Journal of Management Development* 34, no. 4: 476–93. https://doi.org/10.1108/JMD-08-2013-0104.

Gormley, Helen, and Christian van Nieuwerburgh. 2014. "Developing Coaching Cultures: A Review of the Literature." *Coaching: An International Journal of Theory, Research and Practice* 7, no. 2: 90–101. https://doi.org/10.1080/17521882.2014.915863.

Hagen, Marcia, and Maryia Gavrilova Aguilar. 2012. "The Impact of Managerial Coaching on Learning Outcomes Within the Team Context: An Analysis." *Human Resource Development Quarterly* 23, no. 3: 363–88. https://doi.org/10.1002/hrdq.21140.

Hart, E. Wayne. 2003. "Developing a Coaching Culture." *Center for Creative Leadership* 585: 638–8053. http://citeseerx.ist.psu.edu/viewdoc/download?doi=10.1.1.197.234&rep=rep1&type=pdf.

Hawkins, P. 2012. *Creating a Coaching Culture*, Coaching in Practice Series. Maidenhead, Berkshire: Open University Press.

Hsieh, Hui-Hsien, and Jie-Tsuen Huang. 2018. "Exploring Factors Influencing Employees' Impression Management Feedback-seeking Behavior: The Role of Managerial Coaching Skills and Affective Trust." *Human Resource Development Quarterly* 29, no. 2: 163–80. https://doi.org/10.1002/hrdq.21311.

ICF (International Coaching Federation). 2011. "Coached Core Competencies." https://coachfederation.org/app/uploads/2017/12/CoreCompetencies.pdf.

Indeed. 2021. "Coaching vs. Consulting: Overview, Differences and Similarities. Career Development." *Indeed Editorial Team.* www.indeed.com/career-advice/career-development/coaching-vs-consulting.

iPEC. 2020. "What is Coaching? iPEC Coach Training. Pdf." www.ipeccoaching.com.

Jones, Gillian, and Ro Gorell. 2014. *How to Create a Coaching Culture*, vol. 3. London: Kogan Page Publishers.

Jordyn, Betsy. 2020. "Consulting vs. Coaching." www.betsyjordyn.com/blog/consulting-vs-coaching.

Kim, Sewon. 2014. "Assessing the Influence of Managerial Coaching on Employee Outcomes." *Human Resource Development Quarterly* 25. no. 1: 59–85. https://doi.org/10.1002/hrdq.21175.

Lindbom, David. 2007. "A Culture of Coaching: The Challenge of Managing Performance for Long-term Results." *Organization Development Journal* 25, no. 2: 101–06.

Maltbia, Terrence E., Victoria J. Marsick, and Rajashi Ghosh. 2014. "Executive and Organizational Coaching: A Review of Insights Drawn from Literature to

Inform HRD Practice." *Advances in Developing Human Resources* 16, no. 2: 161–83.

McLean, Gary N., Baiyin Yang, Min-Hsun Christine Kuo, Amy S. Tolbert, and Carolyn Larkin. 2005. "Development and Initial Validation of an Instrument Measuring Managerial Coaching Skill." *Human Resource Development Quarterly* 16, no. 2: 157–78.

McLeod, Angus. 2004. "Performance Coaching & Mentoring in Organizations." *Resource Magazine* 1, no. 1: 28–31.

Milner, Julia, Trenton Milner, and Grace McCarthy. 2020. "A Coaching Culture Definition: An Industry-based Perspective from Managers as Coaches." *The Journal of Applied Behavioral Science* 56, no. 2: 237–54.

Pfeiffer, William J. 1990. *Developing Human Resources*. San Diego, CA: Pfeiffer & Company.

Rothwell, William J., and H. C. Kazanas. 2003. *The Strategic Development of Talent*. Amherst, MA: HRD Press, Inc.

Rothwell, William J., Jacqueline M. Stavros, and Roland L. Sullivan. 2016. *Practicing Organization Development: Leading Transformation and Change*, 4th ed. Hoboken, NJ: John Wiley & Sons, Inc.

Saporito, Thomas J. 1996. "Business-linked Executive Development: Coaching Senior Executives." *Consulting Psychology Journal: Practice and Research* 48, no. 2: 96.

Strosinski, Jean. 2003. "Performance Consulting versus Performance Coaching. First Article of Six in the Series: Coaching for Performance." *Constructive Choices, Inc.* www.constructivechoices.com/articles/Art1_Performance%20 Coaching.pdf.

Training Industry. 2018. "What is Performance Consulting?" https://trainingindustry. com/wiki/professional-development/performance-consulting/.

Trochim, William M. K., and James P. Donnelly. 2008. *The Research Methods Knowledge Base*, 3rd ed. Mason, OH: Cengage Learning.

VALUEPROP. 2021. "The Difference Between a Business Coach and a Consultant: Which Do I Need?" www.valueprop.com/blog/the-difference-between-a-business-coach-and-a-consultant-which-do-i-need.

Vesso, Signe. 2014. "Coaching Culture Characteristics in Estonian Companies." *Journal of Management and Change* 32/33, no. 1/2: 109–31.

Vesso, Signe, and Ruth Alas. 2016. "Characteristics of a Coaching Culture in Leadership Style the Leader's Impact on Culture." *Problems and Perspectives in Management* 14, no. 2: 306–18. https://doi.org/10.21511/ppm.14(2-2).2016.06.

Vidal-Salazar, María Dolores, Vera Ferrón-Vílchez, and Eulogio Cordón-Pozo. 2012. "Coaching: An Effective Practice for Business Competitiveness." *Competitiveness Review: An International Business Journal* 22, no. 5: 423–33. https://doi.org/10.1108/10595421211266302.

Whitmore, John. 2009. *Coaching for Performance; GROWing Human Potential and Purpose*, 4th ed. Boston, MA: Nicholas Brealey Publishing.

Whitmore, John. 2017. *Coaching for Performance; The Principle and Practice of Coaching and Leadership*, 5th ed. Boston, MA: Nicholas Brealey Publishing.

Wilson, Carol. 2020. *Performance Coaching: A Complete Guide to Best-Practice Coaching and Training*, 3rd ed. New York, NY: KoganPage.

Worley, Christopher. 2012. "Toward a Relevant and Influential OD." *Journal of the Organization Development Network* 44, no. 2: 5–6.

Zhou, Luisa. 2020. "Coaching Statistics: The ROI of Coaching in 2021." www.luisazhou.com/blog/coaching-statistics/.

Chapter 2

Performance Coaching

Behnam Bakhshandeh

This chapter defines performance coaching, distinguishing its related elements and addresses these questions:

- What is performance?
- What is performance coaching?
- What is the high-performance coaching model?
- What is performance conversation?
- Who is a high-performance coach?
- What are the elements of the high-performance coaching process?
- What conditions are essential for effective performance coaching?
- What competencies do high-performance coaches need?
- What is the relationship between coach and coachee?
- How does high-performance coaching support business competitive advantage?

What Is Performance?

According to the *Merriam-Webster* dictionary (2021), performance is defined as:

- the execution of an action
- something accomplished: deed, feat
- fulfilling a claim, promise, or request: implementation
- the action of representing a character in a play
- a public presentation or exhibition

DOI: 10.4324/9781003155928-3

- the ability to perform: efficiency
- how a mechanism performs the engine
- the manner of reacting to stimuli: behavior

Bailey (1982) defined *performance* as "the result of a pattern of actions carried out to satisfy an objective according to some standard" (4). Performance connotes not just actions or behaviors; rather, it also implies the results achieved. To emphasize that point, "performance is equated with results; behavior is equated only with the actions to achieve results" (Rothwell and Kazanas 2003, 402).

According to Bailey (1982), job performance consists of:

(1) who?—the individual conducting the performance,
(2) what?—the activity, the job, the work, and
(3) where?—the context of the job and work (Rothwell and Kazanas 2003).

But performance may also imply the values demonstrated by the actions and results. What issues are important to the organization? Values underlie the actions and results. Further, performance also implies the ethics or morale stance demonstrated by the actions and results. What is good or bad, and what does morality indicate about the behaviors displayed and the actions achieved? (Rothwell 2015).

According to Whitmore (2009), the dictionary described performance as "the execution of the functions required of one" (95). However, Whitmore (2009) was not satisfied by this simple definition, and he called it "the minimum necessary to get by" (95) and added "that is not performance in my view; it is not what I refer to in coaching as performance" (95). The phrase high performance occurs when individuals, teams, or groups set their own goals and standards at a level beyond what their coaches, managers, or organizations expect of them. Customarily, high-performance individuals and teams establish standards that exceed what others demand or expect of them (Wilson 2020). We call this the Olympian's or champion's quality.

Figure 2.1 displays environmental elements affecting human performance.

What Is Performance Coaching?

The phrase *performance coaching* refers to a category of coaching that advises workers about how they should behave and what results they should

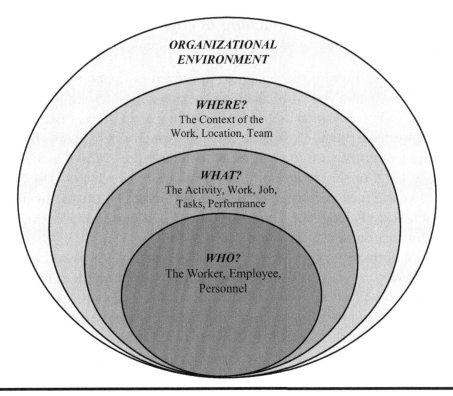

Figure 2.1 The Elements of Human Performance.

Source: Adapted from Rothwell and Kazanas (2003).

achieve. It clarifies the means (behaviors) and ends (results) to be achieved. Unlike nondirective coaching, which prompts coachees to reflect on their own, performance coaching relies on the experience of the coach to direct the coachees' attention to what should be achieved.

Performance coaching can be an important tool for managers faced with workers who do not achieve the results that the organization requires or who behave in ways not aligned with organization policies, procedures, or managerial expectations. Through coaching, managers or experienced coworkers guide workers through what they should do, how they should behave, and how best to measure success. Performance coaching often plays a key role in performance management, performance evaluation, and performance reviews. Workers cannot achieve necessary results if they are unclear what they are. Performance coaching clarifies what measurable results should be achieved.

Application of Directive Coaching in High-Performance Coaching

As we underlined the directive coaching approach in Chapter 1, the coaches are more directly involved with coaching by providing their knowledge, experience, and professional advice because they are a subject matter expert. As we have mentioned previously, the primary benefits of the directive coaching approach are to be used when employees cannot recognize the issue at hand or simply do not know what to do or what else to do, directly affecting their performance. This deficit might be caused by a lack of experience, knowledge, or simply an unmatched performance level required for that particular job, work, or position.

A high-performance coach or a manager-as-coach needs to add one more essential element to your toolbox of experience and knowledge. That is your mindset, which will become one of the most usable tools you can provide for empowering and developing your employees' performances.

Figure 2.2 depicts the three main aspects of what we call the *Directive Coach's Assets Wheels.* Please look at Figure 2.2 and as you read the content,

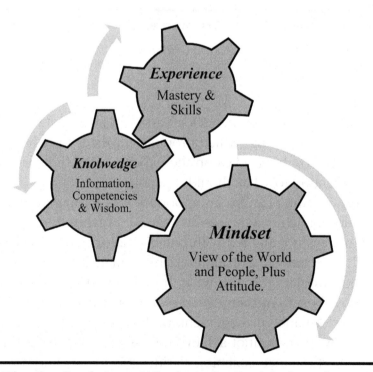

Figure 2.2   Directive Coach Assets Wheels. Author's original creation.

Source: Copyright 2021 by Behnam Bakhshandeh.

try to recognize the level of possession or lack of such elements within yourself.

These three main wheels are source directive coaches' power and ability to understand their workers and be able to provide direct coaching that is sourced by their own coach's mindset, knowledge, and experience.

Mindset

At this segment, we briefly touch on mindset and its effect on our minds and ultimately on our actions and decisions. In the next chapter, we will go a little deeper on the topic of mindset. Mindset is based on one's life events, experiences, upbringing, perceived reality, beliefs, interests, and motivations. The individuals collect these experiences and influence during their cognitive growth and personality development (Bakhshandeh 2009). How you see the world around you affects your decisions and actions for or against that world, environment, or individuals? As a high-performance coach, with outmost honesty and authenticity, you need to get clear about how you view and see yourself (manager, supervisor, coach, boss), others (your employees, subordinates, workers, coachees), and what you do (your job and the work itself) (Bakhshandeh 2015; Bakhshandeh 2009). Your mindset will make or break your relationship with your team and the employees you are coaching. The degree with which your mindset affects your attitude will appear in your relationship with your coachees. For you to be able to be effective with your them and provide them with your information and experience is all dependent on your attitude and the way you are relating to them. Without that positive and uplifting attitude, your knowledge and experience will not be welcome by others. Your mindset is the key to be an effective performance coach.

Knowledge

After developing and establishing a healthy, positive, and productive mindset, the next elements are coaches' knowledge, information, and competencies that they have accumulated and built throughout their careers. The coaches' knowledge will help the coachees to learn new approaches to increase performance and productivity. The performance coaches tell the coachees what needs to get done and the reasons behind what they ask the them to do; that way, the relationship becomes one of learning and development at the same time.

Experience

The Coaches' experiences (personal or professional) are powerful assets of a performance coach. There is something that comes with experience that nobody can buy or just add to their portfolio. These experiences come from hard work, learned skills, accumulated series of "how-to's," and a history of facing challenges that resulted in many breakdowns before finally earning that mastery. Combining the coaches' experiences with their knowledge and their powerful mindsets will yield productive workers and increased levels of performance.

Elements of High-Performance Coaching Process by a Manager-as-Coach

Figure 2.3 displays the general steps in the performance coaching process and intervention from start to finish. Consider this process as a broad approach for encouraging and empowering employees to improve their

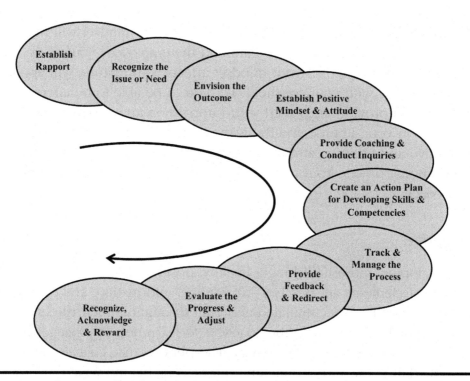

Figure 2.3   Elements of High-Performance Coaching Process by a Manager-as-Coach.

Source: Copyright 2021 by Behnam Bakhshandeh.

productivity. The general steps in this process can be modified to address the needs of specific workers and situations or the type of intervention that is implemented by high-performance coaches or managers-as-coaches. These steps, together or individually, can also be used to manage meetings or just conversations among managers and employees or managers and a team. The wisdom of these steps and process is in their versatility and application in many situations or scenarios and the support they are providing for the implementation of the high-performance coaching model (see Figure 2.6).

Step 1: Establish Rapport

Rapport connects people positively. It means they can relate to each other. *The Merriam-Webster* dictionary (2021) defines *rapport* as a "relation characterized by harmony, conformity, accord, or affinity." Rapport leads to continued communication and collaboration between two people. Sometimes rapport is established immediately; sometimes it takes time to build the trust necessary for a rapport. However, it takes all parties in a relationship to establish workable rapport (Angelo 2012). We will describe rapport in a much deeper fashion in Chapter 4.

The success of performance coaching depends on the depth of the established rapport and how much people trust managers and welcome the coaching relationship (Whitmore 2017; Rothwell, Stavros, and Sullivan 2016; Cummings and Worley 2015; Bakhshandeh 2008).

Step 2: Recognize the Issue or Need

Sometimes people feel the need to improve their performance. Sometimes a manager notices that workers need to change for the better. Sometimes other people in teams or groups note that a coworker needs performance improvement or attitude adjustment because it impacts the team. An issue or need must be recognized before it can be addressed. Chapter 5 builds a deeper understanding of how to clarify the present situation or issue.

Step 3: Envision the Outcome

Once the need or issue is recognized, the coaches need to help the coachees to envision the outcome of the performance coaching process. They must see the future of what would happen when the gap between the present issues or needs are closed and what is possible for them and their teams or departments after going through the performance coaching. This is not a step to miss or cut because coaches want to save time. This step is essential to the success of the process and makes the subordinates partners in the process versus simply resisting the process and just going through the motions because their managers want them to do something. One very important note: If the coaches can't see and envision the outcome, neither will the coachees! When the coaches see the outcome of coaching, and the coaches' goals are clear and owned by the coachees, the processing moves in a productive direction; motivation is the fuel for the coachees' performance (2017, 2016, 2015, 2008).

Step 4: Establish Positive Mindset and Attitude

In this step, coaches recognize as the coachees' mindset through the process of needs assessment. It often results from friendly conversations and informal interviews that avoid stimulating resistance and self-defense. It is very rare for managers to know their subordinates well and understand who they are, what they think, and how they can relate to them. It is easy to judge others based on what we observe on the surface by just seeing their performance and then jumping to conclusions about their mindsets and attitudes. Having good rapport minimizes resistance in this step. Individuals display resistance to change because they don't see the results desired, don't think they need to change, think other people around them need to change, or conclude that change indicates that something is wrong with them. Effective communication and active listening skills are essential to this step's success for coaches (2017, 2016, 2015, 2008). More details about the step will be presented in Chapters 5 and 6.

Step 5: Provide Coaching and Conduct Inquiry

First, the coaches and the coachees need to create a structure for the coaching relationship that describes when they will conduct any session, how long each session will last, and how they will conduct the coaching process without interfering with the coachees' departments or team processes. For this, the coaches/managers need to provide resources to provide a successful process. These resources can be available in length of time, proper time off for the subordinates, training materials, information, equipment, budget for providing outsourced information or third-party involvement, privacy for conducting the coaching, senior managers alignment and support, and the personal commitment from the subordinates/coachees. Coaches should not present themselves as experts or bosses. Nor should they expect coachees to do what they ask without questions.

Step 6: Action Plan for Developing Skills and Competencies

One important element of performance coaching is to understand the competencies that need to be developed. This information can be uncovered during (1) the needs assessment process, (2) informal conversation and interviewing the coachees, (3) reviewing coachees' history and employment records, and (4) confidential interviewing of coachees' direct managers and teammates. After recognizing the needed skills and competencies, coaches should create an action plan on how they will build competencies in the coachees. The managers/coaches should use positive coaching approaches to make sure the coachees are empowered. Many coaching models are available that could provide a framework—and they include appreciative inquiry (AI) coaching, positive psychology coaching, and strength-based coaching. The key to coaching success is for the coaches to know (1) to create an action plan to which the coachees agree, (2) to monitor and assess the progress, (3) to establish responsibilities for both parties, (4) to push, and (5) to hold the coachees accountable for their performances during the coaching process (2017, 2016, 2015, 2008). We will talk about this step in Phase Four (Implementation and Evaluation) of this book.

Step 7: Track and Manage the Progress

Providing coaching is one thing, but tracking and managing the coaching progress is different. Tracking the process helps both parties see what needs to be changed, implemented, or discarded. Managing the process helps the coaches make sure the coachees not only receive new information but also implement, practice, and build skills regarding the new. This is something that many managers miss. Knowing something does not mean managers can coach others about that information or teach how to do it. Researchers have concluded that smoking and eating fattening food are not good health habits, but do these conclusions stop people from smoking or eating fattening food? Some coaching skills that would reinforce the coaching progress are to (1) make a connection between learning skills and implement them for the coachees, (2) have a regular follow up and discussion on the action plan items, (3) review coachees' mistakes or off-track issues, (4) remove nonperformance and irrelevant issues, and (5) provide feedback. We shall have more to say about feedback in the next step (2017, 2016, 2015, 2008). We will also focus on that in greater detail in Phase Four (Implementation and Evaluation) of this book.

Step 8: Provide Feedback and Redirect

Providing good feedback empowers coachees to continue their work constructively. Given the coaches and coachees have established good rapport and establish the structure for their relationship, there exists open communication which enhances the coaching relationship. Giving feedback is a big part of open communication between coaches and coachees. The managers'/coaches' feedback should be done regularly, so the progress would not be interrupted or get on the wrong track. The feedback process could simply be implemented by conducting inquiries and reviewing the coaching process results. Managers can use (1) constructive feedback based on providing feedback on a situation or process related to improving something and (2) positive feedback usually based on recognizing the coachees' efforts. Both forms of feedback can be used during the coaching process to improve the coachee's motivation. Some modifications in the action plan might be in order based on feedback results and what came out of coaching conversations (2017, 2016, 2015, 2008). In further sections of this book, we explain the benefits of feedback for achieving higher employee performance.

Step 9: Evaluate the Progress and Adjust

Another critical element of this process is to evaluate, and when necessary, adjust, the coaching approach periodically. Many forms of employee performance and coaching evaluations are possible. Examples include (1) Self-Assessment, (2) 360 Degree Rating, (3) Skills Evaluation, (4) Goals and Results Assessment, and (5) Graphic Rating Scale (Rothwell et al. 2016; Cummings and Worley 2015). However, the peer review is one valuable, accurate approach to evaluation. It is based on interviewing the coachees' coworkers and teammates about the on-the-job applications of coaching on the attitudes, behaviors, and work performance of the coachee (2017, 2016, 2015, 2008). We will touch on this matter in Chapter 15.

Step 10: Recognize, Acknowledge, and Reward

Coaches should recognize, acknowledge, and reward coachees for their positive progress. Acknowledging coachee progress empowers coachees' progress and creates positive conditioning that will encourage more progress.

Rewarding the efforts could include private and/or public recognition of progress and eventually even a promotion or increased compensation. A reward, therefore, is due to those coachees who successfully undertake changes in attitudes, behaviors, and performance (2017, 2016, 2015, 2008).

Conditions for Delivering Effective Performance Coaching

Performance coaching does not end upon the conclusion of a session or a coaching program. Coaching is a means rather than an end. It is a support system that focuses on empowering individuals and teams to realize their potential (Bakhshandeh 2009). Job performance does not improve on its own or by having individuals participate in performance coaching. In fact, performance coaching is most effective when the organization's leaders and corporate culture support the coaching process. We will touch on organizational and individual commitments to coaching later in this chapter.

A performance coaching culture is established in an organization when the organization's leaders model it, encourage it, discuss it, recognize it, and reward it. Of course, it helps if talent development and learning and development managers use their internal coaches or hire external coaches to train the coaching managers on the following issues:

An Environment of Mutual Trust and Respect

Establishing rapport with trust and respect is a great start to create openness for the coachees—especially if performance issues and tensions exist in the coachees' work environment or department (Whitmore 2017; Bakhshandeh 2009; Pfeiffer 1990).

Manager's Supportive, Compassionate, and Empathetic Attitude

The assigned manager who performs as a coach must have a supportive attitude and display empathy for coachees, who are probably subordinate to this manager-coach or someone in another department. This attitude from coaches helps the coachees to feel safe and understood (2017, 2009, 1990).

Establishing Effective Discussion

Coaching is a collaborative process to finding solutions. It is not a dogmatic view of the issues. Performance coaching will be effective when the coachees' desired goals are consistent with their managers' intentions and the teams' or departments' goals. Intentionality and purposeful discussions make a difference in producing valuable results in the coaching relationship (2017, 2009, 1990).

Emphasizing Work-Related Objectives

The performance coaching process should focus on work-related goals and emphasize how to remove obstacles that coachees face. If unrelated issues surface during the coaching conversations—and they often do surface— the coaches/managers should bring the conversation back to focus on the coachees' roles in their work, department, and organizational settings (2017, 2009, 1990).

No Discussions of Employment Benefits

Employment-related issues including salary, bonus, rewards, raises, days off, or vacations should not become a focus of discussion in a performance coaching session. Attention devoted to these issues will usually distract from performance-related issues and will take away from the intentions to assist the coachees in making work improvements (2017, 2009, 1990).

Potential Objectives for Performance Coaching

Like any other effort to improve goals, performance coaching also needs to have clear objectives. The following objectives should assist coaches or managers in supporting the coachees or subordinates during the coaching process:

- establish a safe, nonthreatening environment for coachees/subordinates to express their concerns and issues
- create and improve the coachees'/subordinates' knowledge and under-standing of their strengths and weaknesses
- support efforts by coachees/subordinates to realize their potential
- improve the coachees'/subordinates' knowledge and appreciation of their work environment and their relationship with coworkers and colleagues
- give constructive feedback on coachees'/subordinates' behavior and attitude to improve their understanding of their own interpersonal effectiveness

- assist coachees/subordinates in analyzing their interpersonal competencies and help them develop what is missing in that domain
- review the coachees/subordinates' personal goals and their relevance to their professional objectives
- detect any obstacles that stand in the way of coachees achieving their goals or delaying their progress
- provide support for the coachees/subordinates in creating action plans for dealing with recognized issues
- support efforts by coachees/subordinates to review and create realistic goals for improving their performance
- be available to the coachees/subordinates for future discussions and support while implementing their action plans

(Whitmore 2017; Bakhshandeh 2009; Pfeiffer 1990)

The Benefit of Coaching for Individuals

The benefits of performance coaching are not limited to mere work-related benefits. Often participants benefit on a personal level and have a positive impact on their lives. People have reported the positive results they have received from coaching. These benefits include:

- increased personal velocity and success
- increased productivity and levels of personal performance
- recaptured interests and passions in life and related activities
- ability to accomplish more in less time with relevantly less efforts
- new imagination and ways of self-expression
- a new life vision and new practices in their lives
- improved communications, understanding, and empathy
- increased personal and professional efficiency and effectiveness

(Bakhshandeh 2015; Bakhshandeh 2009)

What Is Performance Conversation?

Given that the concept of coaching and that the coaching relationship is happening in communication and conversation among the coaches and coachees, it will be beneficial to talk about the role of Performance Conversation, what it is, what it is not, and what to look for when you as a high-performance coach and manager-as-coach are delivering it during the interrelationship with your coachees/employees.

Performance Conversation Is Not a Performance Assessment or Meeting

High-performance coaches understand that the best way to accomplish results during their conversation with their employees is to not feel they are being judged, assessed, or evaluated for their performance but to be directed and coached by someone on their side. Establishing a rapport (we will talk about this in Chapter 4), displaying good intentions and positive attitudes and nonjudgmental behaviors, and not using authoritarian force are helping high-performance coaches to have workable and effective performance conversations that make a difference for employees. As Lee (2021) mentioned, the other alternatives to this approach will be conflicts, continued destructive behaviors, and more separation between managers and employees. "Traditional appraisals do not encourage open conversations or healthy debate because they are too focused on delivering judgment and justifying the power held by a supervisor" (Lee 2021, 21).

The coaches and the coachees need to understand that their performance conversation is a proven technique for high-performance coaching, not a meeting about the employees' performance discussion. The performance conversation has its purposes and operates within a certain framework inside a performance coaching model, using a series of established management practices (Lee 2021; Cardy and Leonard 2011).

Using Positivity for Producing Long-Lasting Outcome

Using positive psychology and AI are proven in the coaching and management practices. These approaches seek what is possible and positive and what works about the coachees and the situations. These coaching approaches are tapping into the "unlimited human potential to create, thrive, build, seek, and innovate. Unlike appraisals, they also build upon strengths and do not focus on deficits or gaps" (Lee 2021, 23). You, as professional high-performance coaches or managers-as-coaches, need to familiarize yourselves with these two powerful distinctions for performance conversations during performance coaching.

The following sections briefly touch on and explain the concepts of (1) Positive Psychology and (2) Appreciative Inquiry as two effective models for conducting Performance Conversations. For further information, please look at "Appendix A" in addition to your own research and reading about these two powerful tools for performance coaching and performance conversation.

Positive Psychology

The term *Positive Psychology* was initially created by Abraham Maslow. Later, Martin Seligman pioneered Positive Psychology as a psychological approach based on scientific research and systematic theories. This innovative approach looks into why people are happy and what it takes to keep the happiness as the main element of their lives and productivity (Seligman 2002). Rao (2013) underlined positive psychology to be considered as the science of "human flourishing" or what could be portrayed as the "anatomy of happiness." According to Gable and Haidt (2005), "It is the study of positive emotions and experiences that contribute to flourishing and optimal performance" (22). As noted by Seligman on the Positive Psychology Website, "Positive psychology seeks to understand and build the strengths and virtues that enable individuals and communities to thrive" (Rao 2013, 209).

Through a series of research and study, conducting massive and extensive questionnaires, Seligman discovered that the most fulfilled and optimistic people were ones who found and utilized what Seligman called their "signature strengths." These strengths included but were not limited to humanity, self-restraint, and persistence. His vision of happiness was backed by the quality and the ethics of Confucius, Mencius, and Aristotle, plus the power of modern psychology, using empowering theories, such as motivation and self-awareness, Seligman concluded that personal happiness in one's life has three proportions that one can develop, nurture, and encourage: (1) the Pleasant Life, (2) the Good Life, and (3) the Meaningful Life (Seligman 2002).

Feelings and emotions have a strong impact on thoughts, which, in turn, cause actions. But which one comes first? Do feelings generate thoughts, or do thoughts create feelings? It is difficult to speak scientifically, and with certainty about which one comes first and affects the other. However, it can be said that either way can be true and could happen. Sometimes when feeling sad, upset, or resentful, negative thoughts filter in about ourselves, others, or the situation itself. Other times, those negative thoughts about some past events or relationships might initiate feelings of sadness, being upset, or even experiencing anxiety. This process also applies to having positive thoughts which generate positive feelings or feelings which bring back some happy thoughts (Bakhshandeh 2015).

Based on the foundation of Positive Psychology, selecting happiness will generate it more often. Positive psychologists focus on the positive side of people's lives and emphasize what is working in their lives versus what is not working. It means looking at the brighter side of the issue, or as an old saying goes, looking at the glass as half full versus half empty. A big movement and a whole new field of research of this empowering approach exist and have a great influence on individual and team coaching approaches with direct and positive results on individual interventions.

Appreciative Inquiry

This segment is an introduction to AI and its related concepts, design, and principles. Many professional consultants are familiar with and use AI in their work as AI Practitioners with organizations and as a form of individual intervention and executive coaching. AI is a process and approach for creating a positive change. This process is applicable to individuals, such as executives or senior/junior managers, a particular department or a team in the company, or to the organization as a whole. AI can be used for strategic planning, cultural transformation, staff training, future building, and leadership development (Cooperrider, Whitney, and Stavros 2008).

According to Cooperrider and Whitney (n.d.), "Appreciative Inquiry is the cooperative search for the best in people, their organizations, and the world around them. It involves systematic discovery of what gives a system 'life' when it is most effective and capable in economic, ecological, and human terms" ("Appreciative Inquiry Commons" n.p.). Fundamentally, AI processes are comprised of asking a series of empowering and positive questions that reinforce and increase the potential for people to raise possibilities in a positive and nonthreatening environment. According to White (1996), "Appreciative Inquiry focuses us on the positive aspects of our lives and leverages them to correct the negative. It's the opposite of problem-solving" ("Appreciative Inquiry Commons" n.p.).

Regardless of how the Appreciative Inquiry Model (AIM) is one of the main approaches of Organization Development (OD), in many ways, it is different from traditional OD. That being said, one can conclude that AI has its own concepts and is operating from its own distinct paradigm. According to Cooperrider et al. (2008), the concept of the AI paradigm is that human beings regularly explore ways to organize their emotions, thoughts, and beliefs into tidy and easy-to-understand contexts in order to better comprehend complex notions and ideas. Because of this, when we gather and organize complex notions and ideas into a simple and easy-to-understand context, then we have formed a paradigm.

The Five Principles of Appreciative Coaching Sourced by Appreciative Inquiry

The appreciative coaching has five fundamental principles, which are the core philosophy for its approach (Oren, Binkert, and Clancy 2007) as follows:

- **The Constructionist Principle.** Throughout the intervention, the coaches should look for statements by the coachees about their understanding of themselves and their perspective and fabric of their lives, their families, and their careers and to keep bringing them back into being whole and complete without any judgments on their past failures and shortcomings. Coaches must make sure to point out their strengths, their gifts, and abilities (Oren et al. 2007).
- **The Positive Principle.** The coaches should keep focusing on presenting or emphasizing the positive effects around the coachees' strengths and achievements. They should keep changing the coachees' language by redirecting their negative and problematic language to positive and resolution-related language (Oren et al. 2007).
- **The Poetic Principle.** The coaches must pay close attention to the coachees' stories that they are saying about themselves. They must use the situations to encourage and assist them to rewrite elements of their stories by establishing themselves in positive ways, distinguishing new possibilities, and transforming their problems into strengths (Oren et al. 2007).
- **The Simultaneity Principle.** The coaches should keep in mind to continue their inquiry as the source of awareness that would guide the coachees to the change. The appropriate questions are helping the coachees see their present challenges or hardships in a new perspective. They should pay attention to the connection between positive inquiry and where it could take the coachees and their experiences (Oren et al. 2007).
- **The Anticipatory Principle.** The coaches could be very instrumental in assisting the coachees to generate positive and empowering views of themselves via self-declarations and visions for their future. It is an innate and natural characteristic of human beings to visualize and anticipate their future (Oren et al. 2007).

Stages of Appreciative Coaching

According to Cooperrider, Whitney, and Stavros (2003), "[t]he Appreciative Inquiry, 4-D Cycle is a dynamic, iterative process of positive change" (101). Besides the philosophical nature of Appreciative Inquiry, it is also an attempt to arrive at a personal and professional change. Please note that later on the fifth stage, the Define stage as the first stage of the process, was added to the original 4-D Cycle, Discovery, Dream, Design, and Destiny and made it a 5-D Cycle (Watkins, Mohr, and Kelly 2011). Regardless of where or for what purpose AI is being used, most of the time the AI approach includes the aforementioned 5-D process, which could vary in duration. Depending on the size of the organization and what needs to be achieved, this process can go from something like two days to a year or more. Overall, the AI process is empowering, positive, effective, and easy to comprehend.

During coaching sessions with clients, the coaches will guide the coachees through the main five stages of AI and ask a set of questions designed to walk them through the 5-D process and assist them in getting present to their dreams and desired future from an empowering perspective versus trying to overcome a possible failure. Basically, it is looking at "What is working?" versus "What is wrong?" The phases of 5-D are as follows.

Figure 2.4 displays the process and relationship between the steps of AI that high-performance coaches or mangers-as-coaches can use to support

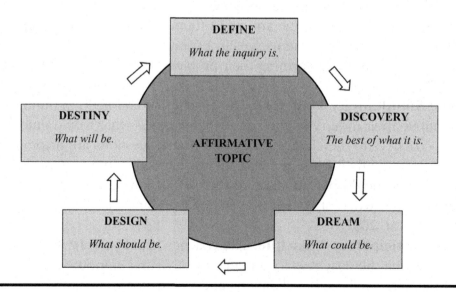

Figure 2.4   Appreciative Inquiry Stages and Model.

Source: Adapted from Rothwell et al. (2016).

the implementation of their high-performance coaching process and questioning process.

- **Define Stage.** In this stage, the coaches assist the coachees in defining their interests and desired topics for the coaching relationship. This stage is about the coachees' topics of interest and on what they are focusing. In this stage, the coaches encourage the coachees to come with ideas of who else needs to be involved and what they need to bring to the game to accomplish their intention and the topic on which they are focusing. The main inquiry in this stage is all about "what it is" and "who is involved?" (Cooperrider et al. 2003).
- **Discovery Stage.** In this stage, coaches establish a positive connection between themselves and the coachees and lead them to an empowering view by confirming the wisdom of what is possible and to look at the best aspects of what it is at this moment. This is the stage during which the coaches will establish a positive connection with the coachees and lead them to an empowering view of themselves. This is the stage for assisting the coachees in creating possibilities and seeing opportunities for themselves and their future. This stage is all about the coachees' discoveries of what is possible and the source of their aspirations. The primary inquiry in this stage is around "why things are the way they are now" (Cooperrider et al. 2003).
- **Dream Stage.** In this stage, the coaches encourage the coachees to generate empowering images of possibilities by inviting them to express and share about their desired futures. The main inquiry in this stage is about "what could be," imagining what is possible for the coachees and their lives. The coaches will encourage the coachees to imagine the future and what their lives would look like in that future. In this stage, the coaches are assisting the coachees to put their aspiring futures into words and verbalize them (Cooperrider et al. 2003).
- **Design Stage.** In this stage, the coaches would support their coachees to bring their desired dreams or futures into light and focus by asserting the realities of those dreams or futures. This is the stage for inquiry in to "how it could become" and defining the idyllic pictures of what the futures could be. At this stage, the coaches assist the coachees to focus on their intentions and confirm the reality of their dreams by supporting the coachees to design an action plan established on reality (Cooperrider et al. 2003).
- **Destiny Stage.** This stage focuses on "what will be," and how to empower, learn, and adjust/improvise (Cooperrider et al. 2003, 101). At

this stage, the coaches help their coachees to distinguish their dreams and realize them in the present time, by empowering them to expand their capacity to create the desired future and inspire them to stick to their action plans. In this stage, coachees learn to keep their dreams alive and in front of themselves. The main inquiry at this stage is about "what it will be" (Cooperrider et al. 2003).

Asking Positive Questions Lead to Positive Inquiry and Change

As Lee (2021) stated, "[t]he statement that 'positive questions lead positive change' should not need any scientific proof to be confirmed" (23). The use of positive psychology and the application of AI bring positivity in performance conversation and a high-performance coaching approach. The Appreciative Inquiry Model with the positive psychology as the background of the coaching approach uses a series of positive questions to uncover and unleash the coachees' potential, while focusing on individuals' or teams' strengths and what is working versus forcing on apparent problems or weaknesses.

Elements of Performance Conversations Framework

The overall concept of the Performance Conversation approach has a framework that utilizes a series of conversations and dialogues that promote a string of positive and effective outcomes for improving individuals, teams, and organizations' performances. Performance Conversation framework assists high-performance coaches in delivering their coaching to an employee or a team to produce greater success, develop more needed skills, and inspire them to aim for gaining an overall professional career (Lee 2021; Cardy and Leonard 2011). Table 2.1 displays these frameworks in regard to the organization as well as to individuals and teams.

Performance Conversation Reflection

Table 2.2 is designed for high-performance coaches to review employees' performance each quarter by asking the employees/coachees to look into what they need to succeed in their performance. You, as high-performance coaches or managers-as-coaches, can modify the quarterly list of questions or ask the employee if they want to add anything new to this list.

Table 2.1 Elements, Purpose, and Benefits of Strong Framework for Performance Conversation.

Elements, Purpose, and Benefits of Strong Framework for Performance Conversation		
For Organizations		
#	**Area**	**Purpose**
1	Rapport	Establishing and building a mutual, effective, and purposeful relationship among the manager and employee resulting in a professional partnership.
2	Coaching	Concentrating on individuals, teams, and developing high performance, productivity, and professional well-being.
3	Alignment	Ensuring consistency in application and direction of coaching efforts with other departments and overall organizational vision and goals.
4	Performance improvement	Discovering pathways to empower individuals, teams, and departments to perform better, faster, and more effectively.
5	Responsibility and accountability	Giving responsibility and holding individuals and teams accountable for their work performance, work progress, results, and overall success or failures.
6	Feedback	Providing input and information as a result of observation, conversation, or collected data concerning past or present efforts, results, and behaviors.
7	Envisioning	Envisioning the possibility of efforts and potential of change interventions to make individual or team performance improvements.
8	Investment	Expending on budget, time, and effort for supporting employees' interest, engagement, and participation.
9	Retention	Working on retaining employees who are providing values, showing appreciation, and being productive and high producers vital to their teams.
10	Developing strengths	Developing and building strength in individuals and teams to produce high performance and effective teams.
For Employees/Coachees		
#	**Area**	**Purpose**
1	Career development	Discussing employees' future with the organization or other career development, giving professional advice for skill-building or improvement opportunities.

(Continued)

Table 2.1 (Continued)

	For Employees/Coachees	
#	**Area**	**Purpose**
2	Affirmation	Confirming employees' correct career pathway and letting them know they are doing well and progressing in their process.
3	Growth and development	Discussing possibility for growth in available formal and informal opportunities to learn more and develop new skills and competencies.
4	Promotability	Defining employees' interests and potential professional growth in taking on promotions and new positions or assignments.
5	Recognitions	Appreciating and acknowledging an employees' work progress, performance, or success.
6	Leadership	Providing space for employees to step into leadership positions or have the opportunity to provide leadership in their teams or departments.
7	Problem Solving	Teaching problem-solving techniques and developing employees to remove obstacles and barriers to their higher performance.
8	Partnership	Developing a working environment that promotes partnership and creativity and acknowledges collaborations.
9	Mentorship	Acting as mentor side by side of the performance coaching relationship and developing employees to mentor one another in productivity and better performance.
10	Reflection	Reflecting on their performance and the coaching relationship to gain insight by reviewing or evaluating their own efforts and gaining empowerment.

Source: Copyright 2021 by Behnam Bakhshandeh.

What Is Performance Management?

Performance coaching helps individuals improve their job performance. Performance management is the process of identifying productivity targets for individuals, teams, departments, divisions, or organizations. Consequently, performance coaching can be a means to the end of improving performance management.

Table 2.2 Quarterly Performance Conversation and Reflection Check List for Employees and Coachees.

Quarterly Performance Conversation and Reflection Check List					
Participant:			Team:		
Supervisor:			Department:		
Directions: This is completed quarterly based on short interviews and performance coaching conversations. These questions are part of a conversation between the coaches and coachees and are designed to focus on all the things employees need to succeed in their job/work and produce the expected performance and results. If you (coaches or coachees) feel something is not mentioned or covered here, bring it up in the conversation and add it for future use.					
Quarter	**Questions/Reflections**	**Yes**	**No**	**Not Sure**	**Comment**
1st Quarter	I know what I need to do to be successful at my job/work.				
	I know the reason for what I do and why it matters.				
	I have all the support I need for completing my job/work.				
	I have enough tools and resources to perform my job/work.				
	I have all the necessary skills and competencies to complete my job/work.				
	I have all the needed training to perform my job/work.				
	Other:				
	Other:				
	What I learned and how do I feel about today's coaching and performance conversation?				
2nd Quarter	**Questions/Reflections**			**Answers**	
	What are the two things I would change if I could change them?			1. 2.	

(Continued)

Table 2.2 (Continued)

	Quarterly Performance Conversation and Reflection Check List				
	Questions/Reflections	***Answers***			
	What are the two actions that would produce a better outcome in my performance?	1. 2.			
	What are the two obstacles that are hindering my job/work?	1. 2.			
	What are the two things that I am enjoying most about my job/work?	1. 2.			
	What are the two challenges in my job/work that make me feel fulfilled?	1. 2.			
	Please explain "why" concerning the above question.	1. 2.			
	Other:				
	Other:				
	What I learned and how do I feel about today's coaching and performance conversation?				
	Questions/Reflections	***Yes***	***No***	***Not Sure***	***Comment***
	I know what I need to do to be successful at my job/work.				
	I know the reason for what I do and why it matters.				
3rd Quarter	I have all the support I need for completing my job/work.				
	I have enough tools and resources to perform my job/work.				
	I have all the necessary skills and competencies to complete my job/work.				
	I have all the needed training to perform my job/work.				
	Other:				
	Other:				

	What I learned and how do I feel about today's coaching and performance conversation?				

4th Quarter	*Questions/Reflections*	*Answers*
	What are the two things I would change if I could change them?	1. 2.
	What are the two actions that would produce a better outcome in my performance?	1. 2.
	What are the two obstacles that are hindering my job/work?	1. 2.
	What are the two things that I am enjoying most about my job/work?	1. 2.
	What are the two challenges in my job/work that make me feel fulfilled?	1. 2.
	Please explain "why" concerning the above question.	1. 2.
	Other:	
	Other:	
	What I learned and how do I feel about today's coaching and performance conversation?	

Source: Adapted from Lee (2021); Rothwell (2015); Cardy and Leonard (2011); Bakhshandeh (2008).

"Performance management is a critical and necessary component for individuals and organizational effectiveness" (Cardy and Leonard 2011, 3). Regardless of the improvement needed or planned, whether it be managing a group, giving feedback to a subordinate, reporting to your senior manager, coaching your employees, or managing your performance, performance management is needed for these actions (2011).

"Performance management is an integrated process of defining, assessing, developing, and reinforcing employee work behaviors and outcomes" (Cumming and Worley 2015, 440).

Often, organizations that implement a well-designed performance management process outperform competitors that ignore these issues.

Performance management incorporates (1) setting goals, outcomes, and declaring intentions; (2) designing well-intentioned performance evaluation and appraisal; (3) incorporating a fair and promotion and reward system; and (4) training and development programs for their workforce in all levels of operation (2015). See Figure 2.3.

The combination of these practices positively influences individual performance, which directly affects the team and group performance, making the organization realize its goals and outcomes. Performance management occurs in the background of three contextual considerations (see Figure 2.3) that determine how the aforementioned four elements of performance management practices change work performance in a better direction: (1) business plan and strategy, (2) workplace systems and technology, and (3) employee involvement and engagement (2015).

Business Plan and Strategy

This element of performance management involves setting goals, creating the outcomes and organization's objectives, designing policies, intentions, and anticipated relationships between the organization and its internal and external environment, and ultimately what it takes to achieve effectiveness (2015).

Workplace Systems and Technology

An organization's systems and their technology affect whether performance management practices and procedures should be established and centered, focusing on the individuals, teams, or groups. On the one hand, when the work activities are low in interdependency, and work procedures are intended for individual job performance, the whole elements of goal setting/ outcomes, performance evaluation/appraisal, development approaches, and promotion/reward systems are intended for the individuals' work and behaviors. But when work is highly interdependent among teams and groups and is designed for team or group work, performance management will concentrate on group behaviors and performance (2015).

Employee Involvement and Engagement

In organizations with highly bureaucratic systems, there are low levels of employee involvement. Goal setting, performance evaluation, workforce development, and promotion/reward systems are mostly overseen by managers. However, in organizations with high employee involvement, performance management is highly participative, involving both employees and managers to set goals, establish a proper promotion and reward system, decide on suitable training and development programs, and create relevant evaluation and appraisal plans (2015).

The High-Performance Coaching Model

The high-performance coaches or a managers-as-coaches need to manage the high-performance coaching, the intervention process, and implementation of changes in order to increase and enhance the individuals' and team's performance. The following model in Figure 2.5 displays the

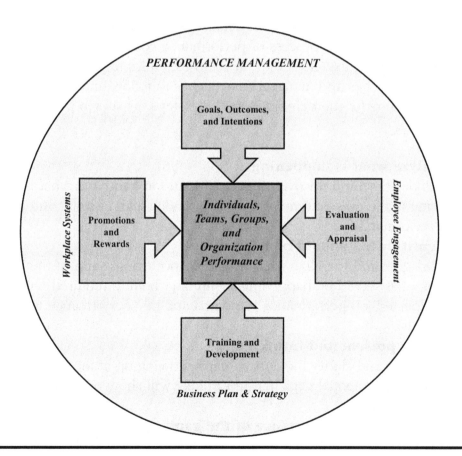

Figure 2.5   Performance Management Model.

Source: Adapted from Cumming and Worley (2015).

performance coaching model we present in this book that is a proven design for assisting the high-performance coaches in applying an effective and manageable model for performance coaching and performance enhancement.

Using this model (see Figure 2.6), the high-performance coaches should pay attention not only to internal factors, such as employees, policies, procedures, and training but also to external factors, such as customers, distributors, suppliers, and other potential stakeholders. The high-performance coaches must always consider all the four environments that affect human performance: (1) Who? The workers, employees, and personnel; (2) What? The activities, the work, jobs, and performances; (3) Where? The context of the work, location, teams, and groups; and (4) organizational environment. The vision, mission, policies, procedures, and culture were displayed in Figure 2.1.

The *Performance Coaching Model* steps presented in this book are discussed, expanded, and explained in detail throughout the chapters. The book chapters follow the process of performance coaching step by step by providing processes, exercises, and business examples to provide clarity for performance coaches and managers-as-coaches to follow and provide education and coaching for their employees. These steps (as shown in Figure 2.6) are as follows:

(1) **Analyze what is happening**
   - Understand and uncover the actual issues at hand and what is occurring at the present time as a result of individuals', teams', and groups' performance.
(2) **Identify what should be happening**
   - Imagine and visualize what should be occurring. Support the idea of what should be happening by linking them to required criteria, expected job performance standards and key performance indicators (KPIs).
(3) **Clarify present and future gaps**
   - Explain and clarify the current gaps showing up at the present time and also potential gaps that most likely will show up in the near future.
(4) **Determine the importance of the gaps**
   - How important are these gaps? Define the importance of these current and potential future gaps and their significance of their impact on the organization.

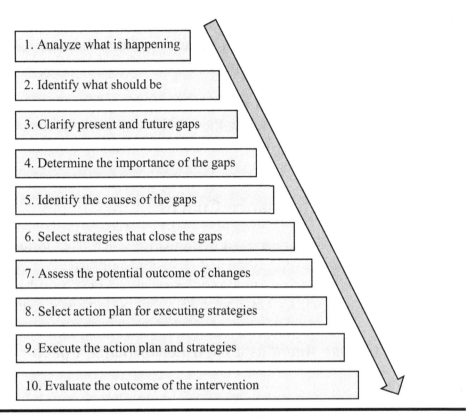

Figure 2.6 The High-Performance Coaching Model.

Source: Copyright 2021 by William J. Rothwell.

(5) **Identify the cause of the gaps**
 – Discover the underlying origins and root cause of these gaps and how they became the issues at hand.
(6) **Select strategies that close the gaps**
 – Conduct brainstorming and problem-solving processes and select high-performance strategies that would close theses current and future gaps.
(7) **Assess the potential outcome of changes**
 – Calculate and evaluate the potential negative and positive outcomes of implementing the strategies and their potential side effects.
(8) **Select an action plan for executing strategies**
 – With the partnership of related managers and supervisors, design a detailed performance-based action plan for executing the high-performance strategies.

(9) **Execute that action plan and strategies**
   – Execute the designed action plan and agreed-on high-performance strategies and manage the process by engaging relevant managers and supervisors.
(10) **Evaluate the outcome of the intervention**
   – Evaluate the progress during the process and postimplementation. Evaluate the final outcomes and provide constructive feedbacks.

Who Is a High-Performance Coach?

Anyone with proper training can be a performance coach. That includes managers, talent development or learning and development practitioners, or even workers. Performance coaches can also be external coaches, consultants, OD practitioners, change agents, or others familiar with performance coaching.

Selecting a Change Agent as a High-Performance Coach

This individual is trying to convince the organization to agree with the needed activities and intervention for a change. Given that the majority of changes' sources originates from dissatisfactions, the most dissatisfied manager or supervisor should take on to be the change agent, "[d]riven by dissatisfaction, change agents seek innovative solutions to tough problems or create improvement strategies to take advantage of opportunities they see" (Rothwell 2015, 65).

The position of the change agents can be an insider (a senior or junior manager, internal OD practitioner, HR director or manager, or the high-performance coach as a manager-as-coach) or a professional outsider (external OD practitioner, HPI or HPE practitioner, business consultant, or an executive coach). By having proper training and knowledge of the work, an internal change agent can fill the position of a performance coach. The external change agents are usually selected by solicitation of a name recognized by an OD practitioner or consultant group, or referral of other organizations' executives or senior managers.

Coaches' Strengths, Skills, and Competencies

Few managers can demonstrate coaching skills without proper training. Talent development and learning and development practitioners need to acknowledge and even embrace, the increasing importance of personal and professional coaching. Coaches need to have confidence in their ability to see through the issues and possess the competencies to keep the clients focused on them (Bakhshandeh 2015; Bakhshandeh 2009; Bakhshandeh 2008).

Compassion

Compassion is one main element of successful coaches. Coaches must recognize that clients would change on their own if they could and that clients are experiencing pain, suffering, or ineffectiveness (2015, 2009, 2008).

Patience

Coaches need patience. Having patience with others is a helpful addition to empowering clients to grow self-aware and achieve self-realization. Not everyone works at the same speed when uncovering their personalities, behaviors, and attitude; not everyone is immediately willing to take complete responsibility for their situations and own who they can become as fast as their coaches or other people (2015, 2009, 2008).

Keen Listening

Coaches must be keen listeners. And they must know to listen for feelings as well as facts. Coaches must know how to listen for facts or mere perceptions of facts (2015, 2009, 2008).

Personal Responsibility

Clients should take responsibility for their choices. The source of suffering for coachees is often avoiding making choices or not being committed to the choices they make. Choosing is easy. What is hard is maintaining and empowering those choices. The world is full of people who don't take responsibility! They just want to blame something or someone for their lack of their personal or professional happiness, fulfillment, or effectiveness (2015, 2009, 2008).

Reality versus Interpretations

People need to be reminded of the differences between reality (what is really happening) and interpretations (how we perceive what is happening). Our interpretations result from our filters of experience (2015, 2009, 2008).

Coaching Competencies According to ATD and ICF

According to the ATD (2014) (Association of Talent Development) and ICF (2011) (International Coaching Federation) websites, coaches should be able to demonstrate eleven competencies. These competencies are designed for regular life or business coaching; however, their value is still relevant for performance coaches.

Establish a Coaching Agreement

A coach can work with coachees to devise detailed and relevant contracts that would provide a safe and workable space. That agreement should outline the relationship between coaches and coachees, their scope of work, and their expectations.

Establish Trust and Intimacy with the Client

No progress is possible without trust and a working bond between coaches and coachees. Trust allows for respect and teamwork among the two parties.

Display Coaching Presence

It is essential to maintain the coaching relationship. It should be clear what the coaching commitments require from coaches and coachees.

Demonstrate Active Listening

Coaches should listen without interruption, judgment, and personal agendas. Coachees talk to their coaches because they trust the coaches. Performance coaches should be present and available to coachees.

Ask Powerful Questions

Present questions as an inquiry and make sure coachees are benefitting from digging deeper versus just providing a potential "coach pleasing" answer. Questions posed by the coach should forward the inquiry and lead to desired outcomes. Coaches should keep the questions on track.

Use Direct Communication

Coaches should not tiptoe around the issues they are finding or to which the coachees are not comfortable facing. Straight, direct, and respectful communication makes a difference. Coaches should establish the rules of communication when negotiating the coaching agreement.

Create Awareness

Coaches should make sure the coachees learn something new about themselves and their behaviors or decision-making processes. Try to make sure that coachees feel that the "light bulb" is going *on* during each interaction.

Design Learning Opportunities

Learning opportunities will occur when direct inquiry happening. Coaches should offer additional materials such as books, articles, and other resources to support coachees' learning progress.

Develop Goals and Plans

Without established goals and action plans to fulfill those goals, coaching sessions are nothing more than friendly conversations. Nothing occurs without structure and planning.

Manage Progress and Accountability

Set deadlines for assignments or inquiries, follow up with the coachees about what they said they would do, hold them responsible for their results, and make them accountable for following your agreements.

Meet Ethical Guidelines and Professional Standards

Follow ethical and professional standards, such as not getting involved with coachees on a personal level, not overcharging them, keeping their information confidential, and other ethical codes of conduct you can find on any professional coaching website.

The High-Performance Coaching Process

The entire book is about guiding and coaching a performance coach to conduct high-performance coaching for individuals, teams, and organizations. The following segment presents (1) a model for general actions required by a performance coach and (2) the performance coaching process from the coach's perspective. In subsequent chapters, we will go through any of these steps in-depth and use tools, processes, and business examples to distinguish these steps further.

A Model for General Actions by a Performance Coach

We can summarize the general view and expected actions by performance coaches on the next general steps, as shown in Figure 2.6. (*Model for Performance Coach Actions*). Obviously, each action and step have their related elements and procedures which will be explained in detail in the chapters of this book.

Performance Coach

Trained and experienced managers-as-coaches are familiar with the work process and have knowledge, skills, and abilities to coach performers to a higher level and increased productivity. There are several skills and competencies that are required for performance coaches to be able to conduct their responsibilities. These required abilities, skills, and competencies will be reviewed in subsequent chapters.

Access the Situation

Performance coaches need a higher manager's support and backing to conduct their work to the best of their abilities. One of these supportive actions is permission to access the situation in hand. For example, sometimes the performance coach is an external agent or an internal agent but not working on a certain department or a team. In this case, a senior manager or a department manager needs to introduce the performance coach and help the coach to assess the current performance situation. This is the time to establish a rapport with any individual in question or the rest of the team that is facing low performance.

Identify the Current Situation

This is the time to start investigating the current situation and recognizing what is actually going on and identifying performance gaps or areas that need a performance improvement.

Compare to the Ideal Situation

At this time, the performance coach needs to understand which ideal performance situations to compare to the actual and current situation and what the team or organization wants to have or achieve.

Plan for Closing the Gap

After the detailed comparison between the current situation and the ideal situation, the performance coach needs to help the individual or team develop an action plan to close the current performance gaps or improve performances. This plan needs to be related to the processes and procedures that individuals or teams are using to perform their tasks, jobs, and work.

Implement a Corrective Plan

Now, the performance coach needs to work with individuals or teams to coach them in how to complement the action plan, manage the process, and evaluate the performance and effectiveness of the action plan.

Figure 2.7   Model for Performance Coach Actions.

Source: Copyright 2021 by Behnam Bakhshandeh.

The Process of High-Performance Coaching from Coach's Perspective

Figure 2.8 represents what high-performance coaches need to conduct step by step to accomplish in the form of questions that they should ask themselves during high-performance coaching. Performance coaches or managers-as-coaches should pose these questions to guide the coaching process productively and effectively.

These twelve questions are designed to direct the high-performance coaches' mindset and focus on step-by-step activities that need to be done to implement an effective high-performance coaching process. We follow

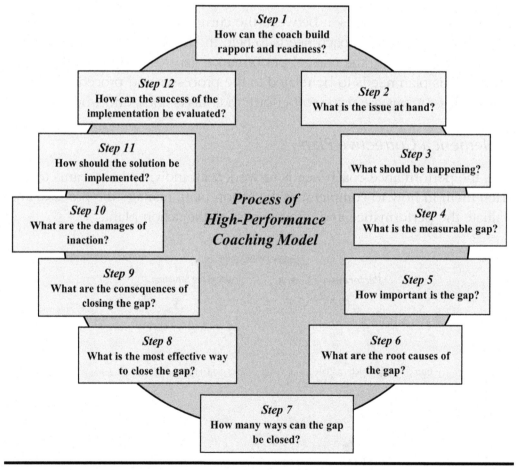

Figure 2.8 The Step-By-Step Process of High-Performance Coaching Model from a Coach's Perspective.

Source: Copyright 2021 by William J. Rothwell.

the order and steps of this high-performance coaching process while developing high-performance coaches and managers-as-coaches in this book.

Table 2.3 presents the twelve steps in Figure 2.8 in much detail for a performance coach to use during the assessment of performance situations. As we have mentioned earlier, we will go through each of the twelve steps in deeper detail during the process of this book.

Table 2.3 High-Performance Coaching Tool.

Performance Coaching Tool Used by a High-Performance Coach	
Directions: For each question listed in the left column below, take notes on what you will do in a specific situation in the right column.	
Questions to Ask in High-Performance Coaching	*Actions to Take for Providing Answers*
1 How can the consultant/manager or a performance coach establish rapport and a contractual relationship with a coachee?	
2 What is the present situation that requires coaching? What is happening? What is the issue at hand? (*Please describe it in detail*)	
3 What should be happening? What is the ideal situation or condition? What are the targets or planned results? (*Please describe the desired target*)	
4 What is the *measurable* gap between what is happening (step 2 above) and what should be happening (step 3 above)? Do you have a job performance standard or KPIs?	
5 How important is the identified gap? How do you determine the importance or significance of these gaps? How do you come up with that conclusion?	

(*Continued*)

Table 2.2 (Continued)

	Performance Coaching Tool Used by a High-Performance Coach	
6	What are the root causes of the identified gap? What happened? What was missed? What are the sources of gaps?	
7	How many ways can the gap be closed by addressing the root causes? What are our options? *(Brainstorm on possible solutions)*	
8	What is the most cost-effective and impactful way to close the gap by addressing the root causes? *(Pick the best or most feasible solution)*	
9	What are the likely consequences, positive and negative, of efforts to close the gap by addressing the root causes? What are the side effects of the solution?	
10	What will happen if the solution is not implemented? What are the likely consequences of inaction?	
11	How can the solution be implemented? How much time, money, and other resources are available for implementation?	
12	How can the results of the solution's implementation be evaluated?	

Source: Adapted from Rothwell (2015).

The Coach–Coachee Relationship

The relationship between the coach and coachee is vital to accomplishing the goals set for the coaching process. Regretfully, there have been few research studies on effective coach–coachee relationships (Baron and Morin 2009). However, we can look at the definition of coaching by the Oxford Dictionary that defines *coaching* as a *verb* to "tutor, train, give hints to, prime with facts."

On the one hand, this definition doesn't help define the relationship between coaches and coachees because tutoring, training, giving hints, and priming with facts can be done in many shapes and forms—and may even occur when no coaching relationship exists. But coaching is related to how these distinctions are delivered, what is delivered, what was hidden, and what was uncovered. The coaching approach provides coachees with access to produce unprecedented results because of the intimate, caring, and supportive rapport between the coaches and the coachees.

Manager-as-Coach

To explain it simply, the manager-as-coach approach means that managers acts as coaches for those reporting to them. Managers may thus serve as coaches to individuals or teams. Effective managers-as-coaches provide support for their employees. Managers-as-coaches facilitate their employees' development instead of controlling and dictating what to do.

As good as it might sound, the fact is this: a manager is also an employee, which creates a paradox. Whitmore (2009) explains this paradoxical issue as

> a paradox because the manager traditionally holds the paycheck, the key to promotion, and also the ax. This is fine so long as you believe that the only way to motivate is to send the stick through the judicious application of the carrot. However, for coaching to work at its best, the relationship between the coach and the coachee must be one of partnership in the endeavor, trust, safety, and minimal pressure. The check, the key, and the ax have no place here, as can serve only to inhibit such a relationship
>
> (20).

Because of this paradox, Whitmore (2009) asks a valid question "Can a manager, therefore, be a coach at all?" (20). And the answer provided by Whitmore (2009) was "Yes, but coaching demands the highest qualities of those managers' empathy, integrity, and detachment, as well as a willingness, in most cases, to adopt a fundamentally different approach to their staff" (20). Besides this quality, managers-as-coaches must find their way through the maze of coaching subordinates, which makes having coached for themselves an ideal resolution for their development as coaches and for developing skills to cope with potential resistance from their employees or the questioning of their approaches from their own higher managers who may compare their approaches with traditional management styles (Whitmore 2009).

Does Coaching Help Businesses' Competitiveness?

"Twenty-first-century organizations face an unprecedented challenge in the form of global competition, changing markets, customer demands, and investor expectations. Management development has grown into a multibillion-dollar industry" (Kochanowski, Seifert, and Yukl 2010, 363). As organizations seek to be part of a global market in their industries, the need for a competent and skillful workforce becomes more evident and supports the argument of providing more effective leadership development of employees. That is why organizations spend approximately fourteen billion dollars a year in employee training and managerial development, and performance coaching, hoping for better work performance and productivity (Kochanowski, Seifert, and Yukl 2010). According to research focused on the influence of coaching in business competitiveness by Vidal-Salazar, Ferrón-Vílchez, and Cordón-Pozo (2012), the results show that "coaching substantially increases the level to which processes of improvement are established within organizations, consequently increasing the competitive capability" (Vidal-Salazar et al. 2012, 423). The evidence of coaching increasing in global organizations shows the influence of managerial coaching due to a constant prerequisite for Workplace Learning and Performance and innovation for modern organizations to stay competitive in their relevant market (Kim 2014).

There is an assumption among business observers that organizational leaders see a positive impact from coaching. It is used as a way to compete for talent as well as to develop managers and workers.

Key Points to Remember

Here are some key points from this chapter:

- ▪ **Trust the process**
  - Performance coaches should inform, support, and encourage coachees to trust coaching and apply the distinctions, practices, and methods designed to empower them (Bakhshandeh 2009).

■ **Manager-as-coach as an instrument**
  – Managers who coach have a big influence on those reporting to them. Managers can provide their knowledge, abilities, and skills to direct, consult, support, and advice to be an effective instrument of the change effort (Cheung-Judge and Mee-Yan 2012).
■ **Authority versus leadership**
  – Running a coaching program as an authority figure is a traditional management approach used in many organizations. Unfortunately, research has shown that a traditional management style can produce more resistance than engagement and participation (Satell 2014).

Coaching and Developmental Questions for Managers

Consider the following questions:
(1) How do you rate yourself from 1 to 10 (1 being the lowest and 10 being the highest) as a performance coach?
(2) How do you rate yourself from 1 to 10 (1 being the lowest and 10 being the highest) on having a meaningful, trusting coaching relationship with your subordinates?
(3) How do your coaching skills and competencies compare to those required for a performance coach?
(4) What competencies do you feel need to be developed for you to be a more effective performance coach?

References

Angelo, Gabriel. 2012. *Rapport; The Art of Connecting with People and Building Relationships*. Middletown, DE: SN & NS Publications.

ATD-Association for Talent Development. 2014. "ATD Competency Model: Talent Development Redefined." *ATD Competency Model Graphic and AOE.pdf*. www.tdcascadia.org/assets/2014/12/ATD-Competency-Model-Graphic-and-AOE.pdf.

Bailey, Robert W. 1982. *Human Performance Engineering: A Guild for System Designer*. Englewood Cliffs, NJ: Prentice-Hall.

Bakhshandeh, Behnam. 2008. "Bravehearts; Leadership Development Training." Unpublished Training and Developmental Course on Coaching Executive and Managers. San Diego, CA: Primeco Education, Inc.

Bakhshandeh, Behnam. 2009. *Conspiracy for Greatness; Mastery on Love Within*. San Diego, CA: Primeco Education, Inc.

Bakhshandeh, Behnam. 2015. *Anatomy of Upset: Restoring Harmony*. Carbondale, PA: Primeco Education, Inc.

Baron, Louis, and Lucie Morin. 2009. "The Coach—coachee Relationship in Executive Coaching: A Field Study." *Human Resources Development Quarterly* 20, no. 1: 85–106. https://doi.org/10.1002/hrdq.20009.

Cardy, Robert L., and Brian Leonard. 2011. *Performance Management: Concepts, Skills and Exercises*. Armonk, NY: Me. E. Sharp Inc.

Cheung-Judge, Mee-Yan. 2012. "The Self as an Instrument: A Cornerstone for the Future of OD." *Journal of the Organization Development Network* 44, no. 2: 40–47.

Cooperrider, David L., and David Whitney. n.d. "Appreciative Inquiry: A Positive Revolution in Change." In *The Change Handbook*, edited by P. Holman and T. Devane, 245–63. Oakland, CA: Berrett-Koehler Publishers, Inc.

Cooperrider, David L., Diana Whitney, and Jacqueline M. Stavros. 2003. *Appreciative Inquiry Handbook: For Leaders of Change*, 2nd ed. Brunswick, OH: Crown Custom Publishing, Inc.

Cooperrider, David L., Dianna Whitney, and Jacqueline M. Stavros. 2008. *Appreciative Inquiry: For Leaders of Change*, 2nd ed. Brunswick, OH: Crown Custom Publishing, Inc.

Cummings, Thomas G., and Christopher G. Worley. 2015. *Organization Development & Change*, 10th ed. Stamford, CT: Cengage Learning.

Gable, Shelly, and Jonathan Haidt. 2005. "What (and Why) is Positive Psychology?" *Review of General Psychology* 9, no. 2: 103–10.

ICF (International Coaching Federation). 2011. "Coached Core Competencies." https://coachfederation.org/app/uploads/2017/12/CoreCompetencies.pdf.

Kim, Sewon. 2014. "Assessing the Influence of Managerial Coaching on Employee Outcomes." *Human Resource Development Quarterly* 25, no. 1: 59–85. https://doi.org/10.1002/hrdq.21175.

Kochanowski, Susan, Charles F. Seifert, and Gary Yukl. 2010. "Using Coaching to Enhance the Effects of Behavioral Feedback to Managers." *Journal of Leadership & Organizational Studies* 17, no. 4: 363–69. https://doi.org/10.1177/1548051809352663.

Lee, Christopher D. 2021. *Performance Conversations: How to Use Questions to Coach Employees, Improve Productivity & Boost Confidence*. Alexandria, VA: SHRM.

Oren, Sara L., Jacqueline Binkert, and Ann L. Clancy. 2007. *Appreciative Coaching: A Positive Process for Change*. San Francisco, CA: Jossey-Bass.

"Performance." 2021. *The Merriam-Webster Dictionary*. www.merriam-webster.com/dictionary/performance.

Pfeiffer, William J. 1990. *Developing Human Resources*. San Diego, CA: Pfeiffer & Company.

Rao, Paulette. 2013. *Transformation Coaching: Shifting Mindset for Sustainable Change*. Brooklyn, NY: True North Resources.

"Rapport." 2021. *The Merriam-Webster Dictionary*. www.merriam-webster.com/dictionary/rapport.

Rothwell, William J. 2015. *Beyond Training & Development: Enhancing Human Performance Through a Measurable Focus on Business Impact*, 3rd ed. Amherst, MA: HRD Press, Inc.

Rothwell, William J., and H. C. Kazanas. 2003. *The Strategic Development of Talent*. Amherst, MA: HRD Press, Inc.

Rothwell, William J., Jacqueline M. Stavros, and Roland L. Sullivan. 2016. *Practicing Organization Development: Leading Transformation and Change*, 4th ed. Hoboken, NJ: John Wiley & Sons, Inc.

Satell, Greg. 2014. "To Create Change, Leadership is More Important Than Authority." *Harvard Business Review*. Harvard Business School Publishing Corporation.

Seligman, Martin E. P. 2002. *Authentic Happiness: Using the New Positive Psychology to Realize Your Potential for Lasting Fulfillment*. New York, NY: Free Press.

Vidal-Salazar, María Dolores, Vera Ferrón-Vílchez, and Eulogio Cordón-Pozo. 2012. "Coaching: An Effective Practice for Business Competitiveness." *Competitiveness Review: An International Business Journal* 22, no. 5: 423–33. https://doi.org/10.1108/10595421211266302.

Watkins, Jane Magruder, Bernard J. Mohr, and Ralph Kelly. 2011. *Appreciative Inquiry: Change at the Speed of Imagination*, vol. 35. New York, NY: John Wiley & Sons.

White, Thomas H. 1996. "Working in Interesting Times: Employee Morale and Business Success in the Information Age." *Vital Speeches of the Day* 42, no. 15: 472.

Whitmore, John. 2009. *Coaching for Performance; GROWing Human Potential and Purpose*, 4th ed. Boston, MA: Nicholas Brealey Publishing.

Whitmore, John. 2017. *Coaching for Performance; The Principle and Practice of Coaching and Leadership*, 5th ed. Boston, MA: Nicholas Brealey Publishing.

Wilson, Carol. 2020. *Performance Coaching: A Complete Guide to Best-Practice Coaching and Training*, 3rd ed. New York, NY: KoganPage.

Chapter 3

Mindset, Attitude, Behavior, and Performance

Behnam Bakhshandeh

How Individual Mindset, Attitude, and Behavior Impact Individual and Team Performance

Coaches help coachees develop awareness of their behaviors and attitudes and spark self-awareness. This approach is made possible by guiding coaching participants from a state of unconscious incompetence to a state of conscious incompetence, which is the first step to coachees' understanding how much they don't know and the necessity of the execution of corrective measures in their behavior and attitude, which will directly and positively influence the organization's strategy for achieving the desired productivity (Vidal-Salazar, Ferrón-Vílchez, and Cordón-Pozo 2012).

This chapter reviews mindset, attitude, behavior, and how they relate to job performance. In this chapter, readers will become familiar with emotional intelligence (EI) and its role in developing individual and team performance. Chapter 3 will cover these issues:

- the influence of coaching on productivity and employees' attitudes• the relationship between mindset, attitude, behavior, and performance
- which one to measure for performance, behaviors, or outcomes
- EI for training and development in high performance
- EI clusters and competencies and its rating system
- the leadership qualities of effective manager-as-coach as its rating system

DOI: 10.4324/9781003155928-4

Influence of Coaching on Productivity and Employees' Attitudes

We can look at the influence of managerial coaching on different elements of the workforce and their relationship to productivity and career:

Career Commitment

Coaching has a positive influence on careers and on career progress for those participating in it. Career commitment refers to how motivated workers are to persist in their career direction and their attitude toward their profession. One critical element of career commitment is the nature of relationships workers experience. Career commitment differs from workers' perspectives on the organization or employee personalities (Kim et al. 2013).

Organization Commitment

Coaching has an impact on organization commitment, which refers to the psychological and emotional attachment that employees feel about the organization for which they are working. This relationship is critical to ensure low turnover and is an important focus of attention for many organizational leaders (Kim et al. 2013).

Job Performance

Coaching influences workforce effectiveness on the job and is directly related to individual productivity. Coaching is thus tied to job performance (Kim et al. 2013).

Sales Increase

The sales of the organization can increase when coaching is used. A coaching intervention in sales is a high-quality interaction between managers and their sales team when managers increase their employees' awareness of many potentially critical elements of their attitude and the impact of attitude on their sales productivity improvement (Pousa, Mathieu, and Trépanier 2017).

Relationship between Mindset, Attitude, Behavior, and Performance

Small events can make a big difference in shaping mindsets, attitudes, behaviors, and achieving performance. For individuals to recognize their mindsets and attitudes, they need to reflect. That is not the same thing as ordinary, day-to-day thinking; rather, it means deep contemplation and intentional inquiries into state of mind.

A primary distinction between humans and other species is that humans can think, choose, and set their minds to what they know they can accomplish.

> To be able to think does not wholly depend on our will and wish, though much does depend on whether we prepare ourselves to hear that call to think when it comes and respond to it appropriately. Thinking is determined by that which is to be thought as well as by he who thinks
>
> *(Heidegger 1968, xi).*

An individual's attitude can be classified as either good or bad, and it can greatly affect individual performance. This simple but powerful phenomenon about attitudes can allow us to see ourselves as winners or losers and can be used to perceive others. According to the general public's viewpoint, the combination of a positive mindset and energetic attitude is one of the best behaviors one can have (Snyder and Tanke 1976). In a simple description, attitude encompasses one's mindset, perceptions, and beliefs. These fundamental components add to the individuals we became and form our skills and behaviors when facing real or perceived challenges (Yashasvi 2019).

This is a simple example from the Buddhist religion and practice in the book *Zen Speaks* by Tsai Chin Chung, which demonstrates the role of mindset and attitude that has an impact on someone's behavior and performance. This is a story of three stonemasons in the Middle Ages. These stonemasons chipped large stones using stone chisels and hammers, chipping away from large pieces of stones to be used in a construction project. They were working hard when a visitor, a stranger passing by, stopped and asked them separately what they were doing. The first mason, who was working hard and sweating fiercely replied while grumbling. "I am chipping this stone."

The second mason, who was comparably less distressed than the first mason sighed deeply and replied, "I am building a road." The third mason, who was doing the same hard stonework, responded with a joyful face, "I am building a beautiful cathedral" (Chung 1994). This short story's moral is this: those three men were doing the same work; however, they had three different perspectives that affected their work. They would have three different experiences of their work, their day, and their performance because of three different behaviors.

Figure 3.1 displays the relationship between mindset, attitude, behavior, and performance.

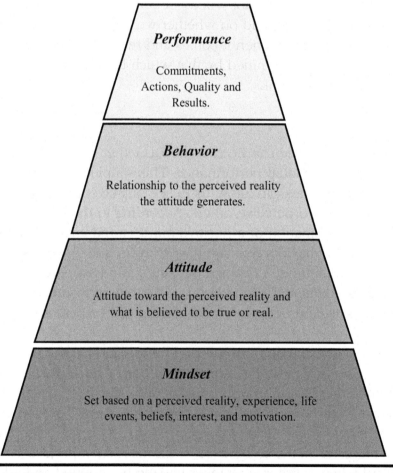

Figure 3.1 Relationship between Mindset, Attitude, Behavior, and Individual and Team Performance.

Source: Copyright 2021 by Behnam Bakhshandeh.

Mindset

Albert Einstein (1879–1955) once said, "reality is merely an illusion, albeit a very persistent one." You and I were born into a world of existing ideas, practices, beliefs, traditions, and rules. Our ideas have been formed by our experiences with life, family, friends, society, media, and work. The future we have had until now is a young child's future shaped and limited by the conditions that our past determined upon that future. A changing world and realities require constant updating of personal and social practices. Those practices and ideas fit an old rather than a new purpose. You and I are accountable for our lives and the results produced in them.

How will we upgrade past thinking to serve our present and future life? By recognizing and distinguishing the source of our beliefs. By getting present to how much of what we believe to be reality is what we have made up! Yes, we have made it up! I am not talking about the physical reality, such as the planet earth being round, the existence of gravity, the human anatomy, or any other proven physical, biological, chemical, or any other scientific reality. I am talking about the realities we have made up about ourselves, others at the workplace, or society in general. "I am not . . . enough," "I can't do . . .," "I am too . . . to do this," and many more; just fill in the blanks the way you are criticizing and limiting yourself. We all have those limiting thoughts and mindsets—not only for ourselves but also about others too.

What have we done as a human race that has defied the common perspective? The invention of the light bulb, reading and writing as a blind and deaf person, man's first step on the moon, and many more! What do these events have in common? Beliefs and mindsets. But what kind of beliefs and mindsets? Invented ones! They are mindset realities that moved so many humans to design, invent, and create realities not even imaginable in the mindsets of present realities of their times. History is full of those invented realities. There are no limits, there is no difficulty, and there is no "I can't" until we say, "It is," or we listen to others saying, "It is!" What is this amazing phenomenon that some people have created a mastery of and for so many others it is still a mystery?" (Bakhshandeh 2009, 19).

Mindset Definition and Types

According to Cherry (2020), individuals' mindsets refer to their beliefs in their attributes such as abilities and intelligence and also their perception of others' attitudes and behaviors. Sometimes these mindsets can be permanent and

stay with individuals for many years or be changeable traits based on perceptions about others or altered issues. Dweck (2016) indicates that most people
are trained in these two types of mindsets in their early stages of life, mostly
through their upbringing and or their experiences in school and life:

- **Fixed mindset**, which is by people who believe that abilities and intelligence are inborn, fixed, and unalterable, and
- **Growth mindset**, which is by people who believe that abilities and
intelligence can be thought, developed, and reinforced through interest,
motivation, and commitment (Dweck 2016).

Attitude

Attitudes demonstrate how individuals think (cognitive expression), how
they feel (affective expression), and how they are inclined to behave (behavioral expression) concerning other people, events, and other subjects
whether it be positively, negatively, or indifferently. Generally, when people
have an optimistic view of themselves and others, feel good about events,
and have constructive beliefs, then they have a positive attitude. When they
behave negatively toward themselves and others and are pessimistic about
events or groups, they have a negative attitude.

Though attitude includes the mind's tendency toward particular people,
ideas, organizations, values, or social systems, behavior correlates to the
definite manifestation of feelings through a form of actions or inactions as
communication and body language (Bainbridge Frymier and Keeshan Nadler
2017). One school of thought points at possible changes in one's attitude,
but gradually. Many organizations have attempted to change their difficult
employees' attitudes and create a workable and productive working environment through a variety of change interventions, training, and development
undertakings (Yashasvi 2019).

Behavior

The by-product of mindset and attitude about one's perceived reality is
one's behavior. Behavior is the activity or action manifested that appears
after the display or recognition of an attitude. It doesn't matter if we address
someone's behavior or attitude first to effectively influence someone or
something. But the recommendation is to first focus on someone's behavior

because it is easier to recognize and alter the perceived change instead of first tackling the attitude which is a much deeper undertaking, takes longer, and given one's mindset might be saddled for a long time (Bainbridge Frymier and Keeshan Nadler 2017).

It is worth mentioning that, unfortunately, there is a fairly large gap about the concept of "attitude-intention-behavior" among professionals who believe attitude does not always result in concurring behaviors. Sometimes individuals are not cognizant of their displayed attitudes which, like implicit attitudes, might cause certain behaviors or not, and not necessarily follow with attitudes (Yashasvi 2019).

Performance

By paying attention to the coachees'/subordinates' states of mind and discovering their mindset through a set of dialogues and conversations within the confines of a safe and free environment, managers can recognize the performance of coachees' linked to their attitudes and behaviors. It is not an easy task, and it might take more than a few coaching sessions. However, when the coaches/managers focus on the coachees' commitments and desired dreams and intentions for working, then the managers can affect their performance by not resisting their attitudes and behavior and keep coaching them to the realization they are the only ones who invented their perceptions, chose their attitudes, and caused their behavior. This process is the main objective of this book, which starts from Chapter 4.

Which One to Measure for Performance, Behaviors, or Outcomes

This question is on the minds of many organizations' managers and supervisors; What are the most important elements to follow and pay attention to: employees, behaviors, or outcomes? This simple but significant question is equivalent to a manager asking whether to pay attention to a process or just to the end results and an outcome. Which one is more important? Clearly, both are critical to a good business process and health organization system; however, in many cases, organizations often choose to focus on one element over the other when attempting to conduct a performance appraisal (Cardy and Leonard 2011). Let's look at a brief description of performance with behavior and performance as an outcome.

Performance as Behavior

From the standpoint of organizations, for the most part, a good job performance consists of good behaviors and attitudes. They are looking at what employees are doing on their jobs and how they conduct their workdays. If you ask many employees what they do on their jobs, most of them will explain their activities and the tasks they are performing at their jobs. In this regard, Cardy and Leonard (2011) pointed that, "[f]rom this perspective, the performance consists of behaviors, and how well those behaviors are executed is a critical performance criterion" (46).

Performance as Outcomes

From the standpoint of managers and supervisors directly dealing with the workforce, job performance mostly involves outcomes, the result, the final product, the achievement of goals, not the activities or even behaviors. Therefore, they are mostly looking at the black and white outcomes, such as:

- What are the sales today?
- What is the total sales amount?
- How many units are being produced?
- How many of them sold today?
- What was the waste today?
- How much time was wasted correcting mistakes?

These are the types of questions that peak performance as outcomes for managers and supervisors (Rothwell 2015; Cardy and Leonard 2011).

Of course, both behaviors and outcomes are important to individuals' and teams' high-performance process and the organization's bottom line, both having advantages and disadvantages for performance measurement; however, many managers pick one over the other based on their own career experiences or the work and productivity philosophy they have gathered during their own careers and based on their personal experiences. Therefore, the best measurement for both elements is to be establishing a set of criteria for both behavior and outcomes.

Establishing performance criteria is important to any operations and producing outcomes. Criteria emphasize and cause attention to what is critical and valued by an organization and its production. Criteria make available a realistic basis for performance measuring and the effectiveness of productions (Rothwell 2015; Cardy and Leonard 2011). "At an operational level, criteria define performance" (Cardy and Leonard 2011, 46).

At this segment, we briefly touched on the concept of criteria and its importance, but we will go much deeper in Chapter 6.

Advantages and Disadvantages of Behaviors and Outcomes as Performance

Table 3.1 presents some advantages and disadvantages of using behavioral and outcome performance criteria. This list is as uncomplicated as possible, with some necessary explanations. You can add any advantages

Table 3.1   Behavioral and Outcome as Performance Criteria—Advantages and Disadvantages.

Behavioral and Outcome as Performance Criteria Advantages and Disadvantages		
Category	*Advantages*	*Disadvantages*
Behavioral	It offers a clear-cut plot of how to alter behaviors and attitude for improving individual and team performance.	Individuals participating in applying corrective behaviors are not necessary guaranteed the preferred outcomes.
	It is under the direct control of employees to alter and modify for improving their performance.	This approach can be costly and time-consuming to develop the required criteria and producing the preferred outcomes.
	It gives the managers and coaches an opportunity to provide directive feedback to individuals and teams.	Some individuals might agree to behavioral changes without having any commitment or interest to maintain the change.
	It has an opportunity to make a difference for individuals in the elements of their personal life.	Some individuals do not like to talk about and dig into their personal behavior and attitudes and find that inappropriate.
Outcome	It is objective and easy to observe and easy to measure.	It is not under the control of individuals and teams because managers and supervisors manage it.

(Continued)

Table 3.1 (Continued)

Category	Advantages	Disadvantages
	Behavioral and Outcome as Performance Criteria *Advantages and Disadvantages*	
	It has potential off improving productivity and increase the bottom line by enhancing the performance of individuals, teams, and organizations.	It is relatively difficult to use directive feedback to individuals and teams by managers.
	It is sort of black and white and managed by quantitative past and present production data or best practices.	Some managers resist black and white numbers management and believe there is no human contact in just outcomes and result-oriented business.
	It has a strong potential to be part of budgeting, planning, designing targets, and managing forecasts.	Numbers need to be reviewed, adjusted, and modified based on the current production and performance compared to past results and future desired outcomes, without accounting for human performance issues.

Source: Adapted from Rothwell (2016), Cardy and Leonard (2011), Bakhshandeh (2008).

or disadvantages you see or experienced to this list as you wish and use them during your high-performance coaching with your employees or coachees.

Critical Incident Worksheet Based on Behavioral and Outcome Performance

Table 3.2 presents a simple example of a form that high-performance coaches or managers-as-coaches can use to manage, direct, and support individuals' or teams' behavioral and outcome performance criteria and adjust such criteria on a quarterly or semiannual basis in order to manage coaching individuals and teams to a high and more effective personal or team's performances.

Note: we will dig deeper into the concept, place, and use of criteria for individual and team performances in Chapter 6.

Table 3.2 Example of Critical Incident Worksheet Based on Behavioral and Outcome Performance.

Critical Incident Worksheet Based on Behavioral and Outcome Performance		
Direction: Use this form every quarter to review an employee's performance critical incidents and evaluate if such incident was related to a behavioral or an outcome performance. Also, this action will assist you and the employee to adjust their behavioral and outcome criteria.		
Participant:	Team:	
Supervisor:	Department:	
Quarter and Year:	Date:	
Job Descriptions and Dimensions:		
Performance Level	*Behavioral Criteria*	*Outcome Criteria*
Weak performance		
Mediocre performance		
Needs improvement on		
Meets the least expectations		
Surpasses the expectation		
Excellent performance		
Note:		

Source: Adapted from Rothwell (2013).

Emotional Intelligence for Training and Development in High Performance

Given that people's mindsets and behaviors determine their underlying attitude and actions and ultimately their interest in increasing their performance and productivity, we propose that Training on EI can positively assist the organization in developing awareness among their workforce while training them in skills, competencies, communication, and leadership (Bakhshandeh 2021). This training has a direct influence on developing leadership competencies among the workforce—including management teams within the organizations. The EI training and development model covers all that would affect leadership development among the workforce and ultimately positively influences individuals' and teams' performance that would increase organizational productivity (Bakhshandeh 2021).

This approach is what we call "Emotional Intelligence Competency-Based Training and Development" (Bakhshandeh 2021). Donahue (2018) described competencies as a combination of a quantifiable and observable collection of knowledge, skills, attitudes, and behaviors (KSABs) that support individuals in performing better at work and achieving their personal and professional goals. Rothwell and Graber (2010) defined competency as "any characteristics of an individual performer that lead to acceptable or outstanding performance." According to Donahue (2018), the term *competency* has become something like a buzzword people are throwing around as something pointless. But in today's Organization development (OD) efforts, competency-based development and education are regarded as the pathway to the future of education/learning, team building, and OD. "Competencies are the measurable and observable knowledge, skills, attitudes, and behaviors (KSABs) critical to successful job performance" (21). Competencies can include the degree of motivation, individual personality traits, people's awareness of certain knowledge and technical skills knowledge, or any abilities and skills for individuals and teams to produce results (Rothwell and Graber 2010). Besides individuals and teams' competencies, in recent years, the competency-based Human Resources Management established its place in organization management and caused growing awareness that has led to innovations in overall competency technology (Dubois and Rothwell 2004).

Emotional Intelligence

The most effective and competent leaders know how to deal with the moods and emotions displayed by the workforce of their organizations by using a peculiar mixture of psychological competencies known as emotional intelligence or EI (HBR 2017). Regarding organization leaders' awareness of EI competencies, the *Harvard Business Review* stated "[t]hey're self-aware and empathetic. They can read and regulate their own emotions while intuitively grasping how others feel and gauging their organization's emotional state" (HBR 2017, 4). EI competencies are defined as "an ability to recognize, understand, and use emotional information about oneself or others that leads to or causes effective or superior performance" (Boyatzis and Sala 2004, 5).

According to the *Harvard Business Review* (2017), EI is a combination of: (1) genetic predisposition, (2) overall personality, (3) professional life experience, and (4) some old-fashioned training. When consciously and compassionately applied, EI encourages organizations, their leaders, and their workforce to achieve exceptional performance (HBR 2017). Our emotions directly influence our mindset, and they rule our daily lives (Bakhshandeh 2015; Hockenbury and Hockenbury 2007). We are deciding based on what we are feeling such as sad, angry, happy, frustrated, or bored; therefore,

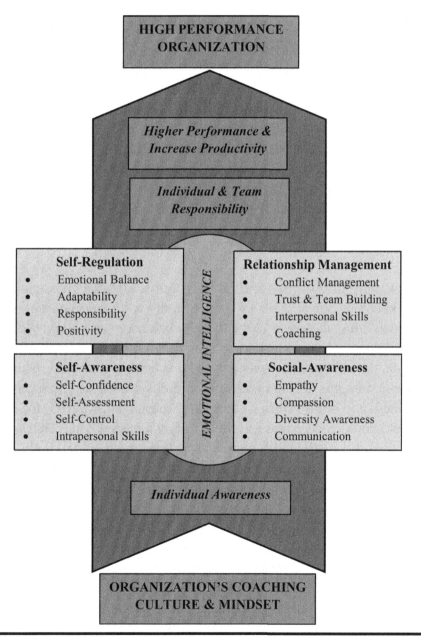

Figure 3.2   Coaching Mentality Produce Higher Performance and Increasing Productivity.

Source: Copyright 2021 by Behnam Bakhshandeh.

unconsciously, we choose reactions based on the emotions we are inflaming (Bakhshandeh 2015; Hockenbury and Hockenbury 2007).

This book has divided and organized the EI clusters and their related competencies (see Figure 3.2) into four clusters:

(1) self-awareness
(2) self-regulation
(3) social awareness
(4) relationship management

Organizational leaders should provide their workers with training on EI and should also participate in that training.

Figure 3.2 displays the four EI clusters and their relevant competencies that could assist organization leaders to implement sets of important and practical EI that would be very helpful to train and develop workforces in high performance and productivity:

Self-Awareness

The view we have of ourselves and others controls our awareness, and our awareness becomes our new reality that naturally will determine our actions (Bakhshandeh 2015). Goleman (2014) depicts behaviors associated with self-awareness with people who recognize how their emotions affect their job performance, those who know when to ask for help, and how to focus on building their strengths and not focusing on their weaknesses. In today's world of mindfulness and self-awareness, there are various pathways to understanding and build competencies around the art of awareness (Zeine 2021). As Zeine (2021) mentioned "[t]his includes many meditations and spiritual paths that teach the skills of becoming intentionally focused on our five senses, bodily signals, mental activities, and relatedness to objects and people around us" (5).

The knowledge of our self-awareness would allow us to recognize others' emotions and states of mind, how they view us, how they perceive our behavior and attitude, and how we respond to them (Rothwell 2015; Goleman 2015). Individual's conscious awareness of their emotions, aspirations, thoughts, desires, intentions, motivations, strengths, weaknesses, and the capacity to act from these elements of self-awareness are distinctive human capabilities (Zeine 2021). "Despite the great importance of self-awareness and the capacity to act from this awareness, many people have not learned the skill of being aware of themselves in their natural environments" (Zeine 2021, 6).

Competencies related to self-awareness include but are not limited to the following.

Self-Confidence

How people view themselves is another important element of EI. Self-confidence is linked to self-assessment, and it is founded further on the perceptions that individuals have of themselves instead of on the measures of their competencies or skills they possess (Goleman 2014). Some attributes of people with self-confidence are (1) trusting their abilities, (2) displaying gratitude, and (3) having inner happiness.

Self-Assessment

Self-assessment is providing awareness into individuals' comprehension of a set of knowledge, skills, and competencies that can provide insights to detect gaps in their area of expertise and knowledge (Goleman 2015). As an important element of creating a feasible and comprehensive self-assessment, some organizations allow individual engagement in the design, redesign, and development of assessment criteria. People who apply self-assessment (1) monitor their learning, (2) monitor their goals' progress, and (3) conduct self-efficacy.

Self-Control

Emotions are a big part of the human psyche. Our emotions are intended to notify us there is something worthy of attention. People with self-control do not make impulsive decisions, control their behaviors, and demonstrate conscientiousness (Goleman 2014).

Intrapersonal Skills

This is the ability of people to distinguish and understand their thoughts, emotions, and feelings. It is a skill for planning and directing their personal and professional lives (Cummings and Worley 2015). Individuals with intrapersonal skills are proficient at looking within, inquiring inward, and sounding out their feelings, emotions, motivations, and objectives. They are characteristically contemplative and thoughtful; by analyzing themselves, they seek self-understanding. Individuals with intrapersonal skills are intuitive and generally introverted. They are mostly learning autonomously and through reflection (Shek and Lin 2015). People with intrapersonal skills demonstrate (1) appreciation for themselves, (2) awareness of their agenda, and (3) elimination of distractions.

Self-Regulation

Self-regulation refers to the ability to recognize, understand, and redirect individuals' distracting impulses, inappropriate reactions, and temperament. Individuals should defer immediate judgment and employ considerations and concerns before acting against others or reacting to ideas (Goleman 2014). Goleman (2014) describes this EI cluster as leaders who can stay "calm and clear-headed under stressful situations" (p. 51). Self-regulation competencies move leaders from emotional awareness to managing their emotional impulses and demonstrating a positivity necessary to get the job done via initiative and instituting trustworthiness and productivity (Goleman 2014; Goleman 1998). Competencies referenced to self-regulation include but are not limited to the following.

Emotional Balance

Being emotionally out of balance is caused by individuals either not allowing themselves to experience their feelings when they arise and then discard and suppress them or being firmly attached to such feelings and being consumed by them (Goleman 2015; Goleman 1998). Emotional balance means to learn about feelings and accept them with no judgments and act on them in responsible ways. Some attributes of people with emotional balance are (1) accurately identifying their emotions, (2) being mindful of their emotions, and (3) managing impulse emotions.

Adaptability

Adaptability refers to strictness and harshness on individuals' ways, mindsets, and approaches and how individuals are efficient in adapting to new ideas, conditions, or environments (Goleman 2015; Goleman 1998). The only way to strengthen teamwork is by planning and creating a cohesive team and demonstrating its inclination to alter its ways. That is a powerful concept for developing leadership in teams and their ability to change (Bakhshandeh 2002). Some attributes of people with emotional balance are

(1) being open to learning new things, (2) adjusting quickly, and (3) embracing new ideas.

Responsibility

Vincent E. Barry, a business historian, has characterized responsibility in the business as "a sphere of duty or obligation assigned to a person by the nature of that person's position, function, or work" (Bivins 2006). From a mindfulness viewpoint, people become responsible when they display their willingness to acknowledge all of their thoughts and assume responsibility for every action they take, good, bad, and ugly, altogether with no justifications (Bakhshandeh 2015). Some attributes of people who practice responsibility are (1) not making excuses, (2) not complaining, and (3) being timely. Integrity and accountability are two competencies supporting responsibility.

Integrity

According to many philosophers, integrity is a lifelong desire to follow people's moral and ethical principles and, as the saying goes, "Do the right thing" in every situation and under any circumstances. It means being true to oneself and not acting in ways that would degrade or disgrace oneself (Goleman 1998). This powerful competency affects every aspect of our personal and professional day-to-day lives. Some attributes of people practicing integrity are (1) being dependable, (2) being honest, and (3) being trustworthy.

Accountability

One who practices accountability is not into the blame game and avoiding their responsibilities by pointing at and blaming others for what happens and how it happens. They are not acting like the victims of circumstances or as a replacement for being responsible. They are not procrastinating in their duties and what they do (Rothwell, Stavros, and Sullivan 2016; Goleman 2015; Bakhshandeh 2015). Some attributes of accountable people are (1) taking responsibility for their actions, (2) not blaming or pointing fingers, and (3) being transparent.

Positivity

A good, positive attitude has a very positive effect in the workplace. This positive impact influences people relating to their peers, how managers are leading, or how organizations are dealing with their clients and customers (HBR 2017). A positive temperament toward other people generates an environment for building relationships, trust, and loyalty among the workforce at every possible organizational level (HBR 2017). On the other side, when we are not displaying our care and commitment to workability and harmony, distrust will arise and cause massive dysfunction in relationships, in the home or at work, personally and professionally (Goleman 2015). Some attributes of people practicing positivity are (1) being optimistic, (2) being resilient, and (3) being grateful. Authenticity comes hand to hand with positivity.

Authenticity

How to become authentic is a mixture of having the courage to admit who we have been, what we have done to deal with challenges of a different situation, and how to take responsibility for it, and then become accountable for the results (Bakhshandeh 2015). "The flip side of authenticity is pretense" (Bakhshandeh 2015, 34). Some attributes of authentic people are (1) being self-reflective, (2) being honest, and (3) not being judgmental.

Calm Manners

Calm manners or composure is the ability to control impulsive reactions—even under heavy pressure. Individuals with composure do not react immediately just because they are not getting what they want or hearing what they do not like. They will reply after careful consideration and critical assessment, demonstrating the application of a conscious effort to stay calm and collected (Wayne 2019; Stevens 2009). Some attributes of people with composure are (1) having confidence, (2) being relaxed, and (3) being insightful.

Social Awareness

Social awareness requires social skills. Even with a business leader's ability to display understanding, empathy, compassion, and control of one's emotions, it is not enough to deal with conflicting and difficult situations arising from the lack of social awareness and related elements (Goleman 2015). Those business leaders understand social awareness elements, such as workplace diversity, and they can perceive differences at the workplace by disregarding stereotypes and generalizations of people. Leaders can demonstrate social awareness results, including their social awareness, throughout the elements of organizational awareness (Handley 2017).

Empathy

This is the ability to focus on others. Business leaders able to effectively focus on others are the ones able to find common ground with others, and their opinions and input carry the most respect and acceptance among their people (HBR 2017). One's propensity to identify and appreciate others' emotional status is by dealing with others relating to the present state of their feelings and emotions (Goleman 2015). Some attributes of empathetic people are (1) recognizing talent, (2) understanding other's emotional states, and (3) being helpful to others.

Compassion

The ability to demonstrate understanding, sympathy, and kindness for others in their time of sorrow, trouble, and hardship is displaying compassion. It is the consciousness of experiencing others' distress and grief and using their interests and aspirations to ease their pain (HBR 2017; Goleman 2015). Compassion is taking empathy a little further and deeper. People with compassion would feel hardship when witnessing another person in hardship and distress and will act to assist them. Some attributes of compassionate people are (1) placing oneself in others' situations, (2) practicing active listening, and (c) being okay with others' failures.

Diversity Awareness

Organizations and individuals can attain diversity awareness when they appreciate and understand the advantages of cultural diversity and differences among people. At the same time, true diversity inclusion also involves a diversity of viewpoints. Oregon Tech (2021) described viewpoint diversity as an act of recognizing others' diverse views that need one's "self-awareness, intellectual flexibility, and broad knowledge" (n.p.) that supports an illuminated perception of the actual diversity in the world via the eyes of people.

A workforce with diversity awareness and diversity of viewpoint can establish an organizational culture built on the foundation of dignity, mutual respect, and acceptance of the differences among people regardless of their cultural background, ethnicity, age, sexual orientation, gender, religion, socio-economic status, and physical abilities (Goleman 2015; Goleman 1998). As Williams (2016) stated, "[d]iversity of viewpoints is essential for the pursuit of knowledge" (n.p.).

Some attributes of people with diversity awareness are (1) embracing uniqueness among people, (2) having mutual respect for everyone, and (3) having universal treatment for everyone.

Communication

This is the ability to act on transferring information from one location, individual, or team to other people or places. All forms of communication include at least one message, one sender, and one receiver (Jones 2015; Bakhshandeh 2004). Steinfatt (2009) expressed his view of communication and its vital role in human connectedness: "[t]he central thrust of human communication concerns mutually understood symbolic exchange" (295). Communication is one concept that has been and continues to be the focus of many theories about human connection (Jones 2015). Without communication, there is no workability or teamwork. Teams are synchronized when communicating effectively (Bakhshandeh 2015; Bakhshandeh 2004). Some attributes of someone with communication skills are (1) being aware of nonverbal communication, (2) delivering clear and concise messages, and (3) showing courtesy and listening keenly.

Active Listening

As an important element of communication, active listening is a valuable skill that can be developed by practicing. One with active listening concentrates completely on the person talking and the content of the conversation and feelings behind the conversation instead of just passively hearing the speakers and their message (Rothwell et al. 2016; Goleman 2015). Practicing active listening helps the listener to gain the trust and respect of speakers by knowing that the listener appreciates their situation. It is an essential first step to neutralize a hard situation and pursue a workable solution to potential crises (Rothwell et al. 2016; Cummings and Worley 2015). Some attributes of people with active listening are (1) paying attention to the speaker, (2) responding appropriately, and (3) providing feedback.

Multiple Perspectives

Park et al. (2000) defined multiple perspectives as a wide term to incorporate many perspectives, statements, and roles that can be adopted in collaborative and noncollaborative frameworks (Park et al. 2000). View an issue from multiple perspectives to observe the whole picture that would improve one's chance to locate the root cause and find a solution that includes the desires and feelings of everybody engaged into consideration (Park et al. 2000). Some attributes of people with multiple perspectives are (1) seeing the whole picture, (2) finding the root cause of an issue, and (3) finding mutually agreed solutions.

Relationship Management

The quality of life is connected and influenced by positive and negative relationships individuals have with others. People aware of EI know this valuable concept. To have a quality relationship, besides looking for values and developing quality, people must also invest in maintaining the relationship and strive to improve it. Similar to a personal relationship, in a professional relationship business leaders need to discover how to effectively employ their intelligence to let them realize and identify opportunities, effectively communicate, attempt to solve problems, and collaborate with their workforce and customers (Goleman 2015).

Conflict management

This refers to the ability to employ practices for solving disputes effectively while it is fair and reasonable. When business professionals properly administer conflict management, they can avoid intensifying the conflicts. Having disagreements among people is natural when people work together. However, when handled with EI, competencies, and conflict management skills, these disagreements can lead the organizations to new ideas, innovative resolutions, and unified professional relationships (Rothwell et al. 2016; Cummings and Worley 2015). Some attributes of someone with conflict management skills are (1) being impartial, (2) being patient, and (3) not playing the blame game (Rothwell et al. 2016; Cummings and Worley 2015). Two EI competencies that would support the managers in their conflict management are Positive Influence and Problem-Solving abilities and qualities.

Positive Influence

In relationship building, positive influence is the impression professionals can employ on themselves or other individuals by indicating their strengths and underlining their qualities to empower and encourage them. Their influence becomes their nature. It will show who they are, what they do, and how they think. Some attributes of those with positive influence are (1) being charismatic, (2) being humble, and (3) striving to help (Longmore, Grant, and Golnaraghi 2018).

Problem-Solving

The problem-solving skill provides business managers with a useful method and effective process for finding the actual problem, realizing a solution or solutions to the problems, and defining a productive course of action to come up with a remedy for such problems (Donahue 2018; Rothwell et al. 2016; Cummings and Worley 2015). That required mindset for someone to attempt the problem-solving approach within organizations means that everyone involved with the problem must be receptive to a new realm of possibilities. Some attributes of those with problem-solving skills are (1) recognizing the perceptions in the problem, (2) redefining the problem, and (3) not being attached to experience (Martz, Hughes, and Braun 2017; Soulé and Warrick 2015).

Trust and Team Building

This competency refers to building trust with others, perhaps lining up with other personality traits and self-concept characteristics (Handley 2017). Forming a foundation of trust is critical to building an effective team because having trust among team members gives an impression of safety. Without trust among teams and groups, there will not be as much collaboration, expressions of creativity and innovation, and little productivity while people devote their time to shielding themselves from others and protecting their interests (Handley 2017; Rothwell et al. 2016). Some attributes of someone with the ability to build trust and teams are (1) being friendly and approachable, (2) being respectful to others' ideas, and (3) practicing integrity and accountability.

Interpersonal Skills

These skills refer to interacting, relating, understanding, and effectively cooperating with others, at home or the workplace. Interpersonal skills are powerful aptitudes for building relationships and establishing cooperation with others (Spencer and Spencer 1993; Boyatzis 1982). While professional position hard skills are very important to workers' ability to perform their work and job-related duties, effectively demonstrating abilities to work with others, delivering clear communication and displaying self-confidence as interpersonal skills are as important as their hard skills, and it can make a difference in one's professional advancement attributes. Someone with interpersonal skills can demonstrate: (1) being aware of themselves and others, (2) being collaborative, and (3) caring about relationships.

Coaching

The professional coaching process concept is about one's performance, and it enhances and increases on-the-job performance. Commonly, professional coaches receive a form of special training to guide people in their professional field for achieving their intentions and goals (Rothwell et al. 2016). There are diverse definitions of coaching by different professional associations. The International Coaching Federation defines coaching as "[u]sing an interactive process to help individuals develop rapidly and produce results, improving others' ability to set goals, take action, make better decisions, and make full use of their natural strengths" (Arneson, Rothwell, and Naughton 2013, 45). Some managers prefer mentoring their employees versus coaching them.

Mentoring

Compared to coaching, mentoring is relatively on the development side, not just working on professional performance and goals but also general career development. Generally, mentoring encompasses no particular or formal training, making it much leaner than coaching (Rothwell et al. 2016). The fundamental difference between a coach and a mentor is in their overall approach; the coach concentrates on the coachee's performance while the mentor concentrates on the mentee's growth (Rothwell and Chee 2013). As a general concept, mentoring is a relationship based on the individuals' development and focuses on mentors passing on their experience, knowledge, and skills to a mentee. In general, mentoring involves teaching and advising. A mentor's job is to encourage the mentee and provide access to "uplifting behaviors" (Rothwell and Chee 2013, 6) motivating, encouraging, and inspiring the mentee with the primary purpose of causing mentee's growth (Rothwell and Chee 2013). Some attributes of someone with mentoring skills are (1) being encouraging, (2) being empowering, and (3) being knowledgeable.

To understand and have a benchmark for training and development of managers coaching their people on EI, this author has designed a rating system for evaluation of "Presence and Use of Emotional Intelligence by Managers." The manager readers can use the tool displayed in Table 3.3 and self-rate their EI (from 1 to 5, 1 being the lowest rate and 5 being the highest rate of presence and use of EI) at the initial date of the rating and then continue rating themselves in six months and then a year after the initial rating.

Table 3.3 Presence and Use of Emotional Intelligence at Work by a Manger-as-Coach Rating System.

Presence and Use of Emotional Intelligence at Work by a Manger-as-Coach Rating System							
Date:		Participant:	Team:				
Month:		Supervisor	Department:				
Rating Scale: *1* = Poor, *2* = Marginal, *3* = Acceptable, *4* = Good, *5* = Excellent							
Categories	*Descriptions*	*Competencies/ Qualities*	*Rating*				
			1	*2*	*3*	*4*	*5*
Self-Awareness	One's capacity to identify and understand one's emotions, temperaments, and motives. Awareness of their impact on other people.	Self-confidence					
		Self-assessment					
		Self-control					
		Intrapersonal skills					
Social Awareness	One's ability to display understanding, empathy, compassion, and controlling one's emotions. Ability to deal with conflicting and difficult situations arising from a lack of social awareness.	Empathy					
		Compassion					
		Diversity awareness					
		Active listening					
Self-Regulation	One's ability to recognize and redirect distracting impulse and temperament. A tendency to defer immediate judgment and to apply considerations before acting against others.	Emotional balance					
		Adaptability					
		Responsibility					
		Positivity					
Relationship Management	One's ability to create and develop a quality relationship and looking for values among others. Ability to invest in maintaining the relationships and strive to improve them.	Conflict management					
		Trust and team building					
		Interpersonal skills					
		Coaching					

Two actions for this month that would bring up my three lowest EI ratings by at least 1 scale on the next month rating:
Action 1:
Action 2:

Source: Copyright 2021 by Behnam Bakhshandeh.

Leadership Qualities of Effective Manager-as-Coach

Besides all the aforementioned skills and competencies, coaching can create a learning environment for developing managers-as-coaches by developing managers in leadership positions that would positively influence their managerial skills and effectiveness in providing coaching for their employees intending to bring up their performance and productivity (Bakhshandeh 2002; Bakhshandeh 2008). The following are some of these qualities for a manager-as-coach:

Shows Respect

Professional managers would display equal respect for everyone in any position in the organization—regardless of their age, race, religion, gender, education, or sexual orientation (2002, 2008).

Thinks Critically

Effective managers would intellectually and skillfully analyze and evaluate gathered information and make their judgments based on evidence and facts, and after all considerations (2002, 2008).

Solves Problems

Facing issues, problems, and breakdowns is the second nature of any business development. Thoughtful managers would approach the problem more thoroughly to realize a greater impact on everyone and the future of the organization (2002, 2008).

Influences Positively

Having the ability to influence their people without creating resistance is one of the most valuable qualities of effective managers (2002, 2008).

Innovates

Nurture and promote innovation and creativity by supporting learning and experimentation. This quality will support an organization's future to compete in their markets (2002, 2008).

Communicates

Foster a strong alliance for actions, resources, and the organization's priorities. Communication is a function of workability, relatedness, and effectiveness and the backbone of smooth operation and production (2002, 2008).

Remains Real

Make informed decisions using numbers, data, and researched facts, and stay away from feeling and emotional-based fast decision-making and drawing immediate conclusions (2002, 2008).

Engages

Be in the trenches with their people and inspire them to express their passions and talents. Be part of the production and engage with people daily. A simple "Please," Thank You," and "job well done" will go a long way (2002, 2008).

Demonstrates Adaptability

Be at ease with volatile and changing circumstances with agility and confidence. Often, the vital need for an immediate change is at the corner and facing the organization or a team. An effective manager can face these adversaries with ease and grace (2002, 2008).

Demonstrates Transparency

Display authenticity, stimulate trust, and build relationships among people. By being transparent, a good manager will build relationships based on trust and respect. Integrity is the backbone of transparency (2002, 2008).

Shows Empathy

Display empathy, humility, and active listening and humility to boost morale. An effective manager displays empathy and compassion for what others are

Table 3.4 Leadership Qualities of Effective Manager-as-Coach Rating System.

Leadership Qualities of Effective Manager-as Coach Rating System							
Day:	Participant:			Team:			
Month:	Supervisor:			Department			
Rating Scale: *1* = Poor, *2* = Marginal, *3* = Acceptable, *4* = Good, *5* = Excellent							
Qualities	*Description*	*Rating*					
		1	*2*	*3*	*4*	*5*	
1	Shows Respect	Displays equal respect for everyone in any position in the organization.					
2	Thinks Critically	Intellectually and skillfully analyzes and evaluates gathered information.					
3	Solves Problems	Approaches the problem more thoroughly to realize a more significant impact on everyone.					
4	Influences Positively	Can influence their people without creating resistance.					
5	Innovates	Nurtures and promotes innovation and creativity by supporting learning and experimentation.					
6	Communicates	Fosters strong alliances for actions, resources, and the organization's priorities.					
7	Remains Real	Makes informed decisions using numbers, data, and researched facts.					
8	Engages	Is in the trenches with their people; inspires them to express their passions and talents.					
9	Adapts	Is at ease with volatile and changing circumstances with agility and confidence.					
10	Demonstrates Transparency	Displays authenticity, stimulates trust, and builds relationships among people.					
11	Shows Empathy	Displays empathy, humility, and active listening, and humility to boost morale.					
12	Learns Continuously	Regularly obtains updated knowledge, learns effective practices, and sharpens skills.					

Two actions for this month that would bring up my 3 lowest leadership qualities ratings by at least 1 scale on the next month rating:

Action 1:

Action 2:

Source: Copyright 2021 by Behnam Bakhshandeh.

facing day today. Being empathetic takes nothing away from being account-able; it just makes it easier to deal with (2002, 2008).

Learns Continuously

Constantly obtain updated knowledge, learn effective practices, and sharpen skills. A committed manager will learn every day and not afraid to say, "I don't know, but I am willing to learn" (2002, 2008).

Key Points to Remember

Note the following important points:

- **There is a direct correlation between mindset and performance**
  - Coaches have to understand their mindsets and how they manage their perceptions. Create a safe and trusting environment so workers can open up and inform the coaches about their mindset.

- **Everyone is facing gaps in the emotional intelligence**
  - In some shape or form, everyone is dealing with a total lack in their understanding and use of EI. Educate yourself in elements and clusters of EI so as manager-as-coach you have understanding and compassion for others who lack or demonstrate a shortage in EI's understanding.

- **Coaching is a quality leadership**
  - Coaching other people is a privilege given to managers to provide an opening for employees to walk into a whole new possibility for personal and professional growth. Do not take this privilege for granted.

Coaching and Developmental Questions for Managers

As manager-as-coach, consider these questions:

(1) Looking at the relationship between mindset, attitude, behavior, and individual and team performance and productivity, how do you assess your understanding of this concept and ability to explain them to your

coachees? Rate yourself from 1 to 5 (1 being the lowest and 5 being the highest).

(2) Looking at the four EI clusters and their relevant competencies, how do you assess your understanding of these competencies and ability to explain them to your coachees? Please use Table 3.1 and rate yourself.

(3) Looking at *Leadership Qualities of Effective Manager-as-Coach Rating System* how do you assess your leadership qualities in being a manager-as-coach and rate your understanding of these competencies? Please use Table 3.2 and rate yourself.

(4) According to your self-assessment and rating, design an action plan to educate yourself and expand your knowledge in the concept of the relationship between (1) Mindset and Performance, (2) EI, and (3) Manager-as-Coach qualities and effectiveness.

References

Arneson, Justin, William J. Rothwell, and Jennifer Naughton. 2013. "Training and Development Competencies Redefined to Create Competitive Advantage." *T + D* 67, no. 1: 42–47.

Bainbridge Frymier, Ann, and Marjorie Keeshan Nadler. 2017. *Persuasion: Integrating Theory, Research, and Practices*, 4th ed. Dubuque, IA: Kendall Hunt Publishing.

Bakhshandeh, Behnam. 2002. "Business Coaching and Managers Training." Unpublished Workshop on Coaching Businesses and Training Managers. San Diego, CA: Primeco Education, Inc.

Bakhshandeh, Behnam. 2004. "Effective Communication." *Audio CD Set and Workshop*. Carbondale, PA: Primeco Education, Inc.

Bakhshandeh, Behnam. 2008. "Bravehearts; Leadership Development Training." Unpublished Training and Developmental Course on Coaching Executive and Managers. San Diego, CA: Primeco Education, Inc.

Bakhshandeh, Behnam. 2009. *Conspiracy for Greatness; Mastery on Love Within.* San Diego, CA: Primeco Education, Inc.

Bakhshandeh, Behnam. 2015. *Anatomy of Upset: Restoring Harmony.* Carbondale, PA: Primeco Education, Inc.

Bakhshandeh, Behnam. 2021. "Perception Of 21st Century 4cs (Critical Thinking, Communication, Creativity & Collaboration) Skill Gap in Private-Sector Employers in Lackawanna County, NEPA." An Unpublished Dissertation in Workforce Education and Development. The Pennsylvania State University.

Bivins, Thomas H. 2006. "Responsibility and Accountability." In *Ethics in Public Relations: Responsible Advocacy*, 19–38. Thousand Oaks, CA: Sage Publication.

Boyatzis, Richard E. 1982. *The Competent Manager: A Model for Effective Performance*. Hoboken, NJ: John Wiley & Sons.

Boyatzis, Richard E., and Fabio Sala. 2004. "Assessing Emotional Intelligence Competencies." In *The Measurement of Emotional Intelligence*, edited by Glenn Geher, 147–80. Hauppauge, NY: Nova Science Publishers.

Cardy, Robert L., and Brian Leonard. 2011. *Performance Management: Concepts, Skills and Exercises*. Armonk, NY: Me. E. Sharp. Inc.

Cherry, Kendra. 2020. "Why Mindset Matters for Your Success." *Very Well Mind website*. www.verywellmind.com/what-is-a-mindset-2795025.

Chung, Tsai Chin. 1994. *Zen Speaks*. Translated by Brian Bruya. New York, NY: Anchor Books Doubleday.

Cummings, Thomas G., and Christopher G. Worley. 2015. *Organization Development & Change*, 10th ed. Stamford, CT: Cengage Learning.

Donahue, Wesley E. 2018. *Building Leadership Competence. A Competency-Based Approach to Building Leadership Ability*. State College, PA: Centerstar Learning.

Dubois, David, and William J. Rothwell. 2004. *Competency-Based Human Resource Management*. Polo Alto, CA: Davis-Black Publishing.

Dweck, Carol S. 2016. *Mindset; The New Psychology of Success*, updated ed. New York, NY: Ballantine Books.

Goleman, Daniel. 1998. *Working with Emotional Intelligence*. New York, NY: Random House.

Goleman, Daniel. 2014. "What it Takes to Achieve Managerial Success." *TD: Talent Development* 68, no. 11: 48–52.

Goleman, Daniel. 2015. *Emotional Intelligence; Why It Can Matter More Than IQ*. New York, NY: Bantam Books.

Handley, Meredith. 2017. "An Interpersonal Behavioral Framework for Early-career Engineers Demonstrating Engineering Leadership Characteristics Across Three Engineering Companies." Unpublished Doctoral diss., The Pennsylvania State University, Pennsylvania, USA.

HBR (Harvard Business Review). 2017. *Harvard Business Review Guild to Emotional Intelligence*. Boston, MA: Harvard Business Review Press.

Heidegger, Martin. 1968. *What is Called Thinking?* Translated by Glenn Gray and J. Glenn. New York, NY: Harper Perennial.

Hockenbury, Don H., and Sandra E. Hockenbury. 2007. *Discovering Psychology*. New York, NY: Worth Publishers.

ICF (International Coaching Federation). 2011. "Coached Core Competencies." https://coachfederation.org/app/uploads/2017/12/CoreCompetencies.pdf.

Jones, Virginia R. 2015. "21st Century Skills: Communication." *Children's Technology and Engineering* 20, no. 2: 28–29.

Kim, Sewon, Toby M. Egan, Woosung Kim, and Jaekyum Kim. 2013. "The Impact of Managerial Coaching Behavior on Employee Work-related Reactions." *Journal of Business and Psychology* 28, no. 3: 315–30. https://doi.org/10.1007/s10869-013-9286-9.

Longmore, Anne-Liisa, Ginger Grant, and Golnaz Golnaraghi. 2018 "Closing the 21st-century Knowledge Gap: Reconceptualizing Teaching and Learning to

Transform Business Education." *Journal of Transformative Education* 16, no. 3: 197–219. https://doi.org/10.1177/1541344617738514.

Martz, Ben, Jim Hughes, and Frank Braun. 2017. "Creativity and Problem-solving: Closing the Skills Gap." *Journal of Computer Information Systems* 57, no. 1: 39–48. https://doi.org/10.1080/08874417.2016.118149.

"Oregon Tech." 2021. *Oregon Institute of Technology. Diverse Perspectives.* www.oit. edu/academic-excellence/GEAC/essential-studies/eslo/diverse-perspectives.

Park, Kyoung S., Abhinav Kapoor, Chris Scharver, and Jason Leigh. 2000. "Exploiting Multiple Perspectives in Tele-immersion." *IPT '00: Proceedings of the 4th International Immersive Projection Technology Workshop.* http://citese erx.ist.psu.edu/viewdoc/summary?doi=10.1.1.5.7925.

Pousa, Claudio, Anne Mathieu, and Carole Trépanier. 2017. "Managing Frontline Employee Performance Through Coaching: Does Selling Experience Matter?" *International Journal of Bank Marketing* 35, no. 2: 220–40.

Rothwell, William J. 2015. *Beyond Training & Development: Enhancing Human Performance Through a Measurable Focus on Business Impact*, 3rd ed. Amherst, MA: HBR Press, Inc.

Rothwell, William J., and Peter Chee. 2013. *Becoming and Effective Mentoring Leader.* New York, NY: McGraw Hill.

Rothwell, William J., and James M. Graber. 2010. *Competency-Based Training Basics.* Alexandria, VA: ASTD Press.

Rothwell, William J., Jacqueline M. Stavros, and Roland L. Sullivan. 2016. *Practicing Organization Development: Leading Transformation and Change*, 4th ed. Hoboken, NJ: John Wiley & Sons, Inc.

Shek, Daniel T. L., and Li Lin. 2015. "Intrapersonal Competencies and Service Leadership." *International Journal on Disability and Human Development* 14, no. 3: 255–63.

Snyder, Mark, and Elizabeth D. Tanke. 1976. "Behavior and Attitude: Some People Are More Consistent than Others." *Journal of Personality* 44, no. 3: 501–17.

Soulé, Helen, and Tatyana Warrick. 2015. "Defining 21st Century Readiness for All Students: What We Know and How to Get There." *Psychology of Aesthetics, Creativity, and the Arts* 9, no. 2: 178–86. https://doi.org/10.1037/aca0000017.

Spencer, Lyle M., and Signe M. Spencer. 1993. *Competence at Work. Models for Superior Performance.* New York, NY: John Wiley and Sons, Ed.

Steinfatt, Tom. 2009. "Definitions of Communication." In *Encyclopedia of Communication Theory*, edited by Stephan W. Littlejohn and Karen A. Foss, vol. 1, 295–99. Thousand Oaks, CA: Sage Publication, Inc.

Stevens, R. 2009. *Emotional Intelligence in Business: EQ, The Essential Ingredient to Survive and Thrive as a Modern Workplace Leader.* Middletown, DE. Self-Published.

Vidal-Salazar, María Dolores, Vera Ferrón-Vílchez, and Eulogio Cordón-Pozo. 2012. "Coaching: An Effective Practice for Business Competitiveness." *Competitiveness Review: An International Business Journal* 22, no. 5: 423–33.

Wayne, Jenny. 2019. *Emotional Intelligence 2.0. A Guide to Manage Anger, Overcome Negativity ad Master Your Emotions.* Middletown, DE. Self-Published.

Williams, Joanna. 2016. "Social Science Space." *Website. Diversity of Viewpoint.* www.socialsciencespace.com/2016/09/diversity-of-viewpoints-is-essential-for-the-pursuit-of-knowledge/.

Yashasvi, G. 2019. "Styles at Life.com." *4 Different Types of Attitudes of People as Per Psychology.* https://stylesatlife.com/articles/types-of-attitudes/.

Zeine, Foojan. 2021. *Awareness Integration Therapy: Clear the Past, Create a New Future, and Live a Fulfilled Life Now.* Newcastle: Cambridge Scholars Publishing.

BUILDING RELATIONSHIP AND RECOGNIZING THE SITUATION

Establishing rapport and building relationships with employees is one of the most important elements of management, which helps understand "what is happening" with them, their productivity, and their overall performance. Throughout this phase, we are trying to educate and increase the knowledge and understanding of high-performance coaches and managers-as-coaches about:

Chapter 4—Step 1: How to Establish Relatedness and Building Rapport?

How can the consultant/manager establish rapport and a contractual relationship with a coaching client?

Chapter 5—Step 2: What Is the Issue at Hand?

What is the present situation that requires coaching? What is happening? Describe it in detail.

Chapter 6—Step 3: What Should Be Happening?

Describing the desired target, results, and outcome.

DOI: 10.4324/9781003155928-5

Chapter 4

Step 1: How to Establish Relatedness and Building Rapport?

Behnam Bakhshandeh

Most people care about their relationships with family, work colleagues, customers or clients, and friends. People who care about the quality of their relationships know those qualities do not happen without work—and continuing cultivation. Quality relationships are created and developed over time. Relationships grow when people display interest, create open communication channels, and establish strong rapport based on mutual respect and understanding. That is true with home and work relationships.

In today's organizational cultures, in some shapes and forms, management is losing the ability to establish a good, authentic rapport with their workforce. Contrary to some corporations trying to establish a more meaningful work environment and create deeper connections with their employees, some are trying to diminish emotional connections from the work environment. Because of that, many workplaces became automated (Gilmore 2019)—or even toxic. We are not saying this because we are against automation and high productivity due to mechanical and technological advancement, but it is because of the disappearing deep connection and strong rapport between organizational leaders and the workers.

This book and its chapters are based on the relationships between managers-as-coaches and their subordinates and what it takes to create high-performance workers through high-performance coaching relationships.

DOI: 10.4324/9781003155928-6

Throughout this chapter, we educate managers-as-coaches about what rapport is and how they can practice using it with their subordinates and coachees to start high-performance coaching on a strong foundation.

This chapter looks at what rapport is, how to establish rapport, and how to form a contractual relationship with subordinates or coaching clients. In this chapter, readers will grow familiar with the general concept of rapport. Chapter 4 covers these topics:

- What is rapport and the importance of it?
- What are relatedness, empathy, and compassion?
- Rapport and basic psychological needs
- Rapport and synchrony
- Fundamental states of being and competencies for establishing relatedness and rapport
- Role of organization values and culture on rapport
- Key factors to remember from this chapter
- Some discussion questions to support manager-as-coach development

Some Definitions and Descriptions

These terms will be used in this chapter:

Rapport

Briefly stated, rapport means to have a positive connection with others. Here are some carefully chosen definitions of rapport:

- "The relation characterized by harmony, conformity, accord, or affinity" (Merriam-Webster 2021).
- "Rapport is a positive connection with another person, one that involves caring and understanding" (Angelo 2012, 11).
- "I like to define rapport as a deep emotional connection and understanding between two people" (Gilmore 2019, 2).
- "Colloquially, rapport is the emotional experience of high-quality interactions. While the emotional experience of a high-quality interaction may often be associated with objective measures of high-quality interactions, this will not always be the case" (Baker, Watlington, and Knee 2020, 330).

■ "Rapport is a process, a happening, an experience between two persons. It may not be a mutual affair at first, but the sharing of the experience and participation in it grows as each individual unfolds him or herself in the interpersonal situation" (Travelbee 1963, 70).

■ "Rapport is one's capability to establish a background of relatedness and connecting with others" (Bakhshandeh 2002, n.p.).

According to Angelo (2012), rapport means "clicking" with one another, which would cause continued communication and collaboration between two people. Sometimes rapport is established immediately, and other times, it takes time to build the trust necessary to establish rapport. However, it takes two people to develop workable rapport. The successful performance of managers-as-coaches hinges on the rapport and trust existing between managers and those they coach (Whitmore 2017; Rothwell, Stavros, and Sullivan 2016; Cummings and Worley 2015; Bakhshandeh 2008).

Rapport means more than polite displays of friendship or casual civility and acquaintanceship. Establishing rapport is about showing emotional awareness—that is, having empathy, compassion, and connecting to others through understanding of another person's emotions (Gilmore 2019; Whitmore 2017; Bakhshandeh 2009). "It is a connection that puts those on the same page and opens the door for collaboration, communication most importantly, deeper understanding" (Gilmore 2019, 2). Looking at all the presented definitions, it is safe to conclude that rapport is the individuals' emotional connections and relationships with others in their lives. Establishing rapport is the step on which to build such connections and relationships based on mutual experiences or perceptions. When formed, it can persist for many years (Gilmore 2019; Angele 2012; Bakhshandeh 2009). As Travelbee (1963) underlined, "rapport is a particular way in which we perceive and relate to our fellow human beings; it is composed of a cluster of inter-related thoughts and feelings, an interest in, and a concern for others, empathy, compassion, and sympathy, a nonjudgmental attitude, and respect for the individual as a unique human being" (Travelbee 1963, 70).

Relatedness

Many people cannot manage their relationships because they are jumping into a relationship with another person before knowing how to relate and understand the deep meaning of relatedness. This phenomenon happens in both personal and professional environments (Bakhshandeh 2009).

Lexico dictionary of Oxford University defined relatedness as "the state or fact of being related or connected." For example, "subjects reported a significant increase in the sense of relatedness to nature" (n.p.). Keller (2016) described relatedness as a reference "to the social nature of human beings and the connectedness with others. Both can be considered as being part of the panhuman psychology, and both are intrinsically intertwined" (1). Keller (2016) combined relatedness with autonomy as two basic human needs;

> the definition of self and others can be regarded as embodying the two dimensions of autonomy and relatedness. Autonomy and relatedness are two basic human needs and cultural constructs at the same time. They may be differently defined yet remain equally important. The respective understanding of autonomy and relatedness is socialized during the everyday experiences of daily life routines from birth on

(1). According to Aristotelous (2019), there is convincing proof in the research literature suggesting that fostering relatedness among people through the formation of deeper human connections provides positivity in organizations and work settings. However, Aristotelous (2019) continued with, "at the same time, preserving our humanity and our sense of relatedness with one another at such times of unprecedented technological development seems a daunting task" (53).

Rapport and Basic Psychological Needs

While the purpose of this chapter is not about digging into individuals' psychological states and needs, there is a direct correlation between individuals' basic psychological needs and their mindsets, attitudes, and behaviors.

According to research conducted by Baker et al. (2020), the satisfaction of a person's psychological needs is crucial for his or her day-to-day functions, operational behaviors, and causes for high-quality interactions with other people. "Rapport is essential to high-quality interactions and may be one way that various relationship types can provide the nutriments of healthy functioning" (Baker et al. 2020, 329). Baker et al. (2020) describe findings of the Self-Determination Theory (SDT) that individuals' goal-focused behaviors are motivated by these three innate characteristics of the psychological needs in every human: (1) autonomy—the need for owning their behavior and actions, (2) competence—the need for producing their desired results or goals and to experience achieving mastery in their producing the desired outcome), and (3) relatedness—the need, feel, and desire to connect to other people (329). Baker et al. (2020) continued to underline the psychological need by referring to Hadden et al. (2016), "[g]iven the compelling evidence that satisfaction of one's needs for autonomy, competence, and relatedness are fundamental to well-being and ill-being as well as behavioral, relational, and personal outcomes, need satisfaction as an outcome in-and-of-itself deserves more attention" (329).

Research conducted by Martela and Riekki (2018) based on the SDT suggested that meaningful work is a vital component of employees' positive operations and performance. Based on research findings on (1) SDT, (2) basic psychological needs, and (3) prosocial impact, the researchers suggested that "there are four psychological satisfactions that substantially influence work meaningfulness across cultures: autonomy (sense of volition), competence (sense of efficacy), relatedness (sense of caring relationships), and beneficence (sense of making a positive contribution)" (1). Given that interactions with other people are so important, one's ability to considerably affect others is directly related to his or her ability to establish rapport and build relationships. Baker et al. (2020) research developed findings by studying how people's interactions (not only with others with whom one has an established relationship) may affect individuals, particularly how rapport and relatedness in the framework of people's day-to-day social connections predict the realization of people's basic needs for autonomy, competence, and relatedness.

Rapport and Synchrony

As it has been established previously, rapport might be believed to be linked to the individuals' need for satisfaction in a type of radiance of positivity and productivity. However, some factors or parts of rapports may suggest that, most likely, there are other reasons associated with success in establishing rapport. For example, both parties should have mutual interests, display mutual competence during their interactions, or have similar skills in communication, which naturally create mutual synchrony, affiliation, respect, and natural relatedness (Hove and Risen 2009).

When a sense of synchronization is created, people are easily acting naturally and authentically with much fewer concerns about how the other party perceives them. This mutual understanding and connection will naturally lead to enhanced autonomous satisfaction because both parties do not feel pressured to engage in the interactions or change to improve the relationship (Baker et al. 2020).

Role of Organization Values and Culture in Establishing Rapport

Correlations between how employees react to their managers and the organization's values have a direct link to the working environment and the organizational culture. In some form, managers' mindsets, attitudes, and behaviors toward productivity and employees' performances connect to their personal and professional values and how the organization's values and culture impact the work environment (Bakhshandeh 2021).

Degree of Organizing in Organizations and Rapport

The degree of an organization's engagement in creating a powerful set of values, operational principles, and culture is related to the degree and level of practicing systematically organized practices in management, operation, and norms. Establishing rapport is one missing element in such an organization. On the other side of the equation, as Cummings and Worley (2015) underlined, in over-organized business systems operating in highly automated and bureaucratic systems, there is a rigid relationship to the organization structure, management styles, structure, and implementation of policies and procedures established for an effective job and task performance.

Often this rigid work environment might be a barrier to establishing relatedness and creating rapport between managers and their subordinates. However, experiences have shown organizations' values, and culture has much to do with the organizations' openness to give managers a chance to establish a healthy rapport with their subordinates, which (in turn) results in higher performance.

Organization Values and Rapport

Organization values are a set of beliefs about personal or socially desired principles that influence action (Schwartz 1992). Organizational values demonstrate what the organization regards as important. Values are related to ethical principles, what is considered right or wrong.

Organizational values help workers to establish a clear path toward results. Values are building blocks to creating an organizational culture based on empowering the working environment and high productivity and performance. An organization's values are crucial in guiding employees' attitudes and behavior. In fact, "organizational values must be able to meet the needs of different employees, and organizations need to clarify their work values and expectations with staff" (Cennamo and Gardner 2008, 891).

Organizational Culture and Rapport

> Mindset is to individuals what culture is to organizations. A strategy to change culture is often required, one that assesses which aspects of the current culture already support the desired future, which block it, and what may need to be created to better serve it
>
> *(Rothwell et al. 2016, 73)*

Organizational culture is a dynamic strength embedded in various aspects of personal (employees) and professional (organization structure and business strategies), comprising deeply rooted behaviors, a history of interactive employee–employee dynamics, and sensitivities for traditions and norms of an organization and its workforce. According to Aristotelous (2019), given this overall dynamics, organizational culture and its business strategy should be aligned with all stages of an organization to guarantee the execution of its goals and the desired outcome by its workforce involved with assisting the organization in achieving its vision, mission, and purpose (Aristotelous 2019).

We are spending more time on organizational culture and values because they have a deep influence on managers and the employees' abilities and desires to establish a rapport among themselves. It is hard to pinpoint a specific definition for what organizational culture is! Research on organizational culture has delivered over 50 different definitions and descriptions of it! Many organization managers define the views of their culture as "the way we do things around here" (Colquitt, LePine, and Wesson 2015). But we all know there is much more in developing an organizational culture intentionally or just by the force of time and sets of organizational processes, practices, and norms. About this concept, Colquitt et al. (2015) invited us to look at one reason for various definitions for organizational culture. He noted that differences stem from the people who have researched it. For example, sociologists who have studied organizational culture used anthropological investigation models and the methods employed to study social cultures such as nationalities, tribes, and civilizations. Psychologists are inclined to study cultures by conducting survey methods.

Colquitt et al. (2015) defined organizational culture as "the shared social knowledge within an organization regarding the rules, norms, and values that shape the attitudes and behaviors of an organization" (534). This definition underlines several important issues about organizational culture:

- **First:** Given culture is a social knowledge between employees of an organization, they learn essential facets of the organizational culture through their interactions with each other through observation and communication, which creates consensus about their culture.
- **Second:** Organizational culture is communicating what the organization's values, rules, and norms are, which assist with an employee's mindset, attitude, and behavior about the organization and their relationships.
- **Third:** Organizational culture is shaping and strengthens certain employee mindsets, attitudes, and behaviors by engaging them in some organizational systems that would have control over employees. This approach causes employees' goals and values to align with the organization's goals and values.

(Colquitt et al. 2015)

Fit and Match Person in Organizations

Establishing a good rapport among managers and employees as the concept of "fit and match person and organization" is essential to workability and realization of the organization's culture and vision. Amos and Weathington (2008) empirically investigated the correlation between a fit and match with individuals and organizations. "Overall findings have supported the existence of a positive relationship between the congruence of employee and organizational values with employee attitudes toward the organization" (615). The research results indicated that employees' view of employee–organization values is positively related to (1) employees' satisfaction with their job, (2) their satisfaction with the organization, and (3) their organizational commitment. Research findings indicated a negative link between what organizations claim as their values and the results of high employee turnover (Amos and Weathington

2008). Again, we can see the importance of organizational value and culture in managers' abilities to establish good rapport with their employees.

The Leadership Role in Values

The organization's leaders demonstrate the organization's values through their attitudes and behaviors and spread the culture by holding their subordinates (lower managers, supervisors, and so on) accountable for behaving in ways consistent with the leaders' values (Rothwell et al. 2016; Bakhshandeh 2008). Therefore, establishing a good rapport between managers and their employees is essential to establishing credibility and trust. Managers can lose credibility and undermine trust by cutting corners to save time instead of following proper procedures. If managers do not follow the organization's rules, policies, and procedures, then workers will lose respect for the rules.

Role of Competencies, Skills, and Training

To establish good rapport, a high-performance coach needs to develop specific competencies as mentioned in Figure 4.1. But before we get to the six competencies that need to establish relatedness and rapport, let us talk a little about what we mean by competencies.

Defining Competencies, Skills, Knowledge, and Training

In this section, we review definitions and descriptions of several key terminologies in professional business and Organization Development (OD) and training, which assist readers in understanding the differences among the terms (1) competency, (2) skills, and (3) training.

Competency

The term competency has been commonly used without clear awareness of its meaning or the context in which it was used. In organizational development, business, and education, the term competency describes individual proficiency, such as knowledge, skills, attitudes, and behaviors against a set of guidelines and established standards (Donahue 2018). The following are definitions of competency by several professionals:

■ "Measurable and observable knowledge, skills, attitudes, and behaviors (KSABs) critical to successful job performance. Competencies refer to the specific KSABs that a person can readily show. They include not only technical skills but also what are known as soft skills" (Donahue 2018, 21).

■ "An underlying characteristic of an individual that is causally related to criterion-referenced effective and or superior performance in a job or situation, where 'criterion-referenced indicates that competency will predict performance" (Spencer and Spencer 1993, 9).

■ "Certain characteristics or abilities of the person [that] enable him or her to demonstrate the appropriate specific actions" (Boyatzis 1982, 12).

■ "A personal capability that is critical to the production of a quality output or outputs" (McLagan 1988, 374).

Often the words competency and competence are used interchangeably. Organizations depend on the qualifications of their workforce, especially their managers, who are trying to develop rapport with their subordinates to coach them to improve productivity.

Skills

Skill is the ability to execute an action or task with established results within a time frame. Skills mean know-how. In fact, a skill is an ability to do something. Skills are what make individuals confident in their life and career pursuits (Rothwell 2015). As much as developing skills requires willpower and practice, almost any skill can be learned, developed, and improved (Donahue 2018).

Skillset

A skillset is the mixture of personal qualities, knowledge, and abilities that individuals develop through their life spans personally and professionally. It typically included two types of skills: (1) soft skills and (2) hard skills.

Soft Skills

Soft skills cover interpersonal skills or people skills. It is difficult to quantify these skills; however, in a general sense, they are an individual's personality and ability to work with others. These skills include being detailed-oriented, using critical thinking, being a problem solver, possessing good communication skills, listening without prejudice, displaying empathy and compassion, and many more ("The Balance Career," n.d.).

Hard Skills

Hard skills are tangible, quantifiable skills. They include some specific technical and profession-related knowledge and abilities required for conducting a job or task. Hard skills could be accounting, computer programming, mathematics, or data analysis ("The Balance Career," n.d.).

Knowledge

Knowledge refers to a theoretical, conceptual, or functional understanding of a trade or a subject matter (Donahue 2018). According to Krathwohl (2002), knowledge is classified into four categories:

- factual knowledge,
- conceptual knowledge,
- procedural knowledge, and
- metacognitive knowledge.

It is essential to understand the characteristics and categories of our knowledge base and its strengths in our personal and professional endeavors. Being a knowledgeable manager-as-coach is no different.

Training

Training has been defined in several ways:

- "Training helps individuals meet minimally acceptable job requirements or refine, upgrade, and improve what they presently do. When employees finish their training, they should be able to apply it immediately" (Rothwell and Sredl 2014, 9).
- "Learning, [is] provided by employers to employees that are related to their present jobs (Nadler and Nadler 1989)" (Rothwell and Sredl 2014, 9).
- "Change in skills (Lawrie 1990)" (Rothwell and Sredl 2014, 10).
- "Its major focus is providing basic knowledge and skills for familiar tasks tied to present jobs (Bartz, Schwandt, and Hillman 1989)" (Rothwell and Sredl 2014, 10).

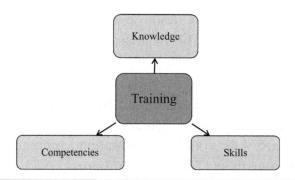

Figure 4.1   Relationship between Accruing Knowledge, Competencies, and Skills in Training.

Source: Adapted from Rothwell and Sredl (2014).

Training is also described as a short-term learning intervention intending to construct people's knowledge, skills, and attitudes to assemble their work requirements at their jobs. In this context of an organization, business, and education, knowledge refers to the realities, facts, standards, and information essential for executing a job or task while skills are the individuals' abilities linked to a successful performance at work, and individual attitudes refer to their feelings and emotions, as expressed by the individuals (Rothwell and Sredl 2014). As a manager-as-coach, we need to clearly understand distinctions between competencies, skills, and training so we can imply them appropriately to enhance our competencies and skills through training and education.

Regardless of industries or types of organizations, a business, a performing team, or even individuals running their businesses as technicians, the outcome of proper training relevant to a particular concept (e.g., rapport) will be the relationship between competencies, skills, and knowledge (see Figure 4.1).

Fundamental State of Being and Competencies for Establishing Relatedness and Rapport

Now that we established what competencies, skills, and training are, we move on to what it takes to establish relatedness and rapport. See the details of this segment in Figure 4.2.

Manager/Coach State of Being

For performance coaching to work, the managers-as-coaches need to pay attention to their state of being while approaching employees or teams. We are making the most significant difference in what we are prepared to do with them during our approach to people. Who we are is where we begin with establishing a positive rapport with people (Bakhshandeh 2009). On average, 75% of all change efforts in organizations fall significantly below management's desired expectations. Either way, the failure rate is high. Research also indicates that two-thirds of employees in organizations undergoing change activities would choose not to become involved at all (Levi 2016; Rothwell et al. 2016; Rothwell and Sredl 2014). Managers-as-coaches should pay close attention to this type of information.

Why do most people going through a change effort come out unchanged? Why don't these efforts have impact? It may have something to do with the trainer, coach, consultant, or manager's state of being. Managers tend to plan change efforts with a focus on what to do and not how we are (how people perceive us to be). There are two sides to any performance change.

> The *Doing* side is about processes, measurement, tools, structures, and procedures. This side is about *management*. The *Being* side is about relationships, participation, commitment, attitude, creativity, overcoming resistance to change, and self-leadership. This side is about *leadership*
>
> *(Primeco Education, n.d.)*

When implementing high-performance coaching interventions, we remind the management team that doing good management cannot generate sustainability and growth in the organization or in the team they are trying to restore and rebuild. They need to adjust the being of an individual to ensure the sustainability and longevity of individuals because what they are being (resentful, regretful, or disappointed), directly influences what they are doing (performance, communication, or productivity) (Bakhshandeh 2009). In one of Martin Heidegger's books, *Being and Time* (1953), the German philosopher and ontologist, expressed his views on the transparency of being as "the self-evident concept. Being is used in all-knowing and predicting, in every relation to being, and every relation to oneself, and the expression is understandable without further ado" (3).

One important, influential element of OD is the role modeling of organization leaders by displaying positive behavior aligned with desirable behavior associated with implementation (Rothwell et al. 2016). This personal development effort by organizations is possible through behavioral coaching for individuals who have a direct and impactful influence on an organization's well-being. Behavioral coaching is not a new phenomenon in applying OD. As part of behavioral coaching, coaches use the model of person-centered psychology based on "holding up a mirror" (Rothwell 2015) for the individuals to get to know themselves on a much deeper level and know how they behave (and how others perceive and interpret their behavior) through the years.

Usually, self-realization is somewhat bad news. However, it is a good thing to know sooner rather than later. For example, some may discover that they are opinionated, and they are always judging and evaluating others. Nobody wants to be known as that judgmental person (the bad news). But it is also a good thing, a good opportunity to face it, own it,

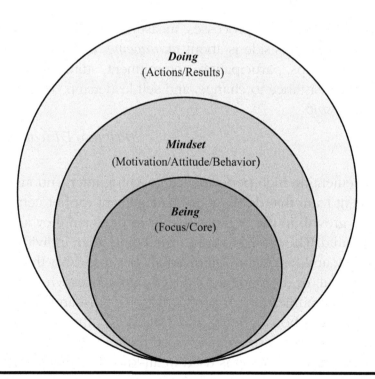

Figure 4.2   Being, Doing, and Mindset Relevancy.

Source: Copyright 2021 by Behnam Bakhshandeh.

and do something about it. This way, this behavior has no power over those individuals; now, they have a choice to continue behaving that way or change their behavior given they see the cost of this behavior on themselves, their families, and people around them, such as people at work (Bakhshandeh 2009).

You can see the relevance between *Being* and *Doing* in Figure 4.2.

We are attempting to shed light on some state of *being* under the *leadership* part we think makes a big difference in establishing rapport. We are using the following display (Figure 4.3) to walk our readers into establishing a rapport with individuals or teams needing to increase their productivity using the steps mentioned in Figure 4.3.

Business Case Examples throughout the Chapters

Throughout this book, we will continue using different organizations from different industries as case examples for each step to create high-performance teams. This way, we are displaying the unified implementation and the use of *High-Performance Coaching for Managers* in different situations in various industries. As a manager-as-coach, you should pay attention to the context of steps and how they will affect your team or individuals you are coaching.

In this segment of Chapter 4, we use a business case example of working with a manager and his team to establish a background of relatedness and rapport to increase the productivity and performance at their jobs. However, in this chapter, the emphasis will be on the consultant/coach's state of being that made a difference in establishing rapport with the individuals in this team. Pay attention to who the consultant/coach was *being* that would support what he was *doing*. Some of the following content was in the last chapter as part of understanding the EI (Emotional Intelligence). But it is beneficial to address several elements again in this chapter briefly.

Background

In 2012, we received an invitation from MBD, an organization that has participated in the beauty supply distribution industry in Southern California since the early 1980s. The organization had four distribution centers with 112 employees and independent contractors throughout California. The primary job of this workforce was involved in sales and the administration of distributing products to the hair and nail salons, spas and massage businesses, gyms, and motel and hotel chains. The sales managers and sales teams in these three locations were 82 people, including four sales managers and 78 salespersons throughout the four distribution centers. The rest of the team were administrations, accounting, shipping, quality control, marketing/public relation, and IT people. The apparent issue was the decreasing level of quarterly and annual sales for the last two consecutive years. Mike, the owner/CEO, could not make a difference with his sales team, he was not able to get to mindset of his sales team and could not get them to discuss the issues and what is in the way of their performance and productivity. It was a clear breakdown in a channel of communication and understanding of employees' needs and wants in their career with the MBD. Some of the issues were Mike's lack of abilities and competencies to relate to his sales team, and another issue was the fact that members of the sales team were resisting Mike's management style and just avoiding his domination from their point of view.

Note: We will use the MBD case throughout the entire book to make an example of how we use our performance coaching model (see in Chapter 3) to coach and walk the MBD team through spaces of the performance model to find fundamental issues in their performance and productivity as well as to develop them as a high-performance team. That being said, you will see examples of the MBD team throughout other chapters of this book, plus possibly other examples from performance development issues with other organizations and some examples of coaching dialogs and performance conversations.

Since this part of this case is about establishing rapport and building relatedness, the case is not about collecting data, analysis, and the process of the change intervention. However, we are walking you through how we conduct building rapport and getting to understand the issues that MBD has missed in communication and relatedness with the sales teams. Two things to consider here are as follows: (1) In this book, we are covering creating a high-performance environment and coaching a manager to become a high-performance coach and make a difference in their performance as a manager-as-coach. (2) If you are interested in understanding the levels of the individual, team, and organization change interventions and their processes, we highly recommend our book *Organization Development Interventions, Executing Effective Organizational Change* by Rothwell, Imroz, and Bakhshandeh (2021) published by Routledge (Taylor and Francis). These two books can work together.

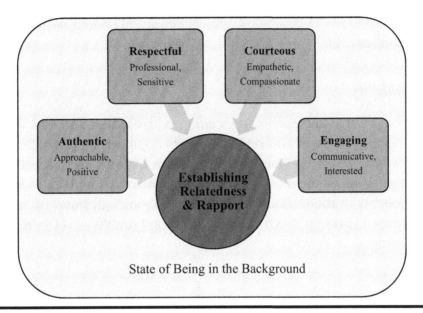

Figure 4.3 The Fundamental State of Being and Competencies for Establishing Relatedness and Rapport.

Source: Copyright 2021 by Behnam Bakhshandeh.

We are looking at how to establish rapport with people to establish a workable foundation for creating a breakthrough for participants and bring them back to their productive performance and establish a good relationship with their manager Mike.

We had a one-day workshop on a Sunday with all the 82 sales team members—including Mike, the owner, and the CEO. Besides establishing rapport for our work with the sales team, we offered executive coaching to Mike and worked to empower his current and possible future team members about their performance and productivity.

In the following part of this chapter, we explain the fundamental state of being, competencies, and skills we used to establish a strong rapport with the MBD sales team. We also indicated "Coaches' Actions" for each part.

Being Authentic

Being authentic means that coaches own who they are and what they stand for. It is a mixture of having the courage to be real and avoid pretending to be someone else just to please people (Bakhshandeh 2015). "The flip side of authenticity is pretense" (Bakhshandeh 2015, 34). Some attributes of authentic people are (1) practicing self-reflection, (2) being honest, and (3) not being judgmental.

Approachability

Approachable people are easy-going, calm, and collected, and they are friendly. They are pleasant and open to others approaching and talking to them. You would sense no resistance from them by your approach and your interest in speaking to them or engaging them in some inquiries. It is effortless to connect with them (Bakhshandeh 2009). Some attributes of approachable people are (1) no presence of ego, (2) being humble, and (3) being open and welcoming.

Positivity

Being positive has a big impact on others. A positive person influences other people by easily relating to them. A positive temperament toward other people creates an environment for building relationships, trust, and loyalty among the workforce at every possible organizational level (HBR 2017). Thinking negatively, displaying negative body language, and expressing judgmental and crude language only results in others resisting and becoming suppressed. When that happens, other people will not talk. People who practice positivity are (1) optimistic, (2) resilient, and (3) grateful.

Coaches' Actions

- Acknowledge them for their time and their commitment to their work and the organization.
- Be real but do not try to act in charge and dominate the process.
- Adopt a friendly and professional approach to minimize the resistance.
- Use self-deprecating humor so they can laugh with you.
- Share stories about your shortcomings and breakthroughs in learning high performance and productivity.
- Make yourself real.
- Be calm and collected and do not get hooked on their differences.
- Make sure they know that nothing is wrong with them or the situation.
- Assure them you and the organization are counting on their strengths and what is great about them.

- Ask the owner/CEO to give his word he will not retaliate based on what the participants are exposing and communicating.
- Ask the owner/CEO to share stories about how he built up the organization, the hardship and struggles of establishing a good business, and his dreams and vision for his organization and his employees.
- Acknowledge them when sharing their issues—and do not water them down.

Being Respectful

Respectful managers and coaches are open to different communication styles and are sensitive to other differences, such as diversity by age, sex, gender, race, ethnicity, nationality, religion, or any other irrelevant differences to their duties.

Professionalism

Professional managers or coaches are keenly aware of their boundaries with their subordinates or coachees. They do not extend their welcome to their employees and act like they know better or have the answers. Being professional means demonstrating respectful manners and calming behaviors. Some attributes of people with professionalism are (1) using formal language, (2) avoiding drama, and (3) displaying ethical behavior.

Sensitivity

Sensitive managers or coaches will acknowledge and recognize the diversity and practice inclusion in their organizations, workplaces, and teams. They attain diversity awareness when they appreciate and understand the advantages of cultural diversity and differences among people. A workforce with diversity awareness can establish an organizational culture built on the foundation of dignity, mutual respect, and acceptance of the differences among people regardless of their cultural background, ethnicity, age, sexual orientation, gender, religion, socio-economic status, and physical abilities (Goleman 2015; Goleman 1998). Some attributes of people with diversity awareness are (1) embracing uniqueness among people, (2) having mutual respect for everyone, and (3) having universal treatment for everyone.

Coaches' Actions

- Use professional and proper language.
- Avoid profanity.
- Mention no differences among participants.
- If any dramatic display occurs, bring the participants back to what they will accomplish out of the coaching event and what the owner has expressed about his intentions.
- Display respect and regards for everyone at the same professional level.
- Ask everyone if, for their comfort, they need any special accommodations.
- Do not compare their issues with other issues or your own experiences.
- Remember that all their issues are real for them.
- Do not interrupt their sharing and expressions.

Being Courteous

Managers and coaches committed to being fair will practice courtesy and empathize with others' past, showing compassion to how they might act or react to past or present situations. They show empathy and compassion because of who they are at that moment.

Empathy

The simplest definition of empathy is understanding and consciousness of other's feelings and emotions (Goleman 2015). An empathetic person can focus on others and could develop personal, social, and professional relationships. Managers and coaches able to focus on others effectively are the ones who can find common ground with others (HBR 2017). One's propensity to identify others' emotional status is in dealing with others relating to the present state of their feelings and emotions (Goleman 2015). Some attributes of empathetic people are (1) recognizing talent, (2) understanding other's emotional states, and (3) being helpful to others.

Compassion

A compassionate person demonstrates understanding, sympathy, and kindness for others in their time of sorrow, trouble, and hardship. It is the consciousness of experiencing others' distress and grief and interests and aspirations to ease their pain (HBR 2017; Goleman 2014). Compassion takes empathy further. People with compassion feel hardship when witnessing another person in distress. Some attributes of compassionate people are (1) placing oneself in others' situations, (2) practicing active listening, and (3) being okay with others' failures.

Coaches' Actions

■ Let them complete what they have to say—regardless of how harsh it is or the pain it provokes.
■ Keep acknowledging them for what they have provided for the organization.
■ Let them know what they think is "their failure" is not a failure but a hiccup in the process, and it does not just belong to them but also belongs to the team and the owner.
■ Ask them to share about their obstacles and difficulties in their lives and what it takes for them to perform their duties.
■ Listen actively while controlling facial expressions and body language.
■ Make sure they know they can have any emotions that might come up—and that includes showing anger and resentment.

Being Engaging

Engaging managers or coaches display their desire to communicate and understand others. They are communicating to produce relationships and results, not just manipulating to make their people do something they want them to do. They show interest in how others communicate while also paying attention to the facial expressions and body language of others.

Communication

To be engaging and connecting with others is to communicate and be communicative. This means to express your message in a well-mannered fashion and listen to the replying person with the same respect and courtesy you demand from them when they listen to you. This is the ability to transfer information from one location, individual, or team to other people or places. All forms of communication include at least one message, one sender, and one receiver (Jones 2015). Steinfatt (2009) expressed his view of communication and its vital role in human connectedness: "The central thrust of human communication concerns mutually understood symbolic exchange" (295). Communication is one concept that continues to be the focus of many theories about human connection (Jones 2015). Without communication, there is no workability or teamwork. Teams are synchronized when communicating effectively (Bakhshandeh 2015). Some attributes of someone with communication skills are (1) being aware of nonverbal communication, (2) delivering clear and concise messages, and (3) showing courtesy and listening keenly.

A communicative person knows that harmony and fulfillment can arise in communication. They know that peace of mind is a function of communication. They know that, without communication, there can be no efficiency or effectiveness in the organization. When communicating with others, remember:

■ Stay present to the purpose of your communication.
■ Be responsible for your communication and for how your listeners receive it.
■ Be clear, precise, and effective in your communications.
■ Speak the truth without causing upsets for others or yourself.

(Bakhshandeh 2015; Bakhshandeh 2004)

Interest

To be interested is to be engaged with the people talking and showing legitimate interest in their message. Coaches committed to being interested in the speakers are practicing active listening. Active listening is one essential element of communication. Active listening is a valuable skill that can be developed by practicing. One with active listening concentrates on the people talking and the content and feeling displayed in the conversation instead of just passively hearing speakers and messages (Rothwell et al. 2016; Goleman 2015). Practicing active listening helps the listeners gain the speakers' trust and respect by knowing the listeners appreciate their situations. It is an essential first step to neutralize a hard situation and pursue a workable solution to potential crises (Rothwell et al. 2016; Cummings and Worley 2015). Some attributes of people with active listening are (1) paying attention to the speaker, (2) responding appropriately, and (3) providing feedback.

Coaches' Actions

- Pay attention to the body language.
- Directly connect with them by looking at their eyes while they are talking and being aware of their facial expressions.
- Listen to what they say as it is the most important thing you need to hear.
- Show interest in the issues they communicate.
- Make sure your responses are related to what they have communicated.
- Ask their permission to provide feedback.
- Do not interrupt or correct their delivery.
- Summarize and/or paraphrase what they say to demonstrate that you really understood what they said—and, if you did not, the paraphrase or summary will give them a chance to correct it.
- When mismatches between stated messages and apparent feelings occur, follow up to ask for why that apparent disparity exists.

Table 4.1 displays a self-rating system that managers-as-coaches can use to realize their level of the fundamental state of being and the coaching competencies for establishing relatedness and rapport and planning properly for expanding their knowledge, skills, and abilities to provide such competencies during their high-performance coaching with their subordinates or coachees.

The next step is taking the team to what we call the interview process for uncovering the reality of relationships.

The Interview Process for Uncovering the Reality of Relationships

As part of the workshop with the MBD, we conducted the interview process to uncover *the reality of relationships* to reveal personal and professional issues in establishing strong rapport.

Effective leadership is essential to any organization's performance. Coaching is a planned intervention to develop people. "Traditionally, coaching has focused on individual empowerment and achievements. Organizations are now beginning to rely on team coaching to enhance organizational performance" (Maseko, Van Wyk, and Odendaal 2019, 1).

Table 4.1 Fundamental State of Being and Competencies for Establishing Relatedness and Rapport.

Fundamental State of Being and Competencies of Effective Manager-as-Coach Self-Rating System

Day:		Participant:				
Month:		Supervisor:				
		Team:				
		Department:				

Rating Scale: 1 = Poor, 2 = Marginal, 3 = Acceptable, 4 = Good, 5 = Excellent

State of Being and Competencies	Descriptions and Attributions	Rating				
		1	2	3	4	5
1	**Being Authentic**	A mixture of having the courage to be real and being oneself without consideration to submit to something to just please someone else.				
1.a	Approachability	(1) There is no presence of ego with them, (2) being humble, and (3) being open and welcoming				
1.b	Positivity	(1) Being optimistic, (2) being resilient, and (3) being grateful.				
2	**Being Respectful**	Display equal respect for everyone in any position in the organization regardless of age, gender, race, ethnicity, nationality, religion, or any other differences.				
2.a	Professionalism	(1) Using proper language, (2) avoiding drama, and (3) display ethical behavior				
2.b	Sensitivity	(1) Embracing uniqueness among people, (2) having mutual respect for everyone, and (3) having universal treatment for everyone				

3	**Being Courteous**	Committed to be fair and practicing courtesy to others past or situation. They show empathy and compassion not because they have an agenda but because who they are being now.					
3.a	Empathy	(1) Recognizing talent, (2) understanding other's emotional state, and (3) being helpful to others					
3.b	Compassion	(1) Placing oneself in others' situations, (2) practicing active listening, and (3) being okay with others' failures					
4	**Being Engaging**	Displaying their desire in communication and understanding of the other party in communication. They are not pushing their agenda and they are not attached to a certain prefabricated solution.					
4.a	Communication	(1) Being aware of nonverbal communication, (2) delivering clear and concise messages, and (3) showing courtesy and listening keenly.					
4.b	Interest	(1) Paying attention to the speaker, (2) responding appropriately, and (3) providing feedback					

Two actions for this month that would bring up my two lowest states of being and competencies ratings by at least one scale on the next month self-rating:

Action 1:

Action 2:

Source: Copyright 2021 by Behnam Bakhshandeh.

Although organizations depend on their teams to accomplish their goals and targets, numerous organizational leaders are unclear about how to effectively advance their teams to develop necessary skills and competencies to improve productivity (Maseko et al. 2019).

As we have mentioned throughout this book, we emphasize how important it is to develop individuals and team members to understand the relevance between their mindsets, attitudes, and behaviors to their performance (see Chapter 3, Figure 3.1). Because of this distinction, at this point of working with the MBD, we introduced the interview process for uncovering the reality of relationships. This interview was presented as a team coaching by presenting these steps:

(1) Explain the interview context and intent.
(2) Express the nondisclosure and confidentiality nature of the interview process.
(3) Assure everyone that they can be free and communicate their issues with no fear of retaliation or being treated differently.
(4) Walk the team through the entire interview setup and questioner's process and explain the intent behind the process and each question.
(5) Ask the team to write notes and ask questions to understand the intent of the interview completely.
(6) Instruct them to interview them and answer the questions privately while taking time to think and answer the questions.
(7) Ask them to call their direct supervisor or the owner/CEO and make a one-hour appointment to interview them in absolute privacy and confidentiality.
(8) Allow them to express all their issues, concerns, resentments, or emotional hardships.

How do we know if our relationships with others (personally or professionally) are the way we think they are? How do you know what you think of someone? How do you know something is correct or even real? How do you know what you *think* they think of you is even accurate? You do not! You might say to yourself, "Unless you ask, right?" Wrong! How often have you asked others to tell you the truth about your relationship, and they just said something that sounded good—but was not true? You have done the same thing, right? So just asking will not do it.

There are many reasons why people may not tell you the truth. Perhaps, they wish to avoid conflict. Perhaps, they are worried how you will react.

Perhaps, they simply do not wish to take the time to work out the reasons for conflict.

So how do we know where we stand with others? To get to that level of understanding of others, we need to ask questions. We just said asking questions makes no difference because people will not always tell the truth.

This process of uncovering the reality of relationships is a very effective tool for managers and to establish strong rapport and start a new, authentic relationship based on mutual respect. Table 4.2 explains how to set up for the interview by the owner, manager, or supervisor. Table 4.3 displays all the interview questions submitted to the team members in advance to prepare their answers to questions that their managers or supervisors would ask to Mike, the owner, and the CEO of MBD company.

Table 4.2 Powerfully Setting Up the Interview Process for Uncovering Reality of Relationships.

Setting Up the Interview Process for Uncovering Reality of Relationships
Part One: What is the purpose of the interview?
■ To face the reality of your relationships with others, how it is for them being with you, working with you, or just being around you.
■ To understand how you have affected others' experiences of life/working with you, around you or when you are with them.
■ To discover how and why they view you the way they do, good, bad, or ugly. All of it.
■ To understand why they respond or react, the way they do to you during day-to-day interactions, communications, or dialogue.
■ To have an opportunity to be related to your team on a higher and more profound level, the level you never knew was available.
■ To have an opportunity to own your mess and clean up your messes in your relationships with others.
■ To start from a whole new starting point with clarity and understanding of each other, personally or professionally.
■ To build a new relationship from a clean slate and build a brighter future, rather than drudging up the upsetting past, trying to hide it, or fix it.
Part Two: Who to interview?
■ People with whom you are not comfortable or with whom you have issues.
■ Someone with whom you have some upset, resentment, regrets, or resistance.
■ The people whom you are avoiding because of some past arguments or difficulty.

(Continued)

Table 4.2 (Continued)

Setting Up the Interview Process for Uncovering Reality of Relationships
■ The people who are the targets of your gossiping, listening to their gossip, or hearing gossip about. ■ These people could be anyone from your manager, colleagues, and business associates.
Part Three: How to set it up?

■ Communicate your commitment to the relationship and how important it is for you to clear the air.
■ Explain that you learned about this process and that it is an effective tool for communication for both parties to understand each other without resistance.
■ Say that it is all about the other person who will also be the only one who will speak and express any opinions.
■ Ask for an appointment. Indicate that at least one hour will be needed.
■ Have privacy, and both of you are comfortable without having to rush to another appointment.
■ Reproduce the "Interview Questions" and have them with you, including a writing pad to take notes.
■ Write their responses in a shortened form so you are focused on what is being said rather than being distracted by writing notes. The purpose of taking notes is so you can accurately reiterate what was said rather than what you thought was said. By doing this, you are preparing for repairing and restoring.
■ When you sit together and based on past damages, create a safe space by making a promise and giving your word that:
  – The other party can say anything with no concerns or fear of your retaliation, not now or later.
  – The other party can be upset, angry, and resentful, or loud if needed.
  – You will not defend yourself for or about anything that was said or done.
  – You will not say, "It was not that way" or, "No, you are wrong," or any other statements that would cast you as defending yourself or invalidating what the other party is saying.

– You will not justify your past actions; you will sit and listen with an open heart and open ears.
Part Four: What not to do?
■ Do not get too involved in your writing. Pay attention to the other party. ■ Do not be attached to how the other person is talking. Just listen with compassion. ■ Do not justify your actions about any issues. ■ Do not defend yourself against criticism or accusatory claims. ■ Do not say, "It was not that way!" ■ Do not interrupt. Be patient and empathetic during the process.

- Do not listen to your inner chatter about what is being said. This is simply the other party's perspective.
- Do not say, "You do not understand me!" It is not about you.
- Do not get upset during the process. Stay present to your commitment.
- Do not leave the interview because "You cannot take it anymore!" Remember, it is not about you. It is all about the commitment to workability and relationships.
- Do not answer your office or cell phone. Give your full and undivided attention and listen without interruptions.

Part Five: What to do?

- Listen as if the other party is telling the truth, regardless of what you think about what you hear, your opinion about the other party, or the issue.
- Remember, it is the truth as the other party sees it; regardless of what you think, the truth is for you.
- Pay attention to what is being said. It is very important. Maybe you are in an upsetting situation because you did not listen.
- Take on everything that is said and exactly the way it is being recounted, just as if you have done it according to how the other party says you did.
- Be responsible for the other party's experience of you. Regardless of what and how you are justifying or explaining your past actions, this experience with you will leave a lasting mark.

- Take accountability for the results you have produced with the other party.
- Establish compassion for the effort put forth to discuss the issue with you. This is especially true about upsetting and sensitive matters.

Part Six: How to be during the process?

- Be patient. Listen as if your life depends on it. Do not rush through the process.
- Be compassionate. Take what is said to heart and try to feel what they have felt.
- Be authentic. Genuinely show interest in the other party, what is being conveyed, and what is being felt.
- Be responsible. Believe that they are correct about their experiences with you.

Part Seven: What to do after the interview?

- Clean up your mess! After the interview is completed, take charge, and apologize for anything you think that you need to apologize for.
- Apologize for any disputed experience with them. It does not mean you agree about what the other party said you have done. But you are showing dignity, class, and interest in resolving the issues.
- Be articulate and detailed about what you are cleaning up. Be specific and speak with clarity. Stay away from generalizing.
- Clean up all your broken promises. Make new ones no matter how small or big. Remember you are cleaning up so leave nothing on the floor.

(Continued)

Table 4.2 (Continued)

Setting Up the Interview Process for Uncovering Reality of Relationships
■ Make new promises authentically and realistically. Do not look good and look committed but then do nothing; otherwise, you will be in the same hole again soon.
■ Ask the other party if it would consider interviewing you. Do not insist, just naturally offer. If agreed, then set it up.
■ Acknowledge the person's commitment and desire to go through this process with you. Ensure that you know how difficult it was for the other party to be open and share and how much you appreciate it. The process is complete.

Source: The content of this table is from the book Anatomy of Upset; Restoring Harmony (Bakhshandeh 2015, 167–78) and used with express permission from Behnam Bakhshandeh and Primeco Education, Inc.

Although these two tables present the interview process in a professional setting, with minor modifications such as a change in questions and directions, this interview can be used on a personal level—such as in relationships, marriages, and friendships.

Table 4.3 displays the set of questions that managers or supervisors would ask participants. The questions are given to participants in advance of a meeting.

Table 4.3   The Questions for the Interview Process for Uncovering Reality of Relationships.

The Questions for the Interview Process for Uncovering Reality of Relationships
Section One: Job and Relationships
1. What do you like the most about working here?
2. What do you not like about working here?
3. How do you envision yourself with this organization?
4. What is your dream for yourself and your life?
5. Do you have a set of goals for yourself and your life? What are they?
6. What obstacles can you see are in your way for fulfilling your dreams?
7. What obstacles can you see in your way of fulfilling your goals?
8. What do you like about your job?
9. What do you not like about your job?
10. What do you like about your location office?
11. What do you not like about your location office?
12. What do you like about this organization?
13. What do you not like about this organization?
14. How do you rate your job performance? And why? (Score from 0 being the lowest to 10 being the highest)

15. Do you have any specific plans for increasing your job performance? What is it?
16. How do you rate your relationship with your direct supervisor (me or others)? And why? (Score from 0 being the nonexistent to 10 being excellent)
17. Do you have any specific plans for improving your relationship with your direct supervisor (me or others)? If yes, what is it?
18. How do you rate your relationship with the organization? And why? (Score from 0 being the nonexistent to 10 being excellent)
19. Do you have any specific plans for improving your relationship with the organization? What is it?
20. What is in your way to perform and be productive?

Section Two: Promises and Targets

1. What did you say you would accomplish in the last year?
2. Which ones did you accomplish?
3. Which ones did you not accomplish?
4. What were your goals and targets for the last year?
5. Which goals and targets were met last year?
6. Which goals and targets were not met last year?
7. How have you been *being* that allowed you to accomplish your goals?
8. What new actions did you create that allowed you to achieve your goals?
9. How have you been *being* that keep you from achieving your goals last year?
10. What could you have done that you have not done yet, that had you done that, you would have met your goals?
11. What could you do differently that would forward your individual performance, team productivity, and the organization's success?
12. What are your new promises for this year?

Section Three: Completing

1. Who do you have a hard time working with? And why?
2. What do you have a hard time working with? And why?
3. What are you willing to do about it?
4. If you could change one thing about your job, what would that be?
5. If you could change one thing about your relationship with your supervisor (me or others), what would that be?
6. If you could change one thing about your relationship with the organization, what would that be?
7. What were your contributions to the team and the organization?
8. What would you like to be acknowledged for?
9. Is there anything you want me to know about you?
10. Is there anything you want me to know about your job or your future?
11. Do you have any requests for me?
12. Is there anything else you need to say?

Source: Copyright 2021 by Behnam Bakhshandeh.

The length of this interview process depends on the number of interviews performed by the manager and how many participants are involved. With MBD, Mike completed all twelve interviews in one week in three locations. The next step for Mike was to organize his notes and create a tally about:

■ What he has discovered during these interviews.
■ What of his relationship with his team?
■ What he needed to alter about his mindset, attitude, and behavior.
■ What training and development he needs to bring to his team for altering their mindset, attitude, and behavior?
■ What he needs to change in his business operations.
■ How he can train and develop his team for greater responsibility and accountability.
■ And more.

The overall result of this rapport-building process was very satisfying for the organization and all the people involved. The work environment changed from a "have to" to a "want to" attitude. Team members communicated the issue publicly, and they came up with new ideas that would empower the organization's vision and mission statement. Having an authentic relationship with others provides the foundation for an effective working environment.

Key Points to Remember

■ **Relatedness is the key to trust and rapport**
  – Effective coaches will not act as if they are better than, or above, their coachees. They will display respect, empathy, and compassion for where the coachees are in their lives and careers.

■ **Be aware of reactions**
  – To consider you as a manager-as-coach is the source of resistance. Not being liked is real but provides a possibility for a more effective approach that results in a better outcome for you.

■ **Who you are being makes the biggest difference**
  – Look at your state of being and be the judge and jury of your self-evaluation.

■ **Values as sources of operations**

- Remember your values. They are the source of healthy business operations and the cause of having healthy rapport.

Coaching and Developmental Questions for Managers

(1) Do you have a good rapport with your subordinates and team members?

    (a) If yes, what are you crediting this good relation to?
    (b) If not, what do you think is on the way?

(2) Do you have a good rapport with your manager or supervisor?

    (a) If yes, to what are you crediting this good relation?
    (b) If not, why do you think it is what it is?

(3) Have you studied and rated yourself on the Fundamental State of Being and Competencies for Establishing Relatedness and Rapport?

(4) What are the areas of building rapport you need to expand your KSAs (knowledge, skills, and abilities)?

References

Amos, Elizabeth A., and Bart L. Weathington. 2008. "An Analysis of the Relation between Employee-organization Value Congruence and Employee Attitudes." *The Journal of Psychology* 142, no. 6: 615–32. https://doi.org/10.3200/JRLP.142.6.

Angelo, Gabriel. 2012. *Rapport; The Art of Connecting with People and Building Relationships*. Middletown, DE: SN & NS Publications.

Aristotelous, Philppos. 2019. *The Marvel of Engagement*. Middletown, DE: Self-Publishing.

Baker, Zachary G., Emily M. Watlington, and C. Raymond Knee. 2020. "The Role of Rapport in Satisfying One's Basic Psychological Needs." *Motivation and Emotion* 44, no. 2: 329–43.

Bakhshandeh, Behnam. 2002. "Business Coaching and Managers Training." Unpublished Workshop on Coaching Businesses and Training Managers. San Diego, CA: Primeco Education, Inc.

Bakhshandeh, Behnam. 2004. "Effective Communication." *Audio CD Set and Workshop*. Carbondale, PA: Primeco Education, Inc.

Bakhshandeh, Behnam. 2008. "Bravehearts; Leadership Development Training." Unpublished Training and Developmental Course on Coaching Executive and Managers. San Diego, CA: Primeco Education, Inc.

Bakhshandeh, Behnam. 2009. *Conspiracy for Greatness; Mastery on Love Within*. San Diego, CA: Primeco Education, Inc.

Bakhshandeh, Behnam. 2015. *Anatomy of Upset: Restoring Harmony*. Carbondale, PA: Primeco Education, Inc.

Bakhshandeh, Behnam. 2021. "Perception of 21st Century 4Cs (Critical Thinking, Communication, Creativity & Collaboration) Skill Gap in Private-Sector Employers in Lackawanna County, NEPA." An Unpublished Dissertation in Workforce Education and Development. The Pennsylvania State University.

The Balance Career website. n.d. "What Is a Skill Set?" www.thebalancecareers.com/what-is-a-skill-set-2062103#.

Bartz, David E., David R. Schwandt, and Larry W. Hillman. 1989. "Differences between 'T' and 'D'." *Personnel Administrator* 34, no. 6: 164–70.

Boyatzis, Richard E. 1982. *The Competent Manager: A Model for Effective Performance*. Hoboken, NJ: John Wiley & Sons.

Cennamo, Lucy, and Dianne Gardner. 2008. "Generational Differences in Work Values, Outcomes and Person-organization Values Fit." *Journal of Managerial Psychology* 23, no. 8: 891–906. https://doi.org/10.1108/02683940810904385.

Colquitt, Jason A., Jeffery A. LePine, and Michael J. Wesson. 2015. *Organizational Behavior: Improving Performance and Commitment in the Workplace*, 4th ed. New York, NY: McGraw-Hill Education.

Cummings, Thomas G., and Christopher G. Worley. 2015. *Organization Development & Change*, 10th ed. Stamford, CT: Cengage Learning.

Donahue, Wesley E. 2018. *Building Leadership Competence: A Competency-Based Approach to Building Leadership Ability*. State College, PA: Centerstar Learning.

Gilmore, Mike. 2019. *The Power of Rapport*. Middletown, DE: Partridge.

Goleman, Daniel. 1998. *Working with Emotional Intelligence*. New York, NY: Random House.

Goleman, Daniel. 2014. "What it Takes to Achieve Managerial Success." *TD: Talent Development* 68, no. 11: 48–52.

Goleman, Daniel. 2015. *Emotional Intelligence; Why It Can Mater More Than IQ*. New York, NY: Bantam Books.

Hadden, Benjamin W., Lindsey M. Rodriguez, C. Raymond Knee, Angelo M. DiBello, and Zachary G. Baker. 2016. "An Actor—partner Interdependence Model of Attachment and Need Fulfillment in Romantic Dyads." *Social Psychological and Personality Science* 7, no. 4: 349–57.

HBR (Harvard Business Review). 2017. *Harvard Business Review Guild to Emotional Intelligence*. Boston, MA: Harvard Business Review Press.

Heidegger, Martin. 1953. *Being and Time*. Translated by Joan Stambaugh. New York, NY: State University on New York Press.

Hove, Michael J., and Jane L. Risen. 2009. "It's All in The Timing: Interpersonal Synchrony Increases Affiliation." *Social Cognition* 27, no. 6: 949–60. https://doi.org/10.1521/soco.2009.27.6.949.

Jones, Virginia R. 2015. "21st Century Skills: Communication." *Children's Technology and Engineering* 20, no. 2: 28–29.

Keller, Heidi. 2016. "Psychological Autonomy and Hierarchical Relatedness as Organizers of Developmental Pathways." *Philosophical Transactions of the Royal Society B: Biological Sciences* 371, no. 1686: 20150070.

Krathwohl, David R. 2002. "A Revision of Bloom's Taxonomy: An Overview." *Theory into Practice* 41, no. 4: 212–18.

Lawrie, John. 1990. "Prepare for a Performance Appraisal." *Personnel Journal* (April): 132–36.

Levi, Daniel. 2016. *Group Dynamics for Teams*, 5th ed. Los Angeles, CA: Sage Publications.

"Lexico.com." 2021. *Powered by Oxford*. www.lexico.com/en/definition/relatedness.

Martela, Frank, and Tapani J. J. Riekki. 2018. "Autonomy, Competence, Relatedness, and Beneficence: A Multicultural Comparison of the Four Pathways to Meaningful Work." *Frontier in Psychology* 9, no. 1157. https://doi.org/10.3389/fpsyg.2018.01157.

Maseko, Badelisile M., Rene Van Wyk, and Aletta Odendaal. 2019. "Team Coaching in the Workplace: Critical Success Factors for Implementation." *SA Journal of Human Resource Management* 17: a1125. https://doi.org/10.4102/sajhrm.v17i0.1125.

McLagan, P. 1988. "Top Management Support." *Training*, May 25, no. 5: 59–62.

"Merriam-Webster Dictionary." 2021. *Rapport*. www.merriam-webster.com/dictionary/rapport.

Nadler, Leonard, and Zeace Nadler. 1989. *Developing Human Resources*. San Francisco, CA: Jossey-Bass.

Primeco Education, Inc. n.d. Website. *Team and Organizational Training*. Accessed April 21, 2021. www.PrimecoEucation.com.

Rothwell, William J. 2015. *Organization Development Fundamentals: Managing Strategic Change*. Alexandria, WV: ATD Press.

Rothwell, William J., Sohel M. Imroz, and Behnam Bakhshandeh. 2021. *Organization Development Interventions, Executing Effective Organizational Change*. New York, NY: Routledge-Taylor and Francis.

Rothwell, William J., and Henry J. Sredl. 2014. *Workplace Learning and Performance: Present and Future Roles and Competencies*, 3rd ed., vol. II. Amherst, MA: HRD Press.

Rothwell, William J., Jacqueline M. Stavros, and Roland L. Sullivan. 2016. *Practicing Organization Development: Leading Transformation and Change*, 4th ed. Hoboken, NJ: John Wiley & Sons, Inc.

Schwartz, Shalom H. 1992. "Universals in the Content and Structure of Values: Theoretical Advances and Empirical Tests in 20 Countries." In *Advances in Experimental Social Psychology*, vol. 25, 1–65. Cambridge, MA: Academic Press. https://doi.org/10.1016/S0065-2601(08)60281-6

Spencer, Lyle M., and Signe M. Spencer. 1993. *Competence at Work: Models for Superior Performance*. New York, NY: John Wiley and Sons, Ed.

Steinfatt, Tom. 2009. "Definitions of Communication." In *Encyclopedia of Communication Theory*, edited by Stephan W. Littlejohn and Karen A. Foss, vol. 1, 295–99. Thousand Oaks, CA: Sage Publication, Inc.

Travelbee, Joyce. 1963. "What Do We Mean by Rapport?" *The American Journal of Nursing* 63, no. 2: 70–72. https://doi.org/10.2307/3452595.

Whitmore, John. 2017. *Coaching for Performance; The Principle and Practice of Coaching and Leadership*, 5th ed. Boston, MA: Nicholas Brealey Publishing.

Chapter 5

Step 2: What Is the Issue at Hand?

Behnam Bakhshandeh

Chapter 5 focuses on the second step after the coach and coachees have established a good rapport and working relationship. The second step is to *understand what is happening*. At this stage, it is necessary to gather information about the situation—and particularly to clarify facts rather than mere perceptions. This chapter reviews what kind of information a high-performance coach needs to know, collect, and analyze to reveal present conditions. In addition, this chapter summarizes what fundamental approaches and models are needed for the process and what competencies are required by a high-performance coach to reveal what is the issue at hand (Rothwell 2013).

Chapter 5 as the second step of high-performance coaching covers:

- Elements of the Human Performance Enhancement approach in organizations
- Environments affecting human performance in organizations
- Manager's understanding, clarifying, and awareness of the performance environment
- The distinction between goals and values, and how we determine our values
- What a High-Performance Coach can learn from an HPI practitioner
- Reviewing, collecting, and documenting information
- An inductive and deductive approach to collecting facts and perceptions
- A business case example, useful tools, and key factors to remember from this chapter

DOI: 10.4324/9781003155928-7

Start by Examining "What Is Happening," Facts or Perceptions?

The first question for realizing "What is happening" or "What is the issue at hand" is to contemplate: "What are we looking for?" Given the human psyche, it is to have perceptions. Are we interested in digging up the (1) facts, (2) perception, or (3) both simultaneously? Facts are indisputable and can be independently authenticated. Examples of facts include the organization's name, starting date, hierarchy and structure, name and position of the executive team, balance sheet, income statement, inventory, and list of products and services (Rothwell 2015a). Facts can be checked—and verified (shown to be true) or falsified (shown to be false). While some facts may be changed over time—such as account receivable information, which could change by the minute—facts can be shown as true or false.

Perceptions, on the other hand, are shaped by opinion. They may be influenced by experience, beliefs, values, principles, mindsets, and emotions. They cannot be independently authenticated.

Examples of perceptions include an employee's opinions about the organization's values, morale, accountability, key work processes, management actions or lack thereof, HR policies, customer service, and satisfaction, and what the organization should do in the present or future (Rothwell 2015b). These opinions run both ways, from employees to managers and from managers to employees. "Managers and employees lack complete facts on which to base decisions. They rely on perceptions. Moreover, perceptions affect reality" (Rothwell 2015a, 86). Perceptions can create a *self-fulfilling prophecy* in which what is perceived is to be true (or false) actually becomes true or false. If a bank is perceived to be on the edge of bankruptcy, a run on the bank can lead to bankruptcy; if the stock market is believed to be crashing, panicked stockholders selling their shares can lead to a crash. Perception can affect facts. If workers are perceived to be poor performers and are treated as poor performers, they may become poor performers because others have discouraged them from achieving results. That can happen even when the facts—actual performance data on workers—demonstrates that the worker perceived to be a poor performer is actually average or even exemplary.

Performance coaches must separate perceptions from facts. It is wise to follow the simple advice to "listen to what people say based—but get the facts anyway." Perceptions cannot be completely trusted because they can be influenced by who likes whom, who dislikes whom, and by other issues that may shape feelings but not facts.

Experienced performance coaches know that the organizational environment shapes worker job performance far more than individuals do. That is an important point to remember at the outset of an investigation into worker job performance. While managers tend to blame employees for poor job performance, the reality is that organizations (and managers themselves) create many obstacles to performance. As W. Edwards Deming once observed, "managers create most of their own problems."

It is not difficult to cite examples. If workers have to secure the permission of their immediate superiors before they can take action, then their actions will be predictably slow. If the managers chose the wrong person to carry out a job—someone lacking the appropriate motivation or skills—then the results may not be good. If managers save money by scrimping on company-provided tools, equipment, or software, then workers can scarcely be expected to perform at peak when lacking necessary resources. If managers establish a pay system that rewards "going along to getting along," then they have incentivized mediocrity.

Coaches should thus begin investigations by gathering information on:

■ What is common or typical performance by other, similar performers?
■ What is outstanding performance?
■ What is recommended performance?
■ What is the past performance of the individual or team?
■ What is the present performance of the team?
■ What is the performance trend line of the individual or team?
■ If time permits, what can be found out about common or typical performance in the same job in other teams, departments, divisions—or even in other organizations?

Environments Affecting Human Performance in Organizations

As we have established in the previous section, these four areas (Figure 5.1) affect human performance in organizations. The corresponding questions would assist the internal or external practitioners in gathering needed background information that can shape the performance investigation. These questions can be modified, if necessary, but provide a good place to begin:

The Organization Environment

■ What does the organization do best?

■ How does the organization compete in its market?
■ What is the biggest challenge facing the organization and its managers?
■ What are the clients'/customers' perceptions of the organization?

The Work Environment

■ What are the biggest internal challenges of the organization?
■ What has occurred recently?
■ What are the causes of these changes?
■ How well do workers and managers work to achieve common goals?

The Work

■ How does the organization produce results?
■ How does the organization serve clients/customers?
■ How up to date is the organization's technology and services?
■ What factors affect the work?

The Workers

■ What are the strengths of the organization's people?
■ What is the reputation of the organization among its people?
■ What are the turnover and absenteeism rates, and what causes them?
■ What is the biggest dissatisfiers among workers?

(Rothwell, Stavros, and Sullivan 2016)

Often organization environment and performance are associated with organizational assessment, that arise from organizational diagnosis, which is the process of a systematic examination of how well an organization is functioning and how well their workforces are performing. Understanding the organization's environmental forces (organization environment, the work environment, the work, and the workers) and their relevancy for change grants a management system to swiftly come up with ideas that would support the change effort's success. Unfortunately, in some cases, change intervention efforts flunk given that an organization is not prepared for change intervention, and for one reason or another, are not ready to take on changes (Rothwell, Stopper, and Myers 2017).

Sometimes, especially when using an external consultant, it would be very useful if practitioners become familiar with the organization's culture and structure before collecting performance data.

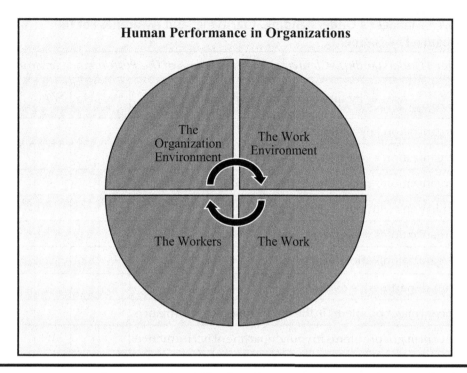

Figure 5.1 **Four Environments Are Affecting Human Performance in Organizations.**
Source: Adapted from Rothwell et al. (2016).

Table 5.1 assists internal or external performance coaches by conducting an inquiry to their level of familiarity with the organization and design their action plan to get to know what they need to know for better data collecting and analysis process.

Individual's High-Performance Is the Results of Their Choice

While it is true that most performance problems stem from management decisions, it is also true that workers sometimes have a tendency to blame others rather than take responsibility for what they can do and what they can control in their own job performance. People can *choose* to be productive. They can focus on what they can control and take proactive action rather than delegate problems upward or bewail their fate rather than act.

The choice of *being* productive is completely generated from individuals' interests on what they are *doing* along with their mindset about their individual values and principles. We talk about the relevance between who people

Table 5.1 Manager's Understanding, Clarifying, and Awareness of the Performance Environment.

Manager's Understanding, Clarifying, and Awareness of the Performance Environment					
#	Area of Inquiry—Are You Familiar with	Yes	No	N/A	Action Needed
The Organization Environment					
1	Organization's vision, mission, and core values				
2	Organization's reputation in the community				
3	Affiliations with other organizations				
4	Organization's long-range goals				
5	Organization's short-term goals				
6	Your department's overall goals				
7	Recent major problems in the organization's performance				
8	Recent major problems in your department performance				
9	Human resources policies and procedures				
10	Diversity, equality, and inclusion policies and practices				
11	Recruitment practices				
12	New hire orientation				
13	Employees' appreciation and social events				
14	Compensation and benefits				
15	Organization's presence in the market				
16	Succession planning				
17	Profit-sharing plan				
18	401K and retirement plan				
19	Bonus plan and structure				
20	Expansion plan				
The Work Environment					
1	Current products or services				
2	Recent changes in products and services				
3	Issues with suppliers or distributors				

4	Core competencies and strengths of the organization				
5	Core competencies and strengths of your department				
6	Any weakness of the organization				
7	Any weaknesses of your department				
8	Clear management hierarchy				
9	Job descriptions				
10	Work responsibilities and accountabilities				
11	Annual or quarterly performance evaluations				
12	Disciplinary policies and actions				
13	Age of facilities and building safety				
14	Age of equipment and inspections				
15	OSHA and safety policies				
16	Comparison between intended plan and actual results				
17	Composition of groups and teams				
18	Absenteeism and turnover records in your department				
19	Rate of accidents and their causes				
20	Training and development opportunities				
21	Promotion opportunities				
22	Educational reimbursement				
23	Supervision and management style				
24	Communication and information distribution systems				
25	Open door policy				
26	Amount of gossip and drama				
27	Work hours, overtime, and holidays off				
28	Social events				
29	Fairness and respect				
30	Rapport, relatedness, and communication				

(Continued)

Table 5.1 (Continued)

	Manager's Understanding, Clarifying, and Awareness of the Performance Environment				
	The Work				
1	Distribution of workers among groups and teams				
2	Quality of products and services				
3	Reputations of products and services				
4	New products training				
5	Hard skills training				
6	Soft skills training				
7	Customer complaints about the products and services				
8	The reputation of products and services in the community				
9	Use of new technologies and relevant training				
10	New products and services plan				
	The Workers				
1	Number of employees in your department				
2	Employees' diversity				
3	Employees' tenure and history with the organization				
4	Employees' ages and closeness to retirement				
5	Employees' turnover rate and causes				
6	Management and supervisors' perception of employees				
7	Employees' perception of management and supervisors				
8	Employees' exit interviews				
9	Employees' complaints and resentments				
10	Camaraderie and team attitude				

Source: Copyright 2021 by Behnam Bakhshandeh.

are *Being* and the quality of what they are *Doing* in Chapter 4 (see Figure 4.2) and the role of people's mindset in this process. For this process to work its magic, there is a need for leaders who understand the place of *interest* and *choice* in their workforce and organization systems. To understand this process, the organization management and leadership need to understand the workforce's individual and team doubts and concerns and what is in their way to fulfill their interests. This relationship requires merging the interests of all the three elements of high performance: (1) individuals, (2) teams, and (3) the organization (Davis 2001). For this reason, just coming with some fast fix and rational solutions to convince the workforce to be faster or better has not produced any inspiring results yet! "All of these were seen as legitimate and honored by the process used, which was designed to build on and integrate the strengths of individualism, teamwork, and leadership. These, I believe, are the three primary forces operating in all organizations at all times whether we acknowledge them or not" (Rothwell 2015a, 27).

Distinction Between Goals and Values?

Individual interests are emerging from their values and what they care about; the things that are drivers of their choices. We hear about goals a lot, but what is the distinction between goals and values? *Goals* are things individuals want to have or accomplish; they are objectives. While *Values* form our character and define us, they shape who we are for ourselves and others. Our values are what make us unique and memorable and what makes us distinct from others. Our values give our life meaning, determine our purpose, and give us direction in life. Ultimately, values determine our choices and guide our mindset, attitude, and behaviors (Bakhshandeh 2008). As Roy Disney said, "[w]hen your values are clear to you, making decisions becomes easier."

How Do We Select Our Values?

As individuals are growing, they are experiencing the presence of values from the following sources:

■ In their home, by observing their parents, grandparents, siblings, and other family members, they learn to care for certain values that are passed down through family generations.
■ Learned through process of being at school and interactions with other children and influence of teachers.
■ National pride, as some values come from being raised in a culture we are proud of and love.

- Participating in any faith-based groups and churches.
- Learning from society, media, politics, and global events.
- Effects of professions and careers on selecting values based on professional positions.
- What they think is the right thing to do, such as moral, ethics, and integrity.

(Bakhshandeh 2009)

Values that Exist in Our World

In this section, we are looking at what values exist in our own world, our environment, our lives in general, and how they define us from others. Clearly, as we mentioned in the previous sections, our values determine our choice in the matter of our actions and behaviors, which directly influence our productivity and performance in personal and professional environments. As a manager-as-coach, if we can understand our workforce's values, then we can have a window to the source of how the workforce operates, makes decisions, the reasons for their actions or inactions. This awareness allows us to be effective performance coaches (Bakhshandeh 2008).

Personal Values

These are values that define who we are as individuals and how to relate to ourselves and guide us in relationships with others. Some examples of personal values are (1) integrity, (2) honor, and (3) respect.

Social Values

These are values that define how we relate to groups of people, such as a team. They define how we are connecting with the communities around us and the people with whom we often interact. Some examples of social values are (1) fairness, (2) diversity, and (3) equality.

Cultural Values

These values define how we relate to other people in the world in general, our place in the world that guides our general interests and behaviors around other cultures and customs, and the degree of our interests or the acceptance of them. At the same time, they define how we relate to people with similar backgrounds as we have. Some examples of cultural values are (1) family, (2) traditions, and (3) celebrations.

Professional Values

These values define how we relate to ourselves in affiliation with the professional work we are doing. They are guiding our mindset, attitude, and behaviors in the work environment and situations. They are determining how we relate to others with whom we work, such as managers, supervisors, and coworkers. Some examples of work values are (1) loyalty, (2) teamwork, and (3) responsibility.

How to Determine What Our Values Are

This simple but effective little practice would bring up individuals' values that might be hidden from their view, or they have not given enough weight or the determination to understand them or even be aware of them. As we are trying to understand what is happening or the issue at hand, understanding individuals who are engaged with the potential issue is valuable for uncovering the source of the problem.

When you value productivity, your work becomes more prominent. When you value serenity, your home becomes more important. When you value your family, you spend more time with them. When you value your faith, you practice it more often. When you value health, you pay more attention to your body. Value your ideas, your time, and your money, and they become more valuable. It is all in your hands and in your mind. Value is not determined by a price tag or any other monetary system. The value of anything is the value we give it. What do you value most? What do you want to grow and become abundant in your life? Give more of yourself to the things you value, and they will flourish and become more present in your day-to-day life (Bakhshandeh 2009).

Simply ask individuals of interest to write what is their (1) personal, (2) social, and (3) cultural and work values by having an inquiry on (1) what are important to them as an individual, (2) what are important to them in life in general, and (3) what is important to them at work.

You can use Table 5.2 for conducting this process and allowing the employees or clients to record their values in one place. At the same time, you can ask the employees to come with some ideas of actions that would bring up the presence of the values in their lives and professions. Continue

Table 5.2 How to Determine Your Values.

Determining Your Values			
Date:	Participant:		Team:
Month	Supervisor:		Department:
Area of Values	**Type of Values**	**Answers**	**Actions to Take**
What are important to you as an individual?	Personal		
	Social		
	Cultural		
	Professional		
What are important to you in life in general?	Personal		
	Social		
	Cultural		
	Professional		
What are important to you at work?	Personal		
	Social		
	Cultural		
	Professional		

Source: Copyright 2021 by Behnam Bakhshandeh.

working with individuals to determine their values and work on having these values. Practicing them assists the high-performance coach in discovering problems and designing an action plan to resolve the problems based on individuals' values and determinations.

What a High-Performance Coach Can Learn from an HPI Practitioner

All the coaching models and practices to enhance one's performance are worthy and effective if they are applied and managed for effectiveness and relevance to increase performance and productivity. One effective way to make these models and practices systematic is to use them as the source of an individual, team, and group high-performance and enhancement coaching (Rothwell 2015a).

This would bring us to the roles of high-performance coaches and what they can learn from an HPI practitioner and the "Six Steps of the Human Performance Improve Process Model" that is defined in ASTD Models for Human Performance Improvement. Clearly, the High-performance coaching model differs from the Human Performance Improve Process Model in some ways. However, they have characteristics that can assist and help one another to improve individuals' and teams' performances in other ways.

These steps are: (1) performance assessment, (2) cause assessment, (3) change intervention, (4) action plan execution, (5) change management, and (6) evaluation and measurement. This model has included the four important roles of the HPI practitioner and, in our case, the high-performance coach as the (1) analyst, (2) intervention specialist, (3) change manager, and (4) evaluator. Figure 5.2 displays the relationship between HPI practitioners' roles that high-performance coaches can apply to their process of coaching employees (Rothwell and Sredl 2000).

Describing the Four Roles

The following is a brief description of each of the four roles according to Rothwell, Hohne, and King (2018) and Rothwell and Sredl (2000) for the high-performance coaches to learn from HPI practitioners and to apply in coaching subordinates, individuals, or team coaching:

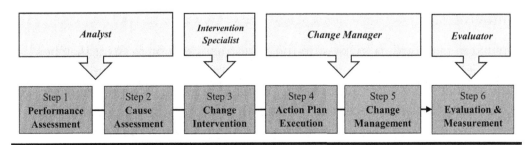

Figure 5.2 What a High-Performance Coach Can Learn from Elements of Human Performance Improvement (HPI) Process.

Source: Adapted from Rothwell et al. (2018).

Analyst

The role of the analyst is considered the most important role, involving individuals', teams', groups' or organizations' performance and cause analysis. In the analyst role, the high-performance coach is performing troubleshooting and cause/effect procedures to uncover the causes of performance gaps or needs for improvements (Rothwell and Sredl 2000). "The process of analysis helps the HPI practitioner to accurately and thoroughly diagnose the problem or situation before recommending and implementing the appropriate solution system" (Rothwell et al. 2018, 12).

Intervention Specialist

Many human performance improvement strategies and interventions are available to the high-performance coach or the HPI practitioner that consist of training or management solutions. It will be the choice of the high-performance coaches to select the appropriate intervention based on what they have determined to cause problems in human performance and as the natural results of analysis (Rothwell and Sredl 2000).

Change Management

Managing the selected interventions and related action plans to implement changes resulting from the intervention requires short- and long-term change management. The change manager's role is to ensure that the results of the change interventions are executed appropriately and follow the intention to produce the desired results by individuals, teams, groups, or organizations (Rothwell and Sredl 2000).

Evaluator

Evaluation is critical to make sure the performance improvement matches the expected results of the intervention. The emphasis of evaluation is making sure that the issues caused by the original performance problems recognized in the analysis process are dealt with effectively and are resolved, or there remains a need for additional interventions. The evaluator

> assesses the impact of interventions and follows up on changes made, actions taken and results achieved to provide participants

and stakeholders with information about how well interventions
are being implemented

(Rothwell et al. 2018, 13)

Supporting the Change Intervention

In every potential change intervention, the most important and almost the
hardest phase is to convince decision-makers and stakeholders to accept that
there is a need for a change, either individually or as a team or an organization. This convincing act is vital to the success of the change intervention
because if people involved with the change effort are not aligned with the
action, it will be challenging to collect data, analyze, and implement the
change, and it will fail (Rothwell et al. 2016). Regarding resistance to change
"people are unwilling to change unless they see worthwhile reasons for
doing so. When making a case for change, someone or some group will
need to be convinced early" (Rothwell 2015a, 65). The convincing individual or group that are the change agents and facilitators for needed change
should gather compelling evidence that supports the necessity of such
change (Rothwell et al. 2016; Rothwell 2015b).

Seeking Evidence of the Need for Change Intervention

We need to point out that someone's or a group's dissatisfaction with something about an individual in a team or an organization is not enough to convince the decision-makers to agree with the change efforts or even create a
strong base for the change. It is a reasonable and appropriate place to start the
process, but it is not all that is needed. Usually, the second act is to organize
an open-ended pursuit for collecting evidence that supports the need for the
change to support the case for the change intervention. The techniques of
obtaining evidence are based on the change agent's knowledge and creativity.
The followings are possible strategies for the change agents, high-performance
coaches, and managers-as-coaches to gather evidence for the potential needed
to change interventions (Rothwell et al. 2016; Rothwell 2015b):

Data from the High-Productive and High-Performance Organizations

During past decades, many organizations have changed their approach
from making workforce training to only enhancing performance. Asking for

interviewing executives of these organizations is a great strategy; questions like the following can open doors for change implementation: What kind of problems triggered the changes in your organization? What kind of issue triggered the change in human performance enhancement? What opportunities arise during or after implementing changes?

Data from the Related Industries or Local Organizations

Given the competition, some organizations are not willing to share their data and strategies for their change efforts with other organizations and their representatives. In these cases, the change agent may prefer to discuss the need for change with organizations in their industry or some organizations operating near their organization. The change agent should look for workability, productivity, and higher performance from other organizations' efforts and strategies, using the same questions mentioned in the previous section.

Investigate the Organization's Strategies and Action Plans

How effective were the organization's strategies and action plans for enhancing the workforce's performance in the past several years? How were the decided action plans for training and development of the workforce to increase productivity performance to a higher level?

Clients'/Customers' or Stakeholders' Requirements

Another good place to investigate for gathering data is the organization's clients, customers, and stakeholders about their requirements and needs and their satisfaction about receiving quality products or services. How might problems with the clients and customers be evidence for the need for a change intervention?

Evidence from Previous Training by the Organization

Were there any previous attempts to implement changes using training and development programs? What resulted from such an attempt? Any evidence of success or failure of such attempts, and why? Maybe the collected evidence about the failure of previous attempts is a fresh starting point for supporting a new change intervention attempt.

Distinguishing Underlying Sources of Current Crises

Connect references and evidence collected to determine underlying causes for crises in the organization. Could these causes be prevented by utilizing some holistic approach to enhancing the workforce's performance? Or is there a need for different approaches and methods to be implemented?

Distinguishing Occurring Problems

What are the most current and urgent challenges confronting the organization? Can traditional training make a difference? Or should we implement high-performance coaching and approach our enhancing human performance issue as a form of change intervention?

Develop Based on Decision-Makers' Values

What are the decision-makers' values and what do they see as problems in the organizations? What do they see as high priorities for the organization? Could the desired change intervention provide a new work environment and high-performance matching with the decision-makers' values and priorities?

Reviewing, Collecting, and Documenting Information: Facts and Perceptions

Whether the change agent is internal or external, fact-finding, and perception hunting are the keys to understanding what is happening. But what approaches should be used to gather and document facts and perceptions? Essentially, there are two approaches to collecting such information, which are not necessary and mutually exclusive: (1) the inductive approach and (2) the deductive approach (Rothwell 2015a).

Before we get to explain the mentioned approaches, at this point, it is beneficial to our readers, including performance coaches and managers-as-coaches to discuss and distinguish differences between meanings and interpretations of facts, perceptions, plans, and norms in public as well as in any organizations independently (see Table 5.3). However, as we are all aware, making interpretations and coming with different meanings about any topic, incident, and concept is a normal human psyche and thinking process (Bakhshandeh 2009).

Table 5.3 Definitions and Meanings of Facts, Perceptions, Plans, and Norms.

Definitions and Meanings of Facts, Perceptions, Plans, and Norms			
Distinctions	*Dictionary Definitions*	*Scientific or Academic Definitions*	*In Performance*
Facts	(1) "a thing that is known or proved to be true." (2) "information used as evidence or as part of a report or news article." (3) "the truth about events as opposed to interpretation." Oxford Language (2021).	[Fact: In science, an observation that has been repeatedly confirmed and for all practical purposes is accepted as "true." Truth in science, however, is never final and what is accepted as a fact today may be modified or even discarded tomorrow] (NCSE 2016).	What is actually being done. The way it is.
Perceptions	(1) "the state of being or process of becoming aware of something through the senses." (2) "a way of regarding, understanding, or interpreting something; a mental impression." (3) "intuitive understanding and insight." Oxford Language (2021).	"Perception is a mode of apprehending reality and experience through the senses, thus enabling discernment of figure, form, language, behavior, and action. Individual perception influences opinion, judgment, understanding of a situation or person, meaning of an experience, and how one responds to a situation" (SAGE Research Methods 2012).	How we like it to be. It should be that way.
Plans	(1) "a detailed proposal for doing or achieving something." (2) "an intention or decision about what one is going to do." (3) "a detailed map or diagram." Oxford Language (2021).	"A plan is typically any diagram or list of steps with details of timing and resources, used to achieve an objective to do something. It is commonly understood as a temporal set of intended actions through which one expects to achieve a goal" Wikipedia (2021).	How we want to do it in the future. How we thought it should be.

| Norms | (1) "something that is usual, typical, or standard."
(2) "a standard or pattern, especially of social behavior, that is typical or expected of a group."
Oxford Language (2021). | "Norms are a fundamental concept in the social sciences. They are most commonly defined as rules or expectations that are socially enforced. Norms may be prescriptive (encouraging positive behavior, or proscriptive (discouraging negative behavior)." Oxford Bibliographies (2021). | How we have always done it this way. |

Inductive Approach to Fact and Perception Finding

"Induction means arriving at general principles from specific facts or circumstances" (Rothwell 2015a, 95). With a performance coach not knowing much about the organization or team issues and not being aware of what is happening or the issues at hand at the current time, an inductive approach is the most appropriate approach to finding facts and perceptions from people. To do so, the High-Performance coach, HPE practitioners, or the manager-as-coach will start by spotting individuals concerned about the apparent problem or issue at hand.

The questions that might be used during an inductive approach can be used regardless of the size or dimensions of perceived or recognized problems or the fact of using internal or external practitioners. These questions in Table 5.4 are asked of individuals, teams, or groups who are most involved and concerned in solving a problem(s):

A similar approach should be used to examine possible performance improvement opportunities. HPE practitioners should begin by identifying those who are likely to be most interested in the opportunity. They should then pose these questions:

Deductive Approach to Fact and Perception Finding

In the deductive approach, "[t]he investigator begins with a theory—sometimes never articulated but evident from the pattern of an investigation—about what caused the problem or led to the opportunity" (Rothwell 2015a, 99).

Table 5.4   Inductive Questions for Finding Facts and Identifying Perceptions about Problem(s).

	Set of Inductive Questions for Separating Facts from Perceptions			
#	Questions	*Answers*	*Fact*	*Perception*
1	What do you think the problem is?			
2	Who is part of the problem?			
3	What is occurring now?			
4	What events led to the situation?			
5	What do you think assisted the progress of the problem?			
6	What consequences have arisen from the problem?			
7	When did the problem first appear?			
8	How did you first notice the problem?			
9	Where did the problem first emerge?			
10	Can you track the problem to one source or location?			
11	Why do you think the problem was happening?			
12	How did you notice the impact of the problem?			
13	Can you cite any situation that was palpable to the problem?			
14	How much is this problem costing the organization in tangible (hard) measures of performance?			
15	How much is this problem costing the organization in intangible (soft) measures of performance?			

Source: Adapted from Rothwell (2013).

In contrast to the inductive approach, which depends on series of open-ended and instinctive inquiries, a deductive approach conducts a more focused investigation of the problem(s). This approach is steered by a sense of "what should be happening" (which is the focus of the following chapter). Here, the high-performance coach or the HPE practitioner starts the investigation by theorizing about what potentially has caused the problem(s) by individuals, teams, or organizations or offered opportunities to the individual, team, or organization (Rothwell 2015b; Rothwell 2013). The deductive approach and its reasoning is valuable and benefits the investigators for facts and perception. Progressively, it has been suggested to professionals to follow specific norms and suggested guidelines for their investigations. Examples of such recommended guidelines include (1) ISO Standards, (2) Six Sigma, (3) Lean Manufacturing, (4) the Malcolm Baldrige National Quality Award, (5) the Deming Prize, and (6) the US Department of Labor's criteria for High-Performance Workplaces (Rothwell 2015a).

Table 5.5   Inductive Questions for Examining and Finding Opportunities.

	Questions for Discovering Possible Performance Improvement Opportunities	
#	*Questions*	*Answers*
1	What is the apparent opportunity?	
2	Why do you think this opportunity occurred?	
3	Who will be affected by this opportunity?	
4	What are the results in discovering this opportunity?	
5	What do you think assisted the discovery of this opportunity?	
6	The costs of pursuing this opportunity.	
7	What are the organization's main competitive strengths?	
8	How can the organization's strengths be used for a bigger competitive advantage?	
9	When did the evidence of the opportunity show up?	
10	How did the evidence of the opportunity show up?	
11	Why do you think this opportunity came to the surface?	
12	What would be valuable about this opportunity if it were realized?	
13	How did you notice this opportunity?	
14	What trend, business issues, customer needs or expectations, outside of the organization caused the opportunity to occur?	
15	How much would this opportunity be worth to the organization?	
16	What is this opportunity's value in tangible (hard) measures for the organization?	
17	What is this opportunity's value in intangible (soft) measures for the organization?	
18	How would the value of this opportunity be an asset to the organization?	

Source: Adapted from (Rothwell 2013).

Table 5.6 represents deductive methods for gathering data about "what is happening" or "what are the issues at hand." There are no orders to using these methods of collecting data. Professionals use some or all these methods relevant to be the internal or external facilitator or the organization's size, or the level of the change efforts and intervention.

Table 5.6 Deductive Methods for Gathering Data about "What Is Happening?"

Deductive Methods for Gathering Data		
#	*Method*	*Description*
1	**Extend Data**	It is recommended to review any existing data related to the problem or potential gap. These potential data can be discovered in many forms and shapes. To begin, reviewing vision and mission statements, organizational values and principles, business plans and goals, previous surveys, and marketing reports can add useful awareness for assessing the situation.
2	**Historical Document Review**	Examine historical forms, such as exit interviews, HR complaints, employment promotions, demotions and firings, accident reports, profit and loss reports, safety training records, sexual harassment training records, or performance evaluations. This would help the practitioner to develop classifications to explain the finding data based on what was uncovered by reviewing such documents.
3	**Observation**	This is one of the most helpful methods for recognizing a problem among individuals and their teammates or their managers and will help to conduct a needs assessment process. Teams and group meetings, management weekly or monthly meetings, and planning meetings are good places to observe individuals' and teams' interactions. The observation can be conducted structured or unstructured and uses the data to help with other collected information.
4	**One-on-One Interview**	This method is very useful and is much the backbone of collecting sensitive and confidential information that needs to be gathered quickly. Using this method helps the practitioner collect much more detailed information than document review or conducting a survey. One-on-one interviews can be structured, unstructured, or semi-structured. Preparation and development of interview protocol and questions are vital as the actual interview and practitioner's commitment to a successful data gathering.
5	**Focus Group**	This method is used when the practitioner wants to interview a particular team member or a group in a department working in the same working environment or supervision. The focus group is usually conducted by four to eight participants. The practitioners conducting focus groups need to have skills and competencies to deal with participants' reactions, emotions, and desires to dominate the conversation.

Deductive Methods for Gathering Data		
#	*Method*	*Description*
6	**Surveys and Questionnaire**	Mailed or web-based survey and questions used to collect data from a large group and broad, quantitative, and nonsensitive data. To use this method, the practitioners need to develop thoughtful questions to collect accurate and useful data. The practitioners need to design a valid, reliable, and user-friendly survey to gather valuable and useful information.
7	**Phone Survey**	This over-the-phone method offers a more personal touch and is much faster than written surveys. Similar to interviews and written surveys, they can be structured or unstructured. This survey method will allow the participants to describe current conditions in a much more detailed fashion.
8	**Product Examination**	A production examination is similar to the process of observation. The coach /investigator visits the work site, observes the process of making products or finished goods, how services are provided, and how employees treat customers.

Source: Adapted from Bakhshandeh (2021), Sleezer, Russ-Eft, and Gupta (2014), Trochim and Donnelly (2008).

Business Case Example

In this section, we will present an example of a business case in which a business manager is engaging individuals and teams concerning their performance levels based on an organization's needs for the improvement of individuals' and teams' performance that are not adequate or consistent with the organization's quarterly and annual performance and productivity goals. In this business case example, we emphasize how to find what the issue at hand is and reveal the actual issue that the organization is facing. These chapters direct the readers to the next needed steps for developing a high-performance coach as a manager-as-coach.

Focusing on Improving Performance in the Performance Coaching Process

Profitability and financial growth are the most critical elements of an organization's well-being, success in longevity, and sustainability. To achieve this essential commitment, organizations must be goal-driven and connect their performance and productivity to their strategic and business plans. An organization can recognize its needs for improving performance, increasing productivity, expanding its market, or training to compare its actual results with its committed results, such as goals, outcomes of the strategic plan, and business plan. As Sleezer et al. (2014) explained, "A learning or performance gap between the current condition and the desired condition is called a need" (17). Understanding "what is happening" or "what is the issue at hand" is a major part of the performance coaching model, which naturally links the finding in this step to the next step of "what should be happening." Both steps have links to organizations' goals and desired outcomes which determine teams', groups', and ultimately individuals' performance and productivity goals.

One of the most frequent questions that High-Performance Coach or Manager-as-Coach professionals ask of organization leaders regarding training needs is the apparent performance gap? What is the space or difference between your desired performance (goals or desired outcomes) of your workforce and the workforce's current (actual and in reality) performance?

The vital concepts of goals and performances are very important elements on which High-Performance Coach and Manager-as-Coach professionals should focus. They must pay attention to its impact on the final "Current Performance Level" report or relevant intervention implementation. Without focusing on improving performances, there will be no organization to improve upon as a group or as individuals. Regardless of what type of assessment approaches has been selected for the organization's needs or performance improvement, the outcome of this process is very clear: the performance assessment direction is setting up the organization for improvement in the areas of productivity, performance, learning, training, and development, individually, as groups or teams, and as the organization (Sleezer, Russ-Eft, and Gupta 2015).

Background

As you might remember, we introduced the organization in Chapter 4, using the MBD (a fictional name for protecting an organization's privacy and confidentiality) business and Organization Development cases for examples of using and implementing High-Performance Coaching steps and processes. MBD is a successful organization operating in the beauty industry, providing beauty supplies and products for the last four decades. As we mentioned in the previous chapter, MBD operates from four states with nearly 112 workers, performing in the team and group-based structure, from the management team, administration staff, sales force, technology team, quality control, marketing/public relations, and shipping team.

What Provoked the Inquiry?

Our invitation to get engaged with the organization issues was a direct solicitation because of a history of working with other organizations with similar workforce issues and other previous engagements. According to the President and CEO and the HR director, the MBD was facing (1) significant turnover and absenteeism among their workforce caused by a high level of work dissatisfaction among their employees and (2) the absence of collaboration and teamwork among the employees, especially between the administration, sales teams, and shipping crew.

Start-Up and Preparation

We had various meetings with the organization's management team, including executives, department managers, and team leaders to support them in understanding the purpose of our presence and answer their questions. We invited everyone to express their knowledge of and issues in the organization and welcome any input and perspectives for how they think the turnover and collaboration issues should be handled. This was a good relationship-building effort in establishing rapport with all the management team. We made sure everyone understood we were coming in as a partner, not as an adversary, to minimize their resistance to uncovering "what is happening?" and to offer potential changes that would result from this effort. We asked the organization's CEO to clarify the organization's need for this needs assessment and express his unconditional support and backing for this undertaking. The CEO's demonstration of alignment and support of the project caused greater buy-in from the rest of the management teams.

Selected Diagnostic Models

Individuals make organizations; these individuals form teams and groups which make departments. These individuals influence the organizations' systems, including inputs, processes, and outputs and everything in between. We can confidently say that they are all part of understanding "what is happening" or "what is the issue in hand." For this simple but significant reason, we have selected four diagnostic models that directly involve individuals and teams to design the data collecting approach and analyze the collected data. We used some for the one-on-one interviews of the executive and senior management team, and some were used for the focus group interviews with different teams and groups within departments.

Individual and Group Behavior model (Harrison 2005)

In this model, the high-performance coach is investigating and collecting information based on these elements of the organization's operation:

(1) **Inputs**: Human, material, financial, intangible, etc.
(2) **Outputs**: Goods, services, products, employees' well-being, and satisfaction.
(3) **Organizational behaviors and processes**: Practices the organization has adopted to create outputs.
(4) **Technology**: Equipment, tools, and systems that would transform inputs into outputs.
(5) **Environment**: Local environment, such as organization's competitors, customers, partners, suppliers, and investors. Remote environment, such as political system, the economy, social structures, and technological advances.
(6) **Culture**: Society's shared values, norms, beliefs, and behaviors.

(Rothwell et al. 2016; Sleezer et al. 2014)

The Great Place to Work model (Burchell and Robin 2011)

In this model, the high-performance coach is investigating and collecting information based on these elements of the organization's workforce relationship and collaboration:

(1) **Trust**: Trust involves credibility, respect, and fairness.
(2) **Credibility**: Credibility is achieved through open communication, competence, and integrity.
(3) **Respect**: Respect is reached through support, collaboration, and caring.
(4) **Fairness**: Fairness is achieved through equity, impartiality, and justice.
(5) **Pride**: Pride can be found in personal achievement, team performance, and the company's status in the community.
(6) **Camaraderie**: Camaraderie is built by facilitating intimacy, hospitality, and a sense of community in the workplace.

(Rothwell et al. 2016; Sleezer et al. 2014)

SWOT Analysis (Dosher et al. 1960)

In this model, the high-performance coach is investigating and collecting information based on these elements of the organization's characteristics and environment:

(1) **Strengths**: Positive tangible and intangible attributes internal to an organization. They are within the organization's control.

(2) **Weaknesses**: Factors within an organization's control that reduce its ability to attain the desired goal. Which areas might the organization improve?

(3) **Opportunities**: External or internal attractive factors represent the reason for an organization to exist and develop. What opportunities exist in the environment?

(4) **Threats**: External or internal factors could place the organization's mission or operation at risk. The organization may benefit by having contingency plans to address them if they occur.

(Rothwell et al. 2016; Sleezer et al. 2014)

Environmental Relations Assessment (Harrison 2005)

The environmental relations assessment (ERA) framework was introduced by (Harrison 2005). Conducting an ERA manages an organization's environmental relations more effectively. The following is a six-step procedure for the ERA during an organizational diagnosis:

(1) **Step 1**: Recognize the main conditions that affect the organization's performance. These include competition, technology, markets, and technical conditions.

(2) **Step 2**: Identify other organizations (outside of the organization) that are pressing demands or restrictions on the organization by their influential actors.

(3) **Step 3**: Identity who or what team in the organization (internally, such as HR, PR, marketing, and sales) is interacting with the aforementioned external key actors.

(4) **Step 4**: Inspect the organization's status of environmental relations management: the variables, the actors, and the gap to resolve.

(5) **Step 5**: Evaluate the organization's current environmental relations management's effectiveness to categorize where the gaps are. What are the top management's expectations for the organization's environmental relations management?

(6) **Step 6**: Discover and suggest ways to improve the organization's environmental relations management. Brief the top management team on what needs to get done and who needs to be involved.

(Rothwell et al. 2016; Sleezer et al. 2014)

Critical Role of Data Collection and Analysis in the "What Is Happening" Uncovering Process

Clearly, for any high-performance coach or HPI and HPE practitioners to conclude the client's actual needs, or separate between their wants and their needs, or to select appropriate data collecting and assessment models or approaches to use during implementation of intervention and training, they need to collect reliable and relevant information and data. Then they can start analysis and diagnosis based on the collected data. Regarding the importance of data collecting and analysis of such data, Sleezer et al. (2014) mentioned:

> [t]he results of a needs assessment reflect the methods that were used to collect the data and also the methods that were used to analyze those data. Thus, data collection and analysis are cornerstone skills for any needs assessment project.
>
> (51)

Professional and well-conducted data collecting will separate fact from fiction and draw a line between what is real and the perceptions and interpretation of a situation.

Data Collection Methods (Best Uses, Best Practices, Pros, and Cons)

According to Sleezer et al. (2014), there are five methods of data collecting approaches for a needs assessment project: (1) observation, (2) one-on-one interviews, (3) questionnaire/survey, (4) focus group interviews, and (5) document review (see Table 5.6) The following are four of the five methods we used to conduct our data gathering process.

Historical and Extended Documents Review

This model of collecting data is based on examining HR historical forms and documents and potentially the HRD efforts results and outcome, such as exit interviews, HR complaints, employment promotions, demotions and firings, and accident reports, as we have stated in Table 5.6 (Rothwell 2015a; Sleezer et al. 2015):

- **Best uses:** Examine historical forms, such as exit interviews, HR complaints, employment promotions, demotions and firings, accident reports, profit and loss reports, safety training records, sexual harassment training records, or performance evaluations. Extended data are existing data related to the problem or potential gap. These potential data can be discovered in many forms and shapes. To begin, reviewing vision and mission statements, organizational values and principles, business plans and goals, previous surveys, and marketing reports can add useful awareness for assessing the situation (see Table 5.6).
- **Best practice:** Ask permission from the appropriate executive (CEO, president, HP director) to review these documents. Schedule appropriately and take time to go through all these potential documents. Take necessary notes, but do not photograph or photocopy the documents.
- **Pros:** This would help the practitioner to develop classifications to explain finding data based on what was uncovered by reviewing such documents (see Table 5.6).
- **Cons:** The practitioner might establish a perception of what is happening before conducting the actual data collecting process and developing bias.

The high-performance coach can use Table 5.1 as a guide to collect much information during data collecting using all recommended methods.

Observation

This method is designed to collect data and evaluate it by first-hand observation (Sleezer et al. 2014):

- **Best uses:** Collect data based on actual workforce behaviors or work practices while working in an actual work environment.
- **Best practices:** Observe people from inconspicuous spots to reduce anxiety.
- **Pros:** Minimize work process interruptions, and collect data directly from an actual work environment, to reduce bias.
- **Cons:** Needs a skilled practitioner. The workforce might be concerned because of an observer, and that might affect their behavior. It also can be very time-consuming.

With permission from the executive team and cooperation of the management team, we had a chance to (1) observe several managers and team meetings, (2) observe the employees during their production process in their work environment, and (3) observe their relationship with their supervisors and each other. These observations give us a window to their behaviors, attitudes, and responses during production, dealing with deadlines, their method of communication or lack of, and their collaboration or conflict with their supervisors or with one another.

One-on-One Interview

In this method of data collecting, the workforce performance is evaluated on a one-on-one basis. The best future of this method is human interaction (Sleezer et al. 2014).

- **Best uses:** Face to face is the best approach, but one-on-one interviews are conducted on the phone or via video conference often.
- **Best practices:** Use a moderate tone, speak slowly, and enunciate clearly; keep the discussion focused; and examine the additional responses to the questions.
- **Pros:** Useful at the recognition of details of training needs while the potential trainer can explore any concerns or reservations.
- **Cons:** This method is time-consuming and, sometimes, difficult to analyze due to the practitioner's lack of experience.

We conducted several one-on-one interviews with the top executives and senior managers to collect data from all the top managers to make sure we have included their perspectives on the potential issues. We have used these tables as the source of our background for the interview questions to gather data:

- Table 5.2: How to Determine Your Values?
- Table 5.4: Inductive Questions for Finding Facts and Identifying Perceptions about Problem(s).

Besides the previous set of questions, we designed an interview protocol and questions for the one-on-one interviews with the executives and senior managers based on (1) individual and group behavior model, (2) SWOT analysis, and (3) environment relations assessment (ERA). Table 5.7 displays the actual questions.

Note: Before conducting the interviews, all the interview participants signed a "Non-Disclosure and Confidentiality" agreement.

Table 5.7   One-on-One Interview Questions and Their Sources (for Executives and Senior Managers).

Questions and their Sources to Be Used during One-on-One Interviews with Executives and Senior Managers
I. Basic Organization Information
A. Background to Diagnosis
1. What is your position and history of participation with the organization? 2. What kind of problems are you facing in your position? 3. What kind of challenges (in your position) do you foresee soon? 4. What would you consider as a recent (1–3 years) organization success? 5. What would you consider as a recent (1–3 years) organization failure? 6. What can we do for your organization?
B. Outputs
1. How do you assess the reputation of your organization? 2. How do you assess the quality of products and your services? 3. What is the staff turnover history in your organization? 4. How would you rate your staff or team member's rate of absenteeism?
C. Goals and Strategies
1. What is the organization's vision? 2. What is the organization's mission? 3. What are the organization's core values or principles? 4. What are the top three organization goals? 5. Do you have short- and long-term plans? 6. Are there any new and additional goal(s) for this year? 7. How do you assess the recent changes (1–3 years) in the organization's strategies? 8. What are the top priorities of the organization's budget?
D. Inputs
1. What is the percentage of the budget for providing services? 2. What percentage of the budget is allocated to use and maintain physical space? 3. What percentage of the budget is allocated to employment or human resources? 4. Do you have any training and development programs for your staff or teams?
E. Environment
1. What is the organization affiliation? Public, private, or part of a larger organization? 2. Are there any alliances with other organizations? 3. Are you outsourcing any aspects of your business or production? 4. Are you counting on any grants or exterior public agency support? 5. How do you rate or assess the safety and security around your organization?

(Continued)

Table 5.7 (Continued)

Questions and their Sources to Be Used during One-on-One Interviews with Executives and Senior Managers
F. Technology and Work Processes
1. What are the main processes regarding your offering services or products? 2. What type of information technology is being used in your organization? 3. Are you using any automation technology? 4. Do you have any saved data on operational failures or accidents? 5. Do you have saved data on employee turnover and firing history?
G. Structure
1. What are your main divisions or units? 2. How many levels are in your organizational hierarchy? 3. How many employees are in the organization? Full-time and part-time? 4. Do you have employment/labor contracts? 5. Do you have human resources, labor grievance procedures, affirmative action rules, or quality assurance standards in place?
H. Behavior and Processes
1. What is the pattern of the high-level decision-making process? 2. What are the significant conflicts (labor, staff, and board members)? 3. Is there any level of harshness or militancy in the relationship with staff or team members? 4. Do any conflicts exist among divisions or programs? 5. What are the main styles of communication (oral, written, and meetings)?
I. Culture
1. How do you describe the organization's identity (logo, slogans, or advertising campaign)? 2. What are some of your organization's historical successes or inspirational stories? 3. What are some of your recurring events or annual celebrations? 4. How do you rate the physical space, orderly, tidiness, decorations, or style of your offices, building, or work environment? 5. How are you assessing your work environment (style, hours, and relationships)?
J. System Dynamics
1. What are the most recent (1 or 2 years) significant changes in style or organization systems? 2. What are the past (3–5 years) significant changes in style or organization systems? 3. Are there any recent significant changes in the structural elaboration of the organization?

4. Are there any significant changes in the profit and loss pattern during the last couple of years?
5. Is your organization dealing with deficits? Low or high?

II. SWOT Questions (Strengths, Weaknesses, Opportunities and Threats)

A. General Questions

1. From your viewpoint, how do you describe the organization's performance?
2. How do you assess the organization's position and influence in the community?
3. What are the main challenges that the organization is facing?
4. Without holding back, what would you say attributed to the creation of these challenges?

B. Strengths

1. From your perspective, what are the organization's top three strengths?
2. What would you say attributed to developing these strengths?
3. How does the organization use and utilize its strengths?
4. How could the organization address its challenges to develop more strengths in the short term (1 year) and the long run (5 years)?

C. Weaknesses

1. From your perspective, what are the organization's top three weaknesses or shortcomings?
2. Without holding back, what would you say attributed to the creation of these weaknesses and shortcomings?
3. What are the organization's developmental plans or strategies to transform its weaknesses?
4. How could the organization address its weaknesses or shortcomings in the short term (1 year) and the long run (5 years)?

D. Opportunities

1. What opportunities can be arising for the organization by expanding on its strengths?

2. What opportunities can be arising for the organization by removing its weaknesses?
3. How could the organization address its challenges in the short term (1 year) and the long run (5 years)?
4. Do you see any opportunity for the organization?

E. Threats

1. What do you consider threats to the organization, if any?
2. How can these threats weaken an organization's strengths?
3. How can these threats exploit an organization's weaknesses?
4. How can the organization use these opportunities to defuse any threats?

(Continued)

Table 5.7 (Continued)

Questions and their Sources to Be Used during One-on-One Interviews with Executives and Senior Managers
F. Closing SWOT
1. Do you have any other suggestions for developing the organization as a productive and effective organization? 2. How do you see the future of the organization?
III. ERA (Environment Relations Assessment) Questions
Status of environmental relations management
A. Internal
1. Who within the organization is managing any internal issues or problems? 2. Are there any pressing internal issues in being handled or resolved? 3. Is there any internal issue not handled? Who is to manage it? 4. Are there any planned interventions or resolutions for these internal issues? 5. Are there any reactionary responses to these interventions among internal personnel? 6. Do you anticipate any internal issues in any aspects of the organization's performance, and what are the preventing measures, if any?
B. External
1. Who within the organization is managing any external issues or problems? 2. Are there any pressing external issues in the process of being handled or resolved? 3. Are there any external issues not handled? Who is to manage them? 4. Are there any planned interventions or resolutions for these external issues? 5. Are there any reactionary responses to these interventions among external affiliations? 6. Do you anticipate any external issues in any aspect of the organization's performance, and what are the preventing measures, if any?
IV. Closing
1. Is there anything else you would like to add to this conversation? 2. Do you have questions for me before we conclude this session?

Source: Copyright 2021 by Behnam Bakhshandeh.

Focus Group

Five to eight employees formed them to discuss their points of view, opinions, and information guided by a moderator (Sleezer et al. 2014):

■ **Best uses:** Conducted by a skilled practitioner, formed by people with something in common.

■ **Best practices:** Collect responses with a nonjudgmental behavior. Avoid discussions. Encourage space of confidentiality and respect.

■ **Pros:** Appropriate for complex or debated subjects that only one person might be unable or unwilling to uncover.

■ **Cons:** This method is also very time-consuming due to organizing, the position of participants, and the potential lack of participation.

We also conducted five focus group interviews with not over eight people in each group.

This way, we covered most categories of the workforce involved with the general office and floor production process. We used the general concept of the information found on the same tables we used during the one-on-one interviews, plus we designed an interview protocol and questions for the focus group interviews with the selected teams and groups based on: (1) the great place to work, (2) SWOT analysis methods and (3) relationship and performance. Table 5.8 displays the actual questions.

Note: Before conducting the focus group interviews, all the interview participants signed a "Non-Disclosure and Confidentiality" agreement.

Table 5.8 Focus Group Interview Questions and Their Resources (for Junior Managers and Floor Supervisors.

Questions and Their Sources to Be Used during Focus Group Interview with Junior Managers and Floor Supervisors
I. Great Place to Work Questions
A. Trust
1. What do you think about a trusting work environment? 2. What do you think would add to or take away from a trusting work environment? 3. From your viewpoint, how could someone gain your trust?
B. Credibility
1. What do you feel about the organization's credibility in the community? 2. What do you attribute to such credibility or lack of it, as you have explained? 3. From your viewpoint, what would make this organization more credible?
C. Respect
1. Tell me about your view of respect? 2. What would take away your respect for a coworker? 3. How can another coworker gain your respect?

(Continued)

Table 5.8 (Continued)

Questions and Their Sources to Be Used during Focus Group Interview with Junior Managers and Floor Supervisors
D. Fairness
1. What ideas do you have about fairness in the workplace?
2. What would happen that might make you think this organization is not being fair to you?
3. How do you gauge fairness in your work position?
E. Pride
1. What would make you proud of this organization?
2. What would make you feel proud of what you do?
3. How important is it for you to feel pride in what you do, and why?
F. Camaraderie
1. Without holding back, what do you feel about camaraderie within your team?
2. From your viewpoint, what would add to a desirable team relationship?
3. From your viewpoint, what is damaging to establishing a productive team?
II. SWOT Questions (Strengths, Weaknesses, Opportunity and Threats)
Mixed Questions
1. From your viewpoint, how do you describe this organization's performance?
2. What are the main challenges that the organization is facing in your department?
3. Without holding back, what would you say attributed to the creation of these challenges?
4. From your perspective, what are your department's top three strengths?
5. What would you say attributed to developing these strengths?
6. From your perspective, what are your department's top three weaknesses or shortcomings?
7. Without holding back, what would you say attributed to the creation of these weaknesses and shortcomings?
8. How could the organization address its challenges in your department in the short term (one year) and the long run (five years)?
9. How could the organization address its weaknesses or shortcomings in your department in the short term (one year) and the long run (five years)?
10. How do you see the future of the organization?
11. How do you see the influence of your department on the organization's success?
12. Do you have any other suggestions for developing your department as a productive and effective department?
13. Do you have any other suggestions for developing this organization as a productive and effective organization?

III. Relationships and Performance Questions
Mixed Questions
1. How do you rate your job performance and why? (Score from 0 being the lowest to 10 being the highest) 2. How do you rate your team's job performance and why? Please list them by their names. (Score from 0 being the lowest to 10 being the highest) 3. Do you have any specific plans for increasing your job performance? What is it? 4. Do you have any specific plans for increasing your team's job performance? What is it? Please list them by their names. 5. How do you rate your relationship with the person to whom you are reporting and why? (Score from 0 = nonexistent to 10 = excellent) 6. How do you rate your relationship with your team members and why? Please list them by their names. (Score from 0 = nonexistent to 10 = excellent) 7. Do you have any specific plans for improving your relationship with the person to whom you are reporting? What is it?
8. Do you have any specific plans for improving your relationship with your team members? What is it? Please list them by their names. 9. How do you rate your relationship with the organization and why? (Score from 0 = nonexistent to 10 = excellent) 10. Do you have any specific plans for improving your relationship with the organization? What is it?
IV. Closing
1. Is there anything else you would like to add to this conversation? 2. Do you have questions for me before we conclude this session?

Source: Copyright 2021 by Behnam Bakhshandeh.

Two Analysis Methods (Best Uses, Best Practices, Pros, and Cons)

We thought it would be beneficial to distinguish two of the most used data analysis methods for refreshing the high-performance coaches experience to uncover "what is happening" and "what are the issues at hand." According to Sleezer et al. (2014), for a high-performance coach and manager-as-coach to collect the data and make an assessment, the data need to be analyzed.

There are two general methods of data analysis: quantitative and qualitative. In some cases, practitioners are mixing these two methods.

Quantitative Analysis

This method is used when looking at actual numbers. It's used to get hard data on how people behave and act. In most needs assessment cases, quantitative data analysis is limited to descriptive statistics. However, it can also perform hand in hand with data collecting software such as Excel, SAS, and SPSS (Sleezer et al. 2014; Rothwell et al. 2016).

- **Best uses:** Line workforce performance on a new process.
- **Best practices:** Using charts, tables, and graphs.
- **Pros:** It is easier and quicker to collect and analyze than qualitative data.
- **Cons:** Bias, and collector's opinion.

(Sleezer et al. 2014; Rothwell et al. 2016)

Qualitative Analysis

This method is usually used when looking at the intangible's elements. This is far more subjective, such as understanding why people behave in a certain fashion. It involves the classification of collected data into different categories, which could even have been generated from previous data collecting processes (Sleezer et al. 2014; Rothwell et al. 2016).

- **Best uses:** Behavioral analysis.
- **Best practices:** Open-ended questions. Read and reread the questions and answers. Make notes and underline important sentences. Assign codes to aspects of data.
- **Pros:** Provide much richer and detailed data and information.
- **Cons:** More difficult to gather and analyze the data. It is more time-consuming.

(Sleezer et al. 2014; Rothwell et al. 2016)

For our business case example, during the data collecting phase to uncover what is happening and what is the issue at hand, we used a mixed method of both qualitative (one-on-one interviews, focus groups, and observations) and quantitative (historical records of turnover, performance evaluations, and productivity) data collecting methods.

Presenting Findings on "What Is Happening" and "What Are the Issues at Hand"

Now, it is time to give the organization's executive and senior managers results from collecting data and analysis of potential problems and what is currently happening. It was our recommendation to the organization's executive to share the problem-finding report with the management teams in all tiers of the organization so they can provide their feedback to the organization and each other about the issues uncovered during data collecting about the potential issues at the organization and what are the issues at hand and how they are influencing individual and teams' performances.

After reviewing the collected data, listening to everyone's concerns (mostly being the apparent symptoms of a larger problem), paying attention to pinpoint the source of the problems, analyzing the data, and reflecting on the future of the organization and its well-being, the problem report on "What is happening?" contained numerous issues raised by management and the employees, and what they wanted to address and resolve. However, based on our analysis, we found the following to be the sources of the present organization's issues and what are the issues in hand and their impact on employees' motivation, performance and ultimately productivity and desire to stay with the organization:

■ There was no clear organization's vision, mission, and principal values; just good old pushing the rock up the hill kind of approach.
■ Uncertainty among managers and supervisors due to lack of succession planning.
■ Employees and lower managers' concern about the lack of open communication and sharing planning for the future of their work and career.
■ No structured training and development plan for the managers and workforce.

The aforementioned issues and the absence of creating a workable environment for workers caused the following among the organization's workforce (almost everyone but the executive team):

■ developed an "us" versus "them" mindset and attitude
■ caused low sales performance and consistently missing daily and weekly targets

■ created a lack of work and organization commitments and just getting by and surviving
■ fear of the unknown and uncertainty about their future with the organization
■ being resigned about what is next for them
■ not taking any ownership of the work, product quality, and organization
■ expressing their frustrations on other people, especially their subordinates
■ feeling their efforts not being appreciated

We encouraged the management and the employees to categorize the level of urgency among the discovered issues and take on only two or three pressing issues that are directly influencing lack or performance and productivity within the next six to eight months and confront the remaining issues over semiannual periods.

We suggested training and development specialized for management teams and some other training for the workforce, all-around high performance and productivity, teamwork, effective communication, and accountability.

Key Factors to Remember

Remember these key factors from this chapter:

■ **Create partnership versus resistance**
  – We talked about the importance of establishing rapport in Chapter 4. As a high-performance coach, you need to create a working partnership with your employees and coaches to produce an effective coaching process. Unfortunately, the other side of this coin is resistance and dragging the process through an unworkable relationship. You can create a partnership with your employees through the building rapport process (see Chapter 4) and relating to their values and principles. Taking to them with respect and interest is a magic key to establishing a partnership.
■ **Critical role of data collecting process**
  – Professional, structured, and detailed data collecting processes are essential to the effective and efficient process of finding what is happening. Without the data collecting process to present the facts to us,

whatever we know is only perceptions and interpretations of what is happening. Accurate and relevant data collecting processes, using diagnostic models and analysis methods, are gateways to the factual and real discovery of what is the issue in hand and not all the symptoms of real issues.

■ **Individual values creates organization values**
- People always act based on their personal and professional values. Effective OD practitioners and high-performance coaches will understand the link between individuals' values and their individuals' or team's productivity and performance, increasing or decreasing. Both are related to people and their values and keeping close to their hearts and mind. Individuals are making teams and groups; those teams and groups are making the departments and the organization; there is no way out of this powerful collaboration and human connection that would make or break any organization (Bakhshandeh 2009).

■ **Role of team members in change**
- To implement a change intervention and create high-performance teams, an OD practitioner or a high-performance coach needs to understand the critical roles that the organization's members are playing in the change effort. Employees and team members have an essential role in the velocity of the process, by their accepting the process, by not reacting to it, by not resisting it, and by communicating their needs and concerns (Wittig 2012). An OD practitioner or a high-performance coach needs to understand employees' protential emotions and cognitions (2012). Making employees feel included is one of the most important elements of minimizing resistance.

Coaching and Developmental Questions for Managers

(1) Are you competent in understanding and implementing diagnostic models and analysis methods? If no, why not? What do you need? What would be your way to do so?

(2) Would you consider yourself as someone who can conduct a complete data collecting process? If no, why not? What would be your way to do so?

(3) Are you capable of talking to your team members to see what their values are and if they are performing based on their values? If no, why not? What would be your way to do so?

(4) Do you see any need for conducting an interview process with any key individual or a focus group with a team to discover what is happening with them?

(5) From your perspective and applying what you learned in this chapter, is there any problem within individuals who made your team?

(6) Are you aware of and can see what is happening in your direct team?

(7) What kind of training and development do you think you need to expand your competencies and skills in recognizing individuals and teams' actual problems versus symptoms of a situation?

References

Bakhshandeh, Behnam. 2008. "Bravehearts; Leadership Development Training." Unpublished Training and Developmental Course on Coaching Executives and Managers. San Diego, CA: Primeco Education, Inc.

Bakhshandeh, Behnam. 2009. *Conspiracy for Greatness; Mastery on Love Within.* San Diego, CA: Primeco Education, Inc.

Burchell, M., and J. Robin. 2011. *The Great Workplace: How to Build It, How to Keep It, and Why It Matters.* San Francisco, CA: Jossey-Bass.

Bakhshandeh, Behnam. 2021. *"Perception Of 21st Century 4cs (Critical Thinking, Communication, Creativity & Collaboration) Skill Gap in Private-Sector Employers in Lackawanna County, NEPA".* An unpublished dissertation in workforce education and development. The Pennsylvania State University.

Davis, Larry. 2001. "Performance Breakthroughs Are the Results of Human Choices, Not Technological Wizardry: A Case Study." *The Journal of Quality and Participation* 24, no. 3: 12–47.

Dosher, Marion, Otis Benepe, Albert Humphrey, Robert Stewart, and Birger Lie. 1960. *The SWOT Analysis Method.* Mento Park, CA: Stanford Research Institute.

Harrison, M. I. 2005. *Diagnosing Organizations; Methods, Models, and Processes,* 3rd ed., Applied Social Research Methods Series, vol. 8. Thousand Oaks, CA: Sage Publication.

Rothwell, William J. 2013. *Performance Consulting: Applying Performance Improvement in Human Resources Development.* San Francisco, CA: John Willy & Sons, Inc.

Rothwell, William J. 2015a. *Beyond Training & Development: Enhancing Human Performance Through a Measurable Focus on Business Impact,* 3rd ed. Amherst, MA: HRD Press, Inc.

Rothwell, William J. 2015b. *Organization Development Fundamentals: Managing Strategic Change.* Alexandria, WV: ATD Press.

Rothwell, William J., Carolyn K. Hohne, and Stephen B. King. 2018. *Human Performance Improvement: Building Practitioner Performance,* 3rd ed. New York, NY: Routledge.

Rothwell, William J., and Henry J. Sredl. 2000. *The ASTD Reference Guide to Workplace Learning and Performance: Present and Future Roles*, 3rd ed., 2 vols. Amherst, MA: HRD Press.

Rothwell, William J., Jacqueline M. Stavros, and Roland L. Sullivan. 2016. *Practicing Organization Development: Leading Transformation and Change*, 4th ed. Hoboken, NJ: John Wiley & Sons, Inc.

Rothwell, William J., Angela L. M. Stopper, and Jennifer L. Myers. 2017. *Assessment and Diagnosis for Organization Development*. Boca Raton, FL: CRC Press; Taylor and Francis Group.

Sleezer, Catherine M., Darlene F. Russ-Eft, and Kavita Gupta. 2014. *A Practical Guide to Needs Assessment*, 3rd ed. San Francisco, CA: John Wiley & Sons.

Sleezer, Catherine M., Darlene F. Russ-Eft, and Kavita Gupta. 2015. "Learning, Training, and Performance Timeline: A Walk Through History." *Performance Improvement* 54, no. 2: 7–15.

Trochim, William M. K., and James P. Donnelly. 2008. *The Research Methods Knowledge Base*, 3rd ed. Mason, OH: Atomic Dog, A Part of Cengage Learning.

Wittig, Cynthia. 2012. "Employees' Reactions to Organizational Change." *Journal of the Organization Development Network* 44, no. 2: 21–28. https://cdn.ymaws.com/www.odnetwork.org/resource/resmgr/odp/vol_44_no2.pdf.

Chapter 6

Step 3: What Should Be Happening?

Behnam Bakhshandeh

This chapter focuses on the third step in performance coaching: envisioning what should be happening. To determine the gap between what is happening and what should be happening, it must be clear what the desired target or vision of a desired future must be. That is what this chapter describes. It covers these issues:

- What is sourcing the power for high performance?
- Vision and envisioning
- Vision statement versus mission statement
- Job performance standards and best practices
- Key performance indicator (KPI)
- Best industry practices
- Performance criteria
- Use of Big Data and AI in measuring employees performance
- How to establish agreement on "what should be happening"
- Potential team dysfunctions and conflicts
- Asking powerful and effective questions that will make a difference
- Step-by-step process of conducting a "what should be happening" session for establishing agreed "job performance standards" among managers and employees

DOI: 10.4324/9781003155928-8

What Are the Anchors? What Is Sourcing Your Power for High Performance?

This chapter is about looking at "what should be happening" in contrast to "what is happening." In the last chapter, we discussed how individuals' high-performance results from their conscious choice by understanding, recognizing, choosing, setting their values, and acting on them because they believe operating based on their values and principles are not just honorable but also effective and productive; their values become an anchor that holds them in place and sources their power in life. We also touched on the choice of *Being* productive as generated from individuals' interests in what they are *Doing* and their mindset about their values and principles. We discussed the relevance between who people are *Being* and the quality of what they are *Doing* in Chapter 4 (see Figure 4.2) and the role of people's mindsets in this process. One of the main places that these individuals are looking to see what should be happening is in their lives through their values and principles. The same concept is relevant to professional work and the organizations' operations. Organizations look at two places to determine their anchors about what should be happening in contracts to what is happening and those are:

(1) their set values and principles, which are manifested in their vision and mission statements and
(2) set of operational and performance standards, KPI, criteria, and best industry practices.

This chapter is about distinguishing these two anchors that source organizations', teams', and individuals' power and access to high performance and productivity. It is also about envisioning the future and what should be happening to produce their targets, end results, final outcomes, bottom lines, or any other terminologies they use in their organizations.

Please read the following segment while you have these figures in the background:

(1) Relevancy and a link between one's mindset, attitude, and behavior (Figure 3.1).
(2) Individual's state of *Being* and what they are *Doing* (Figure 4.2).

What Is Vision?

Vision is an anchor for individuals to center their mindset, attitude, and behavior in a productive way, both personally and professionally (Bakhshandeh 2009). Individual vision and organizational vision are intended to motivate individuals, teams, and organizations in their performance and productivity by offering compelling guidance for the future in the organization or one's individual career and progress. An organization's vision helps individuals form a team and creates an environment of teamwork, a point at a productive direction, allows for improvement ideas and generates a shared sense of camaraderie and ownership among employees (Rothwell, Hohns, and King 2012). "a clear, coherent view of how the future should appear. It is essential in providing a point of departure for what is happening" (Rothwell 2015, 106).

Organization's Vision versus Mission

Organizations have many ways to create their visions. However, they are designing, collaborating, and creating their vision statement, an empowering and guiding one will answer these questions for an employee or affiliate:

- ■ Who are we, and what are we about?
- ■ What are we creating and what do we stand for?
- ■ What is the purpose of our organization?
- ■ What are our core values and principles?
- ■ How do we relate to each other?
- ■ How do we relate to our clients or customers?

An organization's vision statement explains its anticipated future and position in the market and communities they are serving. A vision statement is created first, displaying the organization's directions, intents, and goals. Then, an organization would design its mission statement that describes the organization's objectives, how they are fulfilling the organization's goals and outcomes, and how they are getting there. The vision statement is about the *Being*, the *Leadership* (the mindset, attitude, behavior, participation, commitment, creativity, overcoming resistance, implementing change, performance, and self-regulation), and the mission statement is about *Doing*, the *management* (the processes, procedures, measurements, tools, goods, productivity, and structure) (Bakhshandeh 2008; Bakhshandeh 2002).

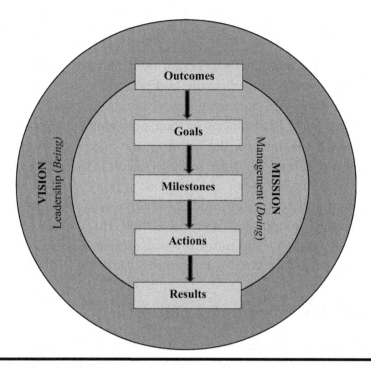

Figure 6.1 Relationship between Organization's Vision and Mission Considering Performance and Production.

Source: Copyright 2021 by Behnam Bakhshandeh.

Figure 6.1 displays the place and relationship between an organization's vision and mission concerning performance and production. For example, the outcome and end results are both related to the organization's vision and mission and supported by the *Being* part of the organization or the leadership that is provided by the management and the structure, while setting goals, designing, and managing milestones, managing action plans are all about the *Doing* part of the organization or management and mission. However, what holds the whole thing together and sources the process of performance and productivity is the vision.

What Are the Characteristics of a Vision?

Let's go through the characteristics of a vision; how do you know if you have a vision and how do you understand how to create one, such as having a checklist for designing a vision and knowing what you have created.

Imagine yourself holding an electrical object in your hands, such as a coffee maker, laptop computer, or hair dryer, and you are trying to use it. What would you do with the two or three prongs at the end of the power cord?

You would connect them to a receptacle on the wall, right? Without the power sourced by electricity, your electrical device would not function. Even if you had a battery-operated device, you would still have to charge it—and for that, you would have to connect to a power source. Without electricity, your devices would have no functionality, which meant they would be no use to you. Your device is *sourced* by electricity. What source is powering your functionality? What are sourcing your choices and actions? Usually, you will see that the only things that have sourced you were your past decisions and experiences in life. You decided about yourself, others, and life mostly polluted by negative, painful experiences. When you plug yourself into the receptacle called your *past*, you keep getting the same results you do not like.

You keep missing the writing on the wall. We worry about what will happen to us and feel nervous about tomorrow or next week because we let our past experiences determine our future moves. We think we are powerless because we do not realize we have another option called "Design your Future." Consider this quote from George Bernard Shaw from one of his plays written in 1893:

> [p]eople are always blaming their circumstances for what they are.
> I don't believe in circumstances. The people who get on in this
> world are the people who get up and look for the circumstances
> they want, and if they can't find them, they make them.

There is another source of power we keep missing. It is the receptacle called the *future*.

What separates something inspirational from a true vision? How can we distinguish a *Mission* statement from a *Vision* statement?

A mission statement is where many businesses and corporations clarify what they do. Their vision statement describes who they are *being* while they are *doing* what they do. These elements of vision characteristics apply to individuals, teams, and organizations. We are mostly pointing at the individual level, as individuals are creating the organization's vision. Let's go through what vision is:

■ **Seeing a future and fulfilling dreams**
   Can you envision a future? Are you fulfilling a dream? Or are you just trying to fix something you do not want to see anymore? Vision represents something in the future and something you are dreaming about.
■ **Being 'at cause'**
   If you are not *at cause* about something, you will be on the other side, at the effect end. Look at your complaints in life. Most are generated

from being 'at effect,' and thinking you cannot do anything about it or feeling powerless around it. Vision moves you to be at the cause of a movement that makes a difference in your life or the lives of others.

■ **Having fun with it and turned on by it**

Fulfilling your vision is fun. It is not something that you would not like to do or to be. It turns you on, and you enjoy doing it. It is obvious to others that you are having fun with it.

■ **Seeing a bigger picture and not doing it alone**

Fulfilling a vision is a much bigger picture. It is bigger than just a task or a project. It might involve different projects and so many tasks you cannot do it by yourself. In fulfilling your vision, you will enroll other people to embrace the possibility of getting those projects completed because your eyes are on the big picture. This is something way bigger than just you. It affects others around you.

■ **Including you but not limited to you**

Fulfilling a vision is not only about you but also about others. It is about everyone around you: your family, your coworkers, your team-mates, your community, and every person with whom you are connected. While your vision is bigger than just you, be sure it includes yourself. You are the cause, and others will enjoy the effect around it.

■ **Why are you doing this, and how will it turn out**

The answer to this question could be a part of your vision. Why are you doing what you do? How will all these things you are doing turn out in the end? Is it just about money and a feeling of security? Or is it for a bigger cause and a bigger plan that will distinguish for others around you and yourself?

■ **It takes you to make it work, and it will inspire others**

A powerful and empowering vision will take you to work every day. You will not be tired of doing what you need to do to accomplish and fulfill your vision. You will not complain that it is hard work. You will not complain and nag because you are inspired and moved by the cause. That will inspire others around you because they can see themselves in you. We always believe that you can live your life based on not failing or live it based on succeeding. Both produce the same results but offer two life experiences.

Notice that nearly all of the aforementioned characteristics are common in the world leaders who inspire you. They describe anyone who inspires you to follow them or respect them for what they do. Notice that your experiences around these people are different. By noticing this about yourself, you will have many great experiences to draw from when inspired and motivated to accomplish something bigger for yourself. That is the magic of being around someone with a vision. When you create and invent your life vision from your future versus from your past, your experience of yourself and the people around you are altered into something more positive and empowering. This brings you inner peace and the freedom to be (Bakhshandeh 2009, 232–35 and 268–71).

As a high-performance coach, you will have your vision about who you are and what you are standing for to coach your people in an inspiring direction directed by the organization's vision and mission statements. The relationship between an organization's values, vision, and mission is depicted in Figure 6.2:

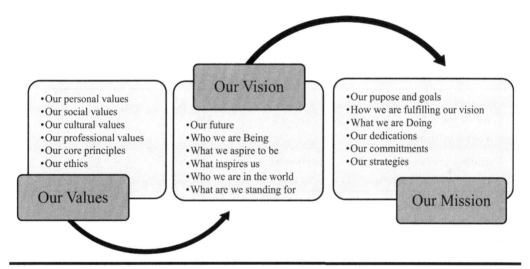

Figure 6.2   Relationship between the Organization's Values, Vision, and Mission.
Source: Copyright 2021 by Behnam Bakhshandeh.

Having teams and groups aligned with the organization's vision, mission, and core values is essential to the cohesiveness and workability of the organization's operations, productivity, and individual and team performance. For this vital reason, a high-performance coach or a manager-as-coach can use one of the useful tools to assess the clarity of the organization's vision among individuals and teams during performance and productivity interventions. Table 6.1 is designed to interview individuals or teams to understand their connection to the organization's vision, get ideas for what is missing or needed, and receive their input.

Establishing rapport with these individuals and teams is critical to the workability of this process.

Table 6.1 Assessing the Current Vision Clarity of an Individual or a Team.

Assessing the Current Vision Clarity of an Individual or a Team							
Day:			Participant:			Team:	
Month:			Supervisor:			Department:	
Rating Scale: *1* = Poor, *2* = Marginal, *3* = Acceptable, *4* = Good, *5* = Excellent							
#	*Clarity on the Organization's Vision by the Team Members*	Rating					*What Is Missing? Actions to Increase Clarity on the Organization's Vision*
		1	*2*	*3*	*4*	*5*	
1	Agrees on the vision of where the organization or the team should go.						
2	Understand and align with the organization and its mission statement.						
3	Understand and align with why their team exists.						
4	Understand and align the functionality of their team to the organization's vision and mission.						
5	Share a vision of how the team should get where it is going.						
6	Understand the plan of progress and agree on how to measure it.						
7	Align with the organization's and their team's values.						
8	Align with what is important and what is not urgent in executing progress plan.						
9	Share the same view about what the organization or their team should be doing best.						

Source: Copyright 2021 by Behnam Bakhshandeh.

Envisioning "What Should Be Happening?"

Recognizing what should be happening begins by *envisioning* what should be happening by the managers who oversee an individual, a team, or a department with the problems.

Envisioning is synonymous with visualizing something, seeing a potential future, picturing what is coming, or dreaming about something.

■ Oxford Languages describes it as to "imagine as a future possibility; visualize" (Oxford Languages" 2021).
■ Merriam-Webster describes envisioning as "to picture to oneself" ("Merriam-Webster" 2021).

In the context of our book and revealing what should be happening, "[e]nvisioning what should be happening means establishing a vision of desired results. The vision established becomes a norm—a prescribed standard or an ideal, the desired end state" (Rothwell 2015, 105). In some shape and form, there is a close similarity between the analysis of envisioning happening and what is happening we went through in the last chapter. Sometimes, examining and analyzing what is and what should be could be done simultaneously. Either separately, or, gathering data and analyzing the data about what is happening and what should be happening have one shared purpose—to reveal gaps to improve individuals, teams, and an organization's performance and productivity (Rothwell and Henry 2014), "[t]he problem is that, without imagination, managers cannot recognize potentially profitable opportunities or predict long-term consequences of their actions" (2014, 218).

Envisioning is similar to the process of environmental scanning, which should be part of an organization's strategic planning that studies and inspects potential exterior future trends with an impact on the organization and how posing future threats or opportunities for the organization (Rothwell et al. 2012). As we have touched on environmental relations assessment (ERA) in Chapter 5, the ERA framework was introduced by Harrison (2005). Conducting an ERA manages an organization's environmental relations more effectively.

> Research indicates that organizations that conduct environmental scanning are more profitable and successful than organizations that do not conduct it. Environmental scanning is the counterpart of internal appraisal, the step in strategic planning that examines existing conditions inside the organization and discovers the organization's competencies (strengths) and areas for improvement (weaknesses)
>
> (Rothwell 2015, 105)

By envisioning what should be happening and comparison between the results of an internal appraisal of an individual, a team, or the organization and the environmental scanning, the high-performance coach or a manager-as-coach can distinguish evidence pointing to the directions that an individual, a team, or the organization is taking. These revealing clues may point at what is seize future opportunities or threats, what could develop on current strengths, or transcend weaknesses, in individuals, teams, and the organization (Rothwell and Henry 2014; Rothwell, Stavros, and Sullivan 2016).

In both cases, the envisioning process and the environmental scanning process are revealing what should be happening and focusing on ideals (what should be) or norms (what it is) instead of actualities or realities. Envisioning and environmental scanning about what should be happening can be based on situations or focused on the potential issues (Rothwell et al. 2016). "Change rarely occurs unless people are dissatisfied with present conditions, can conceptualize ideal alternatives, and are motivated to change" (Rothwell 2015, 105).

What Are the Job Performance Standards?

A minimum degree for the required performance of an employee is known as a job performance standard. A job performance standard is known as the output degree of an average but knowledgeable employee or a worker's average tempo of producing in popular jargon. This description branches out from the perception of McCormick (1979), as a model based on a job analysis, that

> establish[es] the standard or the view, as noted in a classic source on job analysis, that establish[es] the standard or allowed time for a given unit of work . . . based on the amount of time required by a qualified worker, using a standard method and working at a standard work speed, to perform a specified task
>
> (McCormick 1979, 79).

A job performance standard in this way exemplifies a floor level or minimum acceptable level of performance by an employee. The job performance standard is not a goal, outcome, or objective but represents desired minimum expected performance targets or levels by workers (Cummings and Worley 2015).

Key Performance Indicator

During the last two decades, many organizations attempted to associate organizational values, vision, mission, and strategic goals to the KPI and measure it based on elements of the balanced scorecard by establishing performance targets for individuals, teams, departments, and organization.

The balanced scorecard allows a high-performance coach, HPI practitioners, or managers to review the organization's performance from four key perspectives (see Figure 6.3) and offers answers to four basic but essential questions tied to the organization's performance measures on the background of the organization's values, vision, mission, and strategies (Kaplan and Norton 1996; Kaplan and Norton 1992):

(1) **Customer perspective**: How do our clients/customers see us?

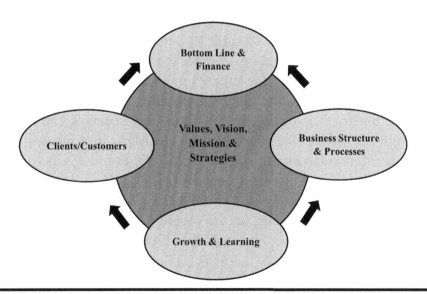

Figure 6.3   Organization's Performance from Four Key Perspectives.

Source: Adapted from Kaplan and Norton (1992).

(2) **Internal perspective**: Business processes' and procedures' efficiency, effectiveness, and level of performance. What are we good at, and what do we stand out for?

(3) **Growth and learning perspective**: Our underlying capabilities and improvements. Are we able to continue growing, improving, and creating values?

(4) **Financial perspective**: How do we appear to the organization's shareholders? Bottom-line measurements as the cost of goods and revenue extremes.

(Kaplan and Norton 1996; Kaplan and Norton 1992)

Though this methodology looks innovative, each of the four classifications of the balanced scorecard is associated with the traditional functioning elements of a health organization and its management structure, such as finance (bottom line and financial), marketing (clients and customer), operations (processes, productions, and structure), and growth and learning (human resources development) (Kaplan and Norton 1996). KPIs are taking an organization's targets and bringing them down to smaller levels on the organization's performance chart that managers and workers can understand (Liraz 2013).

Best Industry Practices

Besides job performance standards and KPI, many organizations are using Best Practices approach to set a benchmark for their workforce's performance indicators. "A best practice is an exemplar, a practice worthy of emulation because it represents the best approach" (Rothwell 2015, 118). Most organizations are practicing searching for and applying the best practices they find throughout their internal benchmarking and what they have learned from external benchmarking. Camp (1989) defined benchmarking as "the search for industry best practices that lead to superior performance" (11). The concept of Best Practices is another possible approach to recognize "what should be happening" in the organizations' dealings with their internal and external environment, including their workforces' performance and productivity.

High-performance coaches and managers-as-coaches can envision "what should be happening" by assessing comparison practices at their teams, departments, and organizations to learn the best practices within their industries' best producers and high performers or even from the same categories outside their industry. Table 6.2 is a good tool to use to determine whether benchmarking

Table 6.2 Evaluating the Needs for Benchmarking the Best Practices in High-Performance Coaching.

Evaluating the Needs for Benchmarking the Best Practices in High-Performance Coaching				
Instructions: Use these inquiries in the left column to determine whether benchmarking for those best practices is justified. For each inquiry in the left column, check, yes, no, or n/a in the middle columns. Come with some actions you can take to get that area moving in a productive direction (or if you need support from senior managers or organization executives) and post them in the right column.				
#	**Area of Inquiry and Interest**	**Yes**	**No**	**N/A**	**Action Needed**
1	Have you explored existing practices in your team?				
2	Have you explored existing practices in your department?				
3	Have you explored existing practices in your organization?				
4	Have you researched practices that have been used for resolving major issues you know about the team's performance?				
5	Have you researched practices that have been used for resolving major issues you know about departmental performance?				
6	Has your organization explained its desired outcome from implementing the best practice in your team?				
7	Has your organization explained its desired outcome from implementing the best practice in your department?				
8	Have you requested from senior managers if they are willing to pay a visit to some high-performance organizations about their best practices in enhancing human performance?				
9	Have you requested from senior managers if they allow you to visit high-performance organizations to learn about their best practices in enhancing human performance?				

Source: Adapted from Lee (2021), Rothwell (2013), Bakhshandeh (2008).

is justified in a team, a department, or an organization. A high-performance coach can use this worksheet (Table 6.2) as a starting point for imagining what should be happening that could positively affect an organization's human performance in an individual, teams, and departments, and an organization.

Criteria

Similar to the KPI, criteria also defining the workforce's performance, measuring performance outcomes, or behaviors are evaluated to be good (acceptable), average (right in the middle), or poor (not acceptable). "Criteria are the yardsticks by which performance is judged. These yardsticks should be based on a systematic consideration of the job" (Cardy and Leonard 2011, 43). Performance criteria have to be related and directed to a job or task which would assist in performing a job or task analysis. Regarding the importance of judging workers' performance against their jobs, Cardy and Leonard (2011) mentioned,

> [i]t would not make business sense to judge someone on criteria that are unrelated to job performance. Yet, this is a common perception among employees, and charges of discrimination in the evaluation and management of performance are made on a routine basis
>
> (43)

Unfortunately, some criteria such as gender, age, and race, even though they are not job-related, occasionally sneak into some employees' performance judgments by their managers or supervisors. These criteria factors are, managers' or supervisors' mental measures, especially when criteria for a job or task performance are uncertain and ambiguous (Cardy and Leonard 2011).

To use criteria in businesses on a daily and practical basis, they need to be as specific, tangible, and functioning as possible. Figure 6.4 presents three basic levels of criteria described by Cardy and Dobbins (1994).

■ **Ultimate level:** This level explains the general purpose of performance, signaling values or strategic intention underlying the job. Recognizing ultimate criteria can orient workers to the customary purposes of their performance at a particular job. Ultimate criteria would assist a high-performance coach in presenting a rationale for

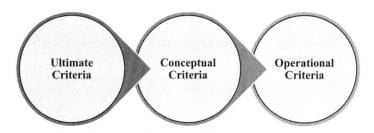

Figure 6.4 Relationship between Levels of Criteria.

Source: Adapted from Cardy and Leonard (2011), Cardy and Dobbins (1994).

maintaining one's performance and continued motivation for a high-performance level (1994).

■ **Conceptual level:** This level explains the attributes of performance. The conceptual level is one step down from the ultimate level and can be the pathway for achieving the ultimate criteria. For example, when 'customer satisfaction' is an ultimate criterion for the organization, then paying attention to product quality, speed of production, delivery of specification, and overall professional customer service could be a conceptual level criterion (1994).

■ **Operational level:** This level is measuring performance. The operational level transforms concepts of the operations into tangible and specific measures. When members of an organization are looking for operational criteria, they are looking for responses to questions such as:

– How do we measure the quality of our products or services?
– How do we measure the speed of our production or the length of our services?
– How do we measure the monetary values of our products or services?
– How do we characterize and enhance our customers' or clients' level of excellent experience?
– How do we know if our efforts to increase the quality of our products or services had the intended impression? (1994).

One way to understand the performance criteria is to interview several managers and supervisors by conducting an inquiry into what should be criteria for human performance in your organization, department, or group. The high-performance coach or the manager-as-coach can use the prompt in Table 6.3 to achieve this intention.

Table 6.3   Inquiries into Identifying Human Performance Criteria.

Inquiries into Identifying Human Performance Criteria		
Day:	Participant:	Team:
Month:	Supervisor:	Department:
Instruction: (1) While you are paying attention to the criteria area in the left column. (2) Answer the inquiry question in the middle column about what should be happening to the best of your ability. (3) Respond to the inquiry in the right column about how you think it should be happening and if it can be measured. There are no right or wrong answers, just your valuable input.		
Criteria	**What Should Be Happening with:**	**How Can It Be Measured?**
Leadership	Your team:	
	Your department:	
	The organization:	
Management	Your team:	
	Your department:	
	The organization:	
Recruitment and New Hire	Your team:	
	Your department:	
	The organization:	
Promotions and Career Opportunities	Your team:	
	Your department:	
	The organization:	
Incentives and Rewards	Your team:	
	Your department:	
	The organization:	
Feedback by Managers and Supervisors	Your team:	
	Your department:	
	The organization:	
Training and Development	Your team:	
	Your department:	
	The organization:	

Tools and Technology	Your team:	
	Your department:	
	The organization:	
Channel of Communication	Your team:	
	Your department:	
	The organization:	
Succession Planning	Your team:	
	Your department:	
	The organization:	

Source: Copyright 2021 by Behnam Bakhshandeh.

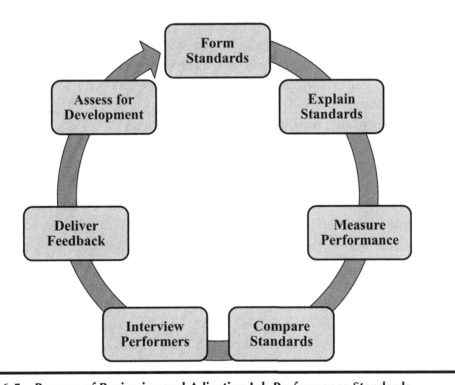

Figure 6.5 Process of Reviewing and Adjusting Job Performance Standards.

Source: Adapted from Rothwell, Hohne, and King (2018), Rothwell et al. (2016).

Reviewing and Adjusting Job Performance Standard

Regardless of what type of job performance standard has been used or planned to be used to understand the performance gap, Figure 6.5 presents general steps and actions from management or a high-performance coach for using a job performance standard. Following these steps are designed to powerfully and professionally support an individual or a team to compare their performance against an ideal and desired performance. Depending on changes in the market, industries, or products and services, there is always a need for adjustments and changes to the job performance standards. Providing feedback and reviewing training and development needs are essential to a successful and relevant job performance standard review.

■ **Forming and establishing the standards**
  The first step is to form the job performance standards to the industry, work, and the job being performed and establish parameters of the desired outcome and results for that job. This is a good time to review the previous standards and records of results and comparisons between the established standards and the actual results and see any discrepancies that might repeat themselves. It is highly recommended to review the newly established performance standards with some experienced managers or supervisors for relevancy and functionality.

■ **Convey, explain, and educate the standards**
  After establishing the desired job performance standards, it is time to communicate and explain them to employees via general announcements and scheduled meetings with related departments, groups, and teams to educate the associated employees and answer questions or concerns about the job performance standards. The employees' input is also valuable to potential adjustments or modifications of such standards.

■ **Measure the actual performance**
  The only way to understand the functionality and accuracy of performance standards is to measure the actual performance. Hence, measuring a one-day or one-week performance block is not an accurate representation of an individual or a team performance. For achieving this step, the manager-as-coach or the high-performance coach needs to review and measure the work/job results for at least a month or even a quarter.

■ **Compare performance with standards**
  At this stage, the manager-as-coach or the high-performance coach needs to compare an individual or team's actual performance measurement with the established job performance standards. This is

the time for some reality checks and perspectives to see if the possible discrepancies are results of (1) the employee's performance level, (2) the influence of internal or external work environments, or (3) unrealistic expectations about the established performance standards. We will discuss this section on a much deeper level in the next chapter.

■ **Interview some performers**

To achieve the previous step, it is highly recommended to interview some of the high producers and some of the lowest producers in a team or group. The data collected from these interviews would shed light on the influence of mindset, attitude, and behavior on individuals' relationships with the organization and their teammates, and their managers and supervisors. Another output of these interviews is understanding the employees' perspectives about the work environment, including the norms, communication channels, physical space, technology, and tools.

■ **Design and deliver the feedback**

After going through the last two steps of (1) comparing the actual performance results with the established performance standards and (2) conducting interviews with the high performers and low performers, it is time to design and deliver your feedback as the manager-as-coach or the high-performance coach. It is recommended to review the feedback with managers and supervisors and consider their inputs before submitting the feedback to the senior management and the organization. Some organizations or managers have the tendency to discuss this step with some high-performance employees to get to reusable, agreeable, and manageable standards or criteria for their job performance standards and "what should be happening."

■ **Assess and potential needs for further developments**

One of the potential feedback results is uncovering needs to (1) make changes in the job performance standards, (2) further develop performance standards, (3) plan some particular technical training, (4) restructure processes or procedures among teams and groups, or (5) rearrange some work or job positions. Again, this is something that could be achieved by involving some of the high-performer and high-producing employees and their inputs.

Table 6.4 is an effective tool for assessing the clarity of job performance standards among individuals and teams. This assessment is useful during performance and productivity interventions at the individual and team levels.

Table 6.4 Assessing the Job Performance Standards of an Individual or a Team.

Assessing Job Performance Standards of an Individual or a Team								
Day:		*Participant:*					*Team:*	
Month:		*Supervisor:*					*Department:*	
Rating Scale: 1 = Strongly Disagree, 2 = Disagree, 3 = Neutral, 4 = Agree, 5 = Strongly Agree								
#	*What to Assess?* *Job Performance Standards Are*	*Rating*					*What Is Missing? What Needs to Get Done About It?*	
		1	*2*	*3*	*4*	*5*		
1	Stated clearly and in the job description without ambiguity.							
2	Distributed and communicated clearly to employees in detail.							
3	Explained by supervisors in measurable terms to employees.							
4	Connected to work/task require-ments for individuals, teams, and the organization.							
5	Revised based on the work methods upgrade or alteration.							
6	Gone through annual review for neces-sary corrections or addition.							

Source: Copyright 2021 by Behnam Bakhshandeh.

This tool gives individuals and teams the means to express their level of clarity about what is expected of their performance and also allows them to evaluate what is missing or what needs to get done about what is missing. But it gives the high-performance coach or manager-as-coach a better under-standing of the existing job performance standards and what potentially needs to alter or modify.

Use of Big Data and AI in Measuring Employees Performance

The use of Big Data for analysis and as a source of information about job performance is already implemented and will be a trend of the future of

Performance Management. In addition, using AI (Artificial Intelligent) for measuring human performance is just around the corner, and it is already in some industries or occupations such as performance improvement and customer service. We thought it would be useful to briefly talk about these two concepts and their roles in recognizing what should be happening by high-performance coaches and organizations who have access to Big Data and AI systems.

Big Data

In these days, from GPS and other types of tracking systems to security cameras everywhere, nearly 80% of organizations and establishments are using some variety of electronic performance monitoring or EPM for short. EPMs are designed to use up-to-date technology for gathering, storing, analyzing, and reporting the workforce's behaviors, such as productivity, performance, use or abuse of the organization's time, or incivility in their actions (Tomczak, Lanzo, and Aguinis 2018). There are other uses for tracking real-time data by EPM systems. Collected data can be used for individual or team performance assessment, selecting proper training and development, tracking logistical objectives, implementing wellness programs, ensuring workers' safety, and most importantly, assessing individuals' and teams' performance and performance-related behaviors.

However, as Tomczak et al. (2018) underlined,

> [d]espite the organizational benefits of EPM, these systems can have adverse effects on employee satisfaction, organizational commitment, fairness perceptions, and employee behavior. Research provides evidence, however, that these downfalls can be mitigated by implementing these systems with employee attitudes and privacy perceptions in mind
>
> (251)

There are other applications for data mining and classification use of the collected data such as (1) Employee Management System (EMS), (2) the process of Knowledge Discovery in Databases (KDD) that classifies substantial data into various categories such as employee performance, disabilities, safety accidents, absenteeism, and more, and (3) the WEKA data mining toolkit classifier model which predicts the workforce's performance on the basis of the workforces' age, date of hire, years of experience, and so forth (Kamatkar et al. 2018). We need to take under consideration that "[d] espite the relevance of data-driven automated decision-making in assessing employee performance and productivity, only limited research has been conducted on this topic" (Wingard 2019, 13).

AI (Artificial Intelligence)

As artificial intelligence (AI) is becoming progressively more intelligent, even in some cases, reaching extraordinary unhuman performance and providing a rapidly growing opportunity for humans to learn from it. However, there are valid concerns about how the human brain approaches problems versus how an AI system attempts at problem-solving (McIlroy-Young et al. 2020). "A crucial step in bridging this gap between human and artificial intelligence is modeling the granular actions that constitute human behavior, rather than simply matching aggregate human performance" (McIlroy-Young et al. 2020, 1677).

That said, several researchers in reasonable and explainable AI that demonstrate that human–AI combined performance on decision-making responsibilities is improving when the AI describes its recommendations. However, several previous studies noted AI performance improvements from explaining with reasonableness only when the AI, without the help of humans, outpaced both the human and the AI–human team (Bansal et al. 2021). "Can explanations help lead to complementary performance, where team accuracy is higher than either the human or the AI working solo?" (Bansal et al. 2021, 1).

Bansal et al. (2021) conducted mixed-method user research on three different datasets. An AI with precision and correctness was comparable to some humans helping participants to resolve and explain a task and explain itself in certain circumstances. The researchers reported that while they noted some complementary improvements from the corresponding AI, there was not much of an increase in improvements when adding explanations. Relatively, added explanations increased the humans' chances when they accepted the AI's recommendation, despite the consequences of its accuracy. In conclusion, Bansal et al. (2021) added, "[o]r result poses new challenges for human-centered AI: Can we develop explanatory approaches that encourage appropriate trust in AI, and therefore help generate (or improve) complementary performance?" (2)

At this point in time, there are considerable documented issues linked to AI automation and several human–machine system mistakes and faults. Reportedly, these issues have been related to various deficiencies in human operator conditions, including self-awareness reductions, increasing complacency and carelessness, and loss of their situation awareness (SA). This nonproductive situation has been observed and discussed at length in various human performance studies (Kaber et al. 2004). "In general, a key underlying factor that has emerged as a contributor to human performance problems in complex, automated systems control is human out-of-the-loop (OOTL) performance (Kaber et al. 2004, 113).

How to Establish an Agreement on "What Should Be Happening"

How do we get managers and employees to reach an agreement on what should be happening? What do we do when managers and employees, or in some cases both managers and employees, do not agree on the elements of anchors or targets? How could managers and employees reach a consensus on what are the job performance standards, including KPIs, best industry practices and criteria? In this segment, we explore the approaches that would bring managers and employees together to establish a working partnership that would benefit all those involved, including managers, employees, and the organization.

The areas that make the biggest difference for creating a robust partnership with employees are (1) leadership, (2) integrity, (3) responsibility, and (4) Accountability, with the support of *Organizations Values, Vision and Mission* that are causing *Organization Culture* as a strong foundation. In the following segments, we look at how to use these elements to cause a strong partnership with the workforce (see Figure 6.6). Organizations need to include these elements in their organizational culture and day-to-day operations to make sure their managers continue influencing the workforce with the presence of these elements.

Again, remember that these distinctions and explanations are brief. There are more sources available for your learning purpose in Appendix A.

Leadership versus Authority

We have briefly touched upon this concept in Chapter 2 (under key points to remember), but we thought we should go deeper and talk about this powerful concept in this chapter too.

The idea of dictatorship and forcing authority is not a foreign concept in the history of human existence. Many kings and repressing governments have tried this way of leading and governing, of which almost none of them survived the free will of people and the desire to be free and make their own choices. Without getting too much into history or politics, running an organization is not much different from running a country. Organizations are made by departments, groups, teams, and individuals; basically, any organization is made by people who naturally avoid dictatorships and authorities which by nature force their ways and their ironclad demands on their workforce. Without going too far, we just use what Satell (2014) brilliantly said about this matter:

> The problem is that, while authority can compel action, it does little to inspire belief. It's not enough to get people to do what you want; they also have to want what you want—or any change is bound to be short lived. That's why change management efforts commonly fail. All too often, they are designed to carry out initiatives that come from the top. When you get right down to it, that's really the just same thing as telling people to do what you want, albeit is [a] slightly more artful way. To make change really happen, it doesn't need to be managed, but empowered. That's the difference between authority and leadership.
>
> (Satell 2014, 2)

Integrity

Integrity is a personal phenomenon. People declare their own personal integrity based on their beliefs, their faith, their upbringing, their values, their principles, and their own choices. However, we all have one thing in common about our integrity. Without integrity, things do not work, and they will fall apart sooner or later.

Individuals practice integrity in different levels, from high levels to very low levels or close to nothing. However, the fact of the matter is this—without integrity, responsibility and accountability mean nothing. We cannot be fully responsible or accountable for our actions if we do not value and practice integrity. This powerful force influences every part of our day-to-day lives, who we are being and what we are doing. To make necessary changes in our lives, we must first start practicing integrity in all we do with others, with our own personal affairs and at work (Bakhshandeh 2015).

Who gives us the power and permission to judge others' integrity? What gives us the right to evaluate others' level of integrity on what we think integrity is, or should be? We judge and evaluate others' decisions, their lifestyle or life choices and anything else we can push our opinions on so we can impose our idea of integrity on them (2015). Unfortunately, when managers exert authority versus leadership, they ignore their employees' perspectives.

When employees do not accept managers' viewpoints, managers become upset and resentful. They distance themselves from their workers. When considering your idea of integrity, I invite you to separate your view of social law, religious beliefs, and/or cultural beliefs from your notion of integrity at this moment. Look at integrity as a personal phenomenon and individual to each person (2015). It is not easy, but by practicing your own integrity and becoming masterful in establishing rapport with others in the workforce, you can establish a partnership of comradery with speed and without holding back. Managers who practice integrity will give their workers the benefit of the doubt and be willing to listen without judgment thereby creating a safe environment for workers to express their concerns and reservations. "Consider integrity as the source of having power, magic and miracles in life" (2015, 28)

Responsibility

When we are responsible, we show our willingness to own every thought we have and own up to every action we take, good or bad, right or wrong, happy or sad, enough or not enough. We did it, nobody else, just us. When we understand this, we realize that we are the ones who make it or break it (2015). This powerful context allows us to live a great life with an abundance of peace of mind and fulfillment. It does not differ from managers who do not take responsibility for the present work environment which is the source of low production and bad performance generated through the years and is the outcome of such an environment on the employees' mindset, attitudes, and behaviors, ultimately affecting the connection of their performance and productivity to the organization.

When we can look back into all the upsetting, sad, dramatic events of our lives and see how we were responsible for the outcome of each event, we are free (2015). This does not differ from a manager who wants to ignore the effect of past bad management policies on the current situations and performances. I am not suggesting that personal or professional upsetting events do not happen in our lives and in our workplaces either on their own or at the hands of others. But what makes the events more upsetting and unfixable is when we drag them along behind us throughout our personal and professional lives like a sack of pain (2015). Our interpretation of these personal and professional events and what we make them mean reflect how we view ourselves, others, work, and life itself; Consequently, it will allow this status quo to continue in our personal and professional lives. "The most important things in life are to continue learning, to thrive on challenges and to fight ignorance" (2015, 30).

Accountability

I do not know about you, but each time we hear *accountability* or *being accountable*, we cannot help but think of something heavy and hard, like something we cannot do, something that is too far from reality, nearly unreachable. It is amazing that when we become present in our own lives, how we come to see just how much we are not being accountable for! Accountability and responsibility go hand in hand. When we practice responsibility, we cannot help being accountable and having integrity. This is the essential component of this combination (2015).

Our power is built on the foundation of our words and promises we make to ourselves and to others. This does not differ from professional promises we made to employers expecting a position at their organizations. The well-being of our integrity and principles depends on how we relate to our relationship to ourselves and the degree to which we keep our words and promises. We have no idea how much our actions impact the world around us. That means that any actions, broken promises, anything we do, and everything we say will influence our relationship with others. Our relationship with others will affect the quality of our personal and professional lives (2015).

Just imagine the possibilities that would arise in our performances and productivity if we all kept promises, worked with integrity, held ourselves responsible for our production, and were accountable for our performances.

This combination of integrity, responsibility, and accountability should be on the list of the most important training for developing professionalism among employees that would directly create an environment of partnership and workability between management and employees. A strong foundation would be built for establishing alignments and agreements in such an environment.

Practice for Establishing Agreement About "What Should Be Happening"

As we have displayed in Figure 6.6, all the organization's *Values, Vision, Mission* and *Culture* support the use of *Leadership, Integrity, Responsibility* and *Accountability* hold the space for management to sit with representatives of their workforce (such as junior managers, supervisors, or floor foremen) to come to an agreement on job and work performance standards and about what should be happening. Obviously, inviting all the employees to these types of meetings is impossible; therefore, managers should always be on the lookout for junior managers, supervisors, and floor foremen who

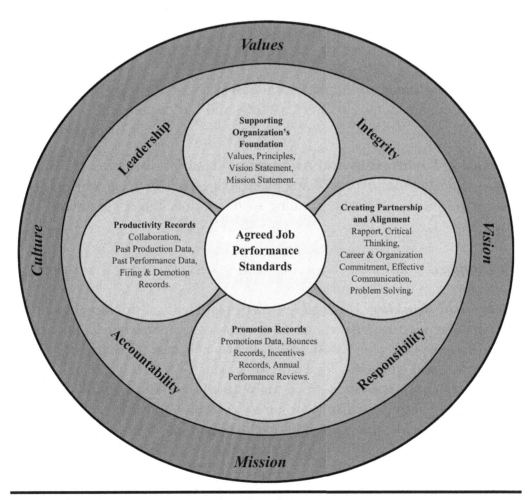

Figure 6.6   How to Come with Agreed Job Performance Standards.

Source: Copyright 2021 by Behnam Bakhshandeh.

are willing to learn leadership qualities and are open to professional discussions that would result in benefiting everyone in the organization. For this reason, the following elements are available for managers in their meetings with employee representatives when trying to get to a consensus on the job performance standards and what should be happening.

Supporting an Organization's Foundation: The conversation between managers and workers should always occur in conjunction with organizational foundations in the background. This background is the anchor that holds the organization together, and they are the source of operations and final outcomes (see Figure 6.6):

- *Values and principles*: What we value the most, and what are the core principles of our relationships and existence as an organization.
- *Vision statement*: Represents and displays who we are being, what we are standing for, where we are going, and what the culture of the organization is.
- *Mission statement*: Represents and displays what we are doing and our commitment to our values, culture, and our customers.

(Bakhshandeh 2008)

Creating Partnership and Alignment: Creating partnership and alignment is critical to the success of any process of establishing agreements. The following elements are vital to creating such a partnership environment (see Figure 6.6):

- *Rapport*: Establishing rapport is the first step of creating a workable relationship (see Chapter 4).
- *Critical thinking*: Using simple elements of critical thinking by paying attention to operational elements of what, why, how, where, who, and when to discuss real occurrences and events instead of perceptions, feelings, and emotions (see Figure 6.7).
- *Career commitment*: Career commitment refers to how motivated workers are to persist in their career direction and their attitude toward their profession. One critical element of career commitment is the nature of relationships that workers experience (Kim et al. 2013).
- *Organization commitment*: Organization commitment refers to the psychological and emotional attachment that employees feel about the organization for which they are working. This relationship is critical to

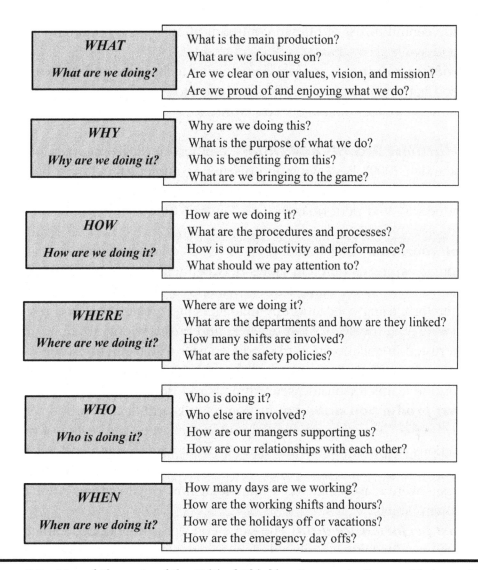

Figure 6.7   Use of Elements of the Critical Thinking Process to Come with Agreed Job Performance Standards.

Source: Copyright 2021 by Behnam Bakhshandeh.

ensure low turnover and is an important focus of attention for many organizational leaders (Kim et al. 2013).

■ ***Effective communication***: Use effective communication techniques and processes, including active listening, to get everyone on the same page. Communication is the source of establishing peace and harmony among people (Bakhshandeh 2004). Steinfatt (2009) expressed his view of communication and its vital role in human connectedness as follows:

"[t]he central thrust of human communication concerns mutually understood symbolic exchange" (295).

■ *Problem-solving*: Using problem-solving techniques and processes
(see Chapter 9) such as conflict resolution to resolve team issues and
conflicts between managers and workers.

Productivity Records and Data: "Numbers never lie, people do!"
(Bakhshandeh 2009). Reviewing and discussing numerical data just helps
managers and employees' representatives to see the reality of past and present productivity and performances (see Figure 6.6):

■ *Collaboration*: Collaboration gives rise to diverse opinions among
groups, expresses different views between team members, and helps to
resolve issues faster than just one person's ideas (Bakhshandeh 2021).
Therefore, using collocation by managers just creates trust and respect
for everyone involved. Most teachers and business organizations are
interested in collaboration to produce faster results among students
in the classrooms and propose different solutions to problems among
working teams for businesses (Ahmadi and Besancon 2017).
■ *Past production data*: Production records and data of productivity
for the past several years can help managers argue the reality of productions by presenting actual data for what was working and what was
not working. This is a realistic comparison for what past productivity
targets were reasonable and workable against organizations' annual
growth targets.
■ *Past performance data*: The same concept as mentioned earlier
about productivity is applicable for individuals', teams', and departments' performance levels and history of job performance standards.
As Albert Einstein once said, "[r]eality is merely an illusion, albeit a very
persistent one."
■ *Firing and demotion records*: With permission from Human
Resources directors or managers, and with absolute confidentiality by
removing names and titles, reviewing reasons for firing or demotions are
good indications for understanding what is happening on the production
floor or among employees. These data can help managers and workers
to see any resistance to productivity and performance standards.

Promotions records and data: This concept is very similar to the
firing and demotion records but in an uplifting way when managers and
worker representatives recognize what would cause promotions. With the

same type of permission from HR, managers and employees' representatives could review what some individuals or teams got promotions or bounces. This perusal helps designing job performance standards because the possibility of a positive forward movement in someone's career is always a good motivation. The following are some examples to review (see Figure 6.6):

- ■ **Promotions data**: The reasons for promotions and relevancy to productivity and performance.
- ■ **Bounces records**: The reasons for receiving bounces and relevancy to productivity and performance.
- ■ **Incentives records**: History of the organization providing incentives linked to productivity and performance and the number of occurrences within the last several years and how they were effective or not and why.
- ■ **Annual performance reviews**: A good step with the same type of confidentiality permission from the HR department.

Role of Critical Thinking Process in Job Performance Standards Alignment

As we have mentioned in the aforementioned segment, the process of critical thinking and its elements is very helpful for managers and employees' representatives to look at the reality of productivity and performance without getting engaged with perception, feelings, and emotions from either side. In this segment, we look at these simple but powerful elements.

Oxford Language Dictionary defined critical thinking as, "the objective analysis and evaluation of an issue in order to form a judgment" (np).

In a study conducted by Moore (2013) called *Critical Thinking: Seven Definitions in Search of a Concept*, Moore presented seven elements which described, pointed at importance, and defined critical thinking as "(i) judgment; (ii) skepticism; (iii) simple originality; (iv) sensitive readings; (v) rationality; (vi) an activist engagement with knowledge; and (vii) self-reflexivity" (506) (Bakhshandeh 2021).

Critical thinking and problem-solving (as one of the outcomes of critical thinking) are qualities that employers look for in their managers and newly hired college graduates (Bakhshandeh 2021).

In the year 2010, American Management Association (AMA) conducted a Critical Skills Survey on 2115 executives and senior managers, asking them to rank the top skills they are looking for when hiring new talent.

Critical thinking was the second most desirable, with communication skills being the most desired (Martz et al. 2017)

(Bakhshandeh 2021).

The six simple elements of critical thinking are *What, Why, How, Where, Who* and *When* (maybe not in the same order, but they are all part of the inquiry). Figure 6.7 displays and digs into them in more detail.

Team's Dysfunctions and Conflicts

Regardless of how good the team is bonding together, or how strong the foundation of the team building is established, from time-to-time, teams are facing some dysfunctions and issues with their team operations; either on an individual level or at the team level while trying to resolve issues. Managers and employees' representatives' meetings about creating an alignment and agreement on Job Performance Standards are not different from potential team dysfunction and conflicts. For this reason, managers need to work on diffusing these potential dysfunctions as they go, quarter by quarter, month by month, and even day by day. It would be very useful if we are aware of the group dynamics within a team that can meddle with the problem-solving progression. The dysfunctions that we are underlining are common within teams and groups; however, they need to deal with and addressed without delay.

The causes of such dysfunctions are identifiable and very much correctable by members' dedication, team strategy, and commitment to the team's purpose and vision. Bottom line, getting a team to function properly and become cohesive again, allows for much easier workability, productivity, and problem-solving process (Bakhshandeh 2004; Lencioni 2002).

Team Dysfunctions

The following are the five potential dysfunctions of a team or a group while they are working together.

Absence of Trust

When the fear of being authentic and real, causing a team member to become vulnerable with other team members will prevent the process of trust-building within the team.

Fear of Conflict

When one or some members of a team not wanting to face any conflict and avoiding confrontations, they maintain a fake harmony with the rest of the team, which suppresses the possibility of productive and professional conflict.

Lack of Commitment

When a team member is not clear about their commitment to the team, or lack of their buy-in to the team's purpose and vision, the team member prevents such team members from making productive decisions, and display commitments they will stick to.

Avoidance of Accountability

When one or more team members are avoiding interpersonal discomfort with team members who are not keeping their promises and commitments, they prevent team members from holding each other accountable for their responsibilities.

Inattention to Results

When team members are pursuing their intentions or desires and pushing for their personal status wearing down the team's focus on the team's purpose and goals and jeopardizing the collective success (Bakhshandeh 2004; Lencioni 2002).

Addressing Dysfunction

Like any other issue in life, when an individual or a team is committed to resolving issues, there are always ways to take on transforming dysfunctions. When a business team or a group is willing to face their dysfunctions and address their issues, the following benefits are achievable. High performing, organized, and unified teams are:

- comfortable asking for assistance and are at ease to receive help from their teammates
- admitting their mistakes and limitations to their team and are open to contributions from their teammates
- taking risks by offering feedback to their teammates for the good of their team
- utilize other team members' skills, competencies, and experiences to better themselves

■ not wasting their time talking about and revisiting the same wrong issue over and over again, just because someone is not buy-in yet
■ making more quality decisions about issues
■ accomplish more productivity in less time with fewer resources
■ facing essential issues and topics for discussion and have productive and professional meetings
■ align the whole team with common outcomes and objectives
■ retaining and rewarding hardworking and producing team members

(Bakhshandeh 2004; Lencioni 2002)

Asking Powerful and Effective Questions

Asking questions is one of the most common tools for obtaining information. Asking powerful and effective questions is the key to the success of performance analysis and discovering *what is happening* as well as *what should be happen*. The high-performance coach's or manager-as-coach's skills and competencies are very important in performance analysis because it takes an expert with good experience to create a set of questions not causing resistance from interviewees (Robinson et al. 2015; Bakhshandeh 2008).

As you remember in Chapter 3, we talked about understanding an individual's mindset, attitude, and behavior, determining an individual's relationship to their performance and productivity. However, designing a set of questions that would not trigger people's resistance or their protecting mindset is essential to conducting an effective performance analysis. Regarding the importance of asking powerful questions, Whitmore (2017) stated,

> [i]t is questions rather than instructions or advice that best generate awareness and responsibility. It would be easy if any old question would do, but it won't. We need to examine the effectiveness of various types of questions

(82)

During the performance analysis process and questioning, the high-performance coach will receive answers from participants that would indicate if the coachee is following the intent of the questions and is on a productive path, aligned with the purpose of the performance analysis objectives (Whitmore 2017).

What to Be Cautious About during Questioning?

It is useful to know what to pay attention to and what to avoid during designing and to conduct questions. The following is a brief review of what to know when asking questions regarding an individual or team performance and productivity:

Productive Questions

Questions should be designed to draw information that would help the coaches or their teams to see you as a high-performance coach who cares about their performance and that of the team's or organization's and shed light on the importance of their roles regarding the organization's purpose (Bakhshandeh 2013). Make sure the questions empower and open an inquiry for better production and performance and not cause the interviewee to feel wrong or to have done something wrong.

Relevant Questions

The questions should relate to the coachees or their team's performance and productivity without moving into personal or professional issues unrelated to the topic and bringing other irrelevant matters, such as their perceptions of HR policies' fairness or coachees' resentment toward them their supervisors. Keep the gossip and hearsay out of the process (Bakhshandeh 2013).

Judgmental Questions

Most coaching process questions commence with *what, where, who, when,* or *how* to turn the concentration inward and support the coachee's thoughts, insights, and feelings, which helps the process to move forward (Rothwell 2015). Wilson (2020) warned coaches to prevent them from questioning *why* because it might cause the interviewees to become defensive and make them feel judged or accused. It would be fine to ask *why* questions when you are not asking for personal information, such as asking about equipment or tools. The nature is not judgmental because it is not aimed at the operator as a person versus the equipment (Wilson 2020).

Leading Question

It is unprofessional and unethical to influence interviewees into responding in a particular way by asking leading questions (Bakhshandeh 2013). This may happen if a performance coach or manager-as-coach does not accept an answer from the coachee or interviewee until it is aligned with what he/she wants to hear. This would cause increasing mistrust, which would direct the data-gathering process in a nonproductive way. "Usually, a question becomes leading because the coach has missed out on exploring a statement from the coachee" (Wilson 2020, 160).

Multiple Questions

Sometimes coachees are unsure what to ask next; therefore, they ask several questions that most probably are not thorough and not part of the original design. Here, it is much better to take time and frame the next questions relevant to the topic (as we touched earlier) and be patient until the coachee provides an answer (Wilson 2020). Do not throw in some questions just to fill the space and uncomfortable silence (Bakhshandeh 2013). It is fine to delay your questioning until you collect what you want to ask; that would be beneficial to the process and the interviewee.

Questions as a High-Performance Management Practice

Designing and implementing a set of simple but elegant questions is an effective practice for delivering the intent of most productivity and increasing performance levels by high-performance coaches or managers-as-coaches. An effective set of questions can offer a perspective for an overview of a need assessment for training, developmental issues, or administrative functions of performance and productivity management. In addition, it could be a productive tool for recognizing the declared and established goals or pathways to realize needed and necessary goals to increase productivity and levels of performance among individuals and teams. Effective and well-designed questions assist during feedback, responsibilities, accountabilities, and overall growth of performance (Lee 2021; Bakhshandeh 2013).

Table 6.5 represents some of these effective questions about establishing or discovering what should be happening. Some of these questions might not be directly linked to the discovery of what should be happening; however, they are forming an environment of trust and respect between managers and employees and therefore can open space for the understanding of employees' mindset and perceptions in order for mangers-as-coaches to provide directions and to coach in order to increase productivity.

Table 6.5 Examples of Effective Questions for Discovering "What Should Be Happening."

Questions Categories	Examples of Effective and Powerful Questions for Discovering "What Should Be Happening"	
	Questions	Potential Outcome
Recreate Rapport	■ How are you? ■ How are your family, children, and their schooling (if applicable)? ■ How is it going with you and your team recently?	Re-establish rapport and ensure a good relationship.
Trust and Respect	■ Is everything okay with your work environment? ■ Is there anything that bothers you about your job? ■ You know whatever we talk about here is confidential. How is your relationship with your direct supervisors or foremen? ■ Are there any issues with your teamwork and team relationship you like to discuss? ■ Do you know you can come to me with any issue or problem you might have, and we will do our best to work them out?	Opening for sensitive conversation.
Ask Permission	■ I would like to discuss and offer some suggestions about the recent individual and team performance. Are you open to it? ■ I have identified some actions that would assist you and your team to adjust your performances positively. Are you open to hearing them? ■ Would you like to know how to increase your professional performance and build up your career in a positive direction?	Creating a safe environment for conversation and build up interests.
Job Performance Standards	■ What have you noticed about your performance? ■ What have you noticed about your team performance? ■ Are you aware of your job performance standards? ■ Do you understand the categories such as KPIs? ■ Is there any ambiguity or confusion on your responsibilities? ■ Are you clear about what is your individual and direct daily productions and team performance? ■ Do you think you will be in better shape if you know all these production and performance targets? ■ What would place you and your team in a better production and performance space?	Re-ensuring clarity on what are the job performance standards.

(Continued)

Table 6.5 (Continued)

Questions Categories	Questions	Potential Outcome
	Examples of Effective and Powerful Questions for Discovering "What Should Be Happening"	
Expectations	■ Do you completely understand what the expectations of your individual and team performances are? ■ Just for clarity, what do you think these expectations are? ■ What are your expectations from your direct manager or supervisor? ■ What are your expectations from the organization?	Remove ambiguity and confusion and get clarity about expectations.
Collecting Suggestions	■ What would you do the best? ■ What would you not be doing so well? ■ What do you find challenging at your job and performance? ■ What do you find challenging at your team performance? ■ What would you do differently at your job to bring up your performance level? ■ What would you suggest your team does differently to bring up your team's performance level? ■ Do you see any need for training? If yes, what kind?	Collect direct information about the reality of performance
Developing Leadership	■ What is your view of your own performance? ■ What do you think your performance should be? ■ Do you have any suggestions for improving your work environment? ■ Do you have any suggestions for potential modifications to job performance standards? ■ What would be two things you would change about your work performance?	Promoting partnership and developing future leaders for the organization.
Closing	■ What did you learn from our discussion? ■ Did you have any insights from our discussion? ■ Do you have any suggestions for improving individuals' and teams' performances? ■ Do you have anything to add before we conclude our conversation? ■ Do you know you can come to me with any additional information or suggestions?	Completing the session and leave opening for future discissions.

Source: Copyright 2021 by Behnam Bakhshandeh.

Business Case Example

In this segment, we use an example of the same organization we used in the previous chapters to show how to understand and discover what should be happening.

Background

As you know, during previous chapters, we introduced and used the MBD as an Organization Development case for examples of using and implementing High-Performance Coaching steps and processes. For more understanding of this organization's issue, review the business example cases in Chapters 4 and 5.

What Provoked the Inquiry?

As we have mentioned on the previous chapters, according to the senior managers, the MBD was facing (1) significant turnover and absenteeism among their workforce caused by a high level of work dissatisfaction among their employees and (2) the absence of collaboration and teamwork among the employees, especially between the administration, sales teams, and shipping crew as the source of what is happening. These issues caused MBD to have lower productivity due to a lack of acceptable performance. That was when MBD management had to bring their managers, supervisors, and foremen to a joint-table discussion and focus on establishing what should be happening.

Setup, Preparation, and Implementation

We invited department managers, several joiner managers, and supervisors from different departments who were trusted by the rest of the teams to join us at a discussion meeting to establish an alignment and agreement on what should be happening and set up job performance standards, including best industry practices, KPIs, criteria, and past records on productivity and performance.

Setup

Given the concern for not stopping the daily routine of running the business or the production without management presence, we decided to conduct the process on two different occasions for a two-day workshop/meeting setting.

Table 6.6 Conducting a Team Meeting and Discussion for Discovery of "What Should Be Happening" and Establishing Job Performance Standards.

What Should Be Happening—Establishing Job Performance Standards
This process is about what should be happening with the production and performance compared to a selected and agreed upon job performance standards among management and employees' representatives. It is highly recommended that high-performance coaches or a managers-as-coaches who are attempting to conduct such a meeting review the following categories and elements to make sure they are ready to hold such meetings with power, confidence, and related competencies.

(a) *Re-establish Rapport*	
1. Get Related	▪ Establishing rapport with these individuals and teams is critical to the workability of this process (see Chapter 4). ▪ Re-establish rapport by getting related to the supervisors and floor foremen on the same level of relating to managers. ▪ Understand that naturally, employees' representatives' mindset differs from managers' mindset (see Figure 4.2); therefore, you can't relate to them as the same. ▪ Review the fundamental state of being and competencies for establishing rapport before the meeting (see Figure 4.3).
2. Discuss Potential Conflicts	▪ Ask everyone to put aside any potential individual or team conflict at this time for the sake of effectiveness and workability that would benefit everyone. ▪ Briefly review some of the potential sources of team dysfunctions that might affect their work in this meeting, such as the absence of trust, lack of commitment, or fear of causing conflict. Let participants talk about them and express their concerns.
(b) *Powerful Setup*	
1. Speak the Commitment	▪ Start by speaking your own commitment to establishing a powerful set of Job Performance Standards that would support the organization's values, vision, and mission, as well as supporting and empowering employees' careers and performance. ▪ Invite the rest of the managers and employees' representatives to express their commitment to the outcome of this process. ▪ Point at the underlying foundation of workability as a team and the mutual commitment to the end results, such as outcome and vision.

2. Explain the Process	■ Briefly explain the process and the core design behind the process by displaying and explaining how to come with agreed job performance (see Figure 6.6). ■ Use the elements of critical thinking (see Figure 6.7) that are being used to empower the process and keep the inquiry on a productive track. ■ Make sure to review the examples of effective questions during your preparations (see Table 6.5).
3. Ground Rules	■ With the partnership of all members, establish a set of ground rules for the meeting. ■ Collect ideas for professional, workable, and effective rules that would support the committed outcome. ■ Try to keep the ground rules to not more than four to six.
(c) *Envisioning Future*	
1. Envisioning	■ Ask all the team members to envision what should be happening in the organization and in their teams. ■ Conduct a sharing session for everyone to hear all their team members' thoughts and desires.
2. Relationship to Vision, Mission, and Values	■ Review the organization's vision, mission, and core values with the team. ■ Ask them to complete individually and rate themselves on the "Assessing the Current Vision Clarity of an Individual or a Team" (see Table 6.1). ■ Conduct a sharing session on what is missing for them to be related to the organization's vision, mission, and values.
(d) *Reviewing the Existing Job Performance Standards*	
1. Evaluate the Existing Practices	■ Conduct a discussion on the existing performance standards or benchmarking among the team members. ■ Use the "Evaluating the Needs for Benchmarking the Best Practices in Human Performance Enhancement" (see Table 6.2).
2. Key Performance Indicator (KPI)	Discuss the existence of KPI among the organization and team members regarding: ■ Customer perspective ■ Internal perspective ■ Growth and learning perspective ■ Financial perspective
3. Criteria	■ Conduct the process of "Inquiries into Identifying Human Performance Criteria" with the team members (see Table 6.3). ■ Collect everyone's input and perspectives on the ten potential criteria in their organization:

(Continued)

Table 6.6 (Continued)

What Should Be Happening—Establishing Job Performance Standards	
4. Assessing Existing Individual Performance Standards	■ Conduct an individual job performance assessment on existing performance standards using the "Assessing the Job Performance Standard of an Individual or a Team" (see Table 6.4). ■ Discover what is missing and what needs to be modified or added.
(e) *Selecting Job Performance Standards*	
***Note* :** The following models are designed to establish "Root Cause Analysis" explained in detail in Chapter 9 of this book. (Read the relevant content of the following three models in Chapter 9.) For example, during the process of "Establishing Agreed Job Performance Standards," high-performance coaches or managers-as-coaches could use the following three Root Cause Analysis Models to bring the deciding team to come to a consensus on their selected job performance standards. In Chapter 9 of this book, we explain several more Root Cause Analysis Models for the use of high-performance coaches or managers-as-coaches to use and implement during their effort to find root causes of problems in their teams.	
1. Brainstorming Session	■ Using the brainstorming session (see Figure 9.3), encourage the team members to come with ideas for a new and relevant job performance standard based on what should be happening and collect ideas. ■ Encourage recognizing what are the "Best Practices" in the market (see Table 6.2).
2. Force Field Analysis	■ Conduct a force field analysis on the best practices and selected job performance standards (see Figure 9.6 and Table 9.3). ■ Ensure the teams' alignment and also the realistic relevancy of the selected new job performance standards (see Figure 6.19 for an example).
3. Nominal Group Technique (NGT)	■ After collecting all the ideas, using brainstorming, using the Nominal Group Technique (see Table 9.1) to evaluate the most popular ideas for the new job performance standards after collecting all the ideas.
(f) *Review and Feedback on the Outcome*	
1. What Is Happening— Problems	■ Provide complete review and feedback to the team on the process of what is happening, including the problem analysis and diagnosis on performance and issues on hand. ■ This review helps the team to refresh their minds on what is happening and have a better understanding of what should be happening.

What Should Be Happening—Establishing Job Performance Standards	
2. What Should Be Happening— Resolutions	Provide complete review and feedback to the key stakeholders and decision-makers on the two processes of: ■ What is happening, including the problem analysis and diagnosis on performance and issue on hand. ■ What should be happening, including the team's proposal on the new job performance standards and all its relevant processes on the above sessions.

Source: Copyright 2021 by Behnam Bakhshandeh.

Preparation

Before starting the event, we had an open discussion about respecting and considering everyone's inputs and ideas. In this setting, all participants are equal with equal voice and equal vote. Clearly, there are different ranking managers, and employees are participating in this workshop, but we all need to consider the fact that we are one team, with one mutual commitment and shared interest.

Implementation

Table 6.6 presents the process of implementation and action taken by the MBD selected team of managers and employees' representatives for discovering what should be happening after they went through the process of what is happening and discovering issues and what they were going to do about it.

As the internal high-performance coaches or managers-as-coaches, you have access to some information that an external practitioner doesn't have. The aforementioned practices for conducting *what should be happening* or establishing effective and realistic job performance standards are directly related to what already exists at the organization. However, as an internal performance coach, you have to decide which of the aforementioned practices are necessary or needed for your team performance enhancement.

Key Points to Remember

Remember these key factors from this chapter:

■ **Gathering around the vision**
  – Use your life vision as an anchor for all aspects of your life and connect it to the organization's vision as an addition to empower your professional performance. If you are not relating to the organization's

vision and mission statement, you are repeating what you already know without bringing something new to your already existing abilities and knowledge (Bakhshandeh 2009). By relating to the organization's vision while providing coaching, you are connecting to your subordinates or coachees from the point of team attitude, partnership, and workability versus being their boss, manager, or supervisor.

■ **Trust your envisioning**
- Trust what you are envisioning for the best of your team or distinguishing for an individual committed to increasing their performance (Rothwell and Kazanas 2003). You or your coachee have nothing to lose by envisioning what it should be as long as you can support it with analysis and comparison with a set of job performance standards created by reasonable comparisons to best practices.

■ **Job performance standards are your guidance**
- Design and promote realistic job performance standards for your organizational criteria or use what is accepted by other organizations in your industry to be your workforce's guidance for what should be happening (Robinson and Robinson 2008). The best approach is to establish your KPIs, so your people know what is expected of them. Review and adjust the performance standards and KPIs annually but keep it in front of your teams as the guidance to individual and team performance checklist for productive and high-performance individuals and teams.

Coaching and Developmental Questions for Managers

(1) How do you relate to your organization's vision, mission, core values, and principles?

(2) How does your team or group relate to your organization's vision, mission, core values, and principles?

(3) Do you have a set of Job Performance Standards for your team members? If yes, what are they? If not, what is in the way to create one?

(4) Do you have a set of Best Practices or Criteria for your team performance? If yes, what are they? If not, what is in the way to have one?

(5) Are you aware of any resistance to the existing Job Performance Standards among your employees?

(6) How do you score yourself (from 1 to 5) on your skills and competencies in conducting an effective questioning for discovering what should be happening?

(7) How do you score yourself (from 1 to 5) on your skills and competencies in conducting brainstorming sessions, force field analysis, and Nominal Group Techniques?

(8) Do you have any problem among your team that any team conflict resolution practices can resolve?

References

Ahmadi, Niluphar, and Maud Besançon. 2017. "Creativity as a Stepping Stone Towards Developing other Competencies in Classrooms." *Education Research International* 2017: 1–9.

Bakhshandeh, Behnam. 2002. "Executive Coaching: For Those of You Who Have Arrived." Unpublished Workshop on Coaching Executives. San Diego, CA: Primeco Education, Inc.

Bakhshandeh, Behnam. 2004. "Effective Communication." *Audio CD Set and Workshop.* San Diego, CA. Primeco Education, Inc.

Bakhshandeh, Behnam. 2008. "Bravehearts; Leadership Development Training." Unpublished Training and Developmental Course on Coaching Executives and Managers. San Diego, CA: Primeco Education, Inc.

Bakhshandeh, Behnam. 2009. *Conspiracy for Greatness; Mastery on Love Within.* San Diego, CA: Primeco Education, Inc.

Bakhshandeh, Behnam. 2013. "Asking Ten Effective Questions." Unpublished Training and Developmental Course on Coaching Executives and Managers. Carbondale, PA: Primeco Education, Inc.

Bakhshandeh, Behnam. 2015. *Anatomy of Upset: Restoring Harmony.* Carbondale, PA: Primeco Education, Inc.

Bakhshandeh, Behnam. 2021. "Perception of 21st Century 4cs (Critical Thinking, Communication, Creativity & Collaboration) Skill Gap in Private-Sector Employers in Lackawanna County, NEPA." An Unpublished Dissertation in Workforce Education and Development. The Pennsylvania State University.

Bansal, Gagan, Tongshuang Wu, Joyce Zhou, Raymond Fok, Besmira Nushi, Ece Kamar, Marco Tulio Ribeiro, and Daniel Weld. 2021. "Does the Whole Exceed its Parts? The Effect of AI Explanations on Complementary Team Performance." In *Proceedings of the 2021 CHI Conference on Human Factors in Computing Systems,* 1–16. https://arxiv.org/abs/2006.14779.

Camp, Robert C. 1989. *Benchmarking: The Search for Industry Best Practices That Lead to Superior Performance.* Milwaukee, WL: Quality Press.

Cardy, Robert L., and G. H. Dobbins. 1994. "Performance Appraisal: The Influence of Liking on Cognition." *Advances in Managerial Cognition and Organizational Information Processing* 5: 115–40.

Cardy, Robert L., and Brian Leonard. 2011. *Performance Management. Concepts, Skills and Exercises.* Armonk, NY: Me. E. Sharp. Inc.

Cummings, Thomas G., and Christopher G. Worley. 2015. *Organization Development & Change,* 10th ed. Stamford, CT: Cengage Learning.

Harrison, M. I. 2005. *Diagnosing Organizations: Methods, Models, and Processes*, 3rd ed., Applied Social Research Methods Series, vol. 8. Thousand Oaks, CA. Sage Publication.

Kaber, David B., and Mica R. Endsley. 2004. "The Effects of Level of Automation and Adaptive Automation on Human Performance, Situation Awareness and Workload in a Dynamic Control Task." *Theoretical Issues in Ergonomics Science* 5, no. 2: 113–53.

Kamatkar, Sadhana J., Amarapali Tayade, Amelec Viloria, and Ana Hernández-Chacín. 2018. "Application of Classification Technique of Data Mining for Employee Management System." In *International Conference on Data Mining and Big Data*, 434–44. Gateway East and Singapore: Springer.

Kaplan, Robert S., and David P. Norton. 1992. "Harvard Business Review" website. *The Balanced Scorecard: Measures that Drive Performance.* https://hbr.org/1992/01/the-balanced-scorecard-measures-that-drive-performance-2.

Kaplan, Robert S., and David P. Norton. 1996. *The Balanced Scorecard: Translating Strategy Action.* Cambridge, MA: Harvard Business Press.

Kim, Sewon, Toby M. Egan, Woosung Kim, and Jaekyum Kim. 2013. "The Impact of Managerial Coaching Behavior on Employee Work-related Reactions." *Journal of Business and Psychology* 28, no. 3: 315–30. https://doi.org/10.1007/s10869-013-9286-9.

Lee, Christopher. 2021. *Performance Conversations.* Alexandria, VA: Society of Human Resources Management (SHRM).

Lencioni, Patrick. 2002. *The Five Dysfunctions of a Team: A Leadership Fable.* San Francisco, CA: Jossey-Bass, a John Wiley & Sons, Inc.

Liraz, Meri. 2013. *How to Implement Management by Objectives in Your Business a Step by Guide to Implementing MBO.* No City: Liraz Publishing.

Martz, Ben, Jim Hughes, and Frank Braun. 2017. "Creativity and Problem-solving: Closing the Skills Gap." *Journal of Computer Information Systems* 57, no. 1: 39–48.

McCormick, Ernest J. 1979. *Job Analysis: Methods and Applications.* New York, NY: AMACO.

McIlroy-Young, Reid, Siddhartha Sen, Jon Kleinberg, and Ashton Anderson. 2020. "Aligning Superhuman AI with Human Behavior: Chess as a Model System." In *Proceedings of the 26th ACM SIGKDD International Conference on Knowledge Discovery & Data Mining*, 1677–87. New Your, NY: ACA.

"Merriam-Webster." 2021. *Envisioning.* www.merriam-webster.com/dictionary/envisioning.

Moore, Tim. 2013. "Critical Thinking: Seven Definitions in Search of a Concept." *Studies in Higher Education* 38, no. 4: 506–22.

"Oxford Language." 2021. *Envisioning.* www.google.com/search?q=envisioning+definition&oq=envisioning&aqs=chrome.1.69i57j69i59j46j0l2j46j0l4.2097j0j15&sourceid=chrome&ie=UTF-8.

Robinson, Dana Gaines, and James C. Robinson. 2008. *Performance Consulting: A Practical Guild for HR and Learning Performance*, 2nd ed. San Francisco, CA: Berrett-Koehler.

Robinson, Dana Gaines, James C. Robinson, Jack J. Phillips, Patricia Pulliam Phillips, and Dick Handshaw. 2015. *Performance Consulting: A Strategic Process to Improve, Measure, and Sustain Organizational Results.* Oakland, CA: Berrett-Koehler Publishers.

Rothwell, William J. 2013. *Performance Consulting: Applying Performance Improvement in Human Resource Development.* San Francisco, CA: John Wiley & Sons.

Rothwell, William J. 2015. *Beyond Training & Development: Enhancing Human Performance Through a Measurable Focus on Business Impact*, 3rd ed. Amherst, MA: HRD Press, Inc.

Rothwell, William J., Carolyn K. Hohne, and Stephen B. King. 2012. *Human Performance Improvement.* New Your, NY: Routledge.

Rothwell, William J., Carolyn K. Hohne, and Stephen B. King. 2018. *Human Performance Improvement: Building Practitioner Performance*, 3rd ed. New York, NY: Routledge.

Rothwell, William J., and H. C. Kazanas. 2003. *The Strategic Development of Talent.* Amherst, MA: HRD Press, Inc.

Rothwell, William J., and Henry J. Sredl. 2014. *Workplace Learning and Performance: Present and Future Roles and Competencies*, 3rd ed., vol. I. Amherst, MA: HR Press.

Rothwell, William J., Jacqueline M. Stavros, and Roland L. Sullivan. 2016. *Practicing Organization Development: Leading Transformation and Change*, 4th ed. Hoboken, NJ: John Wiley & Sons, Inc.

Satell, G. 2014. "To Create Change, Leadership is More Important than Authority." *Harvard Business Review.*

Steinfatt, T. 2009. "Definitions of Communication." In *Encyclopedia of Communication Theory*, edited by S. W. Littlejohn and K. A. Foss, vol. 1, 295–99. Thousand Oaks, CA: Sage Publication, Inc. https://doi.org/10.4135/9781412959384.n108.

Tomczak, David L., Lauren A. Lanzo, and Herman Aguinis. 2018. "Evidence-based Recommendations for Employee Performance Monitoring." *Business Horizons* 61, no. 2: 251–59.

Whitmore, John. 2017. *Coaching for Performance: The Principle and Practice of Coaching and Leadership*, 5th ed. Boston, MA: Nicholas Brealey Publishing.

Wilson, Carol. 2020. *Performance Coaching: A Complete Guide to Best-Practice Coaching and Training*, 3rd ed. New York, NY: KoganPage.

Wingard, Devin. 2019. "Data-driven Automated Decision-making in Assessing Employee Performance and Productivity: Designing and Implementing Workforce Metrics and Analytics." *Psychosociological Issues in Human Resource Management* 7, no. 2: 13–18.

ANALYZING THE GAP

Performance coaching relies on a careful analysis of the gap—positive, negative, or neutral—that gives rise to differences between what is happening and what should be happening. When analyzing the gap, performance coaches should work with coachees and others to set priorities by determining how big is the gap. To that end, setting priorities may depend on determining "what is the *measurable* gap?", deciding how important that gap is and what causes the gap. Sometimes the mere process of clarifying the metrics used to measure a gap will point toward its importance. This phase examines how to analyze the gap by clarifying how to measure that gap, how to assess the importance of the gap to the organization and coachees, and what reasons may exist to explain the gap(s).

Chapter 7—Step 4: What Is the Measurable Gap?
Analyzing the gap between what is happening and what should be
   happening?

Chapter 8—Step 5: How Important Is the Gap?
What are the critical factors of the gap related to their organization?

Chapter 9—Step 6: What Are the Root Causes of the Gap?
What is causing the gap? How did the issue start? What are the main elements of this issue?

DOI: 10.4324/9781003155928-9

Chapter 7

Step 4: What Is the Measurable Gap?

Behnam Bakhshandeh

Recognizing a performance gap sounds easy. But doing so is often overlooked.

Chapter 7 is about finding performance gaps between "What is happening" and "What should be happening" and how to measure such a gap. This step in high-performance coaching is critical. Carrying out this step makes it possible for performance coaches to find, or facilitate others to find, issues that warrant attention.

- This chapter addresses these issues:
- What is analysis?
- What is a performance gap?
- What methods can explain individuals', teams', and organization's present and future performance gaps?
- What are performance gap metrics?
- Some example of gap analysis
- How to measure a performance gap?
- A performance gap assessor's needed competencies and skills
- The potential reasons for lack of acceptable performance
- Leadership and structural problems within the organization
- Different ways to tackle a performance gap in a team
- Performance feedback sessions
- Feedback questions for managers and employees
- Evaluating an organizations and the managers' performance measurement progress

DOI: 10.4324/9781003155928-10

What Is Analysis?

Analysis implies a comparison of what is versus what should be OR between what is possible now and what is needed in the future.

Rothwell, Hohne, and King (2018) described the analysis as "serv[ing] a vital purpose in human performance improvement efforts conducted in organizational settings" (36).

■ Oxford Languages defines *analysis* as a "detailed examination of the elements or structure of something" ("Oxford Languages" 2021).
■ Merriam-Webster describes the *analysis* as: "1a: a detailed examination of anything complex to understand its nature or to determine its essential features: a thorough study doing a careful analysis of the problem. b: a statement of such an examination. 2: separation of a whole into its parts" ("Merriam-Webster" 2021).

Rothwell et al. (2018) defined performance analysis as "the process of identifying the organization's performance requirements and comparing them to its objectives and capabilities (Rothwell 2000)" (39). The following are other names or terminologies used to describe analysis by other researchers and professional practitioners (Rothwell et al. 2018, 38):

■ assess business and performance needs
■ front-end analysis
■ gap analysis
■ performance analysis
■ performance assessment
■ performance audit
■ performance diagnosis
■ training needs assessment
■ needs analysis

What Is Performance Gap?

Rothwell (2015a) explained and described the performance gap as "a difference between what is happening and what should be happening. A performance gap can also be regarded as a difference between the way things are and the way they are desired to be" (133).

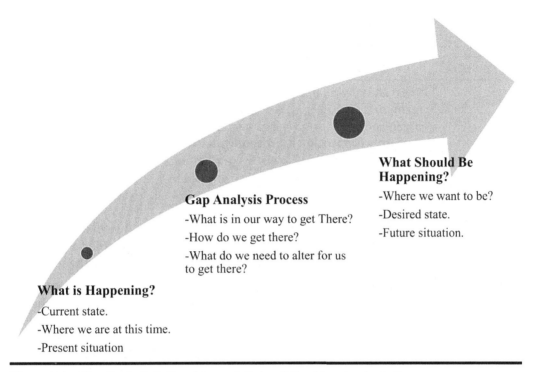

Figure 7.1 The Basic Relationship and Role of the Gap Analysis Process.

Source: Copyright 2021 by Behnam Bakhshandeh.

In more straightforward words, a performance gap is a discrepancy between expected, planned, or expected performance by an individual, a team, or an organization and the actual delivered performance (Colquitt, LePine, and Wesson 2015).

Figure 7.1 displays the fundamental relationship and role of the gap analysis process and what is happening and what should be happening.

Different Performance Gaps

A performance gap is a disparity between what is happening and what should be happening regarding individual, team, and organization performance. At the same time, a performance gap can distinguish between *the way things are* and *the way they are desired to be.* To understand performance gaps among individuals, teams, and organizations, consider six possible ways to distinguish performance gaps (see Table 7.1).

These six categories are organized based on two distinct periods of: (1) the present gaps and (2) the future gaps.

Table 7.1 Possible Approaches to Abstract Performance Gaps.

Possible Approaches to Abstract Performance Gaps			
Period	*Positive*	*Neutral*	*Negative*
Present Time (Current State)	When an individual, a team, or organization presently tops in any or all performance standards and expectations.	When an individual, a team, or organization presently matches relative quotation points in any or all performance standards and expectations.	When an individual, a team, or organization is presently inadequate in any or all performance standards or expectations during the comparison between what is happening and what should be happening.
Future Time (Expected Trend)	If individuals, teams, and organizations resume and maintain their performance and excel as expected by performance standards or expectations.	If present tendencies resume and maintain as expected, causing the organization to match any or all performance standards or expectations.	If present tendencies continue as planned, the organization will ultimately become effective and productive in any or all performance standards or expectations.

Source: Adapted from Rothwell (2015a), Rothwell (2015b), and Rothwell (2000).

At the same time, among these two time periods, the possible kind of gaps are distinguished as: (1) positive gap, (2) negative gap, and (3) neutral gap.

Performance coaches who can recognize these gaps will find better ways to plan and implement improvement efforts.

Present Time

Performance gaps of this kind include the present positive gap, the present negative gap, and the present neutral gap:

Present Positive Gap

A present positive gap is a strategic or tactical strength. It represents the organization's core competency, what it does best. It could also indicate what the division, department, team, or individual does best. The present positive gap distinguishes organizations from competitors. "A positive gap is indicative of internal operations showing a clear superiority" (Camp 1989, 123).

Discovering present positive gaps is important to counterbalance the tendency of managers to focus only on what is going wrong. But

> the burden of proof is greatest when uncovering present positive performance gaps because decision-makers may greet the news with hearty skepticism. When a positive gap is confirmed, the danger also exists that decision-makers will become complacent
>
> *(Rothwell 2015a, 134).*

Present Negative Gap

On the opposite side of the present positive gap is a present negative performance gap that signifies deficiencies. A present negative gap indicates that the individual, team, or organization is not performing up to required job performance standards, key performance indicators, or common business practices. At this point, the organization should conduct further analysis and implement corrective action. Steer clear of quick, glib advice about ways to close negative gaps. Take time, even if conducted quickly, to investigate with a view toward discovering root causes before picking solutions.

Present Neutral Gap

Between the aforementioned two positions, the present neutral gap represents a situation in which individuals, teams, or organizations match job performance standards, key performance indicators, and common business practices. There is really no gap at all when the present situation matches the desired situation.

One issue that emerges when results match intentions is that decision-makers grow complacent. Why change when the performance is adequate? Unfortunately, such thinking can lead to disaster as competitors may choose not to cease efforts to enhance competitive advantage even when present conditions are adequate. Nobody wants to be a "C student." Everyone wants to be an "A student."

Future Time Period

This group of performance gaps includes the future positive gap, the future negative gap, and the future neutral gap:

Future Positive Gap

A future positive gap represents the potential for future competitive advantage. It represents an opportunity to achieve an edge. For individuals, it may mean that people choose to build skills that will be in demand in the future.

Future Negative Gap

A future negative gap represents the potential for future competitive threats. What issues are likely to lead to problems if left ignored. Pinpointing future negative gaps should encourage action plans, tactical approaches, and strategies to avoid the threats.

Future Neutral Gap

Future neutral gaps represent situations in which individuals, teams, or organizations are threatened with future challenges. Job performance standards, key performance indicators, and business practices are appropriate in place and being matched. Competitors pose no threats.

Future neutral gaps can be overlooked by stakeholders because no exceptions to expectations exist. Yet, these gaps may provide an outstanding opportunity for competitive advantages. As a simple example, if a fast-food restaurant does a study and finds that it appears that future waiting time for customers is expected to be just the same as that of competitors—or will meet targets established by owners or corporate headquarters—then waiting time represents a future neutral gap. But if competitors are not paying much attention to waiting time, it can provide a basis for gaining market share and competitive advantage.

What Are Employee Performance Metrics?

The performance gap should be measurable. But how do we measure human performance gaps? What measures are important? What measures are applicable? How should measures be established? The issue is that few organizations have really good objective measures of job performance. The Employee Performance Metrics are answers to these inquiries.

The fact is that Employee Performance Metrics are essential to tracing how well employees are handling and performing at their work/job. Each organization's human resources (HR) department should have methods and metrics to measure the productivity and efficacy of their employees based on their own industry and what they do (Van Vulpen 2021).

Table 7.2 displays the 36 general types of employee performance metrics used by industries in four different categories. Note that not all organizations use all the 35 metrics. Each organization will select some of these matrices for their processes and procedures related to productivity and performances and some will use others, all based on their needs.

The Solitary Analyst Method

One common, relatively easy approach for performance coaches is to undertake, on their own, investigations into actual and ideal conditions. That is the solitary analyst method. It is suitable for finding quick answers.

Note that Chapter 5 focused on finding "what is the issue at hand," Chapter 6 focused on finding "what should be happening," and now Chapter 7 focuses on "what is a measurable gap." Often the most useful data collection approach is to talk to people who have the organization's pulse. Performance coaches may, therefore, set up individual or group interviews for data collection about a problem. Interviews may, of course, be carried out onsite, online, or through hybrid methods that mix real-time (synchronous) and delayed (asynchronous) approaches to data collection.

Table 7.3 offers some basic questions and an opening inquiry into the differences between "what is happening" or "what is the issue in hand" and "what should be happening." By posing these questions, performance coaches can gather information and then sort data as present positive, present negative, present neutral, future positive, future negative, or future neutral performance gaps.

Nuts and Bolts of Performance Analysis

The process of analysis is the highly crucial stage in the high-performance coaching. The purpose of analysis in the high-performance coaching and performance improvement attempts is to recognize the source of issue(s) (what is happening), verify potential cause(s) (comparing what is happening to what should be happening), separate the most severe root cause(s) (see Chapter 9), and overall, make a correct diagnosis that sets in plans and activities as treatments (topics of further chapters). It is crucial to understand there

Table 7.2 Different Categories of Employee Performance Metrics Used by Industries.

Categories of Employee Performance Metrix Used by Industries

Categories	T#*	U#*	Matrices	Descriptions
	1	1	Management by objectives	Structuring managers subjective assessments.
	2	2	Subjective appraisal by managers	Employee performance evaluation based on different criteria.
	3	3	Product defects	The number of defective products per week, month, etc.
	4	4	Number of errors	The number of input errors per day, week, etc.
	5	5	Number of recalls	The number of product recalls, per month, quarter, etc.
A. Work Quality. Based on reflections of employees' individual's, or team's performance.	*6*	6	Number of QC rejections	The number of quality control rejections per month, quarter, etc.
	7	7	Net promoter score	Or NPS is the rate of the willingness of clients to promote a company.
	8	8	360 degree feedback	Feedback score from employees' coworkers, supervisors, subordinates, managers, and customers.
	9	9	180 degree feedback	Feedback score from employees' direct peers, supervisors, and managers.
	10	10	Forced ranking	Or vitality curve is the ranking done with a manager based on the best to the worst employee.
	11	1	Number of sales	How much sales per day, week, etc.
	12	2	Number of phone calls	How many sales calls are done per day, week, etc.

13	3	Number of contacts	How many contacts (actual persons) are done per day, week, etc.
14	4	Number of active leads	How many leads are generated per day, week, etc.
15	5	Number of appointments	How many appointments are made per day, week, etc.
16	6	Number of client visits	How many clients or companies visited per day, week, etc.
17	7	Number of units produced	How many units of products are sold per day, week, etc.
18	8	How much time per day	The ratio of hours per day worked.
19	9	How much time per calls	The ratio of calls per hour.
20	10	How much time per contact	The ratio of hours per contacts
21	11	How much time per appointment	The ratio of hours per appointment
22	12	How much time per contract	The ratio of hours per contract
23	13	How many appointments on the first call	The ratio of making appointments on the first call.

B. Work Quantity. Based on measures on employees' individual or team quantity of performance.

(Continued)

Table 7.2 (Continued)

Categories of Employee Performance Metrix Used by Industries

Categories	T#*	U#*	Matrices	Descriptions
	24	1	Work efficiency	The balance between use of qualitative and quantitative resources.
	25	2	Time	The ratio of utilizing company's time per week, month, etc.
C. *Work Efficiency.* Based on quality and quantity of using the company resources.	**26**	3	Money	The ratio of utilizing company's monetary budget per week, month, etc.
	27	4	Administration	The ratio of utilizing company's administration staff per week, month, etc.
	28	5	Technology	The ratio of utilizing company's technology resources per week, month, etc.
	29	1	Revenue per employee	Revenue per FTE* = Total revenue/FTE
	30	2	Profit per FTE	Profit per FTE = Total profit/FTE
D. *Organizational Performance.* Based on employees' competencies, competitiveness, and professionalism	**31**	3	Human capital ROI (return on investment)	Value of human capital such as knowledge, skills, and social and personal qualities.
	32	4	Absenteeism rate	Rate of employees' absentees per month, quarter, etc.
	33	5	Overtime per employee	Overtime per FTE = Total hours of overtime/FTE

34	6	Number of reported safety valuations	Evaluation of OSHA's safety standards per month, quarter, etc.
35	7	Number of supervisory performance complaints	Employees' supervisor or foremen complaints about quality, behavior, and attitude.
36	8	Number of reported HR valuations	Human resources valuations such as racial commentary, diversity, or sexual harassment complaints.

*T# = total number of metrics; *U# = number of metrics in each category; *FTE = full-time equivalent

Source: Adapted from Van Vulpen (2021), Bakhshandeh (2008), Spitzer (2007), Bakhshandeh (2002).

are two imperial purposes to process human performance improvement: (1) closing gaps or resolving issues regarding an individual, team, or organization's performance and productivity and (2) capitalizing on individuals, teams, and organization's strengths and apprehending opportunities and possibilities (Rothwell et al. 2018; Cummings and Worley 2015). "The purpose of analysis, then, is to diagnose the problem or situation accurately and set the stage so that the appropriate intervention(s) can be selected, implemented, and evaluated to achieve positive performance results and outcomes" (Rothwell et al. 2018, 37). These segments describe elements of the analysis process for recognizing performance gaps and comparisons to happening.

Performance Analysis

Performance analysis is the process of distinguishing between the organization's performance constraints and evaluating them against the organization's objectives and abilities (Rothwell 2000). Performance analysis requires the recognition of gaps and distinguishes discrepancies in performance. A discrepancy is said to be the difference between planned performance levels and actual performance levels (see Figure 7.2). Robinson et al. (2015) refer to this concept as the process of "what *should* be occurring, what *is* occurring, and the root *causes* for these gaps" (p. xxii). "In addition to defining the gap in performance, part of the performance analysis process involves assessing (or at least estimating) the impact, results, or Consequences of the discrepancy" (Rothwell et al. 2018, 37).

Job Analysis

Cardy and Leonard (2011) define job analysis as "a systematic means for describing what constitutes a job" (40). Several approaches exist to conduct a job analysis; however, regardless of the method applied, the ultimate objective is the same: to apprehend the key components of the job, that at this point is about how this job affects what is happening and what should be happening. Some job analysis methods concentrate on (1) the time that would take to complete different tasks, whereas other methods concentrate on (2) the importance of numerous characteristics of the job, and some other methods are focusing on the set of duties and tasks that would deliver the outcome. These fundamental methods underlie nearly all job analysis methods that a high-performance coach or manager-as-coach is expected to run across and use (2011). Job analysis offers a reasonable basis for defining

Table 7.3 The Differences between "What Is Happening" and "What Should Be Happening."

The Differences between "What is happening" and "What should be happening"

1—Organizational Environment Culture, Vision and Mission Statements, Leadership Structure		
Performance Standards, KPIs, Best Practices	**What Is the Issue at Hand?**	**Evidence, Results, Outcomes**	**What Should Be Happening?**

What are the top three significant differences between "what is the issue at hand" and "what should be happening" concerning the organizational environment?

1.
2.
3.

2—Where? The Context of the Work, the Work Environment, Policies, Location, Team		
Performance Standards, KPIs, Best Practices	**What Is the Issue at Hand?**	**Evidence, Results, Outcomes**	**What Should Be Happening?**

What are the top three significant differences between "what is the issue at hand" and "what should be happening" concerning the work environment?

1.
2.
3.

(Continued)

Table 7.3 (Continued)

	3—What?The Work, Activities, Tasks, Jobs, Procedures, Performance		
Performance Standards, KPIs, Best Practices	What Is the Issue at Hand?	Evidence, Results, Outcomes	What Should Be Happening?

What are the top three significant differences between "what is the issue at hand" and "what should be happening" concerning the work?

1.
2.
3.

	4—Who?The Workers, Employees, Personnel, Contractors, Suppliers		
Performance Standards, KPIs, Best Practices	What Is the Issue at Hand?	Evidence, Results, Outcomes	What Should Be Happening?

What are the top three significant differences between "what is the issue at hand" and "what should be happening" concerning the workers?

1.
2.
3.

Source: Adapted from Rothwell, Hohne, and King (2012).

Figure 7.2 Discrepancy and Gap in the Individual, Team, and Organization Performance Level.

Source: Adapted from Rothwell (2013).

how to choose an individual for a job. Without understanding what it takes to perform a job, it is difficult to select individuals who are the best choices to conduct that job (2011).

Level of Analysis

Performance can be regarded from three vantage points: (1) the organization's performance level, (2) the individual performer level, and (3) the process and work level (see Figure 7.3), and therefore, the analysis of such performance also happens on these three levels (Rummler and Brache 2012). Using these levels to define and describe performance levels would assist the high-performance coach or a manager-as-coach in analyzing to clearly outline the scope of their investigation and analysis by understanding the interrelatedness among the different levels of performance and related productivity to uncover what is happening compared to what should be happening (Kaufman 2006).

It is worth mentioning that by analyzing the highest to lowest levels of analysis, the organization's performance level of analysis includes both external and internal standpoints and emphasizes the organization's (1) ability to meet their customers' requirements, (2) ability to compete in their related marketplace, and (3) carry out their strategies, such as production, sales, safety, marketing, expansion, and profitability (Rothwell et al. 2018). "Analysts will sometimes find themselves explaining performance issues at this higher, more strategic level. They may also begin analysis efforts at this organizational level and 'drill down' to isolate key variables at the other levels" (Rothwell et al. 2018, 41).

Role of Analyst

As it has been mentioned on the ASTD Models for Human Performance Improvement, the analyst's role is to "conduct troubleshooting to isolate the cause(s) of human performance gaps or identify areas in which human performance can be improved" (Rothwell 2000, n.p.). As we have mentioned in the last chapter, the role of the analyst (see Figure 5.2) is considered the most important role involving individuals, teams, groups, or an organization's performance-and-cause analysis. In the analyst role, the high-performance coach is performing troubleshooting and cause-and-effect procedures to uncover the causes of performance gaps or needs for improvements (Rothwell and Sredl 2000b).

Analyst Competencies and Skills

ASTD Models define these six key competencies and skills for an HPI practitioner (which also can be used by a high-performance coach) as analysis for Human Performance Improvement. These competencies represent the crucial attributes that support the analyst to perform a professional role and succeed in their role (Rothwell 2000):

(1) **Conducting Performance Analysis (front-end analysis)**: comparing planned and desired performance against present and actual performance to recognize the performance gaps or opportunities.
(2) **Designing and Developing Needs Analysis Survey (open-ended and structured)**: Designing needs analysis surveys such as mail survey

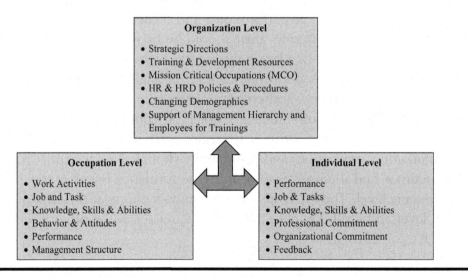

Figure 7.3   Three Levels of Organization's Performance.

Source: Adapted from "U.S. Office of Personal Management" (n.d.), (Bakhshandeh 2021).

(written), phone survey (oral), email survey (electronic), or web-based surveys using a set of scaled questions (close-ended) and responding questions (open-ended) to recognize performance needs.

(3) **Identifying Competencies:** Ability to identify the knowledge, skill, and abilities (KSAs) required from individuals, teams, and groups for conducting their tasks, jobs, tasks, work, or roles at their position.

(4) **Conducting Inquiries and Questioning:** Skills for performing inquiries and questioning individuals and teams for collecting information to inspire insights into the potential issues and recommendations for resolutions.

(5) **Analytical Ability (synthesis):** Ability to break down the collected data and components from greater scales and reconstructing them to impact and improve performance.

(6) **Work Environment Analytic:** Skills for examining internal and external work environments for identifying characteristics and sources of issues affecting performance.

(Rothwell et al. 2018)

Table 7.4 displays the analyst's competencies and skills and what those competencies are producing as outcomes for the analysis process.

Some Examples of Gap Analysis

In today's business world and among organization operations, there are various business areas such as operation, management, sales, accounting, human resources, customer service, and so on. These different areas of business create productivity and performance situations that can utilize the gap analysis process to address different gaps in different areas of business (Weller 2018). Although our book is all about high-performance improvement and recognizing a gap between what is happening and what should be happening, we are taking a moment to briefly introduce several examples of business gaps that exemplify a broad range of ways an organization can use a gap analysis:

■ **Product Introduction**: An organization might use a gap analysis for understanding why after launching a new product, its sales didn't meet the calculated number.

■ **Productivity**: When an organization's productivity does not match general planned targets, expectations, and business requirements using gap analysis can help clarify what needs attention.

Table 7.4 Analyst's Competencies and Skills, and Their Facilitating Outputs.

	Analyst's Competencies and Skills	
#	*Analyst's Competencies*	*Facilitating Outputs*
1	**Conducting performance analysis**	■ Observation. ■ Individual interviews. ■ Focus group interviews. ■ Reviewing documents. ■ Models and tools for troubleshooting of performance gap. ■ Action plan for the performance analysis. ■ Job and task analysis. ■ Identifying potential trends affecting the present and future performance gaps.
2	**Designing and developing needs analysis surveys**	■ Mail survey, email survey, phone survey, and a web-based survey. ■ Administration plan and structure of surveys. ■ Research design and models. ■ Data analysis and data interpretation plan. ■ Finding's analysis and reports. ■ Needs assessment summaries. ■ Analysis results and summaries.
3	**Identifying competencies**	■ Job descriptions. ■ Work and job portfolios. ■ Behavioral issues experience interviews. ■ Critical incidents questionnaires. ■ Competencies models for work process and functionality. ■ 360-degree assessment.
4	**Conducting inquires and questioning**	■ Individual interview protocol. ■ Focus group interview protocol. ■ Structure and admin plan for interviews. ■ Analysis of interview results and collected data.
		■ Plans and agenda for team and group meetings.
5	**Analytical abilities**	■ The root cause analysis strategies and models. ■ Problem-solving model. ■ Fishbone diagram. ■ Force field diagram. ■ Brainstorming diagram.

Analyst's Competencies and Skills		
#	Analyst's Competencies	Facilitating Outputs
6	**Work environment analytic**	■ Business and strategic plans. ■ Internal and external environment scans. ■ Teams, groups, and departmental plans. ■ Human resources policies and procedures. ■ Performance and process improvement plans.

Source: Adapted from Wilson (2020), Rothwell et al. (2018), Pearlstein (2012).

- **Performance:** Organizations use performance gap analysis to identify the source of low performance in individuals, teams, and groups to decide on approaches to enhancing performance.
- **Supply Management**: When some organizations find they are frequently running short of vital supplies or material, they use a gap analysis to detect the cause of this problem.
- **Sales Performance**: Organizations use a gap analysis to define their lack of product sales to distributors, in stores, through catalogs, or online ensure the right mix and/or quality of customer interest.
- **Market Analysis:** An organization or an investor can use a gap analysis for deciding about the desirability and the dynamic forces of a particular market within a particular industry.
- **Individual Assessment**: A manager or team leader can perform a gap analysis on themselves or another individual to improve personal performance and potentially come with some "best practices" that others would adopt.
- **Team Assessment:** Same concept as an individual assessment (see aforementioned individual assessment) but conducted on a team or a group in an organization.
- **Product Assessment**: An organization can use a gap analysis to assess their product or services quality to ensure that all features, characteristics, and outlined functions are present and working as marketed and expected.
- **Customer Service Assessment:** Organizations use gap analysis to determine their customers' satisfaction regarding their customer service practices.

(Weller 2018; Rothwell, Stavros, and Sullivan 2016;
Cardy and Leonard 2011)

Analysis Models for Use by High-Performance Coaches

High-performance coaches or managers-as-coaches can use analysis models to organize their approach and plan a systematic examination into employee performance improvement issues and opportunities. The analytical models used by coaches and practitioners are classified in different ways, depending on the level of analysis, such as the employees' performance (individuals), work and job characteristics (occupations), or an organization level, while they will be used in two possible analyses: (1) performance analysis and (2) cause analysis (Rothwell et al. 2018; Rothwell 2013). However, other models are considered situational models because they focus on a particular issue or situation. In a simpler explanation, some analysis models are generally beneficial for: (1) explaining and distinguishing current conditions, (2) discovering the root causes of crises, (3) portraying the idyllic future state of operation, or (4) desiring optimum performance (Rothwell et al. 2018; Rothwell et al. 2016; Rothwell 2013). In the following segment, we briefly introduce several analysis models that can be used by High-Performance coaches and managers-as-coaches (with some experience in the delivery of them).

The Rummler and Brache Model

Rummler and Brache introduced their model as a framework for performance analysis in their classic book *Improving Performance: How to Manage the White Space on the Organization Chart* (2012). This model of analysis consists of two dimensions:

Performance Level: (1) the organizational, (2) the process, and (3) the individual. These three levels of performance analysis can be compared to the described three organizational levels.

Performance Needs: (1) goals, (2) design, and (3) management.

The three performance levels plus the three performance needs crisscross one another in a grid pattern that would create nine relating variables. This grid-looking matrix offers the high-performance coach the ability to conduct the analysis process systematically and structured to assess the human performance results in dynamic organizational settings (Rothwell et al. 2018).

Gilbert's Three Stages of Analysis

In the human performance industry, Thomas Gilbert is much respected and considered one of the key founders of these fields. In his groundbreaking textbook in 1978, *Human Competence: Engineering Worthy Performance*, he presented several numbers of models, methods, tools, and concepts about human performance improvement, which to his credit, are still used and practiced by HPI and HPE practitioners (2018). This performance analysis model is made up of a matrix analytical framework that follows a three-stage process:

Stage 1: Accomplishment Models: This is the beginning stage of the performance analysis process, by attempting to establish a model for exemplary performance by focusing on a strengths-based or appreciative method that concentrates on possibilities and opportunities. The model of exemplary performance starts by distinguishing the key and best performance results, accomplished goals, or delivery of outcomes among top performers at the individual, team/group, and organization levels (2018).

Stage 2: Measures of Deficiency: Given that the focus is on establishing the current level of the individual, team/group, or organization performance, it is vital to understand and measure the deficiency in performance levels. "Whereas the desired level of performance focused on what should be happening, the current level concentrates on what is happening" (49). When the data about the performance level is collected, it can then be compared to the desired performance level established at stage 1, which would help the analyst to recognize the gap and discrepancies between current and desired human performance levels, as Gilbert called "causal analysis" (2018).

Stage 3: Methods of Improvement: This stage is about proposing models and methods to solve how close the discrepancy gap between current and desired human performance in individual, team/group, and organization levels is needed. This stage is parallel to selecting and conducting a change intervention (2018).

Many intervention models and methods are available for high-performance coaches and managers-as-coaches as a potential solution (see Appendix A).

Gilbert's Performance Matrix

This performance matrix structure combines the three stages of analysis (as has been mentioned as an individual, team/group, and organization) with these three levels of: (1) policies, (2) strategies, and (3) tactics. The result of combining these elements by creating a performance matrix is a comprehensive approach for analyzing human performance issues and determining possible resolutions (2018). As Rothwell et al. (2018) pointed out "[t]he performance matrix expands on the three stages of analysis by introducing three vantage points represented by the three levels. With each level, the matrix is meant to be worked from left to right" (Gilbert 1982, 50).

First Stage: As we have mentioned on stage 1 of "Gilbert's Three Stages of Analysis," an accomplishment model is formed that defines and expresses the desired performance (2018).

Second Stage: The actual and present time performance results are recognized, categorized, and compared with the desired performance (First Stage) to formulate the discrepancies or gaps in performance. It is crucial to detect the causes of the discrepancy or gap by using root cause analysis. Further along in this chapter, we will introduce tools and strategies for the root cause analysis (2018).

Third Stage: At this final stage, in a matrix table, on the far right-hand column, list probable means of performance improvement based on the process of discovered root causes of the performance issues (2018).

Gilbert's performance matrix can be guiding assistance for a performance analyst's diagnostic efforts. "It can thus help to surface and isolate areas in which problems or opportunities exist at each level. Another value is that it points toward potential solutions based on the level of analysis and the problem situation" (Rothwell et al. 2018, 50).

Gilbert's Behavior Engineering Model

The Behavior Engineering Model or BEM for short is another performance analysis model, created by Thomas Gilbert (1978) as another comprehensive model for human performance perspective, analysis, and diagnosis. The BEM comprises two dimensions:

(1) **Environmental Level,** where the emphasis is on the evidence and data at the environmental level.
(2) **Individual Performer Level**, where troubleshooting procedure commencing at the work environment level and then shifting attention (2018).

The BEM design is on the basis which presumes that most individuals are generally capable and wanting to do their jobs and related tasks, or at least they are after they are going through their initiations and job-related training. This theory moves the analysis focus to characteristics of the work environment that potentially are barriers to high performance. Sometimes, this approach is facing resistance from some supervisors or managers, given that usually they are the ones causing these barriers. However, the main focus is on not assigning blame or pointing fingers at individuals, but examining variables in positive or negative influences on both: (1) the work environment and at (2) the individual performer level impacting the total performance (Rothwell et al. 2018; Gilbert 2013). Gathering data in these two levels assist the high-performance coach in better understanding the core issues based on reality versus just perceptions and the blaming game. Rothwell et al. (2018) mentioned, "[a] large number of performance problems relate to lack of information. Some believe that up to 80 percent of performance problems can be traced to this cause" (51).

Mager and Pipe's Model

One of the analysis models that is more situation specific (compared with comprehensive framework models) is the troubleshooting model invented by Robert Mager and Peter Pipe (1997) that is portrayed in their book *Analyzing Performance Problems* (2018). This analysis model resonates with managers because they learn the easy operation and application of the model in situations with which they are dealing. The Mager and Pipe's model is regulated around designing a flowchart with some alternatives to the problems, applying decision points, and looking at branches of the issue to get to the root cause of the problem (2018). This model of the analysis process includes two stages:

First Stage: The analysis process starts with recognizing a particular problem by applying one of the comprehensive analysis models mentioned in this segment. It will be ideal if the problem could be explained with measurable observation and the possibility of performance-based provisions concerning an employee, a customer, an operation process, or management. If possible, illustrate the problem as a description of a discrepancy or a gap between the desired performance and actual present performance (2018).

Second Stage: After defining the problem precisely, either the analyst or managers who participated in the analysis effort have to answer specific questions about the portrayed problem. The first question after discovering the discrepancy is to determine the importance of the problem. The answer to these questions requires collecting inputs from senior management, clients, or key stakeholders to either invest time, capital, or resources to resolve the problem or ignore it for the time being (2018).

Where to Collect the Needed Data?

Similar to other analysis and diagnosis processes, the high-performance and human performance is also data driven, and because of that, there is a need to discuss where the data are collected and what were the sources of the data (Robinson and Robinson 2008). The focus of data gathering for analysis on human performance is mostly on two methods:

(1) **Quantitative data,** or numeric information relating to performance, that is measuring productivity, cost, quality, deadlines, profitability, etc.
(2) **Qualitative data**, or nonnumeric information that exist, such as management and employees' ideas of what the desired situation should be, the current issues, or what they perceive as the best resolution for the current issues. Table 7.5 depicts several potential sources of data among (1) human-related sources and (2) nonhuman-related sources:

Table 7.5   Potential Source of Data for High-Performance Coach, Manager-as-Coach, and Analysts.

Potential Source of Gathering Data	
Human-Related Sources	**Nonhuman-Related Sources**
Employees	HR historical documents
Supervisors	Exit interviews
Managers	Work records
Executives	Help desk logs
Clients	Firing reports
Customers	Absentee reports
Vendors/suppliers	Performance evaluations
Suppliers	Production logs
High performers	Sales logs
Low performers	Safety records
Previous consultants	Survey data
Subject experts	Benchmarking results
Key stakeholders	Quality control reports
Investors	Industry-related articles
Inspectors	Job descriptions
Previous trainers	T & D records

Source: Copyright 2021 by William J. Rothwell.

Needs Assessment versus Performance Gap Analysis

Our commitment is to not only coach our high performance and manager-as-coach readers but also educate these professionals. Many OD practitioners and HPI and HPE professionals have a parallel perspective of similarity between performance gap analysis and needs assessment. Several similarities can be found between needs assessment and performance gap analysis that are used without a complete understanding of those differences. For this reason, we thought to briefly explain the difference between the two approaches.

During the process of needs assessment, individuals', teams', or an organization's needs are regularly regarded as some gaps in their results or accomplishments and consequences of their actions. Needs assessment is defined as "a very valuable tool for identifying where you are ('the current results and consequences') and where you should be ('the desired results and consequences')" (Kaufman, Rojas, and Mayer 1993, 4).

The performance gap is a discrepancy between what is happening and what should be happening or expected to happen. A performance gap can also be considered a disparity between the way things are at present and how they are required, desired, planned, or anticipated to be (Rothwell 2015b) done by individuals, teams, or organizations. See Figure 7.4 for the key elements of a performance gap analysis and the relationship between these interconnected elements of analyzing a performance gap.

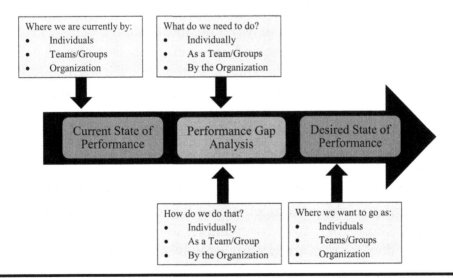

Figure 7.4 Key Elements of Performance Gap Analysis.

Source: Copyright 2021 by Behnam Bakhshandeh.

According to Kaufman et al. (1993), there are two key differences between needs assessment and performance gap analysis:

(1) Needs assessment primarily focuses on individuals and teams: (a) knowledge, skills, and abilities (KSAs) and (b) their mindset and attitude, while a performance gap analysis recognizes any discrepancy or proficiency influencing human performance.
(2) Needs assessment inclines to focus on past and present activities and behaviors while performance gap analysis also considers the future.

Kaufman (2006) viewed performance gaps analysis as opportunities for performance improvement that provides the potential chance to:

(1) improve individuals', teams', and organization's current performance state when it does not match with the desired performance measurements.
(2) enhance or strengthen the current performance state when it is equivalent or surpasses the needed performance measurements by designing and implementing innovations.

People and Systems

Regardless of their size, operation dimensions, or industries, all organizations and businesses are formed on the two fundamental components: (1) people (personal, workers, managers, customers, inspectors, suppliers, contractors, advisors, consultants) and (2) systems (policies, structure, procedures, safety, quality control, marketing, input, output, environment). These two key elements control the business operation and directly influence the organization's well-being. For any organization to achieve their goal, they need to pay equal attention to both components' effectiveness and performance (Cardy and Leonard 2011). "If either component is overlooked for too long, inefficiencies occur. Companies often attempt to overemphasize one lever to compensate for the lack of attention to the other" (Cardy and Leonard 2011, 104). For example, some managers might try to overcome inadequate performance triggered by some sort of problems and unworkability in the system by directing employees to work harder or longer.

Every organization faces some sort of people or system performance issues or challenges to overcome, while every individual or team in that organization must provide sets of skills and competencies to fulfill their job performance requirement to close the gaps (Sharma and Sharma 2019). However, a performance analysis professional, high-performance coach, or manager-as-coach must analyze and diagnose the cause (people or systems) before presenting and implementing a meaningful change. As we mentioned and covered in Chapter 6, most probably, performance gaps are not the actual problem but just a set of symptoms (see Chapter 6, Figure 6.6).

A high-performance coach or manager-as-coach needs to conduct a detailed and relevant action planning, evaluation, analysis, and diagnosis of the actual problems (what is happening) and compare it to the desired outcome (what should be happening) to resolve the performance and productivity issues and get the individuals, teams, and organization back on the sufficient and planned track (Sharma and Sharma 2019).

It is good to apply various data sources besides job performance standards and KPIs to cross-validate the performance problems findings. Some of such additional evaluations and assessments could be leadership effectiveness assessments, employee behavioral assessments, and managers' interpersonal assessments.

Identifying Potential Sources of Performance Gaps

Accurately and properly recognizing individuals, teams, and organization's performance gaps and their potential sources are vital for correcting such gaps. At this point, we are looking at some common reasons for the performance gap among workforces as individuals, teams, groups, and organizations and how a manager-as-coach can overcome these challenges. An organization leader and a high-performance coach who are conducting work as a manager-as-coach must consider the organization's required job

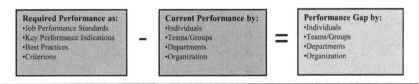

Figure 7.5   Performance Gap According to the Required Performance.

Source: Copyright 2021 by Behnam Bakhshandeh.

performance standards, key performance indicators (KPIs), or best practices and compare these determined requirements and standards to the current and actual performance of the individuals, teams, and departments in their role and responsibilities.

Performance Gap Assessor's Needed Abilities and Core Competencies

Chapter 2 distinguished performance coaches' needed competencies, skills, and abilities to conduct effective performance coaching for individuals and teams. In this segment of Chapter 7, we touch on the needed abilities and competencies for a high-performance coach conducting a gap assessment. To accomplish this intention, we separate the two elements and distinguish them independently as (1) abilities (see Table 7.6) and (2) core competencies (see Table 7.7).

We begin with the first element, the needed abilities for a performance gap assessor (Table 7.6):

Table 7.6 Needed Abilities for a High-Performance Gap Analyst for Comparing "What Is Happening" and "What Should Be Happening."

Needed Abilities for a High-Performance Gap Analyst for Comparing "What is the issue at hand" and "What should be happening."		
#	*Abilities for Comparison in:*	*Descriptions and Activities*
1	Organization's interactions with the external environment	*Issues with meet expectations of:* ■ Customers/Clients ■ Third-party contractors ■ Suppliers/Distributors ■ Inspectors/Governmental agencies ■ Investors ■ Other stakeholders
2	Organization's internal operations	*Issues with elements of internal operations:* ■ Organization structure ■ HR policies/laws (local, state, and federal) ■ General internal policies ■ Leadership structure ■ Cross functioning departments ■ Teams'/Groups' inner relationships

#	Abilities for Comparison in:	Descriptions and Activities
	Needed Abilities for a High-Performance Gap Analyst for Comparing "What is the issue at hand" and "What should be happening."	
3	Work processing	*Issues with the work operations:* ■ Requirements/Standards ■ Procedures/Processes ■ Material/Supplies ■ Inputs/Outputs ■ Safety ■ Labor laws (local, state, and federal)
4	Individual-level performance	*Issues with individuals' performances:* ■ Personal/Family ■ Professional/Experience ■ Managerial ■ Competencies/Skills ■ Educational ■ Performance history ■ Diversity/Inclusions
5	Team or group level performance	*Issues with team/group performance:* ■ Managerial difficulties ■ Policies affecting teams ■ A weak or unfair leadership ■ Inner teams' relevance ■ Appreciation and acknowledgment ■ Deadlines ■ Diversity/Inclusions
6	Tasks and job's related	*Issues related to individuals and their tasks and jobs:* ■ Suitable positions for individuals ■ Matching jobs and competencies ■ Work and job relevance to skills and abilities ■ Job relevancy to individual goals and motivation ■ Labor laws (local, state, and federal) ■ Americans with Disabilities Act ■ Matching with physical and psychological needs
7	Outcomes	*Issues with individuals' and teams' outcomes:* ■ Mindset, Attitude, and Behavior ■ Trainings/Developments ■ Motivations/Interests/Goals ■ Empowerment/Acknowledgment ■ Promotions/Demotions

Source: Adapted from Rothwell (2015a).

And now we look at the second part, the core competencies for a performance gap assessor (Table 7.7).

Table 7.7   Needed Core Competencies for a High-Performance Gap Analyst for Comparing "What Is Happening" and 'What Should Be Happening."

Needed Core Competencies for a High-Performance Gap Analyst for Comparing "What Is the Issue at Hand" and "What Should Be Happening."		
#	Core Competencies	Descriptions and Activities
1	Emotional intelligence	Be aware of one's self-awareness, self-discipline, self-management, and managing relationships.
2	Interpersonal skills	Working closely with others to accomplish common goals and objectives.
3	Leadership skills	Knowledge of leading teams and groups, inspiring them, and positively influencing performance.
4	Industry knowledge	Understanding of industry's culture, trends, and strategies.
5	Technical knowledge	Understanding and working with past and present technology and knowledge of using support systems as needed.
6	Systems understanding	Understanding of the inner relationship between an organization's systems (input, output, subsystems) and relevancy to the performance.
7	Problem-solving skills	Identifying performance gaps and assist individuals and teams in coming up with resolutions to their performance issues.
8	Business understanding	Being aware of the inner functioning of running a business and its fundamental process of producing the results.
9	Organization's knowledge	Being aware of organizations' fundamentals and dynamics, such as structures, social, political, and economics.
10	Performance awareness	Differentiating between activities and results and distinguishing between emotions and actions.
11	Analysis understanding	Knowledge of conducting human performance analysis and understanding of its process and functionality.
12	Diagnosis knowledge	Knowledge of conducting human performance diagnosis and understanding of its process and functionality.
13	Intervention knowledge	Knowledge of performance improvement and planning interventions to implement changes during performance.

	Needed Core Competencies for a High-Performance Gap Analyst for Comparing "What Is the Issue at Hand" and "What Should Be Happening."	
#	*Core Competencies*	*Descriptions and Activities*
14	Communication skills	Understanding elements of effective communication and active listening and how to establish an effective communication channel.
15	Negotiation skills	Understanding of negotiating with workers in teams/ groups, management, vendors, suppliers, and external agencies.
16	Advocacy skills	Establishing ownership in workers' interests and demonstrating support for necessary changes for increasing performance.
17	Coping skills	Understanding how to deal with stress caused by confusion and ambiguity.
18	Visionary view	Looking behind the obvious and keep envisioning possibilities of accomplishment and high performance for everyone involved.
19	Consulting skills	Understanding what the stakeholders need and want to see and showing them what would be possible by implementing well-designed changes to increase performance levels.
20	Coaching and mentoring skills	Demonstrating coaching and mentoring skills and guiding individuals and teams to higher performance and easier productions.
21	Project management knowledge	Understanding planning, hiring, budgeting, organizing, communicating, scheduling, resourcing, and completing a project.
22	Diversity and inclusion	Being aware of diversity and inclusion on the teams and groups and their potentials.
23	HR knowledge	Knowledge of human resources to support individuals and teams in recognizing proper policies and approaches to human performance.
24	HRD knowledge	Knowledge of human resources development for designing and implementing training to influence performance changes.

Source: Adapted from Bakhshandeh (2021), Rothwell et al. (2018), Rothwell, Henry, and Sredl (2000b).

Conducting a Performance Feedback and Discussion Session

After performance assessment and comparison between what is happening or what is the problem at hand and what should be happening, the high-performance coach or manager-as-coach should conduct a performance feedback session with individuals or teams who are not meeting the organization's job performance standards or their established KPIs.

This conversation is critical to improving individuals' and teams' performance. Usually, there is a discussion about how performance coaches carry out the performance gap analysis, what kind of job performance standard they have used to compare the performances, and what were the matrices they considered in such comparison. In summary, how they came with measuring individuals' and teams' performance. As we have mentioned at the beginning of this chapter, different industries use different categories and related metrics to measure their employees' performance gap. For this reason, please review Table 7.2 to select the metrics related to your own industries and what you think are useful metrics for your employees' performances.

It is worth mentioning that the imperial key to a successful and efficient feedback session is the degree of the interviewees' trust, respect, and comfortableness with the coaches or managers. They have to make sure the interviewees are comfortable with them and the process so that they can reveal their issues with their work or process of their job and not hide anything because they are afraid of retaliation.

In today's coaching, management, and the business world, various feedback or performance review models can be found. Coaches can use any model of their choice as long as they have a track record of such model's success and effectiveness. Or they can use what we have offered in this book and its chapters, or they may want to design and develop their performance feedback and discussion sessions based on what they know about the organization and its teams' performance.

One of the early approaches to designing feedback is to contemplate whether the present performance gap has something to do with the organization and its structure or systems that are causing systematic issues before jumping to the conclusion that issues arise because of individuals and teams, especially if there are several complaints from individuals or teams about the same issue throughout the organization (Lees 1996).

During the following segments, we provide some very useful information (listed here) for high-performance coaches and managers-as-coaches to use during the execution of feedback sessions and discussion with their individual employees and teams. Consider the following segments as a proven tool for conducting conversations, discussions, and feedback with your employees, especially during a performance gap discussion.

- Suggestions for speaking to employees about their inadequate performance
- Understanding how to establish rapport
- Elements to consider during design and planning of feedback session
- Questions for yourself as manager-as-coach and interviewer
- General questions for manager-as-coach to ask an interviewee
- Some tips for conducting an effective performance feedback session
- A performance gap analysis tracking sheet

Preparation and Planning for the Feedback and Discussion Session

For designing, planning, and preparing an effective performance feedback session, a high-performance coach or manager-as-coach needs to understand, has competencies and skills on the following elements of design, and prepare for conducting a feedback and discussion session.

Suggestions for Speaking to Employees About Their Inadequate Performance

The following elements are useful tips and suggestions for when a high-performance coach or manager-as-coach faces uncomfortable conversations with employees about their poor performance.

- **Don't postpone the conversation.** Many people postpone uncomfortable confrontations, especially with their employees. Delaying conversations only gives the situation more space to grow out of control potentially.

■ **Re-establish rapport.** Establishing rapport is vital to having an effective conversation about sensitive topics such as poor performance—review elements of establishing rapport in Chapter 4.

■ **Record the meeting in writing.** Provide the employees in question with their performance appraisals. Give them a chance to review it. Write a note to create a meeting minute for the HR department and employment records.

■ **Explain expectations.** Make sure to clarify and explain the issue you are pointing at and have a conversation about it. Always articulate your expectations as you are moving forward in the production or performance conversation. In addition, make sure you have set specific objectives for the conversation and what you want to talk about.

■ **Don't focus on the intent.** Do not emphasize what the employees have done wrong. Their intent is mostly irrelevant; the main problem is their action or dissection because there is no proof of their intent.

■ **Stay away from casual chatter.** Starting an uncomfortable conversation about someone's poor performance with casual chatter is comprehensible, but it will be problematic because it might be considered disrespectful. Instead, treat people respectfully but avoid small talk to put off the actual issue and the main topic.

■ **Avoid discussion about "why."** Conversations about why someone has a poor performance might lead to personal or confidential issues such as employees' physical or emotional conditions. Stay on evidence about the lack of performance related to relevant performance metrics. In the case when an employee references some mental disorder, disability, or faith principles, you must refer the conversation to the HR department for an interactive dialogue.

■ **Present performance examples.** Make sure you support the case by offering the employee examples of their poor performance and specific behaviors and attitudes regarding their performance or productivity that meet the objectives of the conversation.

■ **Make no excuses.** No organization, managers, or employees are perfect in personality or performance. However, avoid making excuses or justifying negative behaviors and poor performance by watering down-ing their negative and poor performance by something like "It's perhaps just as much the company to blame as it is yours." Don't just take responsibility to make the employee feel better unless you are responsible for some or all the performance issues as a manager.

■ **Be careful of bias.** Before conducting any uncomfortable conversation, managers need to ensure they don't have any bias. Even when the organization has a valid and legal cause for their complaint about an employee's performance, sometimes people use some words that may well suggest discrimination. Managers need to be careful about the choice of the words they use in these types of conversations.

■ **Use active listening.** Provide a safe space for employees to have an opportunity to talk about their thoughts and what they want to say without interruptions or expressed judgments. In some cases, the employees have a valid point and are able to provide indications as to why they are underperforming. This attempt could be very well a road map for establishing effective performance improvement.

■ **Avoid generalization and absolute words.** Avoid comments like "always," "never," "ever," "all the time" and any other the absolute words. In difficult and unpleasant discussions, it's much more effective to use words like, "almost always" or "almost never."

(Wilson 2020; Whitmore 2017; Rummler 2007;
Bakhshandeh 2004)

Understanding How to Establish Rapport

In Chapter 4, "Building Rapport," we comprehensively discussed and reviewed how to establish rapport with employees and coworkers. We highly recommend reviewing that chapter and the following figures and tables to prepare as the interviewer. The role of the coach and interviewer is critical to the success of the performance feedback session:

■ Figure 4.3: "The Fundamental State of Being and Competencies for Establishing Relatedness and Rapport."
■ Table 4.1: Rate yourself using "Fundamental State of Being and Competencies for Establishing Relatedness and Rapport."
■ Table 4.2: "Powerfully Setting Up the Interview Process for Uncovering the Reality of Relationships."
■ Table 4.3: "The Questions for The Process for Uncovering Reality of Relationships."

Elements to Consider during Design and Planning of Feedback Session

In this segment, we look at a set of questions coaches can ask themselves to design and plan a practical and effective performance feedback session and discussion:

(1) Do you have an appropriate environment for conducting this feedback session?
(2) Have you established the privacy and confidentiality for this feedback session?
(3) Have you considered enough advanced time for the interviewees to prepare for their feedback sessions?
(4) Are the organization's job performance standards and KPIs completely and publicly communicated?
(5) Have you selected a set of key subjects to give feedback or discuss?
(6) Is the interviewee working for you or directly reporting to you?
(7) Have you reviewed the interviewees' personnel file and employment history?
(8) Have you talked to the HR manager or their direct manager/supervisor about the interviewees' performance?
(9) What is the evidence for their job performance?
(10) Was there any incident linked to the interviewees' performance or behavior?
(11) What is the interviewees' relationship with their teammates?
(12) What is the interviewees' relationship with their manager/supervisor?
(13) What are they doing well?
(14) What are their weaknesses and shortcomings?
(15) Were there any follow-up notes or action plans from their last performance feedback session?
(16) Do you have any history with the interviewees? Good or bad?
(17) Are you prepared to handle disagreements and arguments?
(18) Are you prepared for potential emotional outbursts?
(19) Have you evaluated your own skills, competencies, effectiveness, and performance as an interviewer?
(20) Do you have any bias or harsh opinions about the interviewee?

(Rothwell et al. 2018; Bakhshandeh 2013; Rothwell, Henry, and Sredl 2000b; Lees 1996)

Questions that Are Making a Difference

In this segment, we look at a set of questions that makes the interviewer's job easier, makes the interviewee comfortable and at ease, and ultimately assists the process to be more meaningful and relevant. These questions are designed (1) for the interviewer to be more prepared and (2) for the interviewer to ask the interviewee.

Questions for Yourself as Manager-as-Coach and Interviewer

Another element of preparing for a performance feedback session is asking what a manager-as-coach acting as the interviewer should ask and answer them with utmost honesty and authenticity.

(1) What else do I need to do or to have for effective preparation for this interview?

(2) Where are the interviewees' departmental goals?

(3) What are resources can I provide for the interviewees?

(4) Am I ready to communicate my top priorities about this feedback with the interviewees?

(5) Am I aware of the organization's set performance standards or KPIs?

(6) Do I have some standards for performance success or failure?

(7) Am I aware of available training and development programs for our employees?

(8) Do the interviewees know how to rely on me as their supervisor's support?

(9) Do my management and supervision methods and style support the interviewer?

(10) What could I have done to support the interviewees in their performance?

(11) Have I placed the interviewees at the right/fit job or work?

(12) Have I expressed enough gratitude and appreciation for my team?

(13) Have I expressed empowering and encouraging words to my team?

(14) Do I use enough incentive and reward systems for my team?

(15) Have I noticed any trouble signs about the interviewees or other team members?"

(16) Am I looking for what is not working or what is great about these interviewees?

(17) Am I aware of essential things to track in my team's job performance?

(18) Is senior management aware of what and how my team is doing?

(19) Am I open to my team's suggestions on the team's performance or improvement?

(20) What are the top three challenges I am facing about this performance feedback session?

(Lee 2021; Rothwell et al. 2018; Bakhshandeh 2013;
Rothwell, Henry, and Sredl 2000b; Lees 1996)

After completing the planning and preparing, the coaches should make arrangements to interview the individuals or the teams. It would help if they communicated the session's overview purpose, the main factors of the discussion, and what they were planning to cover during the feedback session. Make sure they have enough time to prepare for the session.

General Questions for Manager-as-Coach to Ask Interviewee

Besides the obvious questions about one's performance and what is in their way to increase their performance or meet their job performance standards and KPIs, some general questions would assist the interviewees in expressing their emotions and perspectives of their work, performance, and employment in organizations or with their team. Sometimes the interview does not know what else to ask! This question supports the manager-as-coach conducting this feedback session to dig deeper and be effective. It is vital to remember this; establishing rapport with the other person is the key to your success in conducting meaningful and effective performance feedback and discussion sessions.

The following represent some of such questions:

(1) What excites you about your job and your team the most?

(2) What else should we be considering about our team's goal?

(3) Is there anything on your mind about your work and your team that might be bothering you?

(4) Is there anything, in particular, you want to discuss today?

(5) From your point of view, what are our team's strengths and weaknesses?

(6) What do you think are the sources of these strengths and weaknesses?

(7) What are the top three challenges in your job?

(8) What challenges are you facing in your responsibilities?

(9) What is your evidence regarding things that are doing well or failing?

(10) From your perspective, what can we do to perform better as a team?

(11) What are the top three KPIs our team should be tracking?
(12) Without withholding, what are my expectations about working or not working in our team's performance?
(13) What new skills have you learned lately?
(14) Do you have ideas that will support our team to meet our goals?
(15) Do you need any additional resources to meet your performance?
(16) What would you change one thing about team processes?
(17) What are the elements of your job performance you are so proud of?
(18) From your point of view, what is holding back our team to achieve all of its goals?
(19) Do you think you are doing your very best at your job/work?
(20) What would be in your way of performing at your best at your job/work?
         (Lee 2021; Rothwell et al. 2018; Bakhshandeh 2013; Lees 1996)

Some Tips for Conducting an Effective Performance Feedback Session

The following is a list of the activity or focuses that would allow for much more effective and meaningful performance feedback and discussion session.

(1) Make sure to conduct the feedback and discussion session in a private environment to ensure the interviewee's comfort.
(2) Try to avoid all potential distractions or interruptions.
(3) Keep yourself on your feedback design and prepared plan.
(4) Encourage and promote an open two-way discussion by engaging the interviewee.
(5) Keep your attention on the issue of performance, not on the performer, and stay objective.
(6) During or after the feedback and discussion session, request interviewees to share their suggestions for the team performance improvement.
(7) If suitable, arrange for the follow-up interview for the possibility of developing a learning and training agreement.
(8) Ensure that the interviewees know there is nothing wrong with their performance; there are only opportunities for improvement.
(9) By the end of the performance feedback and discussion session, write a summary report on the feedback, its findings, and planned actions.
(10) Conduct a self-rating evaluation of your effectiveness and potential improvements.

                    (Lee 2021; Wilson 2020; Rothwell et al. 2018;
              Bakhshandeh 2013; Rothwell & Sredl 2000a; Lees 1996)

Business Case Example

As you might remember in the last business example in Chapter 6, we explored how to discover what should be happening. In this chapter, we are using a business example to display how to find the gap between what is happening and what should be happening and how to measure it.

For this example, we continue to use the MBD again (see more details about this organization in Chapters 4, 5, and 6 business examples).

To ensure the management team understands the progress of performance gap measuring and its relevancy to the actual job performance, we asked the MBD's senior and governing managers, middle managers, and supervisors to conduct a self-rating process (see Table 7.8) of Evaluating Organization and Managers Performance Measurement Progress. This process of self-rating has four primary purposes:

(1) For the organization to understand the degree of implementing actual performance gap processes.
(2) For managers to understand their level of clarity and performing measuring the job performance process.
(3) For managers to come with an action plan to increase the understanding and implementation of current and meaningful job performance measurements.
(4) For managers to understand the performance gap metrics and their relevancy to their profession and industry.

During this process, we had a set of questions and inquiries about (Table 7.8):

A. critical organization criteria
B. job performance standards
C. best practices
D. key performance indicators
E. performance Metrics
F. performance feedback

We recommended reevaluating these elements and conducting the manager's self-evaluation process annually or semiannually.

Table 7.8 Evaluating Organization's and Manager's Performance Measurement Progress.

Date:		**Participant:**					**Team:**	
Quarter:		**Management Position:**					**Department:**	

Rating Scale: *1= Poor, 2= Marginal, 3= Acceptable, 4= Good, 5= Excellent*

#		Categories and Elements	Rating					What is missing?Needed Corrective Actions
			1	2	3	4	5	
		A. Critical Organization Criteria						
1	1	Establishing critical criteria by the organization.						
2	2	A clear understanding of the organization's key criteria.						
3	3	The critical criteria have been announced and communicated to employees.						
4	4	Criteria priorities have been examined and established.						
		B. Job Performance Standards						
5	1	There are established and efficient job performance standards.						
6	2	Supervisors are trained and understand the job performance standards.						
7	3	Individuals and teams are trained on their expected job performance standards.						

(Continued)

Table 7.8 (Continued)

Rating Scale: *1= Poor, 2= Marginal, 3= Acceptable, 4= Good, 5= Excellent*

8	4	The measures for expected job performance standards are designed and established.				
9	5	There are HR policies linked to the failure or success of job performance standards.				
C. The Best Practices						
10	1	There are studies and reviews of the industry's best practices by senior managers.				
11	2	There are plans for implementing selected best practices in the organization.				
12	3	There is a systematic review and measurement of best practices implementation and effectiveness.				
D. Key Performance Indicators (KPI)						
13	1	Individuals and teams are trained and understand their relevant KPIs.				
14	2	KPIs are reviewed and measured by experienced managers or high performers.				
15	3	KPIs are designed and selected based on proven methodologies in the industry.				
16	4	Current KPIs are vetted based on workability or unworkability of past and present measures.				
17	5	There are HR policies linked to the failure or success of KPIs by individuals and teams.				

		E. Performance Metrics					
18	1	There is a set of established industry-related performance metrics.					
19	2	Managers, supervisors, and foremen are aware and trained on their employees' performance metrics.					
20	3	There are annual performance metrics reviews and modifications based on KPIs and other industry-related criterion.					
21	4	There are established methods of measuring performance metrics.					
22	5	There is an approved level of acceptable performance based on related metrics.					
		F. Performance Feedbacks					
23	1	There is established performance feedback for individuals and teams' specialized performances by their supervisors.					
24	2	Performance reviews and feedbacks are empowering and strength based.					
25	3	There are plans for performance enhancement plans available based on the performance review and feedback report					
Total score for each rating							
Total of all above scores							
Final average score (above total scores divided by 25)							
Two actions for this quarter that would bring up my three lowest scores by at least one scale on the next self-rating:							
Action 1:							
Action 2:							

Source: Copyright 2021 by Behnam Bakhshandeh.

Meeting About Deciding on Set of Performance Metrics and Measurement

During an afternoon session using the same group of MBD managers and employee representatives who participated on finalizing the set of job performance standards, we went through a process of (1) selecting relevant performance metrics that were related to MBD's industry and what their teams were doing and (2) how management would measure individuals' and teams' performances and implement the needed correction.

Step 1

Given that the participant has established a rapport and background of relatedness, reestablishing rapport was relatively easy and done in a timely manner. With the use of some sharing about our experiences from the last gathering about setting up an agreed job performance standards and a fun ice breaker process, we were ready to roll the ball.

Step 2

We started with the process of finding differences between what is happening and what should be happening in (1) organizational environment, (2) where, and (3) what and who using Table 7.3. This process offers some basic questions and an opening inquiry into the differences between what is happening or what is the issue in hand and what should be happening. By posing these questions, performance coaches can gather information and then sort data as present positive, present negative, present neutral, future positive, future negative, or future neutral performance gaps (see Table 7.1). The team went through the following main inquiries for each of the categories using Table 7.3:

- What are the agreed-upon job performance standards, including KPIs and best practices?
- What is happening? What is the issue at hand?
- What are the evidence, results, and outcomes related to this issue?
- What should be happening?

Given that we had to go through the process and listen to each participant, their view of the category, their experience and their ideas of what should be happening, this process consumed most of the meeting time.

Step 3

Using nominal group technique (NGT) the team came up with their final assessment for the differences between what is happening and what should be happening. NGT can be used when teams or groups are creating alternate solutions for problem(s) using a quantitative (using numbers) process like the voting process (Rothwell 2000). For example, in Table 7.9, there are several performance gaps (comparisons between What is happening and What should be happening) within the four categories mentioned earlier identified by the MBD team, and now, a team needs to vote on which one has priority. The What should be happening would be voted on by those team members on a scale of 1 to 5 (one being the less priority to five the highest priority for each category) and totaled. The highest score was the selected What should be happening in each category to take on first by the team. The team can select as many results as they wish, whether it be the top two, three, or more. We will explain the NGT in Chapter 9 in a detailed fashion.

Table 7.9 is an example of using the process of NGT for the first category, the Organizational Environment:

As the final decision, the MBD team selected the top two what should be happening: (1) working on more employee engagement and (2) presenting and sharing the power of organizational values, vision statement, and mission statement as the backbone of MBD.

Table 7.9   Example of Result of Nominal Group Technique (NGT) Used on MBD Meeting.

Voting Members	Organizational Environment Performance Gaps What Should Be Happening?		
	Stronger View of Values, Vision, and Mission	More Employees' Engagement	More Leadership Training for Supervisor
John	3	4	4
Patty	2	3	3
Joan	3	4	2
Michael	3	5	3
David	2	5	2
Joseph	4	2	2
Susan	4	5	3
Total	**21**	**28**	**19**

Step 4

At this point, we get to the process of selection and finalizing MBD's job performance metrics and how to measure them, using Table 7.2. After some discussions and looking at the relevancy of the collection of performance metrics to the MBD industry (beauty industry) and the nature of MBD as a business (sales and customer retention and service), the team came to agreements for a series of performance metrics that would cover all the four categories of:

- work quality
- work quantity
- work efficiency
- organizational performance

The team agreed that managing the metrics measurement option should be done by direct junior managers or supervisors with supervision and review by their higher managers on a monthly and quarterly basis.

Step 5

At this point, the only thing left was to come with an idea of how to manage issues caused by performance gaps. As you can see in Table 7.10, the MBD team came with the idea of "Tracking gap analysis management and correction process." They decided to assign a manager or supervisor to a particular performance issue relevant to their team or department, selecting the deadline for resolving it, and using related job performance standards and performance metrics.

Key Factors to Remember

Let's review what lessons we learned from this chapter about what is the measurable gap and what would affect it:

- **Without analysis, it is just an opinion**

Suppose you do not conduct a performance analysis to discover a real issue, what is happening and what should be happening, and the root

Table 7.10 Tracking Gap Analysis Management and Correction Process.

	Tracking Gap Analysis Management and Correction Process	
1	*Project Name*	
2	*Project Manager*	
3	*Starting Date*	
4	*Performance gap Issue*	
5	*Individual or Team*	
6	*Group or Department*	
7	*Performance Category*	
8	*Manager or Supervisor*	
9	*Job Performance Standards*	
10	*Performance Metrics*	
11	*Current State*	
12	*Desired State*	
13	*Completion Due date*	
14	*Level of Priority*	
15	*Corrective Actions*	
16	*Potential Risks*	
17	*Completion State*	
18	*Feedback Provided*	
19	*Reviewed and Signed off by*	
20	*Notes*	

Source: Copyright 2021 by Behnam Bakhshandeh.

cause in an individual or team performance. There, you are only relying on your perception and opinion about that individual or a team, mostly based on your past personal experience or even your view of someone in a personal base (Bakhshandeh 2009). Conducting an analysis is removing guessing and opinion and leaving you with facts and the actual root cause of a problem (Colquitt et al. 2015).

■ Leave it up to professionals
– The high-performance coaches or managers-as-coaches need to have special skills and competencies for conducting analysis, measuring gaps, and assessing performance. Unfortunately, the reality of organizational situations is that not all managers are fit to be performance analysts or have the competencies to conduct a performance diagnosis.

■ **It is not real until the end**

– There are always some stories, interpretations, and perceptions about an individual or a team performance. As a high-performance coach or manager-as-coach, make sure to stay away from the influence of stories and perceptions. On the other hand, listening to stories and perceptions help to understand the organization's environment or team's culture. However, none of these stories and interpretations would impact the actual data gathering, analysis, diagnosis of performances, and the solutions for closing performance gaps.

■ **Analyze the performance based on the type of performance gaps**

– There is always a need for recognizing the relevant performance gap based on the time or level of the negative, positive, or neutral nature of the gap. This step allows the performance gap analysts to invest their time and efforts in proper gaps and to come with relevant corrections and implementation of the action plan.

Coaching and Developmental Questions for Managers

(1) How do you rate yourself from 0 to 10 (0 being the lowest and 10 being the highest) on your knowledge and understanding of Type of Performance Gaps? And what is your action plan to increase your overall rate?

(2) How do you rate yourself from 0 to 10 (0 being the lowest and 10 being the highest) on your knowledge and understanding of conducting a Performance Gap Analysis between what is happening and what should be happening? And what is your action plan to increase your overall rate?

(3) How do you rate yourself from 0 to 10 (0 being the lowest and 10 being the highest) on your knowledge and understanding of recognizing Sources of Performance Gaps? And what is your action plan to increase your overall rate?

(4) How do you rate yourself from 0 to 10 (0 being the lowest and 10 being the highest) on your knowledge and understanding of your Employee Performance Metrics? And what is your action plan to increase your overall rate?

(5) How do you rate yourself from 0 to 10 (0 being the lowest and 10 being the highest) on your knowledge and understanding of your Analysts'

Competencies, Skills and Abilities? And what is your action plan to increase your overall rate?

(6) How do you rate yourself from 0 to 10 (0 being the lowest and 10 being the highest) on your knowledge, skills, and abilities (KSA) to design, plan, and conduct a performance feedback session? And what is your action plan to increase your overall rate?

In the next chapter, we will go through the process of deciding the importance of those identified gaps. Which performance gaps should be handled first? Which gaps have more impact on production and need to be addressed for increasing human performance, budget, and time?

References

Bakhshandeh, Behnam. 2002. "Executive Coaching: For Those of You Who Have Arrived." Unpublished Workshop on Coaching Executives. San Diego, CA: Primeco Education, Inc.

Bakhshandeh, Behnam. 2004. "Effective Communication." *Audio CD Set and Workshop*. San Diego, CA: Primeco Education, Inc.

Bakhshandeh, Behnam. 2008. "Bravehearts; Leadership Development Training." Unpublished Training and Developmental Course on Coaching Executives and Managers. San Diego, CA: Primeco Education, Inc.

Bakhshandeh, Behnam. 2009. *Conspiracy for Greatness; Mastery on Love Within.* San Diego, CA: Primeco Education, Inc.

Bakhshandeh, Behnam. 2013. "Asking Effective Questions." Unpublished Training and Developmental Course on Coaching Executives and Managers. Carbondale, PA: Primeco Education, Inc.

Bakhshandeh, Behnam. 2021. "Perception of 21st Century 4Cs (Critical Thinking, Communication, Creativity & Collaboration) Skill Gap in Private-Sector Employers in Lackawanna County, NEPA." An Unpublished Dissertation in Workforce Education and Development. The Pennsylvania State University.

Camp, Robert C. 1989. *Benchmarking: The Search for Industry Best Practices That Lead to Superior Performance.* Milwaukee, WL: Quality Press.

Cardy, Robert L., and Brian Leonard. 2011. *Performance Management. Concepts, Skills and Exercises.* Armonk, NY: Me. E. Sharp. Inc.

Colquitt, Jason A., Jeffery A. LePine, and Michael J. Wesson. 2015. *Organizational Behavior: Improving Performance and Commitment in the Workplace*, 4th ed. New York, NY: McGraw-Hill Education.

Cummings, Thomas G., and Christopher G. Worley. 2015. *Organization Development & Change*, 10th ed. Stamford, CT: Cengage Learning.

Gilbert, Thomas F. 1978. *Human Competence: Engineering Worthy Performance.* New York, NY: McGraw-Hill.

Gilbert, Thomas F. 1982. "A Question of Performance Part I: The PROBE Model." *Training and Development Journal* 36, no. 9: 21–30.

Gilbert, Thomas F. 2013. *Human Competence: Engineering Worth? Performance*, tribute ed. San Francisco, CA: Pfeiffer.

Kaufman, Roger A. 2006. "Mega Planning and Thinking: Defining and Achieving Measurable Success." In *Handbook of Human Performance Technology*, 3rd ed., 138–153. San Francisco, CA: Pfeiffer.

Kaufman, Roger A., Alicia Mabel Rojas, and Hanna Mayer. 1993. *Needs Assessment: A User's Guide*. Educational Technology.

Lee, Christopher. 2021. *Performance Conversations*. Alexandria, VA: Society of Human Resources Management (SHRM).

Lees, Ian. 1996. *Managing Performance and Goal Achievement*. Sydney, Australia: McGraw-Hill.

"Merriam-Webster." 2021. *Analysis*. www.merriam-webster.com/dictionary/analysis.

"Oxford Language." 2021. *Analysis*. www.google.com/search?q=analysis+definition &oq=Analysis&aqs=chrome.1.69i57j35i39j0i433l3j0i20i263j0i433l4.1430j1j15&so urceid=chrome&ie=UTF-8.

Pearlstein, Richard B. 2012. "What I Think I Know about Performance Improvement." *Performance Improvement Quarterly* 25, no. 3: 3–6.

Robinson, Dana Gaines, and James C. Robinson. 2008. *Performance Consulting: A Practical Guild for HR and Learning Performance*, 2nd ed. San Francisco, CA: Berrett-Koehler.

Robinson, Dana Gaines, James C. Robinson, Jack J. Phillips, Patricia Pulliam Phillips, and Dick Handshaw. 2015. *Performance Consulting: A Strategic Process to Improve, Measure, and Sustain Organizational Results*. Oakland, CA: Berrett-Koehler Publishers.

Rothwell, William J. 2000. *ASTD Models for Human Performance Improvement: Roles, Competencies, and Outputs*, 2nd ed. Alexandria, VA: The American Society for Training and Development.

Rothwell, William J. 2013. *Performance Consulting: Applying Performance Improvement in Human Resource Development*. San Francisco, CA: John Wiley & Sons.

Rothwell, William J. 2015a. *Beyond Training & Development: Enhancing Human Performance Through a Measurable Focus on Business Impact*, 3rd ed. Amherst, MA: HRD Press, Inc.

Rothwell, William J. 2015b. *Organization Development Fundamentals: Managing Strategic Change*. Alexandria, WV: ATD Press.

Rothwell, William J., Carolyn K. Hohne, and Stephen B. King. 2012. *Human Performance Improvement*. New York, NY: Routledge.

Rothwell, William J., Carolyn K. Hohne, and Stephen B. King. 2018. *Human Performance Improvement: Building Practitioner Performance*, 3rd ed. New York, NY: Routledge.

Rothwell, William J., and Henry J. Sredl. 2000a. *The ASTD Reference Guide to Workplace Learning and Performance: Present and Future Roles*, 3rd ed., vol. I. Amherst, MA: HRD Press.

Rothwell, William J., and Henry J. Sredl. 2000b. *The ASTD Reference Guide to Workplace Learning and Performance: Present and Future Roles*, 3rd ed., vol. II. Amherst, MA: HRD Press.

Rothwell, William J., Jacqueline M. Stavros, and Roland L. Sullivan. 2016. *Practicing Organization Development: Leading Transformation and Change*, 4th ed. Hoboken, NJ: John Wiley & Sons, Inc.

Rummler, Geary A. 2007. *Serious Performance Consulting According to Rummler.* San Francisco, CA: John Wiley & Sons.

Rummler, Geary A., and Alan P. Brache. 2012. *Improving Performance: How to Manage the White Space on the Organization Chart.* San Francisco, CA: John Wiley & Sons.

Sharma, R. C., and Nipuna Sharma. 2019. *Human Resources Management; Theory and Practice*, 1st ed. Thousand Oaks, CA: Sage Publishing.

Spitzer, Dean R. 2007. *Transforming Performance Measurement.* New York, NY: AMACOM.

Van Vulpen, Eric. 2021. "AIHR Academy. 21 Employee Performance Metrics." www.aihr.com/blog/employee-performance-metrics/.

Weller, Joe. 2018. "Smartsheet Website. The Complete Guide to Gap Analysis." www.smartsheet.com/gap-analysis-method-examples.

Whitmore, John. 2017. *Coaching for Performance: The Principle and Practice of Coaching and Leadership*, 5th ed. Boston, MA: Nicholas Brealey Publishing.

Wilson, Carol. 2020. *Performance Coaching: A Complete Guide to Best-Practice Coaching and Training*, 3rd ed. New York, NY: KoganPage.

Chapter 8

Step 5: How Important Are the Gaps?

Behnam Bakhshandeh

After measuring the performance gap and recognizing the causes of gaps, it is time to decide the importance of those identified gaps. Which performance gaps should be handled first? Which gaps have more impact on production and need to be addressed for increasing human performance, budget, and time? The organization's management has to decide which gap to attack first, which gap has to be pushed back for a later engagement, and which gap may be ignored.

Chapter 8 focuses on how to clarify issues with present and future performance gaps and prioritize the importance of such gaps by looking at:

- How to measure the importance of gaps
- Key components, related elements, and descriptions of a project research
- Quantitative and qualitative measures of the importance of performance gap
- Organization's strategic objectives and performance measures' importance
- The balanced scorecard
- Critical success factors
- Brainstorming session
- Nominal group technique (NGT)
- Force field analysis (force field diagram)
- Important competencies of performance coaches

DOI: 10.4324/9781003155928-11

- Tools for managers to use for the process of identifying the importance of the gaps
- Key factors to remember from this chapter
- Coaching and developmental questions for managers

Measuring and Deciding on the Importance of Performance Gaps

As we have explained and defined through the last several chapters, the primary use of performance gap analysis is to transfer the **current** (what is happening) performance results to the **desired** (what should be happening) performance results and recoup the control and performance management by identifying those different elements influencing all performance elements with using the collected data.

However, there are two important spaces in this process: (1) the collected data by itself is not sufficient. To conduct a complete and useful performance gap and what gap is more important and must be addressed before others, one must research within the organization and identify the actual priorities and importance of each of the particular performance gaps. And (2) What performance gap is more important than the others depends on "who cares" and where this person "located and sat" on the organization chart.

What is important to different groups is the levels or silos on the organization chart. Ultimately, strategic plans are subjectively determined. What we mean is that importance can change, depending on where you sit on the organization chart. For example, what an organization's President, CEO, or senior management cares about or thinks as a prioritized performance gap is usually more about some items than others, such as salespeople or floor foremen.

Regardless of their positions in the organization's chart and their responsibility and accountability, the process of selecting the importance of performance gaps and which one is more important or prioritized is relatively the same. The difference in the process is that the chosen method and practices depend on the complexity of the matter to choose or the number of people involved. These decisions can be happening within a variety of ranges from top management to teams and groups.

In the following segment, we look at different ways as options to determine the importance of performance gaps and their priorities:

(1) project research. Using elements of project research to identify the importance of gaps

(2) quantitative and qualitative measures of the importance of performance gap

(3) organization's strategic objectives and performance measures' importance

(4) the balanced scorecard

(5) critical success factors

(6) brainstorming session

(7) nominal group technique

(8) force field analysis

It is important to mention that three of the aforementioned eight methods (Brainstorming, Nominal Group Technique, and Force Field Analysis) can be used not only for prioritizing performance gap importance but also for conducting a Root Cause Analysis which we will cover in the next chapter. Given that we have covered these three methods in this chapter, we will present the other methods that could be used for both approaches in Chapter 9 (performance gap importance and root cause analysis).

Using Elements of Project Research to Identify the Importance of Gaps

Research is a careful and thorough understanding and implementation of all elements of a study about a particular topic, phenomenon, or problem utilizing scientifically proven methods (Creswell and Creswell 2018).

This method might not be as usual or commonly used by industries, but it is very detailed and effective. Many people view research as something complex and abstract that needs many years of education and experience to conduct. That perception might be through conducting medical, psychological, scientific, or multidimensions research projects. However, suppose you know the basic elements of research and how to conduct one about something not as complex as any scientific topic. In that case, it is not that hard to conduct ones like any other project that has a beginning, a middle, and an end.

Table 8.1 displays a comprehensive view of the key components, related elements, and descriptions of project research. Clearly, this table could be much more educational, informative, and directional than a manager wants to go through for conducting a research project; therefore, after a high-performance coach understands the process of conducting a research project, he can only use the elements that are relevant to their topic of research. Using this table helps you understand what is needed to conduct a relevant research project to recognize the importance of performance gaps and

Table 8.1 Key Components, Related Elements, and Discretion of a Project Research.

Key Components, Related Elements, and Descriptions of a Project Research

Components	Explanations	Elements	Descriptions
Research Form	In general cases, research projects are conducted in three basic forms.	Descriptive	Primarily design is to describe what is going on or what occurs.
		Relational	Designed to look at the relationships among two or more variables.
		Causal	Designed to verify whether one or more variables cause or affect one or more outcomes.
Research Time	The time or cycle of time that research is being conducted.	Cross-sectional	Takes place at a single point.
		Longitudinal	Takes place over a long period.
		Repeated measures	Takes two or more occurrences of measurement.
		Time series	Many occurrences of measurement.
Levels of Measurement	The level of measurement is a cataloging label that designates the nature of data within the values of the variables.	Nominal	The lowest level in the hierarchy is used for variables measured in categories (male/female, or English/French).
		Ordinal	One level above on nominal scales because it contains more data than a nominal scale (level of education or work experience).
		Interval	It identifies the potential distances between each interval on the scale corresponding to the scale from low to high intervals.
		Ratio	Or scale level is the highest level of variables measurement, and the numbers used to represent variables are real numbers.

Nature of Relationship	The correspondence relationship between two variables.	Correlational	Variables that operate in a synchronized manner.
		Third variable problem	An undetected variable which accounts for a correlation among two variables.
Patterns of Relationships	Variables can be related to one another and correlational in a causal nature or may have different *relationships*.	None	There is no correlation between two variables when values on the variable are known.
		Positive	A correlation among two variables when high values for one variable are linked with high values on another variable and low values are linked with low values.
		Negative	A correlation among variables when high values for one variable are linked with low values on another variable.
		Curvilinear	When the shape of a correlation can be more complicated than the other three relationships.
Variables	Entities can take on various values like age that can be measured as a variable given that age has a variety of values for people at different times.	Quantitative	When variables are in numbers.
		Qualitative	When variables are not in form of numbers.
		Attribute	When variables are specific (generally sex or gender has two specific attributes: male and female).
Property of Variables	Defining properties of variables assists the researcher while assigning attributes to research variables.	Independent	Variables manipulated by the researcher (a program or a treatment).
		Dependent	Variables affected by the independent variable (an outcome).

(Continued)

Table 8.1 (Continued)

Components	Explanations	Elements	Descriptions
		Exhaustive	Variables' properties that arise when the researcher includes all possible answerable reactions.
		Mutually exclusive	Variables' properties that guarantee when the respondent could not appoint two attributes concurrently (it is impossible to claim to be male and female).
Types of Data	Generally, in any research, data and information are collected in two main forms.	Quantitative	Objects or subject's numerical representation. Any variable measured using numbers.
		Qualitative	Objects or subjects' nonnumerical representation. Any variables are not in a numerical form but are in text (photographs, sound bites, explaining feelings, and experience in text).
Hypothesis	A definite statement of research prediction that describes the outcome in solid terms (rather than theoretical), which the researcher anticipates happening.	Alternative	A definite declaration of a research's prophecy usually states what the researcher expects to happen.
		Null	The hypothesis illustrates a possible outcome besides the alternative hypothesis.
		One-tailed	A hypothesis that stipulates a direction (this program will improve the results).
		Two-tailed	A hypothesis that stipulates no direction (this program affects the results, but unclear negative or positive).
Research Quality	Quality of research strength, ethics, and stability. It also underlines the research's	Empirical	Research based on explicit and direct actual observations and reality-based measurements.

	professionalism, accuracy, and transparency.	Validity	How much a concept is accurately measured in research.
		Reliability	The degree that a specific research process generates consistent outcomes.
Research Structure	The main fundamental outlines of the research and its design.	Questions	The crucial issue is being questioned in the research. The research questions are typically couched in the language of theory.
		Theoretical	A blueprint or guideline for research. It is founded on the current and prevailing theories in a field of inquiry, which is connected to and reflects the research questions or hypothesis.
		Conceptual	A structure that the researcher is confident can describe the accepted development of explaining the phenomenon or issue to be researched.
		Operationalization	The action of converting a structure into its manifestation (translating a program into a real program).
Method of Reasoning	A distinction is regularly made between two wide-ranging techniques of reasoning approaches.	Deductive	Top-down reasoning operates from a relatively general conclusion to a relatively precise conclusion.
		Inductive	Bottom-up reasoning starts from precise observations and procedures and ends up as a general conclusion.

Source: Adapted from Bakhshandeh (2021); Creswell and Creswell (2018); O'Sullivan, Rassel, and Berner (2017); Grant and Osanloo (2016); Trochim and Donnelly (2008) and Camp (2001).

which ones have more priority than others. Further investigations and explorations through books and articles can provide additional information that may be needed to go forward with a research project.

Quantitative and Qualitative Measures of Importance of Performance Gap

Table 8.2 briefly represents elements of both quantitative and qualitative measures of elements that would directly affect the overall organization's performance gaps caused by individuals, teams, and departments. Quantitative measures the *hard* measures and qualitative measures the *soft* measures (Rothwell, Stavros, and Sullivan 2016). During the assessment of the importance of existing gaps, one should review these soft and hard measures for determining the impact of existing performance gaps on these measures and which one or ones need to be taken on first.

There is something we need to mention before we go through Table 8.2. As we covered this point at the beginning of this chapter, the importance of the measures, related elements, and relevant details all depend on who is looking at them, what are the positions, responsibilities, and accountability of those who are reviewing them and what type of measures (hard or soft)

Table 8.2   Quantitative and Qualitative Measures of Importance of Performance Gap.

Elements of Quantitative and Qualitative Measures That Affect the Organization's Performance Gaps Caused by Individuals, Teams, and Departments.		
Type of Measures	*Elements*	*Relevant Details*
Quantitative Measures (Hard Measures)	Output	■ Productivity ■ Products ■ Services ■ Profitability ■ Sales ■ Inventory ■ Task's completion ■ Shipping
	Quality	■ Product defect ■ Services rejection ■ Customer retention ■ Errors ■ Timeliness ■ Amount of rework ■ Waste and scrap ■ Recycling

Elements of Quantitative and Qualitative Measures That Affect the Organization's Performance Gaps Caused by Individuals, Teams, and Departments.		
Type of Measures	*Elements*	*Relevant Details*
	Costs	■ Budget ■ Operation cost ■ Fixed costs ■ Flexible costs ■ Cost of goods ■ Overhead ■ Cost reductions ■ Contracts
	Safety	■ Accidents ■ Inspection failures ■ Training records ■ Complaints
	Time	■ Workers' downtime ■ Equipment downtime ■ Overtime ■ Waste time ■ Supervisory time ■ Efficiency ■ Meetings ■ Training
	Marketing	■ Budget ■ Sources ■ Avenues ■ Platforms
	Human resources	■ Absentees ■ Turnovers ■ Incidents ■ Complaints ■ Promotions ■ Demotions
Qualitative measures (Soft Measures)	Skills	■ Decision-making ■ Problem-solving ■ Communication ■ Active listening ■ Conflict resolution ■ Intentionality and focus ■ Relationship building ■ Respectfulness
	Work habits	■ Tardiness ■ Absenteeism

Table 8.2   (Continued)

Type of Measures	Elements	Relevant Details
Elements of Quantitative and Qualitative Measures That Affect the Organization's Performance Gaps Caused by Individuals, Teams, and Departments.		
		■ Professionalism ■ Dependability ■ Accountability ■ Leadership qualities ■ Rules' violations ■ Time offs
	Work environment	■ Complaints ■ Grievances ■ Job satisfaction ■ Discrimination charges ■ Harassment charges ■ Turnovers ■ Litigations
	Attitudes and behavior	■ Harsh behaviors ■ Negative attitudes ■ Loyalty ■ Empowerment ■ Acknowledgments ■ Work refusals ■ Confidence ■ Disciplines
	Development	■ Promotions ■ Pay increases ■ Transfers ■ Training programs ■ Performance appraisals ■ Effectiveness
	Initiative	■ New ideas ■ Effective suggestions ■ Project completions ■ Presenting goals and objectives
	Policies	■ Reviewing policies ■ Updating policies ■ Safety policies ■ Diversity policies ■ Inclusion policies
	Procedures	■ Review procedures ■ Update procedures

Elements of Quantitative and Qualitative Measures That Affect the Organization's Performance Gaps Caused by Individuals, Teams, and Departments.		
Type of Measures	Elements	Relevant Details
		■ New approaches ■ New ideas

Source: Copyright 2021 by Behnam Bakhshandeh.

they are looking at. Basically, "what" is important to "whom" and "why." So, again, as a whole approach, all these elements and details are relevant to the productivity, performance, and bottom-line success and well-being of an organization, but between the elements of quantitative and qualitative measures, which one to emphasize, which one to use, all depends on who are conducting it and in which branch of that organization they belong. Having that on your mind, let's review Table 8.2.

Strategic Objectives and Performance Measures Importance

There is a correlation between the importance of the performance gaps' priority and the organization's objectives and intentions. Look at the relevancy between the organization's goals and objectives and what performance gap needs to be taken on first. And this relevancy should be linked to the organization's critical success factors (CSFs) (we will cover CSFs further in this chapter) and supported by the key performance indicators (KPIs) (please review what we have covered about KPIs in depth in Chapter 6) (see Figure 8.1). Finally, the need for corrective actions will arise as the selection of which performance gap needs to be handled immediately and which ones later.

For designing and implementing corrective actions, the areas of focus for each organization's strategic objectives need to be identified. Figure 8.2 displays

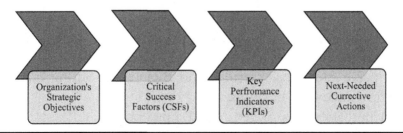

Figure 8.1   Relationship and Process of Strategic Objectives and Performance Measures for Successful Operation.

Source: Copyright 2021 by Behnam Bakhshandeh.

the process of establishing corrective actions related to the organization's strategic objectives, measures, and production targets.

Before we get deeper into this matter, we shall point at something that many consultants or senior managers are missing and that is how to engage employees in the process of selecting the importance of performance gaps and aligning them with this sensitive process so they can also be part of it and not just watching from the sideline. This is an important approach, and it is necessary to appeal to both employees' heads (the hard facts) and their hearts (considering their emotions and feelings).

Throughout this book, we paid attention to individuals' mindsets and their effects on their attitudes and behavior. We took on coaching high-performance coaches and managers-as-coaches to bring up employee engagement levels in their organizations to make sure they create a partnership with them in every step of the process. The following list represents chapters and the relevant topics, figures, and tables that cover the methods and processes that support high-performance coaches and manager-as-coaches to engage employees in understanding:

(1) facts in the matter of business operation, which are not only impacting the organization but also their own direct personal and professional lives and

(2) their heart and their emotions, which are important for individuals to enjoy their work and feel as though their thoughts and ideas matter to their managers and supervisors.

Given our commitment to developing professional high-performance coaches, this book is full of useful and relevant destinations, topics, and practical practices. Therefore, we highly recommend to our readers to use the following list of what is important (so far within the past seven chapters) to review for refreshing their experience for the purpose of engaging employees *Heads* and *Hearts* in establishing correction actions:

- ▪ Chapter 2:
  - What is Performance Conversation?
  - Table 2.1: Elements, Purpose and Benefits of Strong Framework for Performance Conversation.
  - Coaches' Strengths, Skills, and Competencies.

- ▪ Chapter 3:
  - Figure 3.1: Relationship between Mindset, Attitude, Behavior, and Individual and Team Performance.

- Figure 3.2: Coaching Mentality Produce Higher Performance and Increasing Productivity.
- Table 3.4: Leadership Qualities of Effective Manager-as-Coach Rating System.

■ Chapter 4:
  - Figure 4.2: Being, Doing, and Mindset Relevancy.
  - Figure 4.3: The Fundamental State of Being and Competencies for Establishing Relatedness and Rapport.
  - Table 4.1: Fundamental State of Being and Competencies for Establishing Relatedness and Rapport.

■ Chapter 5:
  - Individual's High-Performance Is the Results of Their Choice.
  - Table 5.2: How to Determine Your Values.
  - Table 5.4: Inductive Questions for Finding Facts and Identifying Perceptions about Problem(s).

■ Chapter 6:
  - Table 6.1: Assessing the Current Vision Clarity of an Individual or a Team.
  - Table 6.4: Assessing the Job Performance Standards of an Individual or a Team.
  - How to Establish an Agreement on "What Should Be Happening."
  - Role of critical thinking process in job performance standards alignment.
  - Table 6.5: Examples of Effective Questions for Discovering "What Should Be Happening."
  - Table 6.6: Conducting a Team Meeting and Discussion for Discovery of "What Should Be Happening" and Establishing Job Performance Standards.

■ Chapter 7:
  - Table 7.2: Different Categories of Employee Performance Metrics Used by Industries.
  - Table 7.3: The Differences between "What is happening" and "What should be happening."
  - Conducting a Performance Feedback and Discussion Session.
  - Meeting About Deciding on Set of Performance Metrics and Measurement.

Organization's Strategic Objectives, Measures, Targets and Corrective Actions Process				
Strategic Objectives	Focused Areas	Type of Measurements	Intended Targets	Proposals for Corrective Actions
Financial Well-Being (Bottom Line)	1.	I.	a.	1.
		II.	b.	2.
	2.	I.	a.	1.
		II.	b.	2.
	3.	I.	a.	1.
		II.	b.	2.
Customer Care & Satisfaction	1.	I.	a.	1.
		II.	b.	2.
	2.	I.	a.	1.
		II.	b.	2.
	3.	I.	a.	1.
		II.	b.	2.
Employees' Development (Growth & Learning)	1.	I.	a.	1.
		II.	b.	2.
	2.	I.	a.	1.
		II.	b.	2.
	3.	I.	a.	1.
		II.	b.	2.
Business Structure (Work Processes)	1.	I.	a.	1.
		II.	b.	2.
	2.	I.	a.	1.
		II.	b.	2.
	3.	I.	a.	1.
		II.	b.	2.

Figure 8.2 Process of Establishing Corrective Actions Related to Organization's Strategic Objectives, Measures, and Production Targets.

Source: Copyright 2021 by Behnam Bakhshandeh.

In the example of Figure 8.2, we used the *balanced scorecard's* general four strategic objectives. However, you can use any other strategic objectives you might find necessary for your organization or any other organizations with which you are working. Further in this chapter, we have covered options of using other CFSs dependent on your organization's strategic plans, goals, or desired outcome (review Figure 8.4 and Table 8.4). Some of the individual employees' behaviors are also influenced by strategic objectives. Some examples of these types of behavioral issues are tardiness or levels of absenteeism. There are always opportunities to provide training and development for teams and groups to increase their emotional intelligence and self-awareness. Please review the following two segments of Chapter 2:

(1) Figure 3.1: Relationship between Mindset, Attitude, Behavior, and Individual and Team Performance.
(2) Figure 3.2: Coaching Mentality Produce Higher Performance and Increasing Productivity.

After selecting the relevant organization's strategic objectives, identify the areas of focus for organizations, their departments, and their teams to pay attention to and focus their performance and productivity to cover such objectives. As an example, for financial objectives, the appropriate area of focus could be marketing, sales, and productivity.

The next step is to determine what type of measurement you would use to measure increasing or decreasing performance related to the intended targets for such performance. Intended targets are the raw numbers for weekly, monthly, or quarterly productivity and performance. After all these processes are measured, corrective actions can be designed with the partnership and engagement of individuals and teams who directly influence those areas of focus related to the organization's strategic objectives.

Balanced Scorecard

A balanced scorecard is a metric for job performance used by organizations during their strategic performance management. This tool assists organizations in recognizing needed improvement in their internal operations to help meet the organization's external outcomes. The balanced scorecard structure is based on the balance among the corresponding aspect of internal indicators driving the organization's outcome (Kaplan and Norton 1996).

The balanced scorecard is designed to measures an organization's past quarterly, semiannual or annual productions and performance via displaying correspondent data. The outcome of the balanced scorecard will provide organization management with feedback opportunities on how to alter their approach to productivity and performance and decide for future actions (Kaplan and Norton 1992).

In Chapter 6 (Figure 6.3), we briefly touched on the balanced scorecard and its four main internal elements that support the organization's values, vision, mission, and strategies (Kaplan and Norton 1996; Kaplan and Norton 1992):

(1) **Customer perspective**: How do our clients/customers see us?
(2) **Internal perspective**: Business processes and procedures' efficiency, effectiveness, and level of performance. What are we good at and what do we stand out for?

(3) **Growth and learning perspective**: Our underlying capabilities and improvements. Are we able to continue growing, improving, and creating values?

(4) **Financial perspective**: How do we appear to the organization's shareholders? Bottom-line measurements as the cost of goods and revenue extremes.

Note that the aforementioned four categories of CSFs represent a general perspective of an organization that is looking for a well-run and well-operating business. Although many elements of a well-operating business are not mentioned on these four perspectives, or not displayed in Figure 8.3, it doesn't mean they are not under vision, perspectives, and management of an organization (e.g., the perspective of different divisions, departments, groups, teams, and even individual employees of the organization and what are important to them). These elements could be viewed and examined under number two, the internal perspective. Another example could be the view of personal and professional development for teams and individuals which can be found under number three, the Growth and Learning Perspective. The point is this, the importance of performance gaps is linked to the importance of any of the aforementioned elements of a well-operating business from the perspective of the person in charge of the organization and its divisions and departments for the organization's well-being and longevity that benefits all levels of individual employees and management.

Figure 8.3 displays the main elements of a typical balanced scorecard while Table 8.3 displays the generic measures related to each element and perspective of a general balanced scorecard.

Critical Success Factors

CSFs are as critical and simple as their title. They are defined as follows:

(1) the categories of an organization, a business, or a project that are essential to their growth and success, and

(2) they also point employees to some vital factors to pay attention to and ensure that work, jobs, tasks, and projects are aligned throughout teams, groups, and departments.

Some Definitions and Descriptions

The notion and model of CSF have developed and revolved through the years. For this reason, many organizations may have used and implemented

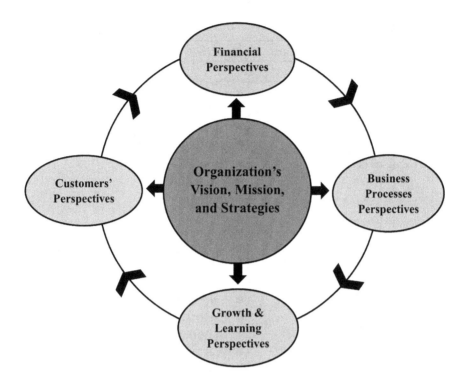

Figure 8.3 Balanced Scorecard.

Source: Adapted from Cardy and Leonard (2011) and Spitzer (2007).

Table 8.3 Elements of Balanced Score Cards, Perspectives and Their Common Measures.

Elements of Balanced Score Cards, Perspectives and Their Common Measures	
Perspectives	*Common Measures*
Financial Perspective	■ Capital ■ Return on investment (ROI) ■ Budget ■ Cash flow ■ Sales ■ Expansion ■ Investment ■ Profitability ■ Salary caps ■ Commissions levels ■ Promotion opportunities ■ Bonus plan ■ Incentives
Customer Perspective	■ Customer retention ■ Customer satisfaction ■ Customer acquisition

(Continued)

Table 8.3 (Continued)

| Elements of Balanced Score Cards, Perspectives and Their Common Measures ||
Perspectives	*Common Measures*
	■ Customer future needs ■ Marketing ■ Market share ■ Reputation
Business Processes Perspective	■ Processes ■ Procedures ■ Hiring ■ Talent recruitment ■ Talent retention ■ Quality ■ Innovation ■ Technology ■ Safety ■ Cost ■ Material ■ Warranty ■ Maintenance ■ Time cycle ■ Defects ■ Recalls ■ Returns
Growth and Learning Perspective	■ Job satisfaction ■ Employees' retention ■ Career development ■ Skills ■ Competencies ■ Training ■ Workplace learning ■ Professional growth opportunities ■ Morale ■ Products ■ Services ■ Communication

Source: Copyright 2021 by Behnam Bakhshandeh.

them in different ways. Here, we have provided some definitions, descriptions, and approaches:

■ "The concept of CSFs (also known as Key Results Areas, or KRAs) was first developed by D. Ronald Daniel, in his HBR article, 'Management Information Crisis'. John F. Rockart, of MIT's Sloan School of

Management, built on and popularized the idea almost two decades later" (MindTools 2021, n.p.).

■ Rockart (1979) defined CSFs as: "[t]he limited number of areas in which results, if they are satisfactory, will ensure successful competitive performance for the organization. They are the few key areas where things must go right for the business to flourish. If results in these areas are not adequate, the organization's efforts for the period will be less than desired" (MindTools 2021, n.p.).

■ Most organizations have some CSFs that are important to them and are central to their focus and indication for their progress and success. CSFs are important results for organizations critical to their success based on their industry, focus, or products, which make the CSFs critical during the decision-making process (Rothwell 2013).

■ "Critical success factor (CSF) is a management term for an element that is necessary for an organization or project to achieve its mission. To achieve their goals they need to be aware of each key success factor (KSF) and the variations between the keys and the different roles key result area (KRA)" (Wikipedia 2021, n.p.).

As Rockart (1979) mentioned in the Harvard Business Review: "[c]ritical success factors for any business are the limited number of areas in which results, if they are satisfactory, will ensure successful competitive performance for the organization" (Rockart 1979, 5). Furthermore, Rockart underlines that CSFs are both internal and external. For example, a comparison of an organization's annual budgets to actual spending capital on the same year would be considered an internal CSF, while the percent of the place of the organization in the market share would be considered an external CSF (Rockart 1979). That being said, from an organization's perspective, CSFs represent performance categories that must achieve strategic objectives and management's expectations in order for organizations to meet their desired outcomes. Like any other business indicator, CSF measurements are used to track any CSFs performance in their categories and success (Evans 2021).

How to Develop Organization's Critical Success Factors

One of the decision-making processes is prioritizing the importance of the selection of performance gaps. Linking the identified performance gaps to any of an organization's CSFs will decide which performance gaps need to be addressed to focus on success factors.

The following are key steps for organizations to identify and develop their critical factors:

■ Develop the organization's strategic objectives and goals.
■ Distinguish the organization's factors needed to accomplish its objectives and goals.
■ List the necessary and related activities relevant to critical factors.
■ Decide the assessment for each critical factor.
■ Monitor the progress of critical success factors.
■ Communicate the identified critical factors to the managers and superiors.

(Parmenter 2020; Rothwell 2013)

In today's market, many websites from different organization developments or business consultants offer different views and perceptions of what should be the set of CSFs or how many CSFs are sufficient for an organization to conduct their business. Followings are two such examples:

According to Lawrimore (2015), "the five Key Success Factors are:

1. Strategic Focus (Leadership, Management, Planning)
2. People (Personnel, Staff, Learning, Development)
3. Operations (Processes, Work)
4. Marketing (Customer Relations, Sales, Responsiveness)
5. Finances (Assets, Facilities, Equipment)"

(n.p.)

According to Quizlet (n.d.), "the six critical success factors are:

1. Achieve financial performance.
2. Meeting customer needs.
3. Producing quality products and services.
4. Encouraging innovation & creativity.
5. Fostering employee commitment.
6. Creating a distinctive competitive advantage."

(n.p.)

So, which one is the correct one? What number of CSFs are sufficient and proper for organizations to conduct their strategies' objectives? We say it all depends on many variables for each organization, what they do, their industry, their market, and their business structure. Basically, there is no magic set of CSFs, but any organizations must pay attention to their commitment and how they want to conduct their operations to achieve their goals and what is relevant to their departments or divisions. Therefore, their selections of CSFs are directly relevant to what is important to them and which would help them select what performance gaps have a priority to improve and fix.

Figure 8.4 displays some of the key elements of the organization's CSFs. We are not committed to stating these elements or categories are customary

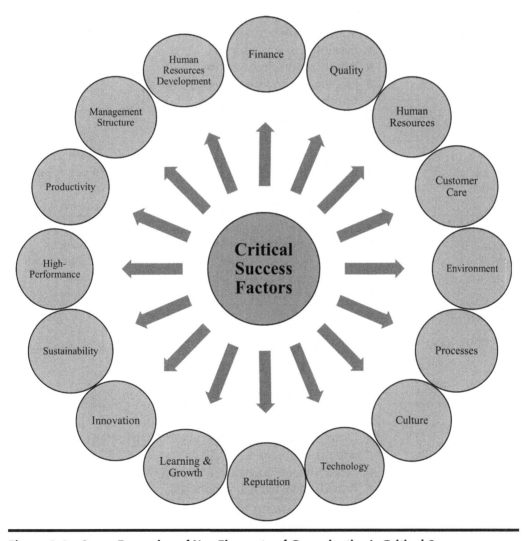

Figure 8.4   Some Examples of Key Elements of Organization's Critical Success Factors.

Source: Copyright 2021 by Behnam Bakhshandeh.

for all organizations, but with a high level of certainty, we can assure clients that many of these elements have been used by many organizations as the focus for indication of their progress and success.

Table 8.4 represents a potential organization's critical success factors and descriptions of necessary actions and relevancy to overall organizations' strategies, processes, and outcomes.

Table 8.4 Potential Organization's Critical Success Factors.

Potential Organization's Critical Success Factors		
#	Factors	Descriptions of Actions and Relevancy
1	*Finance*	■ Strong financial management ■ Feasible business model ■ Wisely controlled cashflow ■ Emphasis on income diversification ■ Cautious investment
2	*Quality*	■ Manage product quality ■ Review the quality of services ■ Promote excellence in the quality of products and services. ■ Back up products and services by offering strong refund policies. ■ Focus on the right product and services for the market.
3	*Employees*	■ Promote partnership among management and workers. ■ Build an environment of respect and appreciation. ■ Promote accountability as means to career advancement. ■ Encourage employee engagement and leadership. ■ Promote morale, and award professionalism and retention.
4	*Environment*	■ Develop strong and systematic safety policies. ■ Promote diversity and inclusion. ■ Establish a safe physical and emotional work environment. ■ Tolerate any harassment behaviors. ■ Promote respecting differences.
5	*Customer care*	■ Demand a robust account management system. ■ Promote service orientation culture. ■ Develop organized and structured customer care policies and procedures. ■ Establish customer satisfaction evaluation and levels. ■ Provide systematic promotions.
6	*Processes*	■ Maintain a strong organizational infrastructure. ■ Review processes' effectiveness. ■ Manage the process strategically. ■ Assure excellent operation. ■ Be open to changes and new ideas for process efficiency.

Potential Organization's Critical Success Factors		
#	*Factors*	*Descriptions of Actions and Relevancy*
7	**Culture**	■ Promote the organization's vision, mission, and core values. ■ Promote and practice leadership qualities. ■ Practice open-door policies. ■ Establish an effective communication channel. ■ Establish a developing, appreciative, and acknowledging environment.
8	**Innovation**	■ Encourage creativity and innovation. ■ Promote entrepreneurial leadership. ■ Reward workable change proposals that save time and money. ■ Implement technological training for employees. ■ Budget for research and development of new approaches.
9	**Technology**	■ Use technology for boosting productivity. ■ Use up-to-date internal communication systems. ■ Support high performance by investing in needed technology. ■ Use automation where needed and feasible. ■ Use automated management reports and evaluations.
10	**Reputation**	■ Practice environmental protection activities. ■ Maintain a strong recycling system in all facilities. ■ Have systematic community services and donations. ■ Promote your productive employees publicly. ■ Have an annual holiday celebration in the community.
11	**Sustainability**	■ Attain a sustainable scale. ■ Have a systematic review of breakdowns and problems. ■ Practice reality versus perception. ■ Have a realistic relationship with the market. ■ Have a strong customer retention system.
12	**Productivity**	■ Promote productivity as access to expansion and profitability. ■ Provide incentives for exceeding metrics and expectations. ■ Provide clear targets, benchmarks, and forecasting systems. ■ Promote efficiency and effectiveness as professionalism. ■ Encourage management involvement with low-productive teams.
13	**High performance**	■ Have a clear and precise performance standard and KPIs. ■ Promote industries' best practices. ■ Promote high performers. ■ Use high performers as instructors for teaching others. ■ Provide necessary training for increasing performance.

(Continued)

Table 8.4 (Continued)

#	Factors	Descriptions of Actions and Relevancy
Potential Organization's Critical Success Factors		
14	**Learning and growth**	■ Support individuals and teams by adding to their knowledge. ■ Develop learning culture. ■ Encourage and promote openness to change. ■ Bring in new business models and skills. ■ Promote growth as means to career advancement.
15	**Management structure**	■ Build a leaders' board. ■ Build a strong management structure. ■ Establish a relationship-based management approach. ■ Establish retention versus turnover scorecards for managers. ■ Be open to lower managers and supervisors' ideas and input.
16	**Human resources development**	■ Provide systematic training and development. ■ Invite and welcome ideas and input for changes.
		■ Broadcast new approaches to work, productivity, and performance. ■ Have systematic training in competencies and skills. ■ Provide soft skills and emotional intelligence skills training

Source: Copyright 2021 by Behnam Bakhshandeh.

Conducting a Brainstorming Session (Brainstorming Diagram)

A brainstorming session is another technique for identifying the importance of the performance gap. Brainstorming would entail deciding which of the performance gaps are more important than others and to set up a priority list to deal with such gaps one after another in an appropriate time. Brainstorming is a method and process of collecting ideas among teams and groups to create solutions for problem(s). The brainstorming process starts with individuals or team/group members spontaneously producing ideas, resulting in inventive ideas to work on the problem(s). A key and crucial principle of this process is to avoid criticism of ideas from any group members and to foster a free-thinking environment that spawns many ideas (Levi 2017).

Brainstorming can be used in a meeting with one worker who is experiencing performance or behavioral problems. It can also be used effectively in a team meeting or a large management retreat. Commonly, performance coaches set ground rules for brainstorming participation. Figure 8.5 provides an example of such ground rules.

Creative Brainstorming Ground Roles

- Avoid criticism of ideas
- Do not discuss ideas
- Do not evaluate ideas
- Do not interrupt expression of ideas
- Keep all ideas equally valuable
- Focus on quantity of idea versus quality
- Welcome everyone's participation
- Build on each other's ideas
- Encourage Creativity
- Establish a time for the process

Figure 8.5   Creative Brainstorming Ground Roles.

Source: Adapted from Rothwell, Hohne, and King (2018), Levi (2017), and Kolb (2011).

Table 8.5   Example of Nominal Group Technique (NGT) for Generating Performance Gap Priorities.

Decision-Makers	Identified Performance Gaps			
	Additional Training	Altering the Process	Change the Supervisor	New Production Schedule
David	3	1	1	2
Suzanne	2	3	1	1
Kim	3	2	1	1
Runny	3	1	2	2
Mike	2	1	1	3
Robert	4	2	1	3
Total	**17**	**10**	**7**	**12**

Using Nominal Group Technique

Another technique for producing a majority's alignment with a subject, such as which performance gap is more important than others or has more urgency, is the Nominal Group Technique or NGT. Again, we have briefly touched on NGT in Chapter 7. NGT can be used when teams or groups are creating alternate solutions for problem(s) using a quantitative (using numbers) process similar to the voting process (Rothwell 2000). For example, in Table 8.5, there are four performance gaps identified going through a diagnosis and analysis process, and now, a team needs to vote on which one has priority. The performance gaps would be voted on by those team members on a scale of 1 to 5 (one having less priority to five the highest priority) and totaled. The highest score was the selected performance gap to take on first by the team (Rothwell et al. 2018).

According to Levi (2017) and Kolb (2011), the NGT process comprises of six steps that encompass a private, silent, and confidential process of voting and ranking of selected ideas and solutions:

(1) silent and confidential generation of ideas by members
(2) mixed reporting of confidential and anonymous ideas with no discussion
(3) clarification and explanation of ideas or solutions
(4) silent and confidential voting and ranking of ideas or solutions
(5) discussion and expression of priorities for solving problem(s)
(6) if necessary or needed, repetition of step 4

While those steps lend themselves to robust root cause analysis, a real-time approach can be used with individuals or teams by simply asking worker(s) to write down ideas about root causes and then voting on them. The result may well be a weighted list of possible causes. At that point, performance coaches can lead coachees to generate possible solutions to address those causes.

Process of Force Field Analysis (Force Field Diagram)

Force field analysis is another way to discuss the importance of the performance gap by engaging relevant personal and discussing the importance of each identified performance gap. Force field analysis, also known as force field diagram, can be used to explore the factors that help or hinder a change program (Lewin 1951). It encourages users to examine connections between *driving forces* (what the team or organization wants to accomplish and the aspects that lessen the problems) and *restraining forces* (the obstacles in the way of success and the aspects contributing to the problems) that influence a change. The force field analysis can be used at various stages of the problem-solving process, but it is often most useful in assessing change implementation issues (Levi 2017).

Levi (2017) explained the underlying dynamics of the force field analysis as "a method for teams to study their problem-solving activities." Teams use group discussions to identify the driving and restraining forces affecting any proposed solution. The team uses this information to decide on strategies for implementation. A cycle of generation, analysis, and application of results is repeated during the implementation process (231). Levi and Lawn (1993) have used this method to analyze the driving and restraining forces that influenced project teams developing new products or services. Figure 8.6 is an example of such a process.

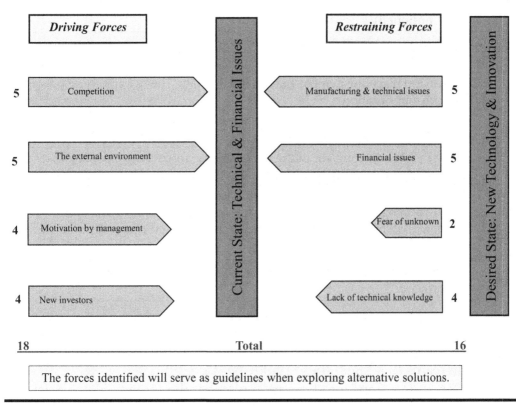

Figure 8.6   Example of Force Field Analysis Process.

Source: Adapted from Rothwell et al. (2018) and Levi (2017).

As can be seen in Figure 8.6, the project teams were motivated by their interest in implementing new technology and enhancement of organizational culture that would promote and encourage innovation (the desired state). However, the success of implementing new technology and marketing any new products was restricted by technological manufacturing issues and by a lack of budget appropriation due to the organization's financial issues (the current state). By understanding these forces, the project team was inspired

Table 8.6   Steps of Performing Force Field Analysis Process.

How to Perform a Force Field Analysis Process	
Steps	Descriptions
1	Invite experts (internal or external) to contribute to your project team's knowledge and expertise.
2	Express and place the desired state on the right side. This is what the team or organization wants to see as an outcome.

(Continued)

Table 8.6 (Continued)

How to Perform a Force Field Analysis Process	
Steps	Descriptions
3	Report and place the current state in the diagram. This is happening now in the present situation.
4	Create two columns on both sides of the current state, as driving forces and restraining forces.
5	Discuss and brainstorm about the top restricting forces and rank the impact and influence on them from 0 being nothing to 5 having the largest influence.
6	Repeat the same process for the driving forces by discussing and brainstorming about the top driving forces and rank the impact and influence of them from 0 being nothing to 5 having the largest influence.
7	Total the number of two ratings in their columns and compare them side by side.
8	Discuss the findings with key organization management and submit a report summary.

Source: Adapted from Levi (2017) and Dyer, Dyer, and Dyer (2013).

to include some financial, technological, manufacturing, and marketing to the design teams to address these problems (Levi 2017).

Table 8.6 shows steps into how to implement the force field analysis process:

While force field analysis is most often associated with looking at what helps and hinders change (and thereby reduces resistance to change), it can also lend itself to modification for root cause analysis. Users can choose to consider driving forces as those that cause a problem or create a gap and restraining forces as those that lead to resolutions or that obviate the problem.

Force field analysis of this kind could be used for real-time or robust root cause analysis. When used in real time, performance coaches would draw a fish bone on a napkin—or whatever is handy—and use it to focus individual or team attention on root causes in a simple conversation. A more robust examination using force field analysis would take more time and would direct the attention of larger groups to pinpointing causes or else issues affecting the implementation of solutions.

Important Assessor's Abilities and Competencies

Chapter 2 distinguished performance coaches' needed competencies, skills, and abilities to conduct effective performance coaching for individuals and teams. Chapter 7 displayed the needed Abilities for a Performance Gap

Table 8.7   Needs Abilities for Assessing the Importance of Performance Gaps Priorities.

Needed Abilities for Assessing the Importance of Performance Gaps Priorities	
#	**Needed Abilities to Determine the Importance of Gaps between "What Is the Issue in Hand" and "What Should Be" About the Organization's:**	**Areas of Abilities, Examinations, and Inquiries**
1	Elements of external environment	■ To carry out strategic thinking. ■ To compare and envision the future of the organization to present events. ■ To assess the involvement of the external sectors and stakeholders. ■ Examine present challenges caused by performance gaps on external factors such as customers, stockholders, suppliers, and distributors. ■ Examine potential future challenges caused by the performance gap on external factors such as customers, stockholders, suppliers, and distributors.
2	Elements of internal environment	■ Lead, organize, and participate in the organization's individuals, teams, and departmental performance enhancement efforts. ■ Assess and explore the organization's structure and policies. ■ Uncover real or apparent consequences of performance gaps to the organization and its departments.
3	Work processing and procedures	■ Examine processes, procedures, workflow, required work, inputs, and outputs about the production or delivery of services. ■ Assess the process of workflows of departments, teams, or groups. ■ Assess the flow process of raw materials, employees, and information by departments, teams, or groups. ■ Assess the consequences of performance gaps in the workflow of departments, teams, or groups. ■ Ability to categorize and prioritize the importance of such consequences.
4	Workers' performance and competencies	■ Examine workers' competencies related to their work requirements.

(Continued)

Table 8.7 (Continued)

Needed Abilities for Assessing the Importance of Performance Gaps Priorities		
		▪ Examine available workers' competencies' effectiveness and functionality about the organization's internal and external environment and work processing.
		▪ Examine existing gaps in workers' competencies required or needed and those competencies that are available.
		▪ Examine existing gaps in workers' competencies required or needed and those competencies that are available.
		▪ Assess gaps between workers' competencies and what is potentially needed for future work.
		▪ Examine the importance of existing gaps in workers' competencies.
		▪ Categorize and prioritize workers' competencies' gaps.
		▪ Assess the consequences of competencies' gaps in departments, teams, or groups.

Source: Adapted from Parmenter (2020), Sharma and Sharma (2018), and Rothwell (2013).

Analyst to compare "what is the issue in hand" and "what should be happening." See Table 7.4. In this segment of Chapter 8, we touched on the needed abilities and competencies for a high-performance coach as the assessor for identifying the importance of performance gaps' priorities (see Table 8.7).

Business Case Example

As we have underlined earlier, after measuring the performance gap between what is happening and what should be happening and how to measure such a gap, it is time to decide the importance of those identified gaps. Which performance gaps should be handled first? Which gaps have more impact on production and need to be addressed for increasing human performance sooner?

For this example, we continue to use the MBD again (see more details about this organization in previous chapters' business examples). The MBD team recognized the gaps in their performance and related issues. Now they have to decide which performance gap is more important than others or what is the priority and order of importance among what they had discovered as the root causes of their issues.

Step 1

To do this, they started by using and reviewing "Quantitative and Qualitative Measures of the Importance of Performance Gap" (see Table 8.2) to understand the importance of the measures, related elements, and relevant details because these all depend on who is looking at them, their positions, responsibilities, accountability of those who are reviewing them, and what type of measures (hard or soft) they are looking at.

Step 2

The next step was to go through the "Process of Establishing Corrective Actions Related to Organization's Strategic Objectives, Measures, and Production Targets" (see Figure 8.2), which is directly related to the concept of "The Balanced Scorecard" (see Figure 8.3) and "Elements of Balanced Score Cards, Perspectives, and Their Common Measures" (see Table 8.3).

Step 3

In this step, they reviewed the concept of "Critical Success Factors," and after reviewing how to develop an organization's CSF, they selected the most important and relevant CSFs for their organization and the relevancy to their industry and market. See "Some Examples of Key Elements of Organization's Critical Success Factors" (Figure 8.4) and "Potential Organization's Critical Success Factors" (Table 8.4) for refreshing your memory and the options for selecting CSFs. To do this process, the MBD team chose the Brainstorming Process (see Figure 8.5) and Using Nominal Group Technique (see Table 8.5) again. You can review the use of these two techniques and models by the MBD team in previous chapters.

By the end of this process, the MBD team came with a new and powerful set of CSFs and made a priority list about what performance gaps are more important or necessary to attack first and bring back the team's performance to match their agreed "Job Performance Standards."

Key Factors to Remember

Let's review the lessons in this chapter about measuring the importance of gaps:

- **Prioritize the performance gaps to save time**
  - Identifying the performance gaps and prioritizing the importance of them based on the organization's need and potential consequences of gaps can save time and energy by not interrupting the workflow to fix everything simultaneously.

- **Different ways to determine the importance of gaps**
  - Learning and understanding the different ways to determine the importance of performance gaps and their priorities can help in selecting what method of determining importance is more appropriate for a certain time or production.

- **Build up your competencies**
  - Being honest and authentic about what you know and what you are confident in regarding knowledge, skills, and abilities can help to develop more skills and competencies as a high performance.

- **Reality versus perception**
  - Stay away from analyzing, diagnosing, or determining performance gaps only based on the perception of individuals, teams, or the work. The reality of situations will emerge using a professional approach consisting of conducting proper assessment and proven methods. Having intuitions and perceptions is okay and, sometimes, appropriate, but the best way to back up any perceptions is a reality check (Bakhshandeh 2015).

Coaching and Developmental Questions for Managers

(1) How do you rate yourself from 0 to 10 (0 being the lowest and 10 being the highest) on your knowledge and understanding of different ways of measuring performance gaps?

What is missing or in the way of your understanding?
What is your action plan to increase your overall rate?

(2) How do you rate yourself from 0 to 10 (0 being the lowest and 10 being the highest) on your knowledge and understanding of the importance and prioritizing performance gaps?

What is missing?
What is your action plan to increase your overall rate?

(3) How do you rate yourself from 0 to 10 (0 being the lowest and 10 being the highest) on your knowledge and understanding of quantitative and qualitative measures of the importance of the performance gap?

What is missing or not understood?
What is your action plan to increase your overall rate?

(4) How do you rate yourself from 0 to 10 (0 being the lowest and 10 being the highest) on your knowledge and understanding of CSFs?

What is missing or not understood?
What is your action plan to increase your overall rate?

References

Bakhshandeh, Behnam. 2015. *Anatomy of Upset: Restoring Harmony*. Carbondale, PA: Primeco Education, Inc.

Bakhshandeh, Behnam. 2021. "Perception of 21st Century 4Cs (Critical Thinking, Communication, Creativity & Collaboration) Skill Gap in Private-Sector Employers in Lackawanna County, NEPA." An Unpublished Dissertation in Workforce Education and Development. The Pennsylvania State University.

Camp, William G. 2001. "Formulating and Evaluating Theoretical Frameworks for Career and Technical Education Research." *Journal of Vocational Educational Research* 26, no. 1: 4–21.

Cardy, Robert L., and Brian Leonard. 2011. *Performance Management: Concepts, Skills and Exercises*. Armonk, NY: Me. E. Sharp. Inc.

Creswell, John W., and David J. Creswell. 2018. *Research Design: Qualitative, Quantitative, and Mixed Methods Approaches*, 5th ed. Los Angeles, CA: Sage Publishing.

Dyer, Gibb W. Jr., Jeffrey H. Dyer, and William G. Dyer. 2013. *Team Building*, 5th ed. San Francisco, CA. Jossey-Bass.

Evans, Matt H. 2021. "Critical Success Factors Defined." https://exinfm.com/board/critical_success_factors.htm.

Grant, Cynthia, and Azadeh Osanloo. 2016. "Understanding, Selecting, and Integrating a Theoretical Framework in Dissertation Research: Creating the Blueprint for 'House'." *Administrative Issues Journal: Connecting Education, Practice and Research* 4, no. 2: 7.

Kaplan, Robert S., and David P. Norton. 1992. "Harvard Business Review" website. *The Balanced Scorecard: Measures that Drive Performance.* https://hbr.org/1992/01/the-balanced-scorecard-measures-that-drive-performance-2.

Kaplan, Robert S., and David P. Norton. 1996. *The Balanced Scorecard: Translating Strategy Action.* Cambridge, MA: Harvard Business Press.

Kolb, Judith A. 2011. *Small Group Facilitation: Improving Process and Performance in Groups and Teams.* Amherst, MA: HRD Press Inc.

Lawrimore, Buck. 2015. "The 5 Key Success Factors of Business." www.linkedin.com/pulse/5-key-success-factors-business-3-operations-buck-lawrimore/.

Levi, Daniel. 2017. *Group Dynamics for Teams*, 5th ed. Los Angeles, CA: Sage Publications.

Levi, Daniel, and Marguerite Lawn. 1993. "The Driving and Restraining Forces Which Affect Technological Innovation in Organizations." *The Journal of High Technology Management Research* 4, no. 2: 225–40.

Lewin, Kurt. 1951. *Field Theory in Social Science: Selected Theoretical Papers (Edited by Dorwin Cartwright.).* New York, NY: Harpers.

MindTools. 2021. "Critical Success Factors. Daniel and Rockart's Guild to Meeting Strategic Goals." www.mindtools.com/pages/article/newLDR_80.htm.

O'Sullivan, Elizabeth Ann, Gary Rassel, and Maureen Berner. 2017. *Research Methods for Public Administrators*, 6th ed. New York, NY: Taylor & Francis.

Parmenter, David. 2020. *Key Performance Indicators: Developing, Implementing, and Using Winning KPIs*, 3rd ed. Hoboken, NJ: John Wiley & Sons, Inc.

Quizlet. n.d. "6 Critical Success Factors." https://quizlet.com/100181511/6- critical-success-factors-flash-cards/.

Rockart, John F. 1979. "Chief Executives Define Their Own Data Needs." *Harvard Business Review* 2: 81–93.

Rothwell, William J. 2000. *ASTD Models for Human Performance Improvement: Roles, Competencies, and Outputs*, 2nd ed. Alexandria, VA: The American Society for Training and Development.

Rothwell, William J. 2013. *Performance Consulting: Applying Performance Improvement in Human Resource Development.* San Francisco, CA: John Wiley & Sons.

Rothwell, William J., Carolyn K. Hohne, and Stephen B. King. 2018. *Human Performance Improvement: Building Practitioner Performance*, 3rd ed. New York, NY: Routledge.

Rothwell, William J., Jacqueline M. Stavros, and Roland L. Sullivan. 2016. *Practicing Organization Development: Leading Transformation and Change*, 4th ed. Hoboken, NJ: John Wiley & Sons, Inc.

Sharma, R. C., and Nipun Sharma. 2018. *Human Resource Management: Theory and Practice.* Los Angeles, CA: Sage.

Spitzer, Dean R. 2007. *Transforming Performance Measurement.* New York, NY: AMACOM.

Trochim, William M. K., and James P. Donnelly. 2008. *The Research Methods Knowledge Base*, 3rd ed. Mason, OH: Cengage Learning.

Wikipedia. 2021. "Critical Success Factor." https://en.wikipedia.org/wiki/Critical_success_factor.

Chapter 9

Step 6: What Are the Root Causes of the Gap?

William J. Rothwell

Once the relative importance of a performance gap is clear to stakeholders, then the next step is to try to identify the root cause(s) of the gaps. Discovering root cause(s) is an analytical process. It can be conducted in real time or over a long time span. Pinpointing root cause(s) is critically important—and difficult. Efforts to close measurable gaps are usually fruitless if they do not address the root cause(s) because those efforts will address symptoms only and will not address why the gap exists.

It can be tempting to grasp at straws, looking for easy, quick, and cheap solutions to tough problems. But treating symptoms rather than root causes will rarely be helpful and will quite often make matters worse.

How This Chapter Is Organized

This chapter is organized into the following parts:

- What This Step Means
- Why Is This Step in Performance Coaching Important?
- Examples of This Step in Performance Coaching
- Approaches to Root Cause Analysis
- Competencies Required by Performance Coaches to Identify Root Cause(s)
- Key Factors to Remember
- Coaching and Developmental Questions for Managers
- References

DOI: 10.4324/9781003155928-12

What This Step Means

Step 6 is about investigating to answer the question "*why is the gap happening?*" It is not an easy question. One reason for this question is that those enacting the role of performance coach will be tempted to skip this step and simply jump to finding solutions. Sometimes that happens out of a strong sense of urgency, a desire to "get on with it" to implementing a solution; sometimes that happens because performance coaches think they already know the root cause(s) and do not need to spend the time, money, and effort to explore further; and, sometimes that happens because performance coaches accept the first cause they find without taking the time to investigate more thoroughly. But one thing is clear: it is hard work to find root cause(s)—and sometimes is not even possible.

When gaps are negative, finding the root cause(s) means discovering what is wrong. When gaps are neutral, no causes exist because there is no gap. When gaps are positive, identifying root cause(s) may require finding out why strengths exist.

Why Is This Step in Performance Coaching Important?

This step is important because any performance gap may result from one or many possible root causes. The point worth emphasizing here is that a gap often stems from more than one root cause, but performance coaches may be tempted to believe that any problem has only cause. And sometimes, admittedly, the root cause simply cannot be easily be determined. About the best that may be possible is to reach a *proximal solution*—that is, an educated guess about what could be the possible or even likely cause(s).

Even when causes appear to be unusual, performance coaches should remember that famous observation from well-known British sleuth Sherlock Holmes: *Once you eliminate the impossible, whatever remains, no matter how improbable, must be the truth.*

Avoiding the Mistake of Confusing Signs or Symptoms and Root Causes

Think for a moment about medical doctors searching for the root causes of illness. Their approach is simple: conduct testing until all possible root causes have been considered and either eliminated or verified as the cause of illness. Medical doctors know that any illness may have more than one root cause. A patient experiencing stomach pain may suffer from indigestion and stomach cancer at the same time.

Medical doctors are trained to recognize the difference between signs and symptoms and root causes. A medical *sign* is a result of a root cause that a medical doctor recognizes; a medical *symptom* is a consequence of a root cause that the patient notices. They are not always the same. Best known of medical signs are pulse, blood pressure, temperature, and so forth. These are the so-called *vital signs*. Changes in those may point to health problems to medical professionals. Symptoms can be noticed by anyone. When a woman vomits in the morning, many people—not just medical doctors—might suspect morning sickness.

Yet, few medical doctors are adequately training on diagnosis. Despite the lengthy training that medical doctors receive, misdiagnosis persists as a major problem in modern medicine. It is estimated that approximately 40,000–80,000 deaths in the United States Annually are attributable to misdiagnosis ("Does a Med School Degree Guarantee Diagnosis Skills?" 2015). About 5% of autopsies shockingly reveal that diagnostic mistakes resulted in patient deaths. One source has found that 1 in 20 outpatients are misdiagnosed annually and that 17% of all adverse medical events stem from misdiagnosis ("Does a Med School Degree Guarantee Diagnosis Skills?" 2015).

Different reasons have been offered as explanations as to why such diagnostic problems occur. Some experts believe that medical schools emphasize treatment of obvious illnesses rather than training doctors to play detectives. Others suggest that misdiagnosis results from patients who conceal important information from their doctors or else offer selected, incomplete, information to avoid embarrassment. Still others suggest that medical doctors misdiagnose because they do not order the appropriate medical tests.

There are different kinds of medical signs. *Diagnostic signs* aid physicians in finding what is wrong. A bone sticking out of a leg is a diagnostic sign of a compound fracture. *Pathognomic signs* are more certain than diagnostic signs. Yellow skin usually indicates jaundice. *Prognostic signs* suggest what will happen to the patient. A lump in a woman's breast indicates cancer—and that suggests clear negative consequences if left untreated. *Anamnestic signs* provide medical professionals with evidence of a past condition. If a patient experiences facial paralysis, for instance, it suggests a past stroke.

Now think about modern management. Even professionally trained managers—that is, those possessing MBA degrees from first-rate business schools—have rarely been trained on how to diagnose what causes human problems. Business education emphasizes skills in finance and marketing and de-emphasizes skills in operations and human resources.

Evidence of this problem is abundant. Managers confuse signs and symptoms for root causes. As a simple example, consider managers who label turnover as a problem when turnover is a consequence of one or more root causes. Misdiagnosis leads to ill-conceived solutions. And bad solutions can often create new problems, which (in turn) prompt more ill-conceived solutions. The result is a downward spiral that robs the organization of productivity and leads to a toxic workplace.

Much information exists to help managers pinpoint root causes of human performance problems. Much has been written about organizational diagnosis (see Alderfer 2010; Bristow and Sandberg 2010; Pershing 2006; Randall and Toplis 2016; Rothwell, Stopper, and Myers 2017). Much has also been written about diagnosing problems with teams or individual performance (Fournies 2007; Gilbert 2007; Lencioni 2007; Mager and Pipe 1997).

The Difference between Performance Problems and Behavior Problems

Note the difference between performance and behavior problems. A *performance problem* is a gap between what work results workers are expected to achieve and what results they do achieve. If workers are to produce fourteen widgets per hour but produce only 3, the gap is eleven. That much is easy to see. But a *behavior problem* is a gap between expected and evident observable actions. If the organization's dress code policy stipulates that men should wear dress shirts and ties but one man wears casual attire to work, the behavioral difference is apparent. But not all performance or behavior problems are immediately obvious. It may also be challenging to pinpoint root causes. If a worker is late for work every day, always with a good excuse, a behavioral problem exists. But even the worker may not know, or may not be willing to offer, the root causes leading to that behavioral problem.

Yet, the best solutions can be implemented only when (or if) the real root cause(s) are found and action is taken to address it or them.

Why Most Change Efforts Are Failing

Earlier, we talked about individuals' mindsets, attitudes, behaviors, and how they determine their thinking and decision-making processes. What made people think differently from others is their perspectives on life and work and how they envisioned the world around them. They knew they could get over any circumstance and obstacles. "If there was a limit, it was not a limit they imposed on themselves, but rather it was what others insisted on!" (Bakhshandeh 2009, 19). There is this amazing mental phenomenon and state of *Being* that many people are practicing and have created a level of mastery around it; for many others, it is still a mystery to figure out. "There are no limits, there is no difficulty, and there is no 'I can't' until we say, 'It is,' or we listen to others saying, 'It is!'" (Bakhshandeh 2009, 19).

Why do we keep talking about this mental phenomenon? The state of *Being* has a positive influence on people's process of thinking. The reason for this is because the individuals' state of mind and the way they are looking at issues are determined by their mindsets. It is directly related to locating the actual problem with individuals, teams, and the organization. Effective and productive people have a vision for what they do. They see a future; they are planning and designing their actions to be connected to the future they saw, and they know it is possible, not like fantasy or some "pie in the sky." Often, they didn't know how to do it or how to get there, but they had no doubt they could reach their objectives because they were in control of their mindset (Bakhshandeh 2009).

As we talk about how to convince the decision-makers and stakeholders to see the need for change, it is important to underline a fact in change intervention; there is no guarantee that any change interventions, including the team-building intervention, would work or will be sustainable. There are many reasons change efforts fail; here is a variety of reasons that account for these failures by people or organizations according to Rothwell and Graber (2010):

■ They see no reasons or need to change.
■ They feel no urgency for change.
■ They don't agree on how they should change.
■ People who are involved don't agree on what to change or how to change.
■ They don't know who should change.
■ Managers think others should change, but not themselves.
■ People who are involved don't know what successful change should look like.
■ They don't know when to change.
■ They don't know where to change.

- They don't know why they should change.
- They don't know how to change.
- They are resisting the change because they worry about what they must give up.

Knowing this will help the individual or group pointing to the necessity of a change intervention know which decision-makers and stakeholders are potentially viewing the change.

Examples of This Step in Performance Coaching

Perhaps, an example will help to clarify what this step means in practice.

The situation: Larry Edwards is the manager of the customer service department of his company, Ajax Chemicals. He has an employee, Letitia James, who is a customer service representative. James' job involves fielding customer complaints by phone. Edwards has received many complaints about James from customers. She has been called "uncivil," "impolite," "mean," and even "surly."

In Edwards' company, customers are randomly selected and then surveyed weekly to assess their relative satisfaction levels with the service they received from Ajax. The survey results for most customer service representatives averages a bottom-line satisfaction score of 6 on a 7 scale. But James averages a score of 4. It seems that the lower her scores are, the more testy and unhappy James becomes—and those attitudes are reflected in how she deals with customers.

The conversation between the performance coach and coachee: Edwards decides to have a performance coaching session with James. He follows the steps of the performance coaching process. When he reaches step 6, the conversation goes as follows:

Edwards: [*He stops a moment to think about the situation. Then he considers how to proceed based on the body language and general mannerisms of the coachee.*] What do you think might be the reason that you seem to get the scores that you do on the weekly customer satisfaction surveys?

James: I honestly don't know. It is true that I am stressed out by the volume of calls I get—and the level of customer unhappiness I encounter. I think I end up with customers who are more upset than the other customer representatives seem to get. I am not sure why that happens.

Edwards: That seems unlikely. As you know, calls are routed from a central place. As your phone line comes free, you are automatically assigned the next caller. I could just tell you what to do, but I think that approach would be counterproductive. I believe it would be better now if you told me why you think other people regard you as unfriendly.

James: I just don't know what causes these problems or what I should do differently.

Edwards: Let's do this. Why don't you pick one of your colleagues to sit at the phone with you for one day and monitor the course of your conversations with customers as they come in. I will then schedule a meeting with you and the person you choose into my office and we will debrief the situation. I will rely on the judgment of one of your colleague on the root cause(s) of these customer complaints.

James: Fair enough. Let's try it.

Note that, in the previous discussion, Edwards refuses to jump to conclusions about root causes. He does suggest a way to investigate the issue and then return to decide what to do based on more information. While that will take time and cost money to carry out, it will likely lead to better results than jumping to conclusions about why the problem exists.

Approaches to Root Cause Analysis

Now, we touch on the number of common tools for uncovering the root cause of problems with human performance effectiveness and its related level of productivity.

> They provide the methods by which to examine performance problems and opportunities, and they provide the foundation by which subsequent improvement and evaluation efforts are organized and implemented
>
> *(Rothwell, Hohne, and King 2018, 45).*

One of the most importance of an analyst's ability to establish the root causes of performance problems with individuals', teams', and organizations' encounters (Rothwell 2013). Often, the symptoms or visible indications of issues display themselves as the actual issue! In these cases, the management may focus on these symptoms of issues, while the actual, imperial cause continues, undiscovered and unaddressed (see Figure 9.1). This is called the

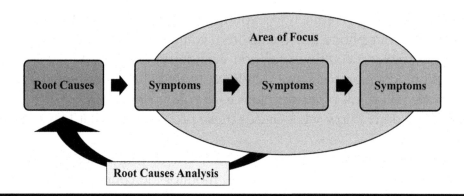

Figure 9.1   Finding Root Causes of Problems versus Looking at the Symptoms.
Source: Copyright 2021 by Behnam Bakhshandeh.

"presenting problems." These symptoms are the consequences or outcomes of another cause, not the actual and real cause itself. The red flag for analysts is confusing the "presenting problem" or the consequence and outcome of the problem with the "underlying reason for the problem" which is the root cause of a problem. This misunderstanding and collapse of concepts can be very wasteful about time, capital, and resources (Rothwell 2018).

There are really two kinds of root cause analysis. One is real-time root cause analysis; the other is robust root cause analysis. *Real-time root cause analysis* is performed "on the fly"—that is, during daily events. *Robust root cause analysis* requires more complete information, more time, more effort, and usually more people.

Many approaches have been suggested to conduct root cause analysis. Often, they suggest that work teams or groups tackle the challenge of discovering root causes. That assumes robust root cause analysis should be used. But performance coaches may use both forms of root cause analysis.

How can root cause analysis be carried out? Consider:

■ fishbone diagrams
■ mind mapping
■ problem-solving Model

Note that the following three methods can also be used for conducting a root cause analysis. These three methods were explained and used in Chapters 6 and 8 for some voting approaches and measuring the importance of performance gaps (refer to Chapter 8 for more details about the following methods).

- Brainstorming diagrams
- nominal group technique (NGT)
- force field analysis

Cause and Effect Analysis (Fishbone Diagram)

Let's look at some good tools and strategies for conducting a root cause analysis. Cause-and-effect analysis identifies and organizes possible causes of performance problems for individuals, occupations, and organizations.

The primary strength of this tool is that it visually organizes information and depicts the linkages between the problem and its possible causes. It is a popular approach to identify the potential causes of the problems. It was designed by Kaoru Ishikawa and is variously known as the "Ishikawa Diagram" or the Fishbone Diagram because of the fishbone shape it takes (as shown in Figure 9.2) (Levi 2017).

For example, Figure 9.2 depicts a manufacturing problem related to the wrong product, such as the wrong size or dimensions or functionality. The problem statement, or the issue, is posted in the box on the left side of the diagram. The large arrow represents the direction of the process; the manufacturing process should produce a correct product. This process can be used to discover root causes for any form of product, service, or even an event.

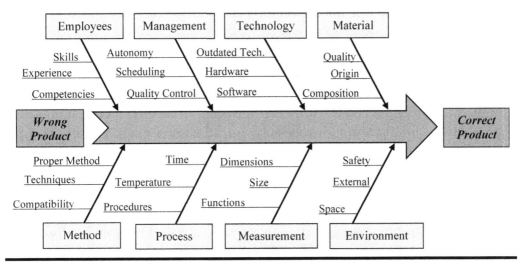

Figure 9.2 Example of Cause-and-Effect Analysis Process Using the Fishbone Approach.

Source: Copyright 2021 by Behnam Bakhshandeh.

Next, the cause categories are defined and written in the boxes on both sides of the large arrow, as you can see in Figure 9.2. A common practice is not to list too many potential causes, given that the fishbone will grow too large for problem identification. It has been recommended to use with problems that likely have between five and eight causes. Here, the causes should be included in categories involved with the manufacturing process—such as employees, materials, measurements, processes, machines, and environment. The next step is to determine potential issues related to these categorized areas and write them between the category and the main arrow, the manufacturing process (as you can see in Figure 9.2). It is possible to use subcauses for the causes related to the process's categories. Users can expand the fishbone diagram and add more details as desired. However, do not make it too complicated to take you away from the key issues, and you chase a rabbit hole called symptoms! As Rothwell et al. (2018) suggested, "[a] more generic example is to ask such simple questions as these: Who? What? Where? When? How? And 'Why?'" (58).

This approach can be used with one worker, a team of workers, or a whole group of people in a management retreat to diagnose one or many issues facing the organization. It can be used in a real-time meeting with one worker and in a robust root cause analysis with a wicked problem (Bentley and Toth 2020). Recall that a *wicked problem* is one that is exceptionally difficult to solve because it is so complicated, because inadequate information is available about root causes, and because interconnected with other problems or issues. Wicked problems, when interconnected, are sometimes likened to a *plate of spaghetti* where each root cause is like one noodle on the plate and they are all tangled up.

Mind Mapping

The mind mapping process is a new approach that bears similarities to brainstorming. It was originated by Tony Buzan (2006). It relies on some traditional approaches to brainstorming process by introducing a graphical display of participants' ideas correlated by areas of concerns (Buzan and Griffiths 2012).

Mind mapping does have unique benefits that distinguish it apart from brainstorming. Mind maps are vivid visual displays portraying issues involved with the problem. Mind mapping lends itself to real-time root cause analysis and to robust root cause analysis. Several mind mapping software packages—some for free—are available to performance coaches and workers (Santos 2013). Table 9.1 summarizes steps in a mind mapping process.

Figure 9.3 illustrates a mind map. It is a good example of following the aforementioned steps (Table 9.1) to create a business plan using the mind

Table 9.1   Steps of Performing a Mind Map Process.

Steps	Descriptions
	How to Perform a Mind Map Process
1	Start with a blank page and start from the middle of the page to expand the ideas.
2	Indicate the main idea or intention with an image or graphical representation (if possible). It will open your imagination and assist you in focusing.
3	Use different colors extensively. Like pictures (if possible), colors also engage your creativity and vitality.
4	Add key categories as the main branches to the main idea to make connections.
5	Add the second- or third-level branches connected to the main branches to expand the idea.
6	Try not using straight lines connecting the ideas and branches unless you are drawing a large mind map. Curved lines are more stimulating than boring straight lines.
7	Use only one keyword for each line, category, or subcategory. Single words allow for more flexibility and strength.
8	Use images and pictures as much as possible. Each additional picture or graphic is worth a thousand words for stimulating imagination and creativity.

Source: Inspired and adapted from Levi (2017), and Dyer, Dyer, and Dyer (2013).

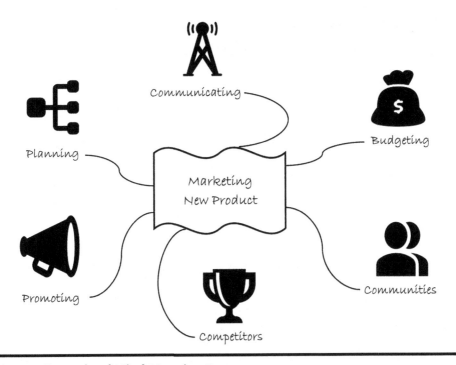

Figure 9.3   Example of Mind Mapping Process.

Source: Copyright 2021 by Behnam Bakhshandeh.

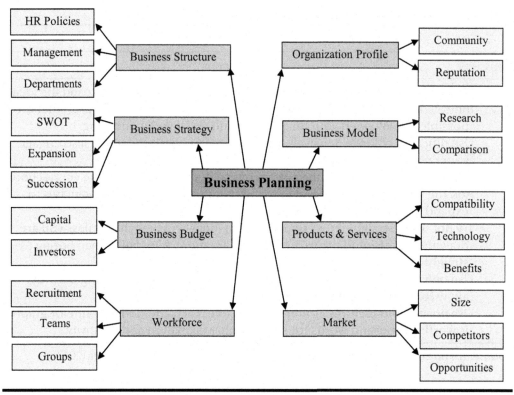

Figure 9.4   Example of Business Mind Mapping Process.

Source: Copyright 2021 by Behnam Bakhshandeh.

mapping process. This approach is beneficial to encourage creativity for relatively simple ideas.

Figure 9.4 displays a more complex mind map. When mind maps are prepared for more complex concepts, straight lines are typically used instead of images.

Problem-Solving Model

Problem-solving is one underlying aspect of teamwork. It is therefore a critical tool for performance coaches working with individuals or teams and facilitating the resolution of their problems and coming to a common conclusion. The team's approaches to the problem-solving process substantially influence the outcome of the problem-solving process (Levi 2017).

The problem-solving model is commonly studied from these three per-spectives (Levi 2017; Kolb 2011):

(1) How teams solve problems?
(2) What behaviors and attitudes support teams to effectively solve their problems?
(3) What tools and techniques enhance the teams to solve the problems?

There are different approaches to a problem-solving process; however, according to Levi (2017) and Kolb (2011), the following are most used and considered as modern problem-solving approaches:

(1) descriptive approach; stages of problem-solving
(2) functional approach
(3) perspective approach; rational problem-solving

Teams usually rush through the problem-solving process and sometimes ignore the process completely. They spend most of their time talking about symptoms and proposing half-baked solutions without digging into what is the primary cause of the problem(s) and understanding the char-acteristics of the problem(s). This ineffective problem-solving undertak-ing harms an organization and their teams' and groups' performance and productivity. It is the role of the manager-as-coach or a high-performance coach as a team facilitator to manage, educate, and guide teams and groups in an effective, productive, and collaborative problem-solving pro-cess (Levi 2017).

Descriptive Approach: Stages of Problem Solving

The problem-solving model and how teams are approaching the problem solving has been researched and implemented by professional OD practi-tioners, high-performance coaches (Rothwell et al. 2018; Levi 2017; Rothwell 2015; Cummings and Worley 2015; Rothwell, Stavros, and Sullivan 2016; Dyer et al. 2013; Kolb 2011; Schein 1988). Understanding different elements of the problem-solving process help high-performance coaches to better position themselves in distinguishing ways to improve the problem-solving perspec-tive and individuals' views of such process.

According to Dyer et al. (2013), during the descriptive problem-solving approach, individuals who have formed a team go through a four-stage process to solve problems while dealing with behaviors and norms at each stage. The four stages are as follows (see Figure 9.5):

(1) Forming
- Teams and their members are trying to understand the depth of the problem.
- Teams are examining the problem and its characteristics.
- Team members are finding their positions and getting familiar with their jobs.

(2) Storming
- This is a stage when conflicts are arising.
- Discussion is high, and emotions are flying.
- Problems are delineated, and solutions are considered.

(3) Norming
- Methods are selected, and approaches are developed to analyze the problem.
- Alternatives are proposed, and action plans are generated.
- Solution(s) are selected, and action plans are conformed.

(4) Performing
- Solution(s) is implemented.
- There is a camaraderie building up among the team members.
- The team is performing productively.

Functional Approach

The functional approach to team problem-solving attempts to identify elements that disrupt and interfere with the team process and strives to

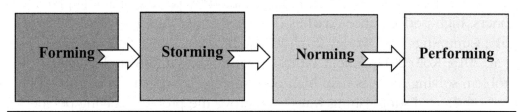

Figure 9.5 Descriptive Approach: Stages of Teams Problem-Solving.

Source: Adapted from Levi (2017).

enhance the team's ability and effectiveness in solving problems. Various constant and hidden internal and external factors influence the team problem-solving process, such as emotional, social, or political factors. The fact is there are several actions that a team can take in response to these internal and external elements that would assist or damage the team's problem-solving process. By examining these elements and related behaviors, a team can manage its problem-solving process and serve as a framework for team interaction (Dyer et al. 2013; Schein 1988).

Figure 9.6 depicts these assisting and damaging factors in the team problem-solving process.

Prescriptive Approach: Rational Problem-Solving

The popular prescriptive approach or rational problem-solving process is a step-by-step technique that utilizes data, observation activities, and a critical thinking process to reach an optimal problem-solving solution. By following and using this systematic, organized, planned, and proven procedure, teams increase their chances of conducting successful problem-solving. The advantages of a structured problem-solving technique differ depending on the dynamics and level of complication of the problem the team is facing. The more difficult and dynamic the problem is, the more advantageous it will be to develop a structured problem-solving approach (Levi 2017; Kolb 2011; Schein 1988).

ASSISTING	DAMAGING
• Viewing challenges from a range of perspectives. • Respecting all ideas and inputs • Collecting data and performing appropriate research. • Pondering both task and interactive factors. • Keeping focused on the challenge. • Valuing and listening to minority opinions. • Not suppressing or discrediting any ideas. • Testing alternative results. • Making decisions based on logical, rational, and conscious ideas.	• Making fast decisions. • Jumping to conclusions • Making decisions based on emotions and intuitive, and prefabricated factors. • Not following a proven and researched and structured problem-solving process. • Disregarding the trade-offs to a resolution. • Entertaining irrelevant information. • Members competing for ideas or recognitions. • Influencing social or political issues on decisions. • Being influenced by group pressure decisions.

Figure 9.6   Factors that Assist or Damage the Team Problem-Solving.

Source: Adapted from Dyer et al. (2013), Bakhshandeh (2009), and Schein (1988).

Figure 9.7 explains the main steps of the process of the rational problem-solving model according to Levi (2017) and Kolb (2011):

Step 1: Identify the Problem

As a team, write a problem statement that recognizes the problem as precise, clear as possible, and is aligned by the entire team. Accurate identification of a problem is a big help in problem-solving. The problem statement works as an anchor for the process. At this step, the team will compare the current state with the desired state to identify the potential gap (2017, 2011).

Step 2: Identify the Causes

List potential causes of the problem. Often, teams and their members have entangled the symptoms or effects of a problem, presenting itself as the key

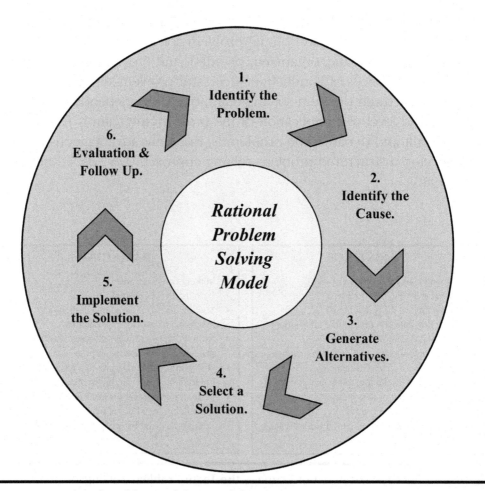

Figure 9.7   Rational Problem-Solving Model Process.

Source: Adapted from Levi (2017).

problem causing and overlooking the root causes. This is the step when teams are looking at the potential causes of the problem. The team can use the cause-and-effect model (fishbone diagram, Figure 9.2) to get the root cause of a more complex problem (2017, 2011).

Step 3: Generate Alternatives

Generate many solutions without being concerned about right or wrong answers. Teams can use creative brainstorming (Figure 8.5), mind mapping (Figures 9.3 and 9.4 and Table 9.2), and the nominal group technique (Tables 7.9 and 8.5) processes to generate more mutually agreeable solutions. To come with a more innovative discussion, the team should conduct inquiries to the who, what, where, when, and how of the causes. The team should have a large list of possible solutions as an outcome of this step (2017, 2011).

Step 4: Select a Solution

Select the best solutions to resolve the problem. This step can become an overwhelming experience. Teams should evaluate the solutions by prioritizing the solutions by using a Pareto Chart. This bar/line illustration combines the team's replies and assists in evaluating and prioritizing potentially large and diverse data. See Figure 9.8 for a sample of the Pareto Chart. Depending on the complexity of the problem(s), the team might implement more than one or two solutions simultaneously (2017, 2011).

Step 5: Implement the Solution

This is the time to get to work and do it! For successful implementation, the team should come with a clear outline and action plan for implementing the solution(s), including the steps, actions, people, schedule, and what tasks must be completed. Factors to consider include lead times, metrics, deadlines, other departments, costs, management, authorizations, contingency plan, and even internal and external political issues, costs, time management, authorizations, and contingency plans. Use the force field analysis process (see Figure 9.6 and Table 9.1) to see the driving and restraining forces pushing and pulling against implementing the solutions as an intervention and change effort (2017, 2011).

Step 6: Conduct Evaluation and Follow-Up

Analyzing the results against the created metrics and adjust if you find it necessary. The team needs to comprehend this final step is a continuing progression following conducting the implementation step. Is this process answering questions such as did the solution(s) work? If it did not work,

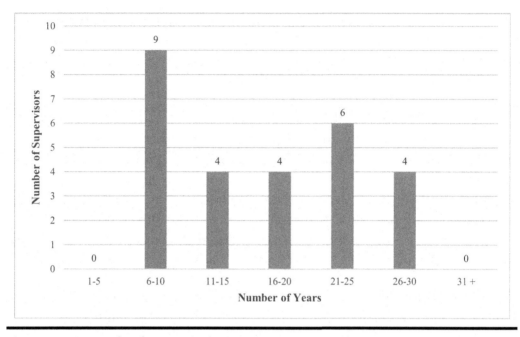

Figure 9.8   Example of a Pareto Chart.

what happened and why? Continuous evaluation, data gathering, and analysis will assist the team and management to ensure positive results and outcomes. Modifications and adjustments are nearly always required and should be monitored (2017, 2011).

Figure 9.8 is an example of a Pareto Chart. Here, the chart is depicting the professional experience among supervisors and floor managers working in a manufacturing organization, comparing (1) how many supervisors are working on that organization and (2) how many would be fit in the seven work experience categories. The Pareto Chart has functions of the Microsoft Excel program and is available in several forms and shapes besides other forms of bars and pie charts.

Competencies Required by Performance Coaches to Identify Root Cause(s)

Performance coaches should be able to:

■ separate signs, symptoms, and root cause(s)
■ apply various approaches to pinpointing root cause(s)

■ facilitate one-on-one, real-time approaches to root cause analysis
■ facilitate robust approaches to root cause analysis

Business Case Example

At this point, the MBD team needed to know what the root causes of their performance issues were. As we have mentioned at the beginning of this chapter, pinpointing root cause(s) is critically important and difficult. Efforts to close measurable gaps are usually fruitless if they do not address the root cause(s) because those efforts will address symptoms only and will not address why the gap exists.

It was important that the MBD team be able to distinguish between the root cause of their performance gaps and the apparent symptoms that might be mistakenly believed to be the actual cause of the pressing issue (see Figure 9.1).

Step 1

Given the sensitivity of these types of discussions and potential disagreements (given the nature of self-protective human mindsets), we conducted a short review of "Descriptive Approach: Stages of Teams Problem-Solving" (see Figure 9.5) and "Factors that Assist or Damage the Team Problem-Solving" (see Figure 9.6). This approach had a good impact on teams' cohesiveness and teamwork to resolve their performance issues as one team, not as individuals who try to make some points for self-protecting agendas.

Step 2

After that, we reviewed the "Rational Problem-Solving Model Process" to ensure the foundation of their teamwork for recognizing the root causes of their issue in a rational and nondefensive approach (see Figure 9.7). This was a productive way to build up their inner relationships and to looking at the team issues as a whole.

Step 3

The MBD used the brainstorming process to gather needed information and feedbacks for conducting the fishbone diagram for their "Cause-and-Effect Analysis" (see Figure 9.2). The primary strength of this tool is that it visually organizes information and depicts the links between the problem and its possible causes.

By the end of this work session, the MBD team recognized three potential root causes of their team's performance gaps and some of their issues in communication and teamwork,

Key Factors to Remember

Let's review the lessons in this chapter about generating ways to identify root cause(s):

- Think like a detective when identifying root cause(s)
- Avoid confusing symptoms and root cause(s)
- Realize that most problems in organizations will have more than one root cause
- Realize that some root cause(s) can never be identified, though it is highly desirable to make the effort to do so
- Be willing to take the time to investigate root causes rather than jumping to action with little to no information because that can make matters worse

Coaching and Developmental Questions for Managers

(1) How do you rate yourself from 0 to 10 (0 being the lowest and 10 being the highest) on your knowledge and understanding of separating signs, symptoms, and root cause(s)?
  - What is missing or in the way of your understanding?
  - What is your action plan to increase your overall rate?

(2) How do you rate yourself from 0 to 10 (0 being the lowest and 10 being the highest) on your knowledge and understanding of approaches to pinpointing root cause(s)?
  - What is missing?
  - What is your action plan to increase your overall rate?

(3) How do you rate yourself from 0 to 10 (0 being the lowest and 10 being the highest) on your ability to facilitate one-on-one real-time root cause analysis?
  - What is missing or not understood?
  - What is your action plan to increase your overall rate?

(4) How do you rate yourself from 0 to 10 (0 being the lowest and 10 being the highest) on your ability to facilitate team or work group efforts to do robust root cause analysis?
  – What is missing or not understood?
  – What is your action plan to increase your overall rate?

References

Alderfer, Clayton. 2010. *The Practice of Organizational Diagnosis: Theory and Methods*. New York: Oxford University Press.

Bakhshandeh, Behnam. 2009. *Conspiracy for Greatness; Mastery on Love Within*. San Diego, CA: Primeco Education, Inc.

Bentley, Joseph, and Michael Toth. 2020. *Exploring Wicked Problems: What They Are and Why They Are Important*. Avon, MA: Archway Publishing.

Bristow, Nigel, and Sarah Sandberg. 2010. *The Corporate Culture Audit*. Charmouth, Dorset, UK: Cambridge Strategy Publications.

Buzan, Tony C. 2006. *The Ultimate Book of Mind Maps: Unlock Your Creativity, Boost Your Memory, Change Your Life*. London: HarperCollins.

Buzan, Tony C., and Chris Griffiths. 2012. *Modern Mind Mapping for Smarter Thinking*. Cardiff: Proactive Press.

Cummings, Thomas G., and Christopher G. Worley. 2015. *Organization Development & Change*, 10th ed. Stamford, CT: Cengage Learning.

"Does a Med School Degree Guarantee Diagnosis Skills?" 2015. www.medpagetoday.com/primarycare/generalprimarycare/52991.

Dyer, Gibb W. Jr., Jeffrey H. Dyer, and William G. Dyer. 2013. *Team Building*, 5th ed. San Francisco, CA: Jossey-Bass.

Fournies, Ferdinand. 2007. *Why Employees Don't Do What They're Supposed to and What You Can Do About It*, 2nd ed. New York: McGraw-Hill.

Gilbert, Thomas. 2007. *Human Competence: Engineering Worthy Performance*, tribute ed. San Francisco, CA: Pfeiffer.

Kolb, Judith A. 2011. *Small Group Facilitation: Improving Process and Performance in Groups and Teams*. Amherst, MA: HRD Press Inc.

Lencioni, Patrick. 2007. *Overcoming the Five Dysfunctions of a Team: A Field Guide for Leaders, Managers, and Facilitators*. San Francisco, CA: Jossey-Bass.

Levi, Daniel. 2017. *Group Dynamics for Teams*, 5th ed. Los Angeles, CA: Sage Publications.

Mager, Robert, and Peter Pipe. 1997. *Analyzing Performance Problems: Or You Really Oughta Wanna: How to Figure Out Why People Aren't Doing What They Should Be, and What to do About It*, 3rd ed. Carefree, AZ: Center for Effective Performance.

Pershing, James, ed. 2006. *Handbook of Human Performance Technology*, 3rd ed. San Francisco, CA: Pfeiffer.

Randall, Gerry, and John Toplis. 2016. *Toward Organizational Fitness: A Guide to Diagnosis and Treatment*. New York: Routledge.

Rothwell, William J. 2013. *Performance Consulting: Applying Performance Improvement in Human Resource Development*. San Francisco, CA: John Wiley & Sons.

Rothwell, William J. 2015. *Beyond Training & Development: Enhancing Human Performance Through a Measurable Focus on Business Impact*, 3rd ed. Amherst, MA: HRD Press, Inc.

Rothwell, William J., and James M. Graber. 2010. *Competency-Based Training Basics*. East Peoria, IL: ASTD Press.

Rothwell, William J., Carolyn K. Hohne, and Stephen B. King. 2018. *Human Performance Improvement: Building Practitioner Performance*, 3rd ed. New York, NY: Routledge.

Rothwell, William J., Jacqueline M. Stavros, and Roland L. Sullivan. 2016. *Practicing Organization Development: Leading Transformation and Change*, 4th ed. Hoboken, NJ: John Wiley & Sons, Inc.

Rothwell, William, Angela Stopper, and Jennifer Myers, eds. 2017. *Assessment and Diagnosis for Organization Development: Powerful Tools and Perspectives for the OD Practitioner*. New York: Routledge.

Santos, Diogo M. F. 2013. "Top 10 Totally Free Mind Mapping Software Tools." *IMDevin.com*, Published February 15.

Schein, Edgar H. 1988. *Process Consulting Volume 1. Its Role in Organization Development*, 2nd ed. New Your, NY: Addison-Wesley.

ANALYZING THE SOLUTION

Performance coaching can require some creative thinking. The reason is simple: gaps can be closed in many ways, and coaches—working with coachees—should consider ways to close gaps, select the "best" way to close the gap, and reflect on the likely consequences of efforts to close gaps. Any problem can be solved in more than one way, though some ways may be more appropriate, cost-effective, or faster than others. This phase addresses the issues described in the following:

Chapter 10—Step 7: How Many Ways Can the Gap Be Closed?
Finding ways to close the gap requires creative thinking, often in real time, and precedes the decision about which solution is best.

Chapter 11—Step 8: What Is the Most Effective Way to Close the Gap?
Finding the most effective way to close the gap is important because that means choosing the solution.

Chapter 12—Step 9: What Are the Consequences of Closing the Gap?
This step is akin to thinking forward, trying to anticipate the possible results or consequences of implementing a solution

DOI: 10.4324/9781003155928-13

Chapter 10

Step 7: How Many Ways Can the Gap Be Closed?

William J. Rothwell

Once the cause of a performance gap is clear—or at least approximated—then closing the gap becomes the next step in performance coaching. Finding ways to close the gap requires creative thinking, often in real time, and precedes the decision about which solution is best. Creating a list of possible solutions before selecting one is the focus of this chapter. Think of this step as brainstorming solutions. Any problem can be solved in many ways, and this step requires performance coaches to brainstorm what solutions are possible.

How This Chapter Is Organized

This chapter is organized into the following parts:

- What This Step Means
- Why This Step in Performance Coaching is Important?
- Examples of This Step in Performance Coaching
- Brainstorming Solutions to Performance Problems
- Pushing Idea Generation of Possible Solutions into Real Time
- Brainstorming Ways to Innovate Beyond Present Performance
- How This Step Can Go Wrong—and How to Avoid the Missteps
- Competencies Required by Performance Coaches to Generate Ways to Close Gaps

DOI: 10.4324/9781003155928-14

■ Key Factors to Remember
■ Coaching and Developmental Questions for Managers

What This Step Means

Step 7 is about generating as many creative ways to close performance gaps as possible. Recall that gaps can be *negative* (i.e., a deficiency between what is and what should be), *neutral* (i.e., actual results match targets), or *positive* (i.e., a strength in which present conditions are better than desired targets).

When gaps are negative, closing them requires corrective action. When gaps are neutral, no action is warranted. However, performance coaches should consider possible creative ways to take advantage of neutral conditions to achieve competitive advantage. When gaps are positive, any action involves intensifying strategic strengths—or getting better at what the organization, team, or individual already excels at.

Why This Step in Performance Coaching Is Important?

This step is important because any performance gap may be closed in many possible ways. It must be emphasized that no problem has just one solution; no performance gap can be closed in just one way. Additionally, some problems—what some call "wicked problems" (Bentley and Toth 2020)—may require multiple steps, and multiple solutions (Williams and Van't Hof 2016), to solve.

Avoiding the Temptation to Jump to Conclusions

Most people have an unfortunate tendency when they confront a problem to jump to the first solution they can think of. That is particularly true of busy managers who are pressured to perform and are therefore eager to solve a problem quickly when they spot one. Performance coaches and their coachees are no different from other people. It is thus tempting—particularly for anyone feeling a strong sense of urgency—to grasp at the first solution they can identify. Yet, hastily chosen actions will often exacerbate a problem rather than alleviate it because the consequences of those actions may be ignored in a bid to choose expediency to effectiveness.

Pause and Consider

While many contemporary business observers claim that modern times are more pressure-packed than the past, the reality is that people have always been tempted to jump to conclusions.

When performance coaches and coachees encounter performance gaps, they should briefly *pause and consider what to do.* The first step in that process is to stop. Call a time out. The second step is to reflect, even if only momentarily, on the issue. The third step is to generate as many possible solutions as possible. Those three steps can be taken quickly and in real time. But it is important to carry out those steps rather than short-circuiting them in a bid to make decisions fast.

Examples of This Step in Performance Coaching

Perhaps, some examples will help to clarify what this step means.

A Performance Coach Dealing with a Negative Performance Gap

The situation: John Smith, a manager, is confronting a problem with Mary Georgeson. Georgeson works on an assembly line. Her coworkers complain that she is not keeping up with the production line and that means that the line itself is not meeting the production standards. The plant engineers have set the standard at 400 products per hour. But the line is producing only 380. Additional investigation and observation verify that Georgeson's performance is causing the performance gap. And it is measurable. Each product is worth $3.74. A gap of 20 products per hour costs $74.80 per hour. That translates into $598.40 per shift and $2,992 per five-day week. It Is thus important because it leads to a sizable loss of money.

The conversation between the performance coach and coachee: Smith decides to have a performance coaching session with Georgeson. He follows the steps of the performance coaching process. When he reaches step 7, the conversation goes as follows:

Smith: [*He stops a moment to think about the situation. Then he considers how to proceed based on the body language and general mannerisms of the coachee.*] How do you think you might be able to improve your work with your co-workers on the assembly line?

Georgeson: I am not quite sure. You have not given me enough training, and this meeting is the first time I have heard about the production problems. While my co-workers have complained to you about me—apparently—they said nothing to me. You are the manager. You tell me what you want me to do, and I will try to do it.

Smith: Well, of course, I can tell you what to do. Given that we have determined the root causes of the problem that you feel that you were not given adequate training and were not informed of the problem, I think we should begin by giving you the training. Do you agree? You are also informed of the production standard and the perception that you are causing the assembly line production shortfalls. Do you agree? Can we brainstorm on other possible solutions to the problem?

Georgeson: Sure. I think you should also look at the capping machine on the production line. Every time I work on that, I find that it is not performing properly. You should have the assembly line mechanics look at it.

Smith: Fair enough.

Note that, in the previous discussion, Smith encourages Georgeson to brainstorm on possible solutions. He does that to encourage her to take responsibility for solving her own problems. But he could have gone steps further by probing Georgeson for more solutions and more discussion about what might be causing her performance problems. He could also have offered pointed suggestions based on his own assessment of the situation.

A Performance Coach Dealing with a Neutral Performance Gap

The conversation in the previous section would have been different if the assembly line had been meeting production standards. Under traditional management thinking, the principle of *management by exception* would dictate that no conversation should occur between the performance coach and coachee for the simple reason that no problem exists (Blokdyk 2018).

Management by exception is based on the view that managers should prioritize their time use. They should, according to the principle, focus only on solving problems. If results match plans, then managers should do nothing. After all, no problem exists.

But a neutral performance gap could also present an opportunity to improve. Consider the revised conversation between Smith and Georgeson in the following.

The conversation between the performance coach and coachee: Smith decides to have a performance coaching session with Georgeson. He follows the steps of the performance coaching process. When he reaches step 7, the conversation goes as follows:

Smith: [*He stops a moment to think about the situation. Then he considers how to proceed based on the body language and general mannerisms of the coachee.*] What are your thoughts on the production levels expected of the assembly line you are working on?

Georgeson: I think it could be better. But it meets the targets managers— and engineers—set for it. I suppose they knew what they were doing when they set those targets.

Smith: I suspected as much. I always say that, if you do only what is expected, you will end up mediocre at best. Pinpointing opportunities for improvement—even when they are not necessarily needed—can offer unique chances to outsmart competitors.

Georgeson: I agree with you. But I also think the workers are doing about as well as they can.

Smith: Sure, sure. But are you willing to spend a few minutes to brainstorm with me on ways that the production levels might be increased? What about involving your co-workers in the same kind of brainstorming?

Note that performing in alignment with targets, or expectations, does nothing to give the organization a competitive advantage. It is just not good enough. While workers should know what is expected and take steps to meet the minimum standards, they should also be told they are expected to engage their minds to find ways to give their organizations advantages. That can be done by constantly questioning how performance could be better.

A Performance Coaching Dealing with a Positive Performance Gap

Performance coaches should be prepared to go beyond mere efforts to close negative performance gaps or prompt new, creative thinking about neutral gaps. The conversation in the previous section would have been different if the assembly line had been exceeding production standards. Using strengths-based management, performance coaches might prompt workers to think about how they could build on their strengths even when individuals, teams, or organizations exceed expectations.

Strengths-based management is the view that what people enjoy doing most may indicate their strengths (Clifton 2008). It is easier, the theory holds, to enhance performance if it is already a strength (Orem, Binkert, and Clancy 2007). Doing so requires *visioning,* a process of thinking forward about an optimistic view of the future in which individuals or teams have leveraged their strengths to maximum advantage. What would that look like? The answer to that question is a strengths-based future vision.

Performance coaches can encourage people—in real time—to think about what they enjoy most and what they do best. That can lead to a tactical (daily) view of how to leverage strengths.

A positive performance gap presents an opportunity to build on strengths. Consider the revised conversation between Smith and Georgeson in the following.

The conversation between the performance coach and coachee: Smith decides to have a performance coaching session with Georgeson. He follows the steps of the performance coaching process. When he reaches step 7, the conversation goes as follows:

Smith: [*He stops a moment to think about the situation. Then he considers how to proceed based on the body language and general mannerisms of the coachee.*] What do you feel you do best on your job every day? What do you believe are the strengths of your workgroup on the assembly line?

Georgeson: I think our production levels are very high. And they are consistent.

Smith: That is a strength. But do you enjoy achieving such high levels of production? How much do you feel your co-workers take pleasure in such super-production?

Georgeson: I can't speak for others. But it does give me a sense of satisfaction to see that our team outperformed the rest of the plant!

Smith: How do you think we could give you that feeling more often? You say you sense it daily. But could we give you that feeling of accomplishment more often?

Georgeson: I suppose so. Maybe we could hold periodic discussion groups at break time about how things are going?

Smith: That is an excellent idea. How would you see that working?

Georgeson: I think we should schedule daily brainstorming sessions to generate ideas—and intensify our feelings achieved from the day's production levels.

Smith: Brainstorming might get old after a few days.

Georgeson: Maybe we should involve the workers in coming up with a list of ways that we could use to generate ideas. That way we would not wear any of them out quickly.

A Tool to Guide Performance Coaches through Brainstorming

Use the tool appearing in Table 10.1 as a job aid to help you carry out this step.

Brainstorming Solutions to Performance Problems

To carry out step 7, performance coaches and coachees must be able to brainstorm solutions to performance gaps.

There are three ways to do that.

Table 10.1   A Tool to Guide Performance Coaches through Brainstorming: How Many Ways Can the Gap Be Closed?

A Tool to Guide Performance Coaches through Brainstorming: How Many Ways Can the Gap Be Closed?		
Directions: For each step in the left column below, indicate in the center column if you have considered it or not. Check the appropriate box. In the right column, take notes about what you could do in that step.		
Have You, as Performance Coach, Done the Following:	**Your Answer** **Yes** √ / **No** √	**Notes About What You Can Do**
1 Identified the performance gap or else guided the coachee to identify the performance gap?		
2 Paused a moment?		
3 Considered ways to close gaps in real time (such as real-time brainstorming) or else guided the coachee to consider ways to close the gap?		
4 Created a lengthy list of possible ways to close the gap?		

Source: Copyright 2021 by William J. Rothwell.

The first way is to rely on traditional approaches to finding creative solutions to problems. Typical approaches include:

■ brainstorming
■ mind mapping
■ the Delphi technique
■ nominal group technique

In brainstorming, group members first pick a problem. Then, they create a list of as many ideas as they can think of. Finally, they discuss solutions and vote for one. In mind mapping, group members draw pictures to illustrate what concepts they associate with an issue—and thereby generate associations, which may prompt possible solutions. In the Delphi technique, which takes its name from the ancient temple of Delphi in Greece, a panel of experts are assembled. They are individually asked to offer solutions. Then, the combined list is handed back to them, and the experts are prompted to vote for the best solutions while also offering more ideas. This cycle of voting and generating ideas is carried out over four rounds. The nominal group technique (NGT) relies on silent idea generation from a group and then group voting to pick the best idea.

Much has been written about such methods of channeling creative thinking at a time when leadership in innovation has grown to become key to competitive advantage (Gliddon and Rothwell 2018). More than 105 ways for individuals or groups to generate creative ideas are listed in Van Gundy's classic book *Techniques of Structured Problem Solving* (1988).

Some of the well-known approaches to idea generation described earlier (and at greater length in an earlier chapter) can be adapted for give-and-take, real-time discussions with workers. For instance, a manager and worker can work together over a table in the company break room to list out many possible ways to solve a problem. That does not require expensive software or even a work group; rather, one manager and one worker could do it if they set their minds to it. Likewise, the same manager and worker could draw a picture on a napkin of ways to solve a problem. That does not require a group or even an office or conference room. Two people—the manager and a worker—can each write their own list of solutions and then share them to see on what solutions their lists share in common and what solutions might differ across lists. That method can prompt discussions to generate more solutions.

The second way is to apply a growing number of virtual ways to gener-ate ideas. These ways are sometimes called *group decision support systems, collaborative software solutions, idea management software, creative proj-ect management software*, or sometimes *creative management software*. They often encourage asynchronous, workgroup idea generation; they encourage collaboration; they sometimes permit idea ranking; they allow crowdsourcing for ideas; they allow status tracking; and much more. It is thus possible to do virtual coaching to improve performance—as well as to improve how well people in teams work together to achieve results (Rothwell and Park 2021).

The third way is to find creative solutions *in real time*. Time is becoming the only real source of competitive advantage. While traditional approaches to finding creative solutions often require time to apply, real-time efforts to discover creative solutions must be carried out "on the fly" (in normal con-versation and on the job). Linkner's (2021) book *Big Little Breakthroughs: How Small, Everyday Innovations Drive Oversized Results* gives ideas about how to do that and is aligned with other real-time approaches—such as those geared to developing talent daily (Rothwell, Chee, and Oi 2015) or microlearning approaches designed to meet immediate learning needs (Torgerson 2020). Many of the approaches suggested in "Idea Generation" (2021) can also be adapted to real-time applications by performance coaches.

Pushing Idea Generation of Possible Solutions into Real Time

How can performance coaches speed up the process of generating a list of possible solutions to performance problems into real time? Often the goal is not to apply *rigorous* approaches to problem-solving; rather, the goal is to generate a long list of *possible* solutions.

Performance gaps can exist for organizations, work groups or teams, or individuals. Consider an example of how to generate a lengthy list of solu-tions with a team.

The Situation

Rolanda Dirksen is the team leader of a customer service team that takes care of the Northeastern United States for a well-known insurance company. The team answers customer questions and any insurance policy problems that may arise. The team has been experiencing declining customer satisfaction measures as indicated by weekly customer surveys. It seems clear that the measures are declining because the team is pressured to service increasing calls.

The Conversation with the Team

The conversation between the performance coach and the team (coachees): Dirksen decides to have a virtual performance coaching session with her team. All team members work from home. Some are based in the U.S.; some are based in Asia or Europe. Dirksen follows the steps of the performance coaching process. When she reaches step 7, the conversation goes as follows:

Dirksen: [*She stops a moment to think about the situation. Then she considers how to proceed.*] What ideas do you have, as a team, about ways we can bring up our customer satisfaction scores?

Team Member 1 (Lorton Wiles with the webcam off on a videoconference): Why are you asking us? You are the one making the big bucks as manager, which they now euphemistically call "team leader." You tell us.

Dirksen: We need to work together effectively. You are being paid for more than just typing. The organization expects you to give us ideas. Could we focus on the issue please?

Team Member 2 (Cheryl Laddrun): Dirksen is right. I suggest we examine the root cause and then generate a list of possible ways to improve the scores. Since we are paid in part on how we score, I think this is an important issue for us individually as well as for the organization.

Dirksen: Good. Let's do that.

Team Member 3 (Jon Cronson): I think that we are stressed out. I know I am. I think we need to do some quick research, perhaps a quick google search, on best ways to maintain civility while under pressure and while stressed out.

Team Member 4 (Laura Bach): I don't know what to suggest. It is lunch time here. [*She giggles.*]

Note that, in the previous discussion, Dirksen prompts the team to do real-time problem-solving to close the gap in customer service scores revealed by the weekly customer satisfaction surveys. That is a way to demonstrate step 7 for a team. Dirksen, as performance coach, does that to tap into team creativity while also building ownership in the problem and solutions.

Brainstorming Ways to Innovate Beyond Present Performance

Performance coaches can use many ways to brainstorm how to innovate beyond present performance. The trend is, of course, to do that in real time. Real-time idea generation for the performance coach—and performance coachees—is the key to success. An alternative is to spin off problems to committees or team that will study a problem at greater depth and then offer solutions. But handing off problems to committees often delays action. While it may be an excellent way to kill action—or the motivation to take action—the demands of today's workplace often requires immediate, if only adequate, solutions.

Among the ways that ideas may be generated include:

- observing people perform and reflecting on what they do to discover new ideas to address performance issues
- reading newly published books and/or journals and reflecting on how to apply new ideas to address performance issues
- surfing the web with random keywords to generate ideas to apply to performance issues
- meditating on ideas to address performance issues
- using structured approaches, such as mind mapping, to generate ideas to apply to performance issues
- talking to people you do not know and asking their opinions about ways to solve performance issues
- rephrasing your performance problem and then seeing if that offers new solutions to performance problems
- intensifying performance problems and then seeing if that offers new ideas
- thinking about the performance problem overnight ("sleep on it")
- brainstorming solutions to problems and then seeing which ones might fit the performance problems you are facing

Use the assessment shown in Table 10.2.

Of course, other innovative ways exist to solve performance problems or leverage strengths. Consider, for instance, changing:

- who does the work
- What work is done

Table 10.2   An Organizational Assessment of Approaches to Find Creative Solutions to Problems in Real Time.

An Organizational Assessment of Approaches to Find Creative Solutions to Problems in Real Time

Directions:

Use this instrument to assess how well you feel your organization's performance coaches are generally able to apply *real-time* approaches to generating solutions to performance problems.

Use this scale: **0 = Not at all; 1 = Performance Coaches Do This Very Poorly; 2 = Performance Coaches Do This Poorly; 3 = Performance Coaches Do This Somewhat Well; 4 = Performance Coaches Do This Well; 5 = Performance Coaches Do This Very Well.** Rate the items. When you finish, add up the scores in the right column and place the total below. Then consult the scoring interpretation.

	How Well Do You Feel That Performance Coaches in This Organization Are Generally Able to Apply Real-Time Solutions to Generating Solutions to Performance Problems?	Ratings					
		0	1	2	3	4	5
1	Observing people perform and reflecting on what they do as means to discover new ideas to address performance issues						
2	Reading newly published books and/or journals and reflecting on how to apply new ideas to address performance issues						
3	Surfing the web with random keywords to generate ideas to apply to performance issues						
4	Meditating on ideas to address performance issues						
5	Using structured approaches, such as mind mapping, to generate ideas to apply to performance issues						
6	Talking to people you do not know and asking their opinions about ways to solve performance issues						
7	Rephrasing your performance problem and then seeing if that offers new solutions to performance problems						
8	Intensifying performance problems and then seeing if that offers new ideas						
9	Thinking about the performance problem overnight ("sleep on it")						
10	Brainstorming solutions to problems and then seeing which ones might fit the performance problems you are facing						
	Total per column						
	Grand total (total of six columns divided by 10)						

Source: Copyright 2021 by William J. Rothwell.

Scoring (for Table 10.2)	
If your score is	*Then*
50–41	Congratulations. Your organization is doing a good job, in your opinion, of generating solutions to performance problems.
40–31	Give your organization a grade of B. You have some work to do, but it appears that you are headed in the right direction in generating real-time ideas to solve problems.
30–21	Give your organization a grade of C. It is about average. Work on the issues you rated low.
20–11	Give your organization a grade of D. It is below average. Work on the issues you rated low.
10–0	Fail your organization. Take immediate corrective action.

- When the work is done
- Where the work is done
- How the work is carried out

How to Meet the Special Challenges Posed by This Step

There are several ways this step can pose challenges.

First, performance coaches may be tempted to apply the first solution they can think of. For instance, they may suggest the coachee participate in training—even when training is not warranted or is not an appropriate solution. Suggesting training as a solution is admittedly a fast way to shift a problem to someone else, but training is often the most expensive solution. Further, only 8% of off-the-job training transfers back to a job in changed before, and it is thus rarely an effective, sustainable solution.

Second, performance coaches may fall victim to distractions posed by coachees. The most common distractions offered by coachees when accused of negative performance gaps are to:

- plead that performance gaps are the fault of the organization or coach by not providing sufficient training
- indicate that they were never informed of performance standards; key performance indicators; common or best business practices; organizational policies and procedures; or relevant laws, rules, and regulations
- suggest that other workers are not treated the same way and thus objections to performance are unfair and capricious

Table 10.3   A Tool to Avoid Common Challenges When Considering Ways to Close Gaps.

A Tool to Avoid Common Challenges When Considering Ways to Close Gaps			
Directions: For each step in the left column below, indicate in the center column if you have considered it or not. Check the appropriate box. In the right column, take notes about what you could do in that step.			
Have You Taken Steps to Avoid Each of the Following Common Missteps When Considering Ways to Close Gaps?	**Your Answer**		**Notes About How to Avoid the Mistakes**
Did you :	Yes √	No √	
1 Plead that performance gaps are the fault of the organization by not providing sufficient training?			
2 Plead that performance gaps are the fault of the coach by not providing sufficient training?			
3 Indicate that they were never informed of performance standards; key performance indicators; common or best business practices; organizational policies and procedures; or relevant laws, rules, and regulations?			
4 Suggest that other workers are not treated the same way and thus objections to performance are unfair and capricious?			

Source: Copyright 2021 by William J. Rothwell.

Of course, other missteps can be made. But these are the most important. Consider using the tool appearing in Table 10.3 to brainstorm ways to address these common missteps.

Competencies Required by Performance Coaches to Generate Ways to Close Gaps

Performance coaches should be able to:

■ pause during a performance problem: Coaches should pause and consider a performance problem before jumping to conclusions or providing solutions that sound good but are not. Stop a moment and think when confronted with a problem. Encourage other people, like the coachee, to do likewise. Call and time out and think about the problem and possible solutions. In practice that can be done by asking for a restroom break or a stretch break.

■ reflect and meditate effectively: Do soul-searching. Think about what is going on and how many solutions are possible to a given problem. Take a deep breath or rely on real-time meditation strategies to clear the mind.

■ ponder creatively on ways to solve problems: Do not trust the first idea that pops into the mind. Try to take the first idea and ask "how can that idea be leapfrogged—that is, go one better than that?"

■ ponder creatively on how to find opportunities when confronting neutral performance gaps: Do not ignore performance when it is meeting expectations. Ask what issues could be pushed to advantage by not taking it for granted. Never be satisfied or complacent about how things are. Be willing to ask coachees what they take for granted in their own performance and how that performance could be improved.

■ ponder creatively on how to leverage individual, team, or organizational strengths: Always ask how strengths may be pushed to greater advantage. Always push coachees what they believe they do best and then how they could get even better at what they are already good at.

Business Case Example

Continuing with the MBD case (as in previous chapters), the management team decided to generate a lengthy list of possible ways to close the performance gap. To that end, they chose not to meet in person, which is often a preferred way to do brainstorming or other idea generation approaches, and instead decided to meet online by videoconference.

The MBD team was keenly aware that face-to-face meetings lead to more ideas than face-to-face meetings. One source found that, on average, a face-to-face meeting will generate more than thirteen ideas, but a virtual meeting will generate only 10 ("Face Squared—The Numbers Behind Face to Face Networking" 2021). But the team still decided to choose a virtual meeting because it was far less costly than a residential meeting where travel costs can be excessive.

Step 1

The MBD team began preparing for the virtual meeting by preparing an agenda for the virtual meeting. Team members decided on the agenda—and on how much time would be set aside for idea generation. They arbitrarily chose a one-hour time limit for idea generation. They then sent out a doodle poll to pick the day and time for the meeting, since their schedules are busy. A decision was made on the day and time, and the invitation was sent out to all team members.

Step 2

On the day of the virtual meeting, the team members assembled. They had chosen simple brainstorming as the preferred way to generate as many ideas as possible. A facilitator was brought in from the HR department to help the team come up with as many ideas as possible in the shortest time. The facilitator began by describing what the team members would do, why they would do it, and how the brainstorming process was to be structured.

Step 3

The facilitator led the group in coming up with many ideas. She had cautioned team members that they should not be critical during the first step of brainstorming and simply list as many ideas as they could think of to close the performance gap. When team members started to find issues with the ideas, the facilitator intervened and reminded the group not to be critical during the first step of brainstorming. The facilitator then led the group through a process of discussing the list of ideas.

Key Factors to Remember

Let's review the lessons in this chapter about generating ways to close performance gaps:

- Avoid the temptation to jump to conclusions
- Pause and consider before offering a solution to a performance problem or a vision for leveraging a performance strength
- Focus on conversations, online discussions, or techniques of problem-solving to address performance problems or strengths

- Prompt coachees to create new ideas to solve performance problems or leverage performance strengths
- Provide guidance, as performance coaches, to coachees through creative group sessions, virtual and asynchronous sessions, and one-on-one real-time sessions
- Generate as many ideas as possible before selecting one
- Avoid common mistakes made in generating ideas to close performance gaps

Coaching and Developmental Questions for Managers

(1) How do you rate yourself from 0 to 10 (0 being the lowest and 10 being the highest) on your knowledge and understanding of different ways of pausing when confronting a problem or issue?
   - What is missing or in the way of your understanding?
   - What is your action plan to increase your overall rate?

(2) How do you rate yourself from 0 to 10 (0 being the lowest and 10 being the highest) on your knowledge and understanding of generating many possible solutions to performance problems/negative gaps?
   - What is missing?
   - What is your action plan to increase your overall rate?

(3) How do you rate yourself from 0 to 10 (0 being the lowest and 10 being the highest) on your ability to generate ideas to address neutral performance gaps?
   - What is missing or not understood?
   - What is your action plan to increase your overall rate?

(4) How do you rate yourself from 0 to 10 (0 being the lowest and 10 being the highest) on your knowledge and understanding of creative ways to leverage positive performance gaps?
   - What is missing or not understood?
   - What is your action plan to increase your overall rate?

References

Bentley, Joseph, and Michael Toth. 2020. *Exploring Wicked Problems: What They Are and Why They Are Important*. Bloomington, IN: Archway Publishing.

Blokdyk, Gerardus. 2018. *Management by Exception*, 2nd ed. Virginia Beach, VA: CreateSpace Independent Publishing Platform.

Clifton, Don. 2008. *Strengths-based Leadership: Great Leaders, Teams, and Why People Follow*. Washington, DC: Gallup Press.

"Face Squared—The Numbers Behind Face to Face Networking." 2021. *Great Business Schools*. www.greatbusinessschools.org/networking/.

Gliddon, David, and William Rothwell, eds. 2018. *Innovation Leadership*. New York, NY: Routledge.

"Idea Generation." 2021. *Science Direct*. www.sciencedirect.com/topics/computer-science/idea-generation.

Linkner, Josh. 2021. *Big Little Breakthroughs: How Small, Everyday Innovations Drive Oversized Results*. New York, NY: Poster Hill.

Orem, Sara, Jacqueline Binkert, and Ann Clancy. 2007. *Appreciative Coaching: A Positive Process for Change*. San Francisco, CA: Jossey-Bass.

Rothwell, William, Peter Chee, and Jenny Ooi. 2015. *The Leader's Daily Role in Talent Management: Maximizing Results, Engagement, and Retention*. New York, NY: McGraw-Hill.

Rothwell, William, and Cho Hyun Park. 2021. *Virtual Coaching to Improve Group Relationships: Process Consultation Reimagined*. New York, NY: Routledge.

Torgerson, Carla. 2020. *Designing Microlearning (What Works in Talent Development)*. Alexandria, VA: Association for Talent Development.

Van Gundy, Arthur. 1988. *Techniques of Structured Problem Solving*, 2nd ed. New York: Van Nostrand Reinhold; Brentwood, TN: Post Hill Press.

Williams, Bob, and Sjon Van't Hof. 2016. *Wicked Solutions: A Systems Approach to Complex Problems*. Morrisville, NC: Lulu.

Chapter 11

Step 8: What Is the Most Effective Way to Close the Gap?

William J. Rothwell

Once the root cause(s) of a performance gap is clear to stakeholders and possible ways to close the gap have been brainstormed, performance coaches should pinpoint the most effective way to close the gap. Pinpointing the most effective way to close the gap is a mixture of art and science, since performance coaches must strike a balance between cost, effectiveness, and other consideration (such as organizational politics) when choosing the most effective solution. Finding the most effective way to close the gap is important because that means choosing the solution.

It can be tempting to forego a reasoned choice and simply grab something that looks appealing and can be implemented quickly and perhaps inexpensively. But it is best to do some reasoned analysis to determine what solution choice will strike the balance among cost, speed, business impact, and other considerations (such as sustained management support). Admittedly, that is not always possible for various reasons—and that can include company politics. Indeed, performance coaches will find occasions when expediency simply trumps reasoned action. Still, it is best to aim for the best, rather than the fastest or cheapest, solution when possible.

DOI: 10.4324/9781003155928-15

How This Chapter Is Organized

This chapter is organized into the following parts:

■ What This Step Means
■ Why Is This Step in Performance Coaching Important?
■ Approaches to Determining the Best Solution Choice
■ Competencies Required by Performance Coaches to Select the Best Choice
■ Key Factors to Remember
■ Coaching and Developmental Questions for Managers

What This Step Means

Step 8 is about selecting a solution from the choices generated in step 7. In step 7, performance coaches generate as many possible solutions as they can think of; in step 8, they narrow them down to one or more desirable choices. It may sound easy. But it rarely is. Many factors complicate the choice of what solution to use to solve a problem. While it might seem that cost/benefit analysis—what some people call Return on Investment (ROI)—would be the governing issue to consider (Phillips and Phillips 2006), it turns out that organizational politics is a more frequent issue of concern when selecting a preferred solution.

Organizational politics is a term that covers many notions. Politics is the study of power and authority. Political issues in organizations are not merely rational but are often perceptual and emotional (Dobson and Dobson 2006; Greiner and Schein 1998), having to do with who gains and who loses in any change effort. Implementing a performance coaching solution is an exercise in power, and those affected by that solution may welcome it, detest it, have mixed feelings about it, or have relatively neutral feelings due to personal or professional reasons. Self-interest is the basis of all organizational politics.

Politics itself can sometimes be regarded as a performance problem. In fact, as Hochwarter et al. (2020, 880) note, "demonstrating the continued relevance of office politics, a recent survey of 2,700 individuals from over 100 countries indicated that members of the modern workforce view office politics as one of the top barriers to job performance" (HBR Ascend Staff 2019). Common sense may dictate one course of action or solution, but the self-interest of leaders or other powerful stakeholders may drive other choices. Perhaps that is what is meant by the old joke that "there is a right way, a wrong way, and our way."

Why Is This Step in Performance Coaching Important?

This step is important because any performance gap may be closed effectively through more than one solution. (In fact, some gaps must be closed by multiple solutions.) Negative gaps require solutions; neutral gaps do not require the choice of corrective action but can still prompt action if that action will produce benefits that outweigh the costs or will provide other benefits; positive gaps require efforts from among many choices to leverage strengths and thereby intensify (and build on) success. The point worth emphasizing here is that closing a gap requires decisions to be made about what solution among many should be chosen. Performance coaches take the lead in selecting the solution(s) and implementing them.

Of note is also that any gap may result from more than one root cause and may thus require more than one solution. Multiple solutions have the potential to interact and create new problems—a fact that medical doctors know well when they consider prescribing one medicine to cure illness when the patient is already on other medicines to treat other conditions. Medical doctors call it *contraindication*—meaning that medicine may create harmful side effects when combined with one or more other medicines.

Taking aspirin is a famous example of contraindication. If patients have headaches, medical doctors may prescribe aspirin. But aspirin has a famous side effect: it causes stomach distress. It is thus possible to take medicine to cure one problem only to cause other, different problems. The same principle applies when selecting solutions during performance coaching.

Think about the issues that can arise when coaches set out to address a performance problem. A simple example may illustrate the point. Suppose Manager Anita Thompson wishes to demonstrate an appreciation for dealing with family problems to address expressed concerns on the company's workplace engagement survey. Worker Marita Ortez visits Thompson and requests permission to leave work early because Ortez has a child who is performing in a school play. Thompson grants the request. When the time comes for Ortez to leave early, her coworkers see that she is cleaning up her desk and is preparing to leave work thirty minutes early. They ask where she is going, and she tells them the manager gave her permission to leave so that she could attend her child's play at school. Her coworkers then go to Thompson with many of their own legitimate reasons to leave early. Since Thompson granted Ortez's request, she knows that she cannot deny legitimate requests if she is to avoid charges of favoritism. She grants all the requests and finds that the entire work unit is empty at the end of the day even as customers demand immediate service. The point to the example is that solutions taken to address one cause may lead to other problems that can spiral out of control with results that prompt nightmares.

So, an important point here is to list out the possible solutions to a performance problem and then apply whatever analytical approaches that time permits. While a robust analysis is rarely possible because of intense and immediate pressures to act, such an approach will likely result in better solutions than grabbing and using the first idea that occurs to decision-makers.

What to Consider

When selecting the most feasible solution to a problem, performance coaches will find that they can rely on many ways to do that.

Consider such approaches as:

- What solution(s) will most decision-makers and/or workers like?
- What solution(s) will be most appealing to key (powerful) stakeholder groups and decision-makers?
- What solution is most likely to be implemented?
- What solution will be most likely to yield measurable results?
- What solution(s) will strike a balance between cost and speed?
- What solution(s) will be most sustainable and likely to "stick" in the corporate culture?
- What solution(s) will most likely yield a favorable return on investment?
- What solution(s) will most likely have the most impact on individuals, teams, or organizational goals?

Use the tool shown in Table 11.1 to help reflect on, and answer, the questions appearing earlier.

Many other ways may, of course, be used to reach decisions. But the aforementioned list probably encompasses the most common ways that a decision is reached on how to close performance gaps.

Table 11.1   A Worksheet to Consider the Most Feasible Solution.

	A Worksheet to Consider the Most Feasible Solution	
	Directions: Use this Worksheet to narrow down a brainstormed list of possible solutions to performance problems to the most feasible solution(s). For each question appearing in the left column below, make notes in the right column below.	
	Questions	**Answers**
1	What solution(s) will most decision-makers and workers like?	
2	What solution(s) will be most appealing to key (powerful) stakeholder groups and decision-makers?	
3	What solution is most likely to be implemented?	
4	What solution will be most likely to yield measurable results?	
5	What solution(s) will strike a balance between cost and speed?	
6	What solution(s) will be most sustainable and likely to "stick" in the corporate culture?	
7	What solution(s) will most likely yield a favorable return on investment?	
8	What solution(s) will most likely have the most impact on individuals, teams, or organizational goals?	
9	What other issues, if any, should be considered? (*List them below at line 10, 11, and 12 and then write your answers in the column at right.*)	
10		
11		
12		

Source: Copyright 2021 by William J. Rothwell.

How to Close the Gaps

It is worthwhile to drill down and examine how performance coaches may use each approach mentioned earlier.

What Will Decision-Makers and/or Workers Like?

This approach means nothing more than running a popularity contest of sorts. Ask managers and/or workers what solution they like the most. Be sure to find out *why* they prefer one solution over others. Also note any voiced opposition to a solution, find out *why* that opposition is raised, and consider ways to overcome voiced concerns.

What Is Most Likely to Be Implemented?

Sometimes the best way to select a solution is to think about which one is most likely to be implemented. A good way to do that is to ask veterans of the organization—that is, denizens of the corporate culture who have worked for the same organization a long time and know the decision-makers personally—what solution they believe will be most likely to endure. Often the old timers are good judges of what will work—and what will lead to dismal failure.

To use this approach, call together a group that represents long-service workers. Preferably choose workers who know the company's leaders well. Then brief the workers on what problem you are trying to solve and what range of solutions you have identified. Point to one solution that you believe is best. Then ask for the workers' thoughts on what will happen if that solution is chosen and implemented. Be sure to probe the workers on why they believe that a solution will lead to the results they predict. Note that this approach will work only if the workers trust you and do not believe that you will betray them in ways that will be counter to their own self interests. Use the tool appearing in Table 11.2 to help you carry out the steps just described.

What Will Be Most Likely to Yield Measurable Results?

There are occasions when stakeholders do not care about anything more than solving a problem. They may not care if it yields a favorable cost/benefit ratio or return on investment; rather, their interest centers on solving a problem and getting immediate, measurable results.

Table 11.2   A Worksheet to Determine What Solutions Are Most Likely to Be Implemented.

A Worksheet to Determine What Solutions Are Most Likely to Be Implemented
Directions: Use this Worksheet to determine what solutions are most likely to be implemented. For each step enumerated in the left column below, take notes on what you did and/or the outcomes of what you did in the right column. When you finish, share the results of this Worksheet with others in the organization to build support for the solution and to take steps to avert likely unpleasant side effects caused by solution implementation. (Also note any positive side effects that may be caused by solution implementation and describe how to enhance or intensify their impact.)

Action Steps	What Did You Do?
1 Call together a group that represents long-service workers.	
2 Brief the workers on what problem you are trying to solve and what range of solutions you have identified. (Point to one solution you believe will work best.)	
3 Ask for the workers' thoughts on what will happen if that solution is chosen and implemented. (Note responses at right. Probe for what the participants in the group believe would be the best ways to avoid the likely consequences of implementing the preferred solution.)	
4 Note the list of likely side effects and possible actions to take to avoid the bad side effects of implementing the preferred solution.	

Source: Copyright 2021 by William J. Rothwell.

To use this approach, select a small group and pilot test the solution(s). Try the solutions out. Be sure to measure conditions before and after the pilot test. As a simple example, to try out a new approach to reducing turnover, identify the turnover rate in an organizational unit before a pilot test. Then implement the test (for instance, a new onboarding program). After the test is concluded, measure the turnover rate again over time to see if introducing a new onboarding program has had any impact on turnover. While skeptics may point to other changes in the organizational environment that may have affected turnover rate, the results of a pilot test are often more persuasive than mere speculation. That is especially true if anecdotal evidence—like testimonials from workers—support the causal link between the problem and the solution. Of course, pilot-testing takes time, money, and effort. It is also important to exercise caution when selecting the location of a pilot test, since the support of the manager and workers is often essential to implementation success in any change effort (Sirkin, Keenan, and Jackson 2005).

What Solution Strikes the Balance Between Cost and Speed?

Not all approaches to making decisions need to be data based. While some approaches may be purely subjective, it is possible to find a middle ground between making decisions based purely on intuition ("gut feel") and robust, unassailable facts and figures.

To use this approach, draw a figure like that shown in Figure 11.1. Then plot the solutions to problems you identified in step 7. The idea is to analyze your subjective judgments, looking for the solution that appears to be best at striking a balance between cost and speed.

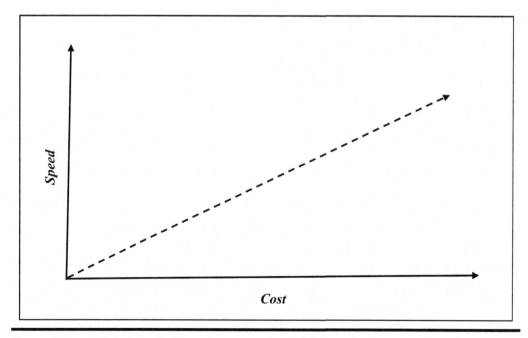

Figure 11.1 Striking the Balance between Cost and Speed.

What Will Most Likely Yield a Favorable Return on Investment?

Calculating return on investment (ROI), sometimes called cost/benefit analysis, is a well-known approach. Often, managers may require a calculation of costs and benefits before an investment is made to solve a problem (Jassy and Kindness 2021). That is especially true if training is the proposed solution, since training is so expensive and often so ineffective (Kong 2010; Kong and Jacobs 2012).

There is not just one way to calculate ROI; rather, there are many. One well-known approach is the *payback method*, which shows how long it takes to repay an initial investment. The payback method is sometimes used to calculate ROI for machine purchases or other capital outlays, such as loans taken to pay off a building or other structure. Its primary advantage is its simplicity; its primary disadvantage is also its simplicity!

There are several ways to calculate ROI. Beattie and James (2021) describe four such approaches and review each one by using a step-by-step description.

But few ROI calculations are immune to criticism. Skeptics often question the results successfully, since the approach may not address every possible issue affecting successful implementation of change efforts such as efforts to close performance gaps. Any implemented solutions may be influenced by other conditions in the organizational setting—such as departing or entering executives, changes in selection methods, changes in the technology used in the work, and much more. Any change that affects people may impact the efficacy of a solution and may impact it more than the solution you chose.

What Will Most Likely Affect Individuals, Teams, or Organizational Goals?

In recent years, much attention has been devoted to establishing measurable goals for individuals, teams, and organizations by using the balanced scorecard or scorecard method. The idea stems from the thinking of Harvard professors Kaplan and Norton (1996). It has also been applied to consulting projects in an approach called the consultant's scorecard (Phillips and Phillips 2011).

Kaplan and Norton's idea is that organizational success should not be limited to profitability alone. Financial success is only one measure. Other measures may also be used to make determinations about organizational success—and about performance. Kaplan and Norton (1996) list four criteria to be considered in a scorecard:

- *Financial success*: How successful is, or should be, the organization with finances?
- *Operational success*: How successful is, or should be, the organization with business operations?
- *Market success*: How successful is, or should be, the organization with serving customers and gaining market advantage?
- *Learning and growth*: How successful is, or should be, the organization with addressing issues associated with organizational or individual learning and growth?

Each cell in the four quadrants can be the basis for establishing measurable strategic planning targets; each cell in the four quadrants can also be the basis for evaluating organizational strategic success. The strategic targets can be cascaded down the organization chart to establish strategic goals for each division, department, team or work group, and worker. Worker targets can be linked to the balanced scorecard organizational goals by establishing key performance indicators (KPIs). KPIs align individual worker performance with organizational performance. Skinner (n.d.) provides examples of KPIs.

The same general approach can be used to set targets and evaluate the relative success of efforts to close performance gaps. In short, any change effort—and efforts to close performance gaps are change efforts—can be planned and evaluated using identifiable measures. An effort to close a performance gap can be the focus of planned targets expressed as KPIs. They can then be measured for achievement just as decision-makers can measure the relative achievement of strategic goals or individual KPIs over time (Thean 2020).

The worksheet appearing in Table 11.3 may be a helpful job aid in setting and tracking targets for closing performance gaps.

How to Select the Most Feasible Approach

Often performance coaches must select the most feasible and not the optimal approach. The optimal approach is the best approach. But the most feasible approach is the one that is the most realistic and most

Table 11.3   Describe What Is the Performance Gap to Be Addresses?

What Is the Performance Gap to Be Addressed? (Describe It)				
Organizational Vision:				
Organizational Mission:				
Division/Department/Work Group or Team Targets:				
Proposed Solution to Close a Performance Gap:				
Financial	Objectives	Measures	Targets	Results (or Results at Milestone Dates)
Market/ Customer	Objectives	Measures	Targets	Results (or Results at Milestone Dates)
Business Processes	Objectives	Measures	Targets	Results (or Results at Milestone Dates)
Learning and Growth	Objectives	Measures	Targets	Results (or Results at Milestone Dates)

Source: Copyright 2021 by William J. Rothwell.

likely to succeed. Choosing the most feasible approach is typically a judgment call.

Use the Worksheet appearing in Table 11.4 to help you decide which approach to identifying the best way to close the performance gap is the most feasible.

Table 11.4   A Worksheet for Selecting How to Close the Gap.

A Worksheet for Selecting How to Close the Gap
Directions:
Use this Worksheet to guide your thinking as a performance coach on how to select a way to close the gap. In Part I, briefly describe the performance problem/gap. In Part II, briefly list all the possible ways you can think of to close the gap. Then, in Part III, for each approach to close the gap described in the left column, offer ideas about what approach might be a good way to close the gap in the right column. The value of this tool depends on the quality of your thinking—or those you involve in completing it.

Part I: What Is the Performance Gap?
Describe the performance gap briefly here:

Part II: Ways You Can Think of to Close the Performance Gap
List many ways to close the performance gap:

Part III: Approaches to Close Performance Gaps	
Approach	**What Solution to the Performance Gap Would the Approach Identify?**
What will decision-makers and/or workers like?	
What is most likely to be implemented?	
What will be most likely to yield measurable results?	
What solution strikes the balance between cost and speed?	
What will most likely yield a favorable return on investment?	
What will most likely affect individuals, teams, or organizational goals?	

Source: Copyright 2021 by William J. Rothwell.

Competencies Required by Performance Coaches to Choose the Best Way to Close Gaps

Performance coaches should be able to:

■ narrow down, from a list of possible solutions, those that strike a balance between cost and speed of implementation: list the options. Weigh the options based on different considerations—such as cost, likelihood of acceptance by various stakeholder groups, time for implementation, likelihood of overall success, and other criteria.

■ narrow down, from a list of possible solutions, those that can work together effectively with a minimum of contraindicators or side effects: list possible side effects of various solutions. Try to predict the likely side effects that will stem from solution implementation.

■ narrow down, from a list of possible solutions, the most feasible solution that will be supported by political issues in the organization: define what is meant by "feasible" in the organization. List out the specific issues that are part of what is meant by the term "feasible."

■ facilitate workers, individually or in teams, to make decisions to narrow down the best solutions to performance problems from a list of possible solutions: involve workers and managers in narrowing down the solutions to identified performance problems. Describe what is meant by "best solution" in the context of a specific organization, group or situation.

■ facilitate workers, individually or in teams, to narrow down the solutions most likely to be successfully implemented from a list of possible solutions to performance problems: describe what is meant by the word "facilitate" in the context of the national culture, organizational culture, and group. Involve workers and managers in narrowing down the solutions to performance problems. Involve workers in selecting the "best" solution to a performance problem.

Business Case Example

The management team of MBD remained committed to following the steps in the performance coaching model. For that reason, the team continued working where the project left off in the previous chapter. After brainstorming many different ways to close the performance gaps identified from previous steps, the team members reached step 8 in which the challenge was to select the *best* way to close the performance gap.

The team members had a lengthy, and some might say contentious, discussion over what is meant by "best." Whose opinion governs what is best? What criteria are used to select the "best" way to close a performance gap or to leverage a performance strength? Should one criterion be used to pick best, or should multiple criteria be considered?

The team members debated this issue in a weekly meeting. When it became apparent that the team could not reach a consensus on what is meant by "best"—or even who should choose the criteria to be used in judging best—the team decided they would devote a retreat to deciding how to select the best way to close the performance gap and who would make that decision.

At the retreat, the team members eventually decided that they would make the decision about what solution(s) would be best and that they would compile a list of the solutions generated in step 7 and simply take a majority vote on which solution should be chosen. It would be up to the team members to decide how they prioritized the solutions.

And so that is exactly what they did.

Note in this description that many ways exist by which to select the "best" way to close performance gaps—or leverage strengths. While studies of best practice or common business practice can help, they take time and cost money to carry out. While it is possible (and often desirable) to poll all stakeholder groups about what solution is preferable, a final decision about what is "best" must ultimately be made. That will always be a subjective opinion, regardless of how much evidence is used to make the decision and how many people are involved.

Key Factors to Remember

Let's review the lessons in this chapter. When choosing the best way to close gaps, performance coaches should:

- rely on what information is available to make a choice—and realize that all relevant information is rarely at hand
- recognize that it is seldom possible to have all necessary information to make the best choice of a solution to close a performance gap
- realize that, since gaps can have more than one root cause, closing gaps may require more than one solution
- be aware that efforts to use multiple solutions to close gaps caused by more than one root cause may prompt new problems as the solutions themselves interact with each other
- realize that the decision to use a solution often hinges primarily on the decision-maker's values, culture, beliefs, and attitudes

Coaching and Developmental Questions for Managers

(1) How do you rate yourself from 0 to 10 (0 being the lowest and 10 being the highest) on your knowledge and understanding of ways to decide quickly yet effectively which solution of many may be most feasible?
- What is missing or in the way of your understanding?
- What is your action plan to increase your overall rate?

(2) How do you rate yourself from 0 to 10 (0 being the lowest and 10 being the highest) on your knowledge and understanding of the best ways to make decisions rather than suffer the paralysis of analysis?
- What is missing?
- What is your action plan to increase your overall rate?

(3) How do you rate yourself from 0 to 10 (0 being the lowest and 10 being the highest) on your ability to facilitate the choice of a good solution to a performance problem with managers, workers, and work groups?
- What is missing or not understood?
- What is your action plan to increase your overall rate?

(4) How do you rate yourself from 0 to 10 (0 being the lowest and 10 being the highest) on your ability to choose multiple solutions when a performance gap is caused by more than one root cause?
- What is missing or not understood?
- What is your action plan to increase your overall rate?

References

Beattie, Andrew, and Margaret James. 2021. "A Guide to Calculating Return on Investment." www.investopedia.com/articles/basics/10/guide-to-calculating-roi.asp.

Dobson, Michael, and Deborah Dobson. 2006. *Enlightened Office Politics: Understanding, Coping with, and Winning the Game—Without Losing Your Soul*. New York, NY: Amacom.

Greiner, Larry, and Virginia Schein. 1998. *Power and Organization Development*. New York, NY: FT Press.

HBR Ascend Staff. 2019. "The Changing Perspectives of Young Professionals on Work and the Workplace." https://hbrascend.org/topics/the-changing-perspectives-work-and-the-workplace-youth-skills-survey/.

Hochwarter, Wayne, Christopher Rosen, Samantha Jordan, Gerald Ferris, Aqsa Ejaz, and Liam Maher. 2020. "Perceptions of Organizational Politics Research: Past, Present, and Future." *Journal of Management* 46, no. 6: 879–907. https://doi.org/10.1177/0149206319898506.

Jassy, Daniel, and David Kindness. 2021. "Calculating the Payback Period with Excel." www.investopedia.com/ask/answers/051315/how-do-you-calculate-payback-period-using-excel.asp.

Kaplan, Robert S., and David P. Norton. 1996. *The Balanced Scorecard: Translating Strategy into Action*. Cambridge, MA: Harvard Business Review Press.

Kong, Y. J. 2010. "Establishing a Comprehensive Model of Cost Analysis of Web-based Training Programs Based on a Systems Approach." In *Proceedings from the E-Learn World Conference on E-Learning in Corporate, Government, Healthcare, and Higher Education*. Orlando, FL. ISBN 978-1-880094-83-9 Publisher: Association for the Advancement of Computing in Education (AACE), Chesapeake, VA.

Kong, Y. J., and R. Jacobs. 2012. "A Comparison of the Practices Used by Human Resource Development Professionals to Evaluate Web-based and Classroom-based Training Programs within Seven Korean Companies." *Human Resource Development International* 15, no. 1: 79–98.

Phillips, Jack, and Patty Phillips. 2006. *ROI at Work*. Alexandria, VA: ASTD Press.

Phillips, Jack, and Patty Phillips. 2011. *The Consultant's Scorecard: Tracking ROI and Bottom-Line Impact of Consulting Projects*, 2nd ed. New York, NY: McGraw-Hill.

Sirkin, Harold, Perry Keenan, and A. Jackson. 2005. "The Hard Side of Change Management." *Harvard Business Review*. https://hbr.org/2005/10/the-hard-side-of-change-management.

Skinner, Ted. n.d. "Balanced Scorecard KPI Examples: A Comprehensive List of KPIs." www.rhythmsystems.com/blog/comprehensive-list-of-179-kpi-examples-for-any-industry.

Thean, Patrick. 2020. "Creating KPIs: How to Create a KPI in 5 Simple Steps." www.rhythmsystems.com/blog/bid/122008/5-simple-steps-to-create-useful-kpi-s.

Chapter 12

Step 9: What Are the Consequences of Closing the Gap?

William J. Rothwell

Once a solution has been chosen to close the performance gap, performance coaches should reflect on the likely consequences that will be created by the solution. This step is akin to thinking forward, trying to anticipate the possible results or consequences of implementing a solution, and then averting negative side effects and maximizing positive side effects. Consequences may be individually focused, organizationally focused, or both.

Perhaps a simple example will illustrate what this step means.

Suppose that an individual is tardy nearly every day. The performance coach suggests that the individual take steps to ensure timely arrival. When implementing the solution, the individual ends up in a marital separation. That might be an individually focused consequence of closing the gap.

In today's organizations, there is often such a sense of urgency to implement a solution that the consequences of implementing that solution may be overlooked at the time it is planned. Yet the consequences could have been anticipated if considered beforehand.

Medical doctors are familiar with the notion of anticipating consequences. When medicine is prescribed or therapy is ordered, physicians know that there may be side effects for any corrective action. Aspirin may cure a headache but may also prompt stomach distress; chemotherapy may reduce cancer's terrible effects but may also prompt the patient's hair to fall out.

DOI: 10.4324/9781003155928-16

Performance coaches, working with their coachees, must strive to anticipate the negative side effects of efforts to close performance gaps and take
steps to avoid or minimize them. If positive side effects are possible, they
should be seized and turned to best advantage.

It should be noted that actions may also have positive side effects.
Medicine taken to heal cancer can lead to weight loss. That weight loss can
be a positive side effect for those wishing to lose weight. It was not the
medicine's intended effect to help people lose weight—but it does. That is
an example of a positive side effect.

How This Chapter Is Organized

This chapter is organized into the following parts:

- What This Step Means
- Why Is This Step in Performance Coaching Important?
- Examples of This Step in Performance Coaching
- Approaches to Anticipating Side Effects
- Competencies Required by Performance Coaches to Anticipate Side Effects
- Key Factors to Remember
- Coaching and Developmental Questions for Managers

What This Step Means

Step 9 is about anticipating the likely side effects or consequences that
will stem from implementing one or more solutions. Carrying out that step
may sound easy. But it rarely is easy. Since organizations are open systems
(Luhmann 1995), that means that actions taken in one part of the organization will have ripple effects that affect the whole system. Much as tossing a
pebble in a pond will lead to ripples throughout the entire pond, so too will
an action taken in one place—or with one person or team—possibly affect
all other people and all other organizational parts. Some people call this the
spider web effect, which refers to the results of yanking one side of a spider
web and seeing the entire web vibrate in response.

Medical doctors are familiar with the notion of side effects. Quite often,
possible side effects of new drugs are identified and/or monitored during
clinical trials (Rosen 2013). In fact, an important issue to consider during

clinical trials is the reaction to a drug or therapy experienced by people of different demographics (such as age, race, gender, pregnancy status, and so forth). As new drugs or treatments are approved for use by the broader population, side effects are noted by physicians and then logged to a centralized system called the Federal Food and Drug Administration Adverse Reporting System. But research has also indicated that another good way to identify emerging side effects is to analyze search engine results, monitoring for how many people conduct searches on google for two or more drugs and the effects of those drugs on each other (Rosen 2013).

Despite the best efforts of physicians to spot and avoid side effects, their impact on health can be severe. One study, for instance, found that

> in the United States, about 750 people 65 and older are hospitalized each day because of them, according to a 2019 report from the Lown Institute, a nonpartisan think tank. Other research has found that almost 80% of people 70 and older experience at least one drug side effect in a six-month period
>
> (Consumer Reports 2020).

The same principle applies to management and to organizations, though no centralized reporting system exists as in medicine to track the impact of management actions. Management actions taken in one place affect others. Often the side effects simply cannot be predicted with precision until they are tried out. But just as clinical trials in medicine may help to identify side effects stemming from new drugs, pilot tests of organizational change efforts can help to pinpoint likely positive and negative consequences of change efforts when time and money permits.

Why Is This Step in Performance Coaching Important?

Most organizational change efforts fail. Efforts to implement solutions in performance coaching are change efforts and are thus prone to possible, and quite often likely, failure.

Many solutions, and many implementation efforts, fail because due consideration was not given to the likely consequences of the solution. To avoid failure, performance coaches should take steps to anticipate what consequences will stem from solution implementation and then take steps to mitigate negative side effects or leverage positive side effects.

What to Consider

When making efforts to anticipate the likely side effects of implementing a solution, consider such issues as these:

- Who will be affected by the solution implementation?
- What will be affected by the solution implementation?
- When will people or organizational issues be affected by solution implementation?
- Where will people or organizational issues be affected by solution implementation?
- Why will people or issues be affected by solution implementation?
- How will people or issues be affected by solution implementation?
- How much will people or issues be affected by solution implementation?

The consequences of solution implementation can affect:

- individuals
- teams or work groups
- departments/divisions
- organization
- community or groups external to the organization such as customers, suppliers, distributors, and others

Use the Worksheet appearing in Table 12.1 to guide your thinking.

How to Anticipate Consequences

There are several ways to anticipate consequences of solution implementation. An informal way is to brainstorm about them. More formal ways is to carry out mind mapping and scenario planning.

An Informal Way to Anticipating Consequences

When performance coaches are about to make a decision to choose the solution to a problem, it is wise to reflect on what might happen as a result.

Table 12.1   A Worksheet to Anticipate the Likely Side Effects of Implementing a Solution.

A Worksheet to Anticipate the Likely Side Effects of Implementing a Solution					
Who will be affected? / **Questions**	Individuals	Teams or Groups	Departments or Divisions	Organization	Community or External Groups
Who will be affected by the solution implementation?					
What will be affected by the solution implementation?					
When will people or organizational issues be affected by solution implementation?					
Where will people or organizational issues be affected by solution implementation?					
Why will people or issues be affected by solution implementation?					
How will people or issues be affected by solution implementation?					
How much will people or issues be affected by solution implementation?					

Source: Copyright 2021 by William J. Rothwell.

The same principle applies in the game of chess. Good chess players learn to think forward, anticipating how opponents will respond to their moves and countermoves. While some people believe that chess geniuses can look thirty moves ahead, research reveals that even the best players can see only fifteen to twenty moves ahead (Markushin 2015). Often it is wise to focus on fewer moves ahead, since trying to anticipate too far into the future leads to mistakes of their own ("Bruce Pandolfini Teaches Thinking, Not Chess" no date).

Simple reflection may be helpful when trying to anticipate the consequences of implementing solutions. Just making the effort to think forward may be enough to prompt ideas about what side effects to expect and avert or what positive side effects may be worthy of seizing to advantage.

Practicing managers—and performance coaches—can probably relate to practical ways to do use simple reflection. If problems arising during the day lead managers or coaches to experience sleepless nights, then they know how brooding on problems can prompt insomnia. Sleeplessness can actually be turned to advantage if the time is productively used to surface different problems that are likely to arise during the implementation of a solution and determine ways to avoid or minimize the negative side effects. Even taking a walk over the lunch hour can clear the head of a manager or coach if devoted to reflecting on work problems, likely consequences of taking action to implement solutions, and how to sidestep the impact of those consequences.

Formal Ways to Anticipating Consequences

While there may be many approaches to structured problem-solving that can be used to anticipate consequences (Van Gundy 1988), mind mapping and scenario planning can be particularly helpful.

Mind Mapping

Mind mapping is a good approach to use in trying to anticipate consequences. A *mind map*, first popularized by Tony Buzan (2020), is a diagram that shows relationships between one idea, concept, action, task and others. A simple mind map may be nothing more than a doodle on the back of a napkin; a more complex mind map may be a collaborative diagram, assembled by a group of people, to illustrate how the implementation of one solution might lead to consequences and those consequences, in turn, may prompt other effects. We covered the process of mind mapping in detail in

Chapter 9. For more information about mind mapping, please review the following figures and tables:

- Figure 9.3: Example of Mind Mapping Process.
- Figure 9.4: Example of Business Mind Mapping Process.
- Table 9.1: Steps of Performing a Mind Map Process.

Figure 12.1 shows a simple blank mind map diagram, and it can be modified for immediate use. Free software exists to guide mind mapping, and it can also be hosted on websites so as to permit participation by teams or work groups from across the globe.

To use the mind map, write in the center of this figure what action you propose to take as a solution for closing a performance gap. Then try to think of what might happen as a result of that action. Realize that consequences may also create chain reactions, sometimes called the "domino effect," in which one action can touch off a chain of events that can spiral out of control.

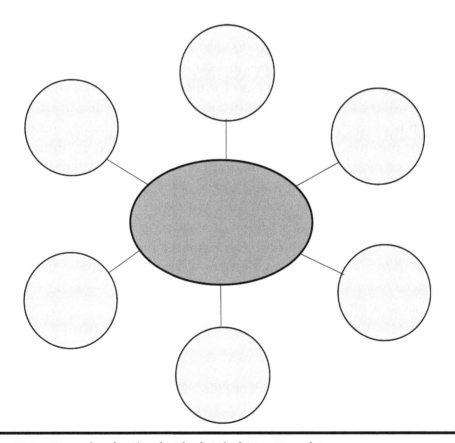

Figure 12.1   Example of a Simple Blank Mind Map Template.

In modern times, the so-called *black swan event* is a good illustration of the issue of a minor problem that touches off a most unfortunate chain of events. A seemingly simple event—like the advent of a virus in a small city in China—can spiral out of control, touching off a global pandemic that threatens the world economy and leads to unexpected side effects that could shut down global supply lines, cost countless people their lives and others their jobs, and prompt thousands of businesses to go broke.

Can performance coaches face black swan events? The answer is "of course they can." A simple action can have monumental consequences. As a simple example, a performance coach who makes a coachee angry enough to quit may prompt a wave of resignations as others follow the departing worker. That wave of resignations, in turn, could lead customers to question their continued relationship with the organization, which could create a crisis in stock price and market share.

Scenario Planning

Scenario planning is based on the notion that the future is uncertain—and is often unpredictable. For that reason, planning necessitates looking at contingencies and then trying to plan for those. A typical scenario planning effort will try to predict the future around three assumptions. One assumption regards the external environment affecting the organization as favorable or positive; one assumption regards the external environment as unfavorable or negative; and one assumption regards the external environment to work out realistically, a best guess of what decision-makers believe will really happen.

A *scenario* represents a description of a situation. *Scenario planning* thus offers contingencies based on different assumptions about how the future will work out for an organization. Scenario planning has grown to be popular in strategic planning. But it can be used in other ways—such as with performance coaching.

To apply scenario planning to identifying the consequences of closing a performance gap, take these steps:

(1) Describe the solution you wish to take to implement solutions to performance problems.
(2) Identify what forces or issues you believe will most affect the implementation of the solution.
(3) Pinpoint areas of uncertainty.

(4) Create descriptions (often "best guesses") of a positive situation that favors your solution's implementation, that is not favorable to your solution's implementation, and that is your best guess of what will happen if business conditions remain unchanged.

(5) Discuss what to do in each situation to maximize results and minimize unfortunate side effects.

Use the worksheet shown in Table 12.2 to help carry out these steps. For more detailed information about scenario planning, see Chermack (2011).

Table 12.2   A Worksheet to Guide Scenario Planning.

A Worksheet to Guide Scenario Planning	
Directions: For each question appearing in the left column below, write your answers in the right column. The purpose of this Worksheet is to help guide your thinking on how to plan a scenario planning activity. There are no right or wrong answers in any absolute sense, but some answers may be better than others.	
Questions to Guide the Preparation of a Scenario Planning Activity	**Your Answers/The Plan**
1 What is the solution you wish to implement to close a performance gap?	
2 What forces or issues do you believe will most affect the implementation of your solution?	
3 What are the areas of uncertainty that may affect implementation?	
4 What positive results may stem from your implementation? What negative results may stem from your implementation? What is your best realistic guess of what results may stem from your implementation?	
5 What should you do if the conditions favor implementation of your solution, if the conditions do not favor implementation of your solution, or if the external conditions turn out to match your realistic best guess of what will really happen?	

Source: Copyright 2021 by William J. Rothwell.

Two Examples of This Step in Performance Coaching

Perhaps two examples will help to clarify what this step means in practice.

Example 1

The situation: Mortina Erickson is the manager of the warehouse at the Orton Company. She faces a problem: one of her workers, Mina Thorson, is very disruptive. Thorson talks very loudly; she uses swear words in the warehouse with the work crew and with customers; and she wears informal clothing (such as halter tops or extreme cutoff shorts). Erickson has had performance coaching sessions with Thorson and still holds out hope that Thorson will change her behaviors. Erickson's discussions with Thorson have not gone unnoticed. Thorson's coworkers feel that Erickson has been "picking on Mina." They side with her. That coworker support was unexpected. Other managers are grumbling, complaining that Erickson's coaching of Thorson may be having a side effect of increasing absenteeism and turnover in other departments. Thorson's behavior, which has not changed much since the coaching began, has also encouraged other employees to wear increasingly inappropriate clothing to work.

Erickson is thinking about what to do next in her performance coaching sessions with Thorson. But she believes it is important to reflect on her action—and their likely consequences—before she does anything. When Erickson reaches step 9 of the performance coaching model, she goes to her office and closes the door. She takes out some paper (out of her computer printer) and draws a mind map circle in the center of several such papers. On the first paper, she writes "Fire Thorson"; on the second paper, she writes "give Thorson an oral warning"; on the third paper, she writes "give Thorson a suspension"; on the fourth paper, she writes "talk to Thorson again—but inform her what the next step might be."

Erickson then draws some circles near the one in the center on each page. She then tries to brainstorm, using the mind mapping method to guide her thinking, what might happen as a result of each action. In each case, Erickson tries to anticipate what consequences might happen with Thorson, her coworkers, and with other stakeholders who might have some reaction to any action Erickson takes. One possible consequence is that Thorson will look for other job opportunities, a consequence that Erickson would not like to see because Thorson is actually a first-rate employee who just happens to have disruptive on-the-job behaviors that need to be corrected.

Based on the results of the mind mapping activity, Erickson decides she will talk to Thorson again to explain what will happen next if she does not mend her ways.

Conclusion: Note that, in the previous discussion, Erickson does not rush to action. Instead, she gives careful thought—albeit without a lengthy delay—to think through what she will do and what might happen as a result of what she will do. Erickson takes special steps to try to think of negative and positive consequences of any action she might take with Thorson.

Example 2

The situation: Howard Rumple was the CEO of a large bank. He has just promoted Jack Lund to Bank President, a title Howard has given up. But Howard is surprised, because he was challenged in his decision to promote Lund by Linda Monson, VP of Human Resources. Monson points out to Rumple that his decision to promote Lund creates many problems. One is that Lund is an alcoholic and often comes to work smelling of alcohol. A second is that Lund is having a love affair with his administrative assistant, which violates the bank's policy that prohibits intimate love relationships between managers and their direct reports. Rumple concedes that these are serious problems with Lund's promotion, which could give the impression to workers that Rumple is sanctioning, and at least ignoring, love affairs and alcohol abuse. Rumple asks Monson what she proposes for him to do after the announcement is made of Lund's promotion. Monson suggests executive coaching.

Rumple calls Lund into his office. He tells him that he will give him one year to treat his alcohol abuse and to cease his love affair with his assistant. Lund agrees to the terms. When Rumple reaches step 9 of the performance coaching model, he invites Lund to consider what consequences may stem from his behavior. Lund admits that his behavior could set an unfortunate, and bad, example for others. He commits to change his behavior and set a positive example.

Conclusion: Note that, in the description given earlier, neither Rumple nor Lund rushes into immediate action with ill-founded solutions and do reflect on how the behavior of a senior executive may influence other people. Lund commits to change.

Competencies Required by Performance Coaches to Choose the Best Way to Close Gaps

Performance coaches should be able to:

- narrow down, from a list of possible solutions, those that strike a balance between cost and speed of implementation: brainstorm possible solutions. Note the least costly solutions. Note the fastest solutions that can be implemented. Then identify solutions that could strike a balance between cost and speed.
- narrow down, from a list of possible solutions, those that can work together effectively with a minimum of contraindicators or side effects: identify possible negative side effects of possible solutions. Identify possible positive side effects of possible solutions. Identify actions that may not have many side effects. Identify possible side effects that could touch off a chain of events or "black swan events."
- facilitate workers, individually or in teams, to make decisions to narrow down the best solutions to performance problems from a list of possible solutions: identify the possible negative and positive side effects of facilitating efforts by managers and workers to narrow down feasible solutions to performance issues. Take steps to minimize the negative side effects and maximize the positive side effects of the consequences of actions taken to solve problems.
- facilitate workers, individually or in teams, to narrow down the solutions most likely to be successfully implemented from a list of possible solutions to performance problems: use collaborative approaches, face-to-face or virtually, to help identify solutions to performance issues. Become familiar with informal and formal methods that can help individuals and groups to work together to narrow down solutions.

Business Case Example

One member of the MBD management team was Clarissa Wardstone. Clarissa was the VP of Human Resources for the organization.

Once the organization selected a course of action—several steps, in fact, in a sequence of efforts to drive down turnover, among other corrective actions—Wardstone suggested to others on the management team that a meeting be held online to "consider the fallout" of what was planned.

MBD managers decided to increase entry-level salaries as one method by which to drive down turnover. That was justified because many exit interviews cited the reason for workers' departure as pursuit of "better pay- ing jobs." Management reasoned that higher salaries, particularly for entry- level staff members, would reduce turnover. After all, most turnover occurs among those who are most recently hired.

In the meeting, Wardstone asked to speak. Then, over a zoom link with other members of the management team, she innocently asked this ques- tion: "[w]hat will be the fallout of increasing entry salaries at all levels of the organization chart without offering a corresponding increase to staff with more experience?" She was making several points without saying it in so many words:

(1) HR should have been consulted before the management team made a decision on increasing salaries but was not consulted;

(2) HR would have described the notion of salary compression (referring to efforts to save money by increasing entry-level salaries but failing to preserve the internal equity of salary across a wage scale); and

(3) HR would have probably advised against the action the management team took because salary compression could lead to increased turnover at higher levels of experience.

There was a long silence after Wardstone asked her not-so-innocent ques- tion. Then other members of the management team asked Wardstone to supply an estimate price tag for increasing all salary levels in a way com- mensurate with the increase at entry level. She did not hesitate a moment and said "at least 10 million dollars annually, not counting an extra 5 million dollars in employee benefit costs." Other committee members gasped, since that was a huge sum for salary and benefits in MBD.

One team member suggested that a subcommittee should be formed to consider the matter further. Wardstone objected, noting that HR had cap- tured a benchline before the new salaries went into effect and discovered a 20% jump in turnover at higher levels of experience on the organization chart.

The meeting continued. Many managers seemed to be reluctant to speak up, and so the CEO asked each member of the team to write an email to predict the likely consequences of a salary increase at entry only and what might be done to avert the negative side effects. The CEO also asked each member of the team to describe what might be the likely positive side effects of a salary increase at entry only and what could be done to leverage those positive side effects.

The meeting was adjourned after one hour. The CEO gave each participant one week to submit the report he requested.

Key Factors to Remember

Let's review the lessons in this chapter. When choosing the best way to close gaps, performance coaches should:

- rely on what information is available to make a choice
- recognize that it is not always possible to have all necessary information to make the best choice of a solution to close a performance gap
- realize that, since gaps can have more than one root cause, closing gaps may require more than one solution
- be aware that efforts to use multiple solutions to close gaps caused by more than one root cause may prompt new problems as the solutions themselves interact with each other
- realize that the decision to use a solution often hinges primarily on the decision-maker's values, culture, beliefs, and attitudes

Coaching and Developmental Questions for Managers

(1) How do you rate yourself from 0 to 10 (0 being the lowest and 10 being the highest) on your ability to anticipate the negative side effects of implementing a solution?
 – What is missing or in the way of your understanding?
 – What is your action plan to increase your overall rate?

(2) How do you rate yourself from 0 to 10 (0 being the lowest and 10 being the highest) on your ability to identify positive side of effects of implementing a solution?
 – What is missing?
 – What is your action plan to increase your overall rate?

(3) How do you rate yourself from 0 to 10 (0 being the lowest and 10 being the highest) on your ability to identify steps to take to mitigate the negative side effects or consequences of implementing a solution?

– What is missing or not understood?
– What is your action plan to increase your overall rate?

(4) How do you rate yourself from 0 to 10 (0 being the lowest and 10 being the highest) on your ability to take steps to seize advantages stemming from efforts to implement a solution to a problem?
– What is missing or not understood?
– What is your action plan to increase your overall rate?

References

"Bruce Pandolfini Teaches Thinking, Not Chess." n.d. *FS Blog*. Accessed August 19, 2021. https://fs.blog/2009/09/bruce-pandolfini-teaches-thinking-not-chess/.

Buzan, Tony. 2020. *Mind Map Mastery: The Complete Guide to Learning and Using the Most Powerful Thinking Tool in the Universe*. Sydney, Australia: ReadHowYouWant.

Chermack, Thomas. 2011. *Scenario Planning in Organizations: How to Create, Use, and Assess Scenarios*. San Francisco, CA: Berret-Koehler.

Consumer Reports. 2020. "How to Recognize and Avoid Drug Side Effects." *The Washington Post*. www.washingtonpost.com/health/how-to-recognize-and-avoid-drug-side-effects/2020/05/15/de438aca-88aa-11ea-9dfd-990f9dcc71fc_story.html.

Luhmann, Niklas. 1995. "The Paradoxy of Observing Systems." *Cultural Critique*, no. 31: 37–55. https://doi.org/10.2307/1354444.

Markushin, Yury. 2015. "5 Chess Myths that Most People Believe." *Attaching Play Secrets*. Accessed August 19, 2021. https://thechessworld.com/articles/general-information/5-chess-myths-that-most-people-believe/.

Rosen, Michael. 2013. "Editorial March 2013." *Journal of Cardiovascular Pharmacology* 61, no. 3: 175. https://doi.org/10.1097/FJC.0b013e318288182d.

Van Gundy, Arthur. 1988. *Techniques of Structured Problem Solving*, 2nd ed. New York, NY: Van Nostrand Reinhold.

IMPLEMENTATION AND EVALUATION

Implementing and evaluating performance coaching can be challenging. It is often cited that many change efforts fail due to poor implementation. Performance coaching can occur quickly (one-minute coaching) or over many years. This Phase focuses on addressing the following questions—the critical issues associated with implementation and evaluation.

Chapter 13—Step 10: What Are the Damages of Inaction?
What will happen if the solution is not implemented? What are the likely consequences of inaction?

Chapter 14—Step 11: How to Implement the Solution?
How can the solution be implemented? In other words, how much time, money, and other resources are available for implementation?

Chapter 15—Step 12: How to Evaluate the Successful Implementation?
How can the results of the solution's implementation be evaluated?

DOI: 10.4324/9781003155928-17

Chapter 13

Step 10: What Are the Damages of Inaction?

William J. Rothwell

Once the likely consequences of implementing solutions have been identified, performance coaches should consider what damages—or other
results—may result from inaction. Not all problems deserve corrective
action; rather, sometimes it is best to ignore problems and focus attention on
other, more pressing issues. The damages—and sometimes legal liability—
that can result from inaction have been studied (Hinkin and Schriesheim
2004; Hinkin and Schriesheim 2008; Moore 2002; Von Bergen 2012).

While performance coaches may be tempted to *act* rather than *think*
(see Lambert 2016; Saltzman 2018; "Why the Things You Ignore Will Only
Grow" 2021), they should instead contemplate whether inaction will prompt
damaging consequences—or else have no effect or even a positive effect.
Sometimes the best way to solve a problem is to step away, even if only
temporarily, because it can help to concentrate a decision-maker's attention
on what really matters to the organization, department, team, or worker
(Swanson 2016). Still, the consequences of inaction should be considered.
At the same time, efforts should be made to avoid a keen temptation felt by
ambitious managers to *do something*—that is, *do anything*—to solve a problem out of a bias for action (Mohrmann 2020; Mueller 2017).

Organizational leaders sometimes complain that any action with people
will be costly. For that reason, they often demand evidence of return on
investment (ROI) with training or other improvement efforts—including performance coaching. ROI is nothing more than cost/benefit analysis in which
the financial cost of taking corrective action is weighed against the financial

DOI: 10.4324/9781003155928-18

value of the benefits received from taking corrective action. But ROI can also be calculated for inaction. What will be the costs of *not* acting to close performance gaps and what will be the benefits of *not* acting? If the benefits of inaction outweigh the costs, then minimal damage will result from doing nothing. By the same token, if the costs of inaction outweigh the benefits, then more damage will result from doing nothing.

Note also that ROI can be considered from a viewpoint that transcends mere considerations of financial issues. That is the logic of the balanced scorecard. Any action taken can have impacts on finances. But actions can also have impacts on customer service and market share, business operations, and the learning and growth of the business. In many organizations today, managers must weigh more than mere financial issues. How will the organization appear to regulators? Customers? Distributors? Suppliers? Union representatives? Interest groups and activists in the community? The point is that inaction can have consequences that go beyond mere financial considerations. If the organization is considered to be a pariah—like tobacco companies have been perceived to be—anything the organization does is suspect.

How This Chapter Is Organized

This chapter is organized into the following parts:

■ What This Step Means
■ Why Is This Step in Performance Coaching Important?
■ Example of This Step in Performance Coaching
■ Competencies Required by Performance Coaches to Select the Best Choice
■ Key Factors to Remember
■ Coaching and Developmental Questions for Managers

What This Step Means

Step 10 is about going the step beyond thinking about likely consequences of corrective actions and taking steps to avoid negative side effects or to leverage positive side effects of action. Simply stated, step 10 means directing attention to what is likely to happen if no corrective action is taken to close a performance gap.

The same idea often surfaces in discussions about training. Some people jokingly paraphrase Shakespeare's quote "to be or not to be, that is the question" in another form: "[t]o train or not to train, that is the question." The point here is to demonstrate awareness that training, while expensive, can have positive consequences. But inaction can also have consequences— both positive and negative. Perhaps, the issue is best articulated in the old joke apparent in the statement that "if you think training is expensive, try ignorance." Failing to train people—or failing to train people properly—can have serious consequences, and often, they are even more dramatic and extreme than training is.

Failure to act is an issue that can arise in a civil law case. The concept of *laches* commonly refers to failure to take action to claim a right. Failing to file a lawsuit when the aggrieved party would otherwise have every right to do so is an example of laches. It refers to a failure to act when taking action is legitimate and warranted. In laches, the aggrieved party delays in filing suit, and the result is that the defendant later has trouble assembling evidence to refute the claim.

The religious have another name for failure to act: it is *a sin of omission,* which means failing to act when acting is appropriate and that failure to act ends up hurting other people. The famous 1964 Kitty Genovese criminal case may be a classic example of a sin of omission. Genovese was a bar tender in Queens, New York. She was stabbed to death by an attacker outside her apartment building as she returned home from work. Later police discovered that 38 witnesses had observed the crime, but nobody chose to help Genovese while she was attacked or even call the police. The failure to act was a sin of omission. Genovese died of stab wounds while unfeeling onlookers casually gawked. When asked why they behaved that way, the witnesses claimed they "did not want to get involved." For the most part, there is no law in the United States that requires witnesses to crimes to report them.

As an example of the legal principle called laches, suppose Georgiana was sexually harassed by her immediate supervisor Jack Nichols. Georgina suffers in silence (perhaps due to shame) and chooses not to inform anyone at her employer but instead waits ten years before complaining. In the meantime, Nichols leaves the organization, starts employment somewhere else and is eventually promoted to CEO of another organization. Perhaps, he leaves many sexual harassment victims in his wake—in part because Georgina failed to report the abusive actions or take steps to get relief ten years prior. If Georgiana wants to file suit against Nichols after such a long period of time, Nichols can raise an affirmative defense of laches. Too much time has elapsed and that will make it difficult for Nichols to raise an adequate defense against the sexual harassment claim because the people involved at the time may be difficult to track down, memories have faded, and written or electronic documents have vanished.

The same logic applies to other possible actions that are intended to close performance gaps. That could include individual, team, department, divisional, or organizational actions. Any action has consequences. Sometimes ignoring a performance gap leads to damage, and the consequences of that damage can grow more severe over time. By the same token, not everything warrants action. Efforts to chase and solve every problem will reveal an inability to set priorities.

Why Is This Step in Performance Coaching Important?

This step is important because performance coaches should not necessarily prefer corrective action to inaction. Instead, any decision to act should be weighed against what is likely to happen if no action is taken. Sometimes problems will solve themselves if nothing is done about them!

Consider a simple example. Suppose a manager is struggling with problematic behavior from a worker. Suppose Marsha Cronson is late to work every day. The manager, Tom Clawson, has spoken to her many times about her tardiness. But the problem persists. The manager, beside himself with concern because he does not wish to encourage other workers to be late by witnessing the ineffectiveness of Clawson's actions to change Cronson's behavior, considers suspending Cronson. But then Clawson learns that Cronson's coworkers have been pressuring her to get to work on time for the simple reason that they cannot leave work until they are relieved by Cronson. So, by not acting, Clawson benefits from the peer pressure applied to Cronson. The problem solves itself when Cronson quits rather than modifies her behavior!

The same issue applies in management when performance coaches weigh the relative advantages of action and inaction. Performance coaches should always ask themselves the question

what will happen if no corrective action is taken? Will there be negative, neutral or positive side effects resulting from inaction, and (if so) what will the side effects be and how can negative side effects be avoided or minimized?

What to Consider

When reflecting on possible damages resulting from inaction to close performance gaps, performance coaches should often contemplate answers to such questions as:

- What is likely to happen if no action is taken to close performance gap(s) or to solve performance problems?
- Who will react, if anyone, if no action is taken?
- What damages will likely result from inaction?
- What kind of damages are likely to be felt from inaction?
- Who will face damages from inaction, and how will they react?
- How can the damages of inaction be minimized?

Many other questions may be posed. But answering the questions appearing earlier may surface many ideas about what damages may (or may not) result from taking no corrective action to close performance gaps.

Use the Worksheet appearing in Table 13.1 to guide your thinking when reflecting on what damages may result when no corrective action is taken.

Table 13.1   A Worksheet to Guide Thinking on the Damages Resulting from Inaction.

A Worksheet to Guide Thinking on the Damages Resulting from Inaction
Directions: Use this Worksheet to structure and organize your thinking. In the space immediately below the Directions, briefly describe the performance gap or performance problem you are trying to solve. Then, in the next section, answer each question appearing the left column by offering your answers in the right column. There are no "right" or "wrong" answers in any absolute sense; rather, there may be better or worse answers given the needs of your organization.
Part I: Describe the Problem
What is the problem/performance gap? Briefly describe it here:

(Continued)

Table 13.1 (Continued)

A Worksheet to Guide Thinking on the Damages Resulting from Inaction	
Part II: Questions About Inaction	
Questions	**Answers**
1 What is likely to happen if no action is taken to close performance gap(s) or to solve performance problems?	
2 Who will react, if anyone, if no action is taken?	
3 What damages will likely result from inaction?	
4 What kind of damages are likely to be felt from inaction?	
5 Who will face damages from inaction, and how will they react?	
6 How can the damages of inaction be minimized?	

Source: Copyright 2021 by William J. Rothwell.

Of course, it is possible to apply scenario planning to any situation in which performance coaches contemplate doing nothing. In scenario planning, performance coaches try to make predictions about what will happen based on different assumptions about the future. If future conditions will be favorable, then the scenario is considered optimistic; if future conditions are unfavorable, then the scenario is considered pessimistic; and if future conditions are neither favorable nor unfavorable, then the scenario is considered neutral. Performance coaches may apply the same logic to consider what will happen if no action is taken to address a performance problem. A worksheet like the one appearing in Table 13.2 may be helpful in contemplating what might happen if no action is taken.

Another way to think about reflecting on the possible consequences of inaction is to modify the well-known force field analysis model. In the original model, coaches can use the model to think about the forces driving change and the forces resisting change. Change will occur when steps are taken to weaken the restraining forces or else to strengthen the driving forces.

Table 13.2 A Worksheet to Guide Scenario Planning on the Consequences Resulting from Inaction.

A Worksheet to Guide Scenario Planning on the Consequences Resulting from Inaction	
Directions: Use this table to organize your thinking about what might happen if you do nothing to address a problem situation. In the first box below, describe a problem situation you are confronting. Then, for each question appearing in the left column below, write your best guess or prediction about what might happen if no action is taken to address the problem. When you finish, reflect carefully on next steps and consider what might be the consequences of inaction.	
What is the problem situation you are confronting? Describe it. Try to be specific and answer who is involved, what is happening, what should be happening, and so forth.	
Questions About the Problem Situation	**Your Best Predictions**
1 If no action is taken to address the problem situation described above, what is your best prediction about what *damages* will result if no action is taken to address the problem?	
2 If no action is taken to address the problem situation described above, what is your best prediction about what *neutral* side effects may be experienced by the organization?	
3 If no action is taken to address the problem situation described above, what is your best prediction about what *positive* side effects may be experienced by the organization?	

Source: Copyright 2021 by William J. Rothwell.

But a creative way to reinvent the model is to consider the change effort as a driving force. If action is taken, it will create positive, negative, and neutral side effects or consequences. Likewise, if no action is taken, that will also lead to positive, negative, and neutral side effects. See Figure 13.1 and use it as a way to help organize your thinking about a change effort.

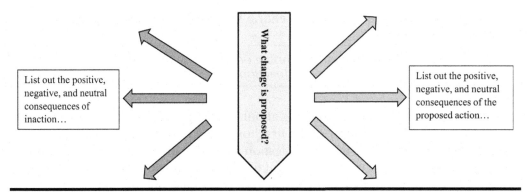

Figure 13.1 A Modified Force Field Analysis for Comparing Proposed Actions versus Inactions.

Source: Copyright 2021 by William J. Rothwell.

Examples of This Step in Performance Coaching

Perhaps, two examples will help to clarify what this step means in practice.

Situation 1

The situation: Marjorie Gulfton works with Harold Fonstor. Harold has been struggling with his job performance. While Marjorie is not Harold's supervisor, she is concerned that his job performance problems will affect her—and the team. To that end, Marjorie decides to play the role of performance coach with Harold. She goes through all the steps of the performance coaching model. When she reaches step 10, she asks herself the question "[w]hat damages are likely to result if no action is taken with Harold?"

How the Performance Coach Addresses This Step in Performance Coaching: Marjorie drives to and from work every day. One day, as she drives home after work, she reflects on the answers to that question. She tries to brainstorm on what will happen if nobody does anything about Harold's inadequate job performance.

She believes that the results are predictable. If no action is taken, she believes that company managers will progress through the typical steps of corrective action—that is, first an oral warning, then a written warning, then a 3-day suspension without pay, and finally a termination for cause. Harold will then apply for unemployment compensation, which the company will fight. At the same time, the team will be affected because time will need to be devoted to making up for the loss of Harold—which will most likely lead to mandatory overtime for all workers, declining morale and employee engagement, and much effort devoted to recruiting, selecting, onboarding, and training Harold's replacement.

Inaction will lead to many damaging consequences to Harold and to the organization's team. Marjorie does not believe that inaction will produce a neutral or positive effect.

Marjorie is also aware that damaging consequences could result that are not immediately apparent. For instance, the department manager may eventually be fired (or else moved to another assignment) because her managers will worry that she has shown she cannot rectify bad employee performance like Harold's when it becomes evident. They might use Harold's situation as evidence that the department manager cannot do his job.

All in all, Marjorie concludes that corrective action with Harold should be taken.

Note that, in the previous discussion, Marjorie refuses the temptation to take corrective action immediately. Instead, she reflects on what damaging impact may result from inaction.

Situation 2

[This situation is based on a true story.]

The situation: Maria Wilson is a senior executive in a large insurance company. She is well-known on the senior team for her ability to meet and exceed the targets established for her department. In fact, her bonuses always exceed her salary by many times each year.

But Maria has a problem that can bedevil many ambitious executives. She has an explosive effect on those who work for her. They detest her. She has a habit of criticizing her direct reports publicly, making fun of their performance, and badmouthing her own workers to her peers on the senior team.

As a direct consequence of her behavior, her direct reports went to see the CEO as a group. Maria's entire department—not including Maria—went along. The CEO was shocked to see a large crowd in his office. To him, it felt like a mass demonstration that one might see on the streets. Several workers even carried placards that bore message like "Maria leaves—or we do" and "Mutiny in Wilson's Department—It is High Time."

The CEO called the meeting to order and asked one of the groups to speak on the group's behalf. Morton Wiler stepped forward and agreed to do it.

The conversation went as follows:

CEO: Could I ask what is the meaning of this show of force?

Wiler: We have had it. We work in Maria Wilson's department, and it is intolerable. She belittles us; she criticizes us in public; she bad mouths us to her colleagues; and she generally is a bad boss. If her behavior does not undergo a radical transformation—and quickly—we will all walk. We don't have other jobs but we will leave anyway! Do something! You are her boss!

CEO: What do you propose I do?

Wiler: The Board pays you a lot of money. I bet you have ideas about how to fix a problem like this one better than we do.

CEO: Well, the thing is that Maria consistently outperforms anyone else we could possibly recruit to take her place. I will not fire her—at least not so long as her job performance is so outstanding.

Wiler: Your inaction has had a price. As you know, turnover in Maria's division is higher than in any other. Every day people are absent. They are gone not because of illness but because they are interviewing somewhere else within the company or in other companies. So, inaction has been damaging.

Worse yet, we have evidence that those who work in Maria's division have been telling the policyholders of our insurance products not to buy them! In other words, Maria's management actions have motivated workers to sabotage the company!

What do you have to say about that? Your inaction has prompted damaging consequences.

CEO (raising his hands as one might do to surrender if people pulled a gun on him): I give up. You have made your point. I actually believe you, too, because she has criticized some of you when I have been in attendance. So, I propose to hire a performance coach to re-direct her behavior.

Wiler: You have to be joking. Do you honestly believe that arrogant, know-it-all Maria will listen to a coach? She has a nutrition coach right now, and she is so overweight that we need to boost the electricity on elevators when she gets on to go upstairs. My point is that she does not have a great track record in listening to other people.

CEO: She will listen to me. I will go to the Board first and get approval to replace her. Then I will meet with her and tell her that she has one chance to work with a coach to improve her behavior in working with other people. But I would ask all of you to give it a chance. Don't quit! Give me—and her—6 months to work this out. We can't expect to change a lifetime's behaviors overnight. That is just not practical. I would also ask all of you to keep this conversation confidential. As you know, personnel actions have to be confidential because workers—even Maria—have privacy rights. We can't tell you any more about the situation.

Wiler (looking at the others in the room): Is this acceptable?
  [*Many people shake their heads in agreement.*]

Note that, in the previous discussion, Wiler does an outstanding job of demonstrating convincingly that the CEO's inaction so far to act on Wilson's behavior has had damaging consequences on workers and company policyholders alike.

Competencies Required by Performance Coaches to Avoid Damages Resulting from Inaction

Performance coaches should be able to:

- reflect on what negative consequences may result from taking no action to close performance gaps: consider possible negative scenarios stemming from inaction.
- reflect on what positive consequences may result from taking no action to close performance gaps: consider possible benefits of inaction.
- balance the relative value of acting to close performance gaps and the relative value of taking no action: weigh the cost of actions to the cost of inaction. Weigh the benefits of action to the costs of inaction. Compare the costs. Consider other issues that go beyond financial considerations—such as the impact of action or inaction on the work group/team, department, division, and organization as well as customers, suppliers, distributors, union members, and other stakeholder groups.
- consider what stakeholders may experience damages from inaction and how to mitigate the effects experienced by those stakeholders: weigh the organizational politics of action versus inaction. Will action produce positive results? Will inaction lead to negligible consequences?

Business Case Example

Before implementing the solutions chosen in earlier chapters, the MBD management team wanted to go a step further than in the previous chapter. Recall that, in the previous chapter, the MBD team brainstormed both negative and positive consequences that might result from implementing solutions to the problems identified.

But members of the management team were worried that they might be biased toward action. VP of HR Clarissa Wardstone warned the group that

> managers tend to *do something* whenever a problem occurs. But sometimes the best course of action is *to do nothing*. Of course, acting can have negative or positive consequences. So too can refusing to act. It is important to give due diligence consideration to both the consequences of taking action and the consequences of not taking action.

CFO Yi Xue agreed with Wardstone. She told the group on a zoom call that

> about 2 years ago I had eye surgery to remove a cancerous growth. If I had done nothing, I may have had additional problems from the cancer. Doing nothing would have long-term negative consequences. But doing nothing would have had at least one positive consequence: I would not have developed the permanent red mark on my eyelid that resulted from surgery and that is quite noticeable to everyone who meets me. My point: taking no action, just like acting, can have consequences that are good, bad, or indifferent. Care should be taken to consider action and inaction and their likely consequences. That does not require a long-term committee to study it; rather, a short and informal assessment is often good enough. In conclusion, I agree with Wardstone.

With that, Wardstone asked the management team over the zoom video-conference to brainstorm about what might happen if no action is taken to reduce turnover. They felt that, if no action is taken on salaries that:

■ Turnover among entry level staff would increase.
■ Turnover among more experienced or more senior staff would also increase.
■ Absenteeism rates would go up because absenteeism rates go up before turnover goes up.

Wardstone suggested that engagement rates might go down because unhappy workers would validate each other that would lead to growing dissatisfaction. Wardstone pointed out that active disengagement among workers was related to growing accident rates, increasing health insurance claims, and many other problems—including increased alcohol abuse and drug abuse.

By the end of the videoconference, the management team agreed that action should be taken to address increasing turnover. The advantages of doing something appeared to outweigh the damages that could result from inaction.

Key Factors to Remember

Let's review the lessons in this chapter. Performance coaches should:

- avoid the temptation to act when inaction may be a viable alternative
- prioritize performance gaps worthy of action
- identify possible negative consequences stemming from action or inaction and take steps to mitigate them
- identify possible positive consequences stemming from action or inaction and take steps to leverage them to advantage

Coaching and Developmental Questions for Managers

(1) How do you rate yourself from 0 to 10 (0 being the lowest and 10 being the highest) on avoiding the temptation to act to solve every problem?
  - What is missing or in the way of your understanding?
  - What is your action plan to increase your overall rate?

(2) How do you rate yourself from 0 to 10 (0 being the lowest and 10 being the highest) on prioritizing what performance gaps to close—and which ones to ignore?
  - What is missing?
  - What is your action plan to increase your overall rate?

(3) How do you rate yourself from 0 to 10 (0 being the lowest and 10 being the highest) on identifying which stakeholder groups might experience the most damaging effects from inaction?
  - What is missing or not understood?
  - What is your action plan to increase your overall rate?

(4) How do you rate yourself from 0 to 10 (0 being the lowest and 10 being the highest) on your ability to mitigate the damages created by inaction on performance problems?
  – What is missing or not understood?
  – What is your action plan to increase your overall rate?

References

Hinkin, Timothy R., and Chester A. Schriesheim. 2004. "If You Don't Hear from Me You Know You Are doing Fine: The Effects of Management Nonresponse to Employee Performance." *Cornell Hotel and Restaurant Administration Quarterly* 45: 362–72.

Hinkin, Timothy R., and Chester A. Schriesheim. 2008. "An Examination of 'Nonleadership': From Laissezfaire Leadership to Leader Reward Omission and Punishment Omission." *Journal of Applied Psychology* 93: 1234–48.

Lambert, Andrea. 2016. "Ignoring Problems Can Lead to Serious Consequences: Learn to Face Challenges Head On." *Andrea Lambert Life Coach*. https://andrealambertlifecoach.com/ignoring-problems-can-lead-serious-consequences-learn-face-challenges-head/.

Mohrmann, Jacob. 2020. "When We Ignore Problems to Avoid Their Solutions." *PeopleScience.com*. https://peoplescience.maritz.com/Articles/2019/When-We-Ignore-Problems-To-Avoid-Solutions.

Moore, Henry. 2002. *The High Cost of Doing Nothing: How to Avoid Troubles and Assure Success*. Kennett, MO: Skyward Publishing Company.

Mueller, Jennifer. 2017. *Creative Change: Why We Resist It . . . How We Can Embrace It*. New York: Houghton, Mifflin & Harcourt.

Saltzman, Jason. 2018. "Here's the Real Cost of Ignoring Your Problems." *Entrepreneur*. www.entrepreneur.com/article/311834.

Swanson, Ana. 2016. "The Incredible Power of Ignoring Everything." *The Washington Post*. www.washingtonpost.com/news/wonk/wp/2016/03/03/the-incredible-power-of-ignoring-everything/.

Von Bergen, C. W. 2012. "The High Cost of Supervisory Inaction." *The Exchange* 1: 1. http://homepages.se.edu/cvonbergen/files/2015/03/The-High-Cost-of-Supervisory-Inaction.pdf

"Why the Things You Ignore Will Only Grow." 2021. *Kletische*. https://kletische.com/amplify-things-ignore/.

Chapter 14

Step 11: How to Implement the Solution?

William J. Rothwell

Once the previous 10 steps of performance coaching have been enacted, performance coaches must implement them. Implementation goes by many names. Some call it *execution*; some call it simply *implementation*; and some call it *intervention*. Whatever the name, it usually involves taking action. The action can occur on a short-term basis—such as a one-minute performance coaching session. Or it may occur on a long-term basis—such as many one-hour session between performance coach and coachee.

Performance coaching sessions share common characteristics. They all have a beginning, a middle, and an end. They all have a relationship established of some kind between the performance coach and the coachee. They all have goals to be achieved, actions to be taken by coach and coachee, and results to be evaluated. In many ways, performance coaching is like any project; in many ways, performance coaching can be directive (run by the coach), nondirective (run by the coachee), or a combination (some features run by the coach and others run by coaches). Performance coaching can rely on discussions only or they can rely in part on instruments. And performance coaching is carried out in a setting, and for that reason, a performance coaching culture is important to establish and maintain.

DOI: 10.4324/9781003155928-19

How This Chapter Is Organized

This chapter is organized into the following parts:

- What This Step Means
- Why Is This Step in Performance Coaching Important?
- Example of This Step in Performance Coaching
- Using Project Management Methods to Guide Performance Coaching Implementation
- Managing Across Coaching Projects
- Using Instruments to Guide or Support Performance Coaching
- Establishing a Corporate Culture that Supports Performance Coaching
- Competencies Required by Performance Coaches to Implement Coaching
- Key Factors to Remember
- Coaching and Developmental Questions for Managers
- References

What This Step Means

Step 11 is about implementing the performance coaching effort. It typically involves clarifying:

- Who will be coached?
- What will the coaching focus on in the short-term and long-term?
- When will the coaching sessions occur?
- Where will the coaching sessions occur?
- Why will the coaching sessions occur?
- How will the coaching sessions be organized and carried out?
- How much time, money, and effort will be devoted to performance coaching?

Like any change effort, performance coaching is heavily dependent on actions and follow-up.

Use the worksheet appearing in Table 14.1 to organize your thinking to plan a performance coaching session.

Table 14.1   A Worksheet to Guide Project Planning for Performance Coaching.

A Worksheet to Guide Project Planning for Performance Coaching	
Directions: Use this Worksheet to Guide you in organizing your thinking about how to implement the solution and how to plan a performance coaching intervention. For each question appearing in the left column below, provide your answer in the right column. While there are no 'right" or "wrong" answers in any absolute sense, some answers may be better than others for you, for those you coach, and for the organizational context.	
Questions	**Answers**
1 Who will be coached?	
2 What will the coaching focus on in the short-term and long-term?	
3 When will the coaching sessions occur?	
4 Where will the coaching sessions occur?	
5 How will the coaching sessions be organized and carried out?	

Source: Copyright 2021 by William J. Rothwell.

Why Is This Step in Performance Coaching Important?

Most change efforts fail. And the root cause of failure can often be found in ineffective implementation. It is one thing to identify the need for performance coaching and select the best solutions; it is quite another thing to conduct and sustain effective performance coaching interventions. But without sustained efforts, results will rarely be achieved.

When performance coaching interventions fail, managers who act as performance coaches will often cite predictable reasons. They will point to the lack of time, money, or staff sufficient to conduct the effort. Some will try to shift blame to the coachee or to others such as the human resources department or other workers. But only by sustained effort, results will be achieved.

It is important to note that people cannot be helped if they refuse that help. For that reason, it is important at the outset of any performance coaching effort to assess the readiness of coaches. Do they want help? Do they see the need for it? Will they be supported in making changes by their immediate supervisor (if not the performance coach), their coworkers, their family members, and other stakeholders who may affect their relative commitment to the coaching experience?

Examples of This Step in Performance Coaching

Perhaps, an example will help to clarify what this step means in practice.

The situation: Juan Johnson is a production manager in the Acme Insurance Company. He is about to meet with his worker Mary Oo. Mary has been having serious job performance problems. They are meeting for the required annual performance review. Juan is planning to discuss the performance problems with Mary and then go through all the steps of the performance coaching process. He does not believe that it can be done in one meeting. Instead, he is thinking that it may require monthly meetings over the next year.

Using the Worksheet appearing in Table 14.1, Juan also uses the steps in the performance coaching model (shown in the Table of Contents of this book) to plan for a series of performance coaching sessions with Mary. In his first meeting with Mary, he begins by conducting the performance review to explain why he believes there are important areas needing improvement in Mary's job performance. Mary does not argue; rather, she signals a willingness to improve. When she does, Juan shares his performance coaching plan with her and discusses how they will work together. Mary leaves the room encouraged and appears to be motivated to improve.

Note that, in the previous discussion, Juan treats performance coaching like a project. While he takes the lead, he does not coerce Mary into the change effort. Instead, he explains why a change is needed in her job performance and shares a plan for performance coaching to help her improve.

Using Project Management Methods to Guide Performance Coaching Implementation

Performance coaches should be familiar with the principles of project management and apply them to performance coaching projects. Effective projects comply with the standards of project management, and performance coaches should be familiar with those. They are set forth by the Project Management Institute (PMI) (see Project Management Institute 2021; Sandhu 2018; Udo and Koppensteiner 2004).

Managing Across Coaching Projects

A common problem in management today is that many organizations have numerous change efforts going on simultaneously. One author of this book asked a client how many major, strategic change efforts were being implemented in the client's organization. The answer was 99 major projects! It is unlikely that so many projects can be successfully implemented at the same time in any organization.

Performance coaches run into the same problem if they try to help too many people at the same time. Coaching effectiveness can melt away when coaches spread themselves too thin across to many clients:

How can that problem be solved?

While there are many answers to that question, one idea is to apply the principles of Whole Systems Transformational Change (WSTC) to performance coaching (Dannemiller, Sylvia, and Tolchinsky 2000; Sullivan, Fairburn, and Rothwell 2002). In WSTC, the idea is to bring together all the key stakeholders involved in change efforts and work with them simultaneously. Individual coaching efforts can be folded into a more systematic approach to large-scale organizational change.

The steps in WSTc have been identified elsewhere. But the idea is to:

- plan a meeting with all the key stakeholders
- assess the needs of the whole group
- set common performance coaching goals that are shared by all members of the group
- work with the group to identify ways to achieve the goal individually and collectively
- work with the group to set targets for achievement at the individual and group levels
- implement the change effort and thereby work to implement solutions to performance problems
- establish methods by which individuals and groups can meet to share concerns, work through issues, leverage strengths, and provide celebrations of successes

Using Instruments to Guide or Support Performance Coaching

Many instruments are commonly used today. Popular instruments include the Myers-Briggs Type Indicator (MBTI), the Disc, the Rokeach Value Survey, and the Kilmann Conflict Resolution Survey (Buros Center 2021; Inc. Coach U 2005); 360-degree assessments are also popular in which individuals rate themselves on a list of criteria, and they are also rated by supervisor(s), peers, subordinates, and members of other groups such as family members, customers, suppliers, and distributors (Rothwell et al. 2015).

Instruments can be powerful in demonstrating to individuals or teams the need to change and specific issues deserving of attention.

Establishing a Corporate Culture that Supports Performance Coaching

While performance coaches and coachees may work together effectively on their own, the coaching effort is more likely to be implemented effectively—and the opportunity for success in implementing solutions to performance problems is likely to be better—if the organization has established an effective corporate culture to support coaching. A culture that supports performance coaching has distinctive characteristics. Use the instrument appearing in Table 14.2 to assess the quality of the corporate culture in your organization. Then, for each area identified as less than optimal, devise action strategies to improve those elements of your organization's corporate culture.

It is also helpful if performance coaches follow best practices in coaching like those shown in the assessment appearing in Table 14.3. (You may wish to assess yourself against the characteristics of an effective performance coach and use those characteristics to identify areas for your own improvement and development).

Competencies Required by Performance Coaches to Implement Solutions

Performance coaches should be able to:

■ assess the relative willingness of coachees to participate in a performance coaching intervention
■ apply effective project management approaches to performance coaching
■ manage across multiple performance coaching interventions as necessary
■ source, use, and provide feedback on various instruments that can be of value in performance coaching sessions
■ manage performance coaching sessions effectively

Table 14.2   Assessing Your Organization's Coaching Culture.

Assessing Your Organization's Coaching Culture					
Directions: For each characteristic of an effective corporate coaching culture appearing in the left column below, rate your organization in the right column. Use this rating scale: **1 = Strongly Disagree; 2 = Disagree; 3 = Neutral; 4 = Agree; and 5 = Strongly Agree**. When you finish, add up the scores from the ratings in the right column. Then read about your rating below.					
Assessing Corporate Coaching Culture	*How Would You Rate Your Organization?*				
I Would Say That My Organization Represents an Excellent Corporate coaching Culture. That Means That Coaching in This Organization	*1*	*2*	*3*	*4*	*5*
1 Is built on interpersonal trust.					
2 Encourages self-disclosure.					
3 Is based on openness.					
4 Enables self-awareness.					
5 Leads to self-development.					
6 Allows people to acknowledge their weaknesses as well as their strengths.					
7 Enables meaningful conversations.					
8 Inspires people to improve themselves.					
9 Demonstrates a willingness of people to give feedback to others and receive feedback from others for improvement.					
10 Is clearly based on the belief that everyone can be developed and can improve.					
11 Is based on a belief that leaders have a responsibility to develop others.					
12 Gives people comfort to challenge issues that are of importance to them.					

(Continued)

Table 14.2 (Continued)

Assessing Corporate Coaching Culture		How Would You Rate Your Organization?				
I Would Say That My Organization Represents an Excellent Corporate coaching Culture. That Means That Coaching in This Organization		1	2	3	4	5
13	Is based on a conviction that it is desirable to have coaches or coachees.					
14	Is not based on status because even senior leaders may need coaching.					
15	Encourages people listen and seek to understand first.					
16	Encourages people to ask questions to discover issues and solutions.					
17	Encourages teams and work groups to be more open and practice team coaching.					
18	Relies on common terminology and understanding of coaching.					
19	Is evaluated in more than one way.					
20	Can build and leverage on strengths as well as solve problems.					
	Total					

Source: Copyright 2021 by William J. Rothwell.

Scoring (for Table 14.2)	
If your score was between	*Then:*
100 and 90	Congratulations. Your organization has an effective corporate coaching culture. Give your organization a grade of A.
89 and 80	Good. Your organization has many correct elements in place to have a wonderful corporate coaching culture. However, your organization also has areas for improvement. Give your organization a grade of B.
79 and 70	Okay. Your organization is about average in its corporate coaching culture. Give your organization a grade of C. Do not rest on your laurels. Get busy to fix the identified areas for improvement.

Scoring (for Table 14.2)	
If your score was between	*Then:*
69 and 60	Your organization is nearly failing. You have significant work to do to improve your organization's coaching culture. Your organization gets a D.
59 and below	Get busy. Fix your organization's coaching culture problems.

Table 14.3   Comparing Your Organization to Best Practices in Coaching.

Comparing Your Organization to Best Practices in Coaching						
Directions: For each best practice linked to coaching in the left column below, rate your organization in the right column. Use this rating scale: **1 = Strongly Disagree; 2 = Disagree; 3 = Neutral; 4 = Agree; and 5 = Strongly Agree**. When you finish, add up the scores from the ratings in the right column. Then read about your rating below.						
Best Practices in Coaching		*How Would You Rate Your Organization?*				
I Would Say That My Organization Aligns with Global Best Practice in Coaching. That Means that Coaching in This Organization		*1*	*2*	*3*	*4*	*5*
1	Aligns with the organization's strategic business plan.					
2	Focuses on achieving business results.					
3	Encourages self-awareness for coachee and for coach.					
4	Begins with an assessment of some kind, either formal (databased using an instrument) or informal (relying on perceived needs)					
5	Takes a holistic approach—which means that it does not limit coaching discussions to business topics only but can also include issues having to do with physical health, mental health, family, and personal issues of the coachee.					
6	Makes the role of the coach clear (directive, nondirective, or both).					
7	Is carried out with confidentiality in mind					

(Continued)

Table 14.3 (Continued)

Best Practices in Coaching		How Would You Rate Your Organization?				
I Would Say That My Organization Aligns with Global Best Practice in Coaching. That Means that Coaching in This Organization		*1*	*2*	*3*	*4*	*5*
8	Can involve others that go beyond the coach and coachee—such as managers, peers, subordinates, or even those off-the-job such as significant others.					
9	Is sensitive to national culture issues.					
10	Is sensitive to corporate culture issues.					
11	Relies on a clear organization of each coaching session.					
12	Is carried out over a defined period of time.					
13	Begins with a contract that lays out expectations.					
14	Must have the support of the coachee throughout the coaching process.					
15	Is regarded as a sign of a leader who wants to improve continuously.					
16	Is supported by important stakeholders in the organization—such as Board of Directors (in a publicly traded company) or owner in a private company, CEO and others.					
17	Often focuses on one issue in each coaching session.					
18	Is not always held "on the job site" because privacy is important.					
19	Can sometimes include impromptu meetings when the coachee experiences a crisis.					
20	Is periodically updated to ensure that the measurable goals sought from the coaching experience/relationship is clear and kept up to date.					
Total						

Source: Copyright 2021 by William J. Rothwell.

Scoring (for Table 14.3)	
If your score was between	**Then:**
100 and 90	Congratulations. Your organization is following best practice. Give your organization a grade of A.
89 and 80	Good. Your organization has many correct elements in place. However, your organization also has areas for improvement. Give your organization a grade of B.
79 and 70	Okay. Your organization is about average. Give your organization a grade of C. Do not rest on your laurels. Get busy to fix the identified areas for improvement.
69 and 60	Your organization is nearly failing. You have significant work to do to improve how coaching is conducted. Your organization gets a D.
59 and below	Get busy. Fix your organization's coaching problems.

Key Factors to Remember

Let's review the lessons in this chapter. When implementing the best solutions and implementing performance coaching, performance coaches should:

- assess the willingness of the coachee to participate
- manage the performance coaching intervention like a project
- manage performance coaching sessions
- manage across performance coaching interventions if necessary with one or more people
- identify, administer, analyze, interpret and provide feedback using instruments helpful in performance coaching

Coaching and Developmental Questions for Managers

(1) How do you rate yourself from 0 to 10 (0 being the lowest and 10 being the highest) on your knowledge and understanding of ways to assess the willingness of individuals or groups to participate in performance coaching interventions?
 – What is missing or in the way of your understanding?
 – What is your action plan to increase your overall rate?

(2) How do you rate yourself from 0 to 10 (0 being the lowest and 10 being the highest) on your knowledge and understanding of ways to apply project management techniques to performance coaching?
   – What is missing?
   – What is your action plan to increase your overall rate?

(3) How do you rate yourself from 0 to 10 (0 being the lowest and 10 being the highest) on your ability to manage a performance coaching session with one or more people?
   – What is missing or not understood?
   – What is your action plan to increase your overall rate?

(4) How do you rate yourself from 0 to 10 (0 being the lowest and 10 being the highest) on your ability to use various instruments in performance coaching?
   – What is missing or not understood?
   – What is your action plan to increase your overall rate?

References

Buros Center. 2021. *The Twenty-First Mental Measurements Yearbook*. Lincoln, NE: Buros Center for Testing.

Dannemiller, Kathleen, James Sylvia, and Paul Tolchinsky. 2000. *Whole-Scale Change*. San Francisco, CA: Berret-Koehler.

Inc. Coach U. 2005. *Coach U's Essential Coaching Tools: Your Complete Practice Resource*. New York, NY: Wiley.

Project Management Institute. 2021. *PMBok Guide: A Guide to the Project Management Body of Knowledge*, 7th ed. Newtown Square, PA: PMI.

Rothwell, William, James Graber, David Dubois, Aileen Zabellero, Catherin Haynes, Ali Alkhalaf, and Sarah Sager. 2015. *The Competency Toolkit*, 2nd ed., 2 vols. Amherst, MA: HRD Press.

Sandhu, Sahil. 2018. "Key Competencies for Project Managers: An Empirical Study." https://digitalcommons.harrisburgu.edu/pmgt_dandt/46.

Sullivan, Roland, Linda Fairburn, and William Rothwell. 2002. "The Whole System Transformation Conference: Fast Change for the 21st Century." In *Rewiring Organizations for the Networked Economy: Organizing, Managing, and Leading in the Information Age*, edited by Stanley Herman, 115–42. San Francisco, CA: Jossey-Bass/Pfeiffer.

Udo, Nathalie, and Sonja Koppensteiner. 2004. "What Are the Core Competencies of a Successful Project Manager?" In *No. 2. Paper Presented at PMI® Global Congress 2004—EMEA, Prague, Czech Republic*. Newtown Square, PA: Project Management Institute.

Chapter 15

Step 12: How to Evaluate the Successful Implementation?

William J. Rothwell

Step twelve in the performance coaching model is evaluation. Evaluation, the process of placing value, should be continuous during the coaching process. In other words, nobody should wait until the end to begin evaluation; rather, evaluation should be planned before coaching begins. Evaluation should also occur before, during, and after each coaching session and before, during, and after a planned sequence of coaching experiences.

How This Chapter Is Organized

This chapter is organized into the following parts:

- What This Step Means
- Why Is This Step in Performance Coaching Important?
- Steps in Evaluating Performance Coaching
- Examples of This Step in Performance Coaching
- Competencies Required by Performance Coaches to Evaluate
- Key Factors to Remember
- Coaching and Developmental Questions for Managers

DOI: 10.4324/9781003155928-20

What This Step Means

Step twelve is about evaluating performance coaching. It means placing value on the coaching experience as it is about to occur, while it is occurring, and after it took place. Evaluation can focus on feelings and perceptions (i.e., how much people liked the experience), on behavioral change (how much people changed their behavior as a result of coaching), on results or productivity, on financial return, on career progress, on goal attainment, or other issues of importance.

Evaluation has become nearly an obsession with many in the learning and development field. Managers often request so-called return on investment (ROI) information about training. While sponsors and clients sometimes do request evaluation information about performance coaching interventions (Bartlett, Boylan, and Hale 2014; Carter, Wolfe, and Kerrin 2005; Ensminger et al. 2015; Gray 2004; Institute for Employment Studies 2005; Lai and Palmer 2019; Leedham 2005), they less often ask for the ROI of coaching in the same way that they do for training. Instead, sponsors and clients more often ask for feedback on how well the coaching experience is achieving desired results. They wish to know if:

- coaching intended to improve job performance is working
- coaching intended to correct behavioral problems is working
- coaching intended to leverage personal strengths is working
- coaching intended to help workgroups or teams is working

The abovementioned issues are much more practical than complicated efforts to demonstrate financial benefits to skeptical managers.

Why Is This Step in Performance Coaching Important?

Evaluation is important to forecast benefits, ensure alignment of coaching efforts with the organization's strategic direction, monitor the continuing progress of coaching interventions, and document results achieved.

Assessment and coaching work together. Assessment identifies the measurable goals to be achieved from the performance coaching effort. Evaluation identifies the results achieved from the performance coaching intervention.

Steps in Evaluating Performance Coaching

To evaluate performance coaching, follow a step-by-step approach. It is also important to consider who or what is evaluated, a topic also treated in the following.

Evaluation Step by Step

The first step in evaluating performance coaching is to determine the purpose of the evaluation. Why is evaluation necessary, and who wants the information from it? Consider:

■ Were the measurable objectives of the coaching session/intervention met?
■ How much did coaching contribute to achieving workers' key performance indicators?
■ How much did coachees benefit from participating?
■ In what ways did coachees benefit?
■ What were the strengths and weaknesses of the coaching experience?
■ How well-satisfied were those who requested the coaching experience?
■ How can future coaching efforts be improved?

The second step is to decide what evaluation method(s) to use. In that step, decide how the information will be collected. Consider:

■ interviewing the coach, coachees, and stakeholders
■ surveying the coach, coachees, and stakeholders
■ conducting focus groups of coaches, coachees, and stakeholders
■ observing coaching experiences
■ reviewing secondary data related to coaching

The third step is to make, buy, or make-and-tailor the data collection methods for evaluation. Should coaches design their methods to collect data, try to purchase some from sources outside their organizations, or purchase off-the-shelf data collection instruments and then try to modify them for their purposes?

The fourth step is to collect data. In short, conduct the interviews, surveys, focus groups, observations, or document reviews. This step is sometimes called administration. Administering data collection can be more difficult than it sounds. For instance, some people may refuse to participate. Data may be collected with a promise of confidentiality, but sensitive data that emerge may be cause for concern. (For instance, if the confidentiality of responses is promised when a survey is administered, what should the organization do if a crime is reported on a survey?)

The fifth step is to analyze the results of the data collection effort. If the data collection instruments were designed to be answered with scaled responses, they are subject to quantitative analysis; if they are designed for open-ended responses, they are subject to qualitative analysis. Sometimes data analysis will require expert help on statistics, thematic analysis, or both.

The sixth step is to apply the results of the evaluation to improving future efforts. There is little benefit to collecting information and then not using it. Often, a good approach is to feedback the information to those who supplied data and enlist their ideas on how to improve the coaching experience.

The seventh and final step is to document coaching results and communicate them to stakeholders. Documenting means "writing it down for future reference." Often, the results of evaluation are reported and then become the basis for plans leading to improvement. Communication is also important. Stakeholders should hear the results of evaluation. In addition, reports—like case studies—of effective coaching experiences are essentially stories that help shape and change the corporate culture (BB & Co 2013).

Who or What Is Evaluated?

When planning the evaluation of performance coaching, consider:

- Who will be evaluated?
- What will be evaluated?
- Who will use the results of evaluation?

Who Will Be Evaluated?

Often, it is assumed that evaluation will focus on coachees—that is, how well they achieved the change objectives established at the outset of a coaching experience. And, indeed, often performance coaches need to show results with those they coach. An evaluation may be a necessity to justify any expenditures on performance coaching or the time and effort devoted to it. Use the evaluation in Table 15.1 as one example of a way to guide a coachee through an evaluation.

Table 15.1 A Tool for Evaluating the Performance Coaching Experience: The Coachee's Perspective.

A Tool for Evaluating the Performance Coaching Experience *The Coachee's Perspective*						
Directions: Use this tool to evaluate the coaching experience. For each step in the 12-step performance coaching process, rate your coach on how well he or she performed as a coach on each step. Use this scale: **0 = Not appropriate; 1 = Not at all well; 2 = Somewhat well; 3 = Adequate; 4 = Well done; 5 = Very well done.** When you have finished completing your assessment, add up the scores. Then interpret them by reviewing the scoring below.						
Steps in the Performance Coaching Model	*Rate How Well You Feel You Performed*					
How Well Do You Feel the Coach Carried Out Each Step in the Performance Coaching Process	*0*	*1*	*2*	*3*	*4*	*5*
1 Step 1: Built rapport and readiness?						
2 Step 2: Determined the issue at hand?						
3 Step 3: Determined what should be happening?						
4 Step 4: Clarified the measurable gap between what is (step 2) and what should be (step 3)?						
5 Step 5: Determined how important is the gap?						
6 Step 6: Identified the root cause(s) of the gap?						
7 Step 7: Identified a range of ways to close the gap?						
8 Step 8: Determined the most effective way to close the gap?						
9 Step 9: Considered the consequences of closing the gap?						
10 Step 10: Clarified the damages of inactions?						
11 Step 11: Considered how to implement the solution(s)?						
12 Step 12: Decided how to evaluate the implementation?						
Total Add up the scores and right and place in the box at right						

Source: Copyright 2021 by William J. Rothwell.

Scoring (for Table 15.1)	
If your score is	**Then**
60–51	Grade your coach an A. Good job.
50–41	Give your coach a B. Invite him or her to work on improving the areas you identified for improvement.
40–31	Give your coach a C. Ask him or her to work on improving his or her coaching skills.
30–21	How disappointing. Give your coach a D. Suggest that the coach make it a priority to improve skills as a performance coach.
20 and below	You believe your coach is a failure. Suggest that the coach get some training on coaching.

But it is also possible to focus evaluation on others. An obvious focal point for evaluation is the coach. Was the coach helpful? How well did the coach help the coachee? Was the relationship productive? These and similar questions may be explored during coaching sessions or built in to be discussed at checkpoints along a planned chain of performance coaching sessions. Use the evaluation in Table 15.2 as one example of a way to guide a coachee through an evaluation.

Some performance coaching interventions are requested by one person (the sponsor who pays the bill for it) and carried out by another person (the coach) to help a third person (the client or coachee). Sponsors, whose interests may not necessarily coincide with those of performance coaches or the coachees, may be the focus of attention. Sponsors, when they exist, play an important role and do influence the direction of performance coaching efforts. For that reason, their role and how they enact it should also be evaluated. Sponsors can impact coaching results.

Less often discussed is focusing performance coaching evaluation on how much and what kind of support coachees receive from such stakeholders as managers, significant others (spouse, siblings, or children), friends, coworkers, and even company customers, suppliers, or distributors. It is possible to gather data from such sources in 360-degree assessments. It is also possible to evaluate how much, if at all, these stakeholders help or hinder on-the-job or at-home applications of coaching advice or lessons learned.

Table 15.2   A Tool for Evaluating the Performance Coaching Experience: The Coach's Perspective.

Tool for Evaluating the Performance Coaching Experience *The Coach's Perspective*						
Directions: Use this tool to help you self-assess how well you feel you managed one or more performance coaching interventions. For each step in the 12-step performance coaching process, rate yourself on how well you performed as a coach. Use this scale: **0 = Not appropriate; 1 = Not at all well; 2 = Somewhat well; 3 = Adequate; 4 = Well done; 5 = Very well done**. When you have finished completing your assessment, add up the scores. Then interpret them by reviewing the scoring below.						
Steps in the Performance Coaching Model	*Rate How Well You Feel You Performed*					
How Well Do You Feel You Carried Out Each Step in the Performance Coaching Process	*0*	*1*	*2*	*3*	*4*	*5*
1 Step 1: Built rapport and readiness?						
2 Step 2: Determined the issue at hand?						
3 Step 3: Determined what should be happening?						
4 Step 4: Clarified the measurable gap between what is (step 2) and what should be (step 3)?						
5 Step 5: Determined how important is the gap?						
6 Step 6: Identified the root cause(s) of the gap?						
7 Step 7: Identified a range of ways to close the gap?						
8 Step 8: Determined the most effective way to close the gap?						
9 Step 9: Considered the consequences of closing the gap?						
10 Step 10: Clarified the damages of inactions?						
11 Step 11: Considered how to implement the solution(s)?						
12 Step 12: Decided how to evaluate the implementation?						
Total Add up the scores and right and place in the box at right						

Source: Copyright 2021 by William J. Rothwell.

Scoring (for Table 15.2)	
If your score is	**Then**
60–51	Grade yourself an A. Good job.
50–41	Give yourself a B. Improve the areas on which you rated yourself as wanting.
40–31	Give yourself a C. Develop an individual development plan for improvement.
30–21	How disappointing. Give yourself a D. Make it a priority to improve yourself as A performance coach.
20 and below	You believe you are a failure. A mentor might help you sharpen your ability to carry out the steps in performance coaching.

What Will Be Evaluated?

Performance coaching is a powerful intervention that can achieve far-ranging results. Such powerful change efforts should be guided by planned targets and then results compared to those. Each performance coaching session should have goals; each performance coaching session should have checkpoints during the session; each planned chain of performance coaching sessions should have their own goals; and milestones should be established and examined during the implementation of a long-term performance coaching intervention.

While many issues could be the focus of evaluation, two are of particular importance:

■ What was the problem or issue to be addressed by the performance coaching effort, and how well was it addressed?
■ How did people work together to achieve results, and how were interpersonal relationships affected by the performance coaching intervention?

The first question addresses the task outcomes that were achieved; the second question addresses changes in interpersonal relationships or group dynamics that were achieved. Both the what and the how is important. In some cases—as in working to improve individual or group innovation—the how emerges as most important.

Who Will Use the Results of the Evaluation?

Perhaps, the most important issue to consider in evaluating performance coaching is the answer to the simple question *"who wants the evaluation, and what will they do with it?"*

If it is clear who is the primary audience or customer for evaluation information, that can affect what objectives are set for evaluation, how data are collected, how data are interpreted, and how the results will be used. A simple reason: different stakeholders care about different information.

Coaches care about the effectiveness of the coaching effort. Coachees care about the same, but they may also care about how others perceive the coaching experience and what it might say about perceptions of their ability. Coachees may also worry about the impact of performance coaching on helping them achieve job performance targets, prepare for promotion, or interact with others.

Examples of This Step in Performance Coaching

Perhaps, two examples will help to clarify what evaluation means for performance coaching.

Situation 1: Lysotta Dorfman is a performance coaching. She has been working with Maria Taylor, a promising manager in the VouisDillon Corporation. VouisDillon is a candymaker, and Taylor is the production manager. She has been working with Dorfman for many months in response to complaints from Taylor's direct reports, who claim that she is an abusive manager with a brutal management style. Taylor's supervisor is the CEO of VouisDillon, Li Ming.

Dorfman worked with Taylor to establish an improvement plan to guide the performance coaching intervention. Li Ming was a part of the discussion, offering thoughts on what should be improved in Taylor's management style. Dorfman shadowed Taylor around the plant for one day per month, and that was part of the agreement. At the end of each day, Dorfman would meet with Taylor to offer feedback on what she observed throughout the day. Dorfman offered her views on what Taylor did and what reactions Taylor's behaviors prompted from her direct reports. She also asked Taylor to reflect on her behavior and offer her ideas about what could be improved in her interpersonal interactions with others. At the end of each session, Dorfman would guide Taylor in an evaluation of the coaching experience as well as Dorfman's performance and Li Ming's contributions (if any). The evaluation was thus tightly focused on each session.

After six months of coaching sessions, Li Ming asked Dorfman for a report to address the answer to the simple question "what improvements have been made?"

Comments About Situation 1: Note that, in the previous example, Dorfman establishes plans for each coaching session and then guides a conversation after each coaching session focused on evaluating results achieved. The results of the evaluation then provide information to guide the goals to be set for future coaching sessions. That is one way to think about evaluation in performance coaching.

Situation 2: Martin Marietta has an outstanding worker named Jolson Gunns, who is a security guard. Martin is the manager in charge of an entire region of security guards. He supervises 32 sites in a 50-square-mile area. His workers are on their jobs 24 hours per day, 7 days a week, 365 days per year. Each site is different: some are corporate headquarters; some are industrial plants; some are large retail stores; some are rental companies that rent out automobiles; and many other organizations. The security guards in each location have different responsibilities, which are often dictated by insurance requirements.

Martin wants to call his efforts to groom Jolson "performance coaching." His goal is to build on Jolson's strengths and gradually train him on how to perform every aspect of Marietta's job. They are doing that through daily efforts (Rothwell, Chee, and Oo 2015). He plans the development experiences daily, using his job description as the basis for the plan. And he believes that evaluation of the performance coaching effort should focus on how well the Gunns is developed each day and also over time.

Comments About Situation 2: Evaluation can take many forms and focus on many issues. This example is intended to illustrate that point. Evaluation can be conducted each day against daily targets, and it can be conducted over longer timeframes when plans extend over longer durations.

Competencies Required by Performance Coaches to Evaluate

Performance coaches should be able to:

- identify the measurable results to be achieved from a performance coaching intervention because of an assessment: set measurable targets. Track achievement against targets. Involve key stakeholders in tracking results.
- align performance coaching interventions with the organization's strategic plans and goals: determine the organization's strategic goals. Align coaching goals with the organization's strategic goals. Monitor

achievement of coaching goals—perhaps establishing Key Performance Indicators (KPIs) for the performance coaching change effort.

■ plan for evaluation before a coaching intervention or session is implemented: establish a project plan for the performance coaching effort. Implement the project plan. Monitor project results.

■ monitor coaching sessions and interventions as they occur: establish performance coaching dashboards and other ways of showing results. Meet with coachees to discuss progress. Meet with sponsors (who pay the bills for the coaching) to discuss progress as warranted.

■ pinpoint areas for improvement in coaching efforts because of sessions and establish agendas for improvement in future sessions: create a performance coaching scorecard and meet with the coachee and sponsor regularly to discuss achievement against scorecard targets.

■ document the short- and long-term results of performance coaching: describe the anecdotal evidence of achievement. Describe quantitative, empirical evidence of achievement from performance coaching as desired or requested.

■ communicate the short- and long-term results of performance coaching to such key stakeholders as senior executives, managers, workers, and others who have an interest in coaching outcomes: establish a coaching communication plan. Communicate with the coachee. Communicate with the sponsor. Communicate with others who are in the circle of acquaintance of the coachee as appropriate.

Business Case Example

As Harold Corson worked on preparing a project plan to implement performance coaching at MBD, he considered ways to evaluate the change effort before, during, and after implementation.

Corson was quite familiar with the so-called Kirkpatrick model, widely used in evaluating training. According to that model, training can be evaluated based on:

■ *Reaction*: How much did people like the training?
■ *Learning*: How much did people learn from the training?
■ *Behavior*: How much behavioral change occurred back on the job after people participated in training?
■ *Results*: How much did the organization gain in increased productivity, or else save in reduced costs, from training?

Corson felt that these four levels could be revised to fit efforts to evaluate the benefits of actions taken to reduce turnover and/or to evaluate performance coaching.

Corson's team, at Corson's direction, developed a reaction sheet to administer weekly to managers to ask them how much they liked the salary increases geared to their entry-level workers and how well they felt the salary increases were working to reduce turnover. Corson's team members also interviewed managers to see if they could offer suggestions on what to evaluate to ensure that the performance coaching change effort was successful.

When Corson presented his proposal for evaluation methods to the steering committee, the committee members felt that it was lacking in rigor. The committee members wanted to see evidence that the efforts were securing a positive cost/benefit ratio (i.e., it was gaining a positive ROI). To that end, Corson worked with the Chief Financial Officer and her department to come up with ways to try to measure the change effort.

Key Factors to Remember

Let's review the lessons in this chapter. When evaluating performance coaching, performance coaches should:

- plan for evaluation before sessions are conducted
- monitor each performance coaching session with individuals or groups/ teams
- document the measurable results of coaching
- communicate the measurable results of coaching to interested stakeholders

Coaching and Developmental Questions for Managers

(1) How do you rate yourself from 0 to 10 (0 being the lowest and 10 being the highest) on your knowledge and understanding of ways to plan for the evaluation of performance coaching sessions?
   - What is missing or in the way of your understanding?
   - What is your action plan to increase your overall rate?

(2) How do you rate yourself from 0 to 10 (0 being the lowest and 10 being the highest) on your knowledge and understanding of ways to monitor

performance coaching as it is implemented with individuals and/or groups and teams?

– What is missing?
– What is your action plan to increase your overall rate?

(3) How do you rate yourself from 0 to 10 (0 being the lowest and 10 being the highest) on your ability to document the results from performance coaching?

– What is missing or not understood?
– What is your action plan to increase your overall rate?

(4) How do you rate yourself from 0 to 10 (0 being the lowest and 10 being the highest) on your ability to communicate the results from performance coaching?

– What is missing or not understood?
– What is your action plan to increase your overall rate?

References

Bartlett, James, Robert Boylan, and Jimmie Hale. 2014. "Executive Coaching: An Integrative Literature Review." *Journal of Human Resource and Sustainability Studies* 2, no. 4: 188–95. www.scirp.org/pdf/JHRSS_2014111909115742.pdf.

BB & Co. 2013. "How to Change Corporate Culture with Storytelling." *Strategic Storytelling*. https://bbcostorytelling.com/blog/how-to-change-corporate-culture-with-storytelling/.

Carter, Alison, Helen Wolfe, and Maire Kerrin. 2005. "Employers and Coaching Evaluation." *International Journal of Coaching in Organizations* 3, no. 4: 63–72. https://researchportal.coachfederation.org › Pdf.

Ensminger, David, Leanne Kallemeyn, Tania Rempert, James Wade, and Megan Polanin. 2015. "Case Study of an Evaluation Coaching Model: Exploring the Role of the Evaluator." *Evaluation and Program Planning* 49: 124–36. www.pieorg.org/wp-content/uploads/2016/06/Case-study-of-an-evaluation-coaching-model_-Exploring-the-role-of-the-evaluator.pdf.

Gray, David E. 2004. "Principles and Processes in Coaching Evaluation." *The International Journal of Mentoring and Coaching* 2, no 2: 1–7.

Institute for Employment Studies. 2005. *Practical Methods for Evaluating Coaching*. Brighton, UK: University of Sussex. www.employment-studies.co.uk/system/files/resources/files/430.pdf.

Lai, Ying-Ling, and Stephen Palmer. 2019. "Psychology in Executive Coaching: An Integrated Literature Review." *Journal of Work-Applied Management* 11, no. 2: 143–64. www.emerald.com/insight/content/doi/10.1108/JWAM-06-2019-0017/full/html.

Leedham, Mel. 2005. "The Coaching Scorecard: A Holistic Approach to Evaluating the Benefits of Business Coaching." *International Journal of Evidence Based Coaching and Mentoring* 3, no. 2: 30–43. https://www.researchgate.net/publi cation/228974779_The_Coaching_Scorecard_a_holistic_approach_to_evaluating_ the_benefits_of_business_coaching.

Rothwell, William J., P. Chee, and J. Oo. 2015. *The Leader's Daily Role in Talent Management: Maximizing Results, Engagement, and Retention*. New York: McGraw-Hill.

Rothwell, William J., and Cho Park. 2021. *Virtual Coaching to Improve Group Relationships: Process Consultation Reimagined*. New York: Routledge.

SUPPORT, MAINTENANCE, SELF-EVALUATION, AND SELF-RATING

Performance coaches must be self-aware, since they are the instruments for change that can impact those they seek to help. This part demonstrates that the fundamental foundation of all knowledge, as recognized in the carved motto above the ancient temple of Apollo at Delphi, is to "know thyself." Chapter 16 focuses on building self-awareness and self-knowledge.

Appendix A points the way forward, pointing aspiring performance coaches to resources that can take them to higher levels of competence in practicing performance coaching.

Chapter 16—How Effective Are You?

How do you know if you are effective and productive, mentally? Maintaining and implementing learned disciplines and conducting self-rating and self-evaluation.

Appendix A

Selected resources to support High-Performance Coaching for Managers and related topics.

DOI: 10.4324/9781003155928-21

Chapter 16

How Effective Are You?

Behnam Bahshandeh

Now that we have completed the fifteen chapters and gone through trying to educate, inform, and develop you about conducting an effective high-performance coaching process, we would like you to examine yourself and conclude about how effective you are. How do you know if you are effective and productive, mentally, emotionally, and can actually go through high-performance coaching with your clients and coachees?

This last chapter gives you methods and tools to maintain and implement learned disciplines and tools which were found throughout this coaching book.

This chapter will cover:

- How to generate values for your clients and teams and increase your effectiveness
  - Leadership and management competencies
  - Knowledge, skills, and abilities
  - Who you are being
- The process of self-management and maintenance
  - The self-managing and maintaining list (SMML)
  - Weekly values and practices
- Self-evaluating
  - High-performance coaches self-evaluating
  - Top ten coaching processes self-rating for a manger-as-coach
  - The monthly discipline of coaching self-rating
  - Coaching session evaluation form
- Recommendation for reviewing some of the elements and disciplines of previous chapters

DOI: 10.4324/9781003155928-22

How to Generate Values for Your Clients/ Teams and Increase Your Effectiveness

(Part 1 of 4)

The high-performance coaches' expertise is set in assisting individuals to improve and enhance their ability to conduct and perform their skills while on the job, in a profession, a performance, a sporting event, etc. It may occur while working with different people in a variety of professions, like musicians, attorneys, executives, managers, artists, or athletes.

Our job as high-performance coaches is to uncover and distinguish possible gaps (proficiency gaps) in their skills and abilities, to find "what is happening," then identify "what should be happening" based on their relevant job performance standards in their careers, jobs, or performance. Finally, with their alignment, to come with a set of training and resources (related to their industry) for improving and enhancing their performance.

To achieve this intention, high-performance coaches provide a series of methods and techniques based on proven models, disciplines, and platforms seeking to provide continuous performance enhancements and improvements for individuals, teams, departments, or organizations. The relationship between high-performance coaches or managers-as-coaches is a coaching process and feedback structure between coaches (could be managers) and coachees (could be clients or employees or teams), that provide the learning and the developmental environment through feedback, corrections, and new approach techniques.

When we look at high-performance coaches' responsibilities and their commitment to their work with their clients, it is clear that they need to constantly work on their own development and to make sure they are effective in what they are doing with their clients and coachees.

The following four-part review summarizes what a high-performance coach needs to have, pay attention to, and develop to be able to provide a high level of values for their clients and coachees. Please review these elements:

- Do you have what it takes to generate values for your coachees?
- Are you confident about what you have developed in yourself as high-performance coaches?
- Do you have the leadership and management competencies for conducting effective performance coaching?

- Have you accumulated the knowledge and skills, and abilities to be effective performance coaches?
- Are you aware of who you are being while you are doing the performance coaching?

The following review and summary will assist you in having some answers and will provide some opening for further learning and development for you as effective high-performance coaches who can provide values for their clients and coachees.

Let's start from Figure 16.1.1, the main form of this review and summary process. This process includes two distinct approaches:

(1) **Inquiries** for you to think, process, and come with your own answers. There are no right or wrong answers, no good, bad, or acceptable answers, only you, your authenticity and your honesty, knowing you are not competing with anyone or anything, not trying to win in this process, and only trying to get to know yourself better. When you come with your own honest answers, then you are the ones responsible for planning developmental programs for yourself and designing learning techniques using this book or other available resources to improve and enhance your own performance as coaches.

(2) **Depicting** and breaking down some of elements of this process for your easy review. This attempt will make it easier to think and to stimulate your thoughts for adding what is relevant to you, your career or your industry.

Please Come with Answers for the Following Inquiries for Yourself

- What is *value* to you?
- What comes to your mind when you hear *Generate value*?
- What is your strength in *Generating value* for your clients or coachees?
- What is your weakness in *Generating value* for your clients or coachees?
- What is your fear of *Generating value* for your clients or coachees?
- What is stopping you from *Generating value* for your clients or coachees?
- What is on your way to *Generating value* for your clients or coachees?

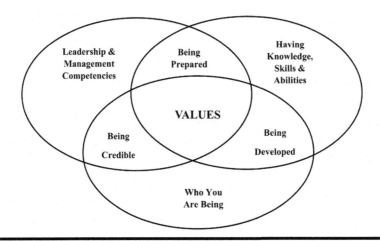

Figure 16.1.1   How to Generate Values for Your Clients/Teams and Increase Your Effectiveness.

Source: Copyright 2021 by Behnam Bakhshandeh.

Knowledge, Skills, and Abilities

■ vision, mission, values, principles, commitment, and stand
■ methods, models, techniques, and services
  – meetings, analysis, diagnosis, feedback, evaluation, planning, and procedures
■ your knowledge
■ your history
■ systems, structures, and approaches
  – training, workshops, seminars, etc.
■ your material
  – handouts, displays, manuals, brochures, and website

Leadership and Management Competencies

■ leading and managing experience
■ managing style
■ effective communication skills
  – active listening
■ having people skills
  – good manners
  – being compassionate
  – welcoming

- having a business coach or mentor
- managing and leading by example
- making a stand for your team and your customers
  - having people realize their greatness versus letting them justify their circumstances

Who You Are Being

- with yourself
  - your look, fitness, appearance, and presentation
  - your dreams, vision, and values
  - owning and learning your failures and successes and being responsible for them
- with others
  - your coachees
  - your partners
  - your team and customers
- about what you do
  - your productivity
  - your planning
  - your structures
  - your disciplines

Knowledge, Skills, and Abilities + Leadership and Management Competencies = Prepared

The combination of your knowledge, skills, and abilities with your leadership and management competencies will make you *Prepared* to:

- lead and produce results in a timely manner
  - schedules, meetings, appointments, and services
- respond to questions and concerns effectively
  - training, developments, clients' issues, and potential upsets
- see and predict what is coming at you
- powerfully deal with what is so and what is real
- take on your coaching business completely
- get to the source of emergencies before they are happening

Leadership and Management Competencies + Who You Are Being = Being Credible

The combination of your leadership and management competencies and who you are being will make you *Credible* with:

■ listening to what you are saying
■ your work and style
■ following your leads
■ making business decisions
■ being an example of success
■ your managing practices
■ your coaching approaches
■ life in general

Knowledge, Skills, and Abilities + Who You Are Being = Being Developed

The combination of your knowledge, skills, and abilities with who you are being will make you *Developed* in being:

■ a powerful person
■ an effective coach, manager and leader
■ someone who can generate versus survival
■ a compassionate and understanding person
■ a productive and efficient person
■ a patient and foreseeing manager and coach

Prepared + Credible + Developed = Generating Value

The combination of you becoming prepared, credible, and developed will help you to *Generate value for your clients and coachees* by:

■ increasing productivity
  – being responsible for educating your clients and coachees
  – being accountable for serving your clients and coachees
■ increasing client base
  – enrolling your clients in your vision and values for what you are doing
  – inventing new games for higher performance

- inventing new services and products
  - finding out what clients or coachees need
  - making it easy for clients and coachees to get what they want
- building reputations
  - for good service, professional behavior, and great attitude
  - for excellent business operations
- expanding business
  - securing future

Set of Coaching Questions for Your Future Activities and Maintaining What You Learned

Note: Before answering some of the following questions, please read the next section, "Explanations. Descriptions and Directions for Answering Some of Above Questions," before answering some of the following questions:

- What aspects of *Knowledge, Skills, and Abilities* do you need to work on or need support with?
- What aspects of *Leadership and Management Competencies* do you need to work on for yourself?
- What aspects of *Who You Are Being* do you need to have more understanding?
- What do you realize or notice about your abilities and skills to generate value?
- What are you willing to do, add, change, or alter to be *Prepared* to generate value?
- What are you willing to do, add, change, or alter to become *Credible* for generating value?
- What are you willing to do, add, change, or alter to be *Developed* in generating value?
- What are you promising to yourself?
- What are you willing to do to keep your promise?
- Who will you discuss this with?

Explanations. Descriptions and Directions for Answering Some of the Above Questions

For your complete understating for what we are looking, we have provided some explanations and directions on how to answer some of the aforementioned coaching questions.

What Do You Realize About Yourself?

What did you learn about yourself by reading and applying the last sections? What was the realization about yourself regarding those topics? Usually, the nature of this realization is the "bad news," but if it is a good thing, how? For example, you might realize you are an opinionated person, and you always judge and evaluate people. That by itself might be the bad news; however, it is a good thing that you got to face it and *own* it, so you have power over *it*, not *it* having power over you! (Bakhshandeh 2009).

What Are You Willing to Add, Change, or Alter?

Now that you realized a few things about yourself, what are you willing to add, change, or alter about your life based on that realization? If you are not adding something new, changing something old, or altering some behaviors and trains of thought, what is the point? If you want something different for yourself, your career, and your life, you have to do something different. Start jotting down the changes. The scariest thing is the one you do not want to write down, the one that you know must be done. For example, if you realized that you are opinionated, what you would change is your view of people. As a result, you alter the way you relate to others. You will not judge them immediately before knowing them (Bakhshandeh 2009).

What Are You Promising Yourself?

Now that you know what needs to be added or changed, or altered, you must make a promise to yourself that you will do something about it! This promise is one of the most important promises of your life because it is a promise to *you*! A goal without a promise and a deadline is nothing but a good idea. So, make a promise and keep it. Do not make a promise just because you do not know how to keep it. Write down your promise based on the changes that need to be done to transform what you realized about yourself. Using the previous example, *I promise not to judge others immediately, Or I promise not to act on my opinion but instead spend time to find the facts* (Bakhshandeh 2009).

What Are You Willing to Do to Keep that Promise?

Now that you have made the promise, you have to come up with a series of actions that will guarantee the fulfillment of those promises! It is black and white. It is something you will do, not just think about. You will take these actions, and you will do them to keep your promise. This is not conceptual; this is real! This has time, location, and format. Using the previous example; *As soon as I judge someone, I will apologize for it, and I will clean it up!* Or *I will keep myself away from opinionated people who do not care about the facts and just want to gossip* (Bakhshandeh 2009).

With Whom Will You Discuss This?

These are people who you like to talk to and with whom you can share your transformation, development, and learning experience. In some cases, these are people you have judged, evaluated, and formed some opinion about! (Based on the mentioned example of insight and realization). As hard as it is, you will gain so much respect for yourself, and they will develop so much respect for you when you clean up your mess with them and acknowledge what you have done. Clean it up and make a new promise to them. At that moment, you will be powerful and extraordinary (Bakhshandeh 2009).

[*Note*: The content of the previous five paragraphs was from the book "Conspiracy for Greatness; Master of Love Within" (Bakhshandeh 2009, 109–12) and used with express permission from Behnam Bakhshandeh and Primeco Education, Inc.]

Leadership and Management Competencies

(Part 2 of 4)

In this second out of four-part summaries (using Figure 16.2.2), we depict the elements of Leadership and Management Competencies:

Please Come with Answers to the Following Inquiries

- What are *Leadership and Management Competencies* to you?
- What comes to your mind when you hear *Leadership or Management Competencies*?
- Where are you weak or not confident in *Leadership and Management Competencies* in what you do?
- Where are you strong or confident in your *Leadership and Management Competencies* in what you do?

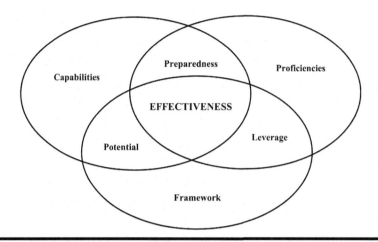

Figure 16.1.2 Elements of Leadership and Management Competencies.
Source: Copyright 2021 by Behnam Bakhshandeh.

■ What is your fear of lacking *Leadership and Management Competencies?*
■ What is stopping you from developing *Leadership and Management Competencies?*
■ What is in your way to develop *Leadership and Management Competencies?*

Proficiencies

■ To respond to the underlying occurring dynamics during coaching sessions.
■ To upgrade your clients' or the teams' primary source of energy.
■ To replace paradigms from which your clients or the teams are operating.
■ To train your clients or the teams to invent solutions for their problems.
■ To train your clients or the teams to add and implement new dimensions to their perceptions and thought processes.

Capabilities

■ To listen without judgment.
■ To respond to the matter at hand.
■ To take your clients' and teams' concerns seriously.
■ To be fully expressed and bring play and fun to the coaching process.
■ To keep up with your clients' and teams' speed and thinking.

Framework

- There is usually a better way.
- Risk is always reducible.
- Success is a by-product of actions and disciplines.
- It's all solvable, or it's not.
- Delay is increasingly expensive.

Proficiencies + Capabilities = Preparedness

The combination of your proficiencies with your capabilities will make you be *Prepare* and *Powerful*:

- to be present versus being mystified
- to look for possibilities versus expectations
- to find resolutions versus complaints
- to be with upset versus to get entangled with emotions
- to be at cause versus to be at effect

Capabilities + Framework = Potential

The combination of your capabilities with your framework will create *potential*:

- to fulfill the personal and professional vision
- to achieve the intended goals
- to expand the operations and services
- to move through obstacles speedily
- to have an effective operation

Proficiencies + Framework = Leverage

The combination of your proficiencies with your framework will give you *Leverage*:

- to increase your productivity
- to have a relationship with your teams or clients
- to demand excellence and structure
- to expand the teams or business
- to have an open and authentic working environment

454 ■ Support, Maintenance, Self-Evaluation, and Self-Rating

Power + Potential + Leverage = Effectiveness

The combination of your developing and having power, potential, and leverage will help you to become *Effective*:

- in producing results
- in relationships with your clients
- in relationships with your team members
- in fulfilling your vision and accomplishing your goals
- in expanding and achieving your future plans

Set of Coaching Questions for Your Future Activities and Maintaining What You Learned

- On what aspect of *Proficiencies* do you need to work, design, or need support?
- What aspect of *Capabilities* do you need to have more understanding?
- What aspect or part of the *Framework* do you need to have, prepare, or provide for yourself?
- What do you realize or notice about your *Proficiencies, Capabilities and Framework* to become more effective in generating value?
- What are you willing to do, add, change, or alter to have power in managing your business and life?
- What are you willing to do, add, change, or alter to have more *Potential* and *Leverage* in your business and life?
- What are you willing to do, add, change, or alter to apply what you learned into your business and life to generate value?
- What are you promising to yourself?
- What are you willing to do to keep your promise?
- Who will you discuss this with?

Knowledge, Skills, and Abilities

(Part 3 of 4)

In this third part out of four-part summaries, using Figure 16.1.3, we depict the elements of knowledge, skills, and abilities.

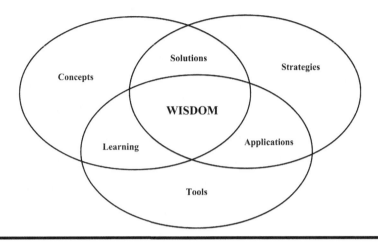

Figure 16.1.3   Elements of Knowledge, Skills, and Abilities.

Source: Copyright 2021 by Behnam Bakhshandeh.

Please Come with Answers for the Following Inquiries

- What is *Knowledge, Skills, and Abilities* to you?
- What comes to your mind when you hear *Knowledge, Skills, and Abilities?*
- Where are you weak or not confident with *Knowledge, Skills, and Abilities* in what you do?
- Where are you strong or confident with your *Knowledge, Skills, and Abilities* in what you do?
- What is your fear of lacking *knowledge* or having *Skills* or *Abilities?*
- What is stopping you from developing *Knowledge, Skills, and Abilities?*
- What is in your way to develop *Knowledge, Skills, and Abilities?*

Strategies

- Short-term business plan (one to four years).
- Long-term business plan (five to ten years).
- Short-term business plan (one year and next quarter).
- Production targets and daily and weekly forecasts.
- Sales plan and velocity of production.
- Appropriate alliances and partnerships.

Concepts

- You are either fulfilling a vision or redoing a past event.
- There is no tomorrow; it is an illusion it will never come; it is only today!

- There is nothing wrong until you say there is.
- You are enrolling others to something powerful or small every day.
- They are not out to get you; relax!
- Stop adding meaning to everything.

Tools

- Policies and dynamics.
- Operation procedures between departments.
- Inside and outside structures.
- Team and client trainings.
- Operations logistics.

Strategies + Concepts = Solutions

The combination of your strategies with your understanding of concepts will give you abilities to *Solving* issues:

- upsetting situations with a team or clients
- operation breakdown during growth time
- growing and expanding obstacles
- team and client's expectations of you or your operations
- your own suffering

Concepts + Tools = Learning

The combination of understanding of concepts with your tools will give you an opportunity for *learning*:

- How to run the business smoothly.
- How to handle issues and situations.
- How to lead your team within your organization's vision.
- How to be responsible for your planned expansions.
- How to live your vision versus avoiding the same past mistakes.

Strategies + Tools = Applications

The combination of your strategies with your tools will give you an opportunity for *Applying*:

- planning the work and working the plan
- practicing principles that make a difference
- implementing procedures that bring up the presence of values in business and performance
- policies and structures for inventing rigor
- what you know is the right thing to do

Solutions+ Learning + Applications = Wisdom

The combination of solving, learning, and applying will help you to develop *Wisdom*:

- to make decisions that are aligned with your vision
- to lead effectively for your team and for your clients
- to cause leadership within your team and for your clients
- to see and design your future and to make it real
- to become responsible for your business and its operations as a whole

Set of Coaching Questions for Your Future Activities and Maintaining What You Learned

- On what aspects of *Strategies* do you need to work, design, or need support?
- What aspects of *Concepts* do you need to have more understanding?
- What aspects or parts of *Tools* do you need to have, prepare, or provide for yourself?
- What do you realize or notice about your *strategies, concepts, and tools* to become wiser to generate value?
- What are you willing to do, add, change, or alter to solve problems or issues in managing your business and life?
- What are you willing to do, add, change, or alter to utilize on learning more about your business and life?
- What are you willing to do, add, change, or alter to apply what you learned into your business and life to generate value?
- What are you promising to yourself?
- What are you willing to do to keep your promise?
- Who will you discuss this with?

Who You Are Being

(Part 4 of 4)

In this fourth and the final part of these summaries, using Figure 16.1.4, we depict the elements of knowledge, skills, and abilities.

Please Come with Answers for the Following Inquiries

■ Who are you for yourself?
■ How do you see yourself? Authentically, with honesty?
■ What comes to your mind when you hear, *Who Are You Being?*
■ Where are you weak or not confident in understanding and distinguishing *Who You Are Being?*
■ Where are you strong or confident in understanding and distinguishing *Who You Are Being?*
■ What is your fear of becoming fully expressed in *Who You Are Being?*
■ What is stopping you from digging into recognizing *Who You Are Being?*
■ What is in your way to distinguish and discover *Who You Are Being?*

Your Qualities

■ your vision of the world
■ your perceptions
■ your life principles
■ your personal integrity

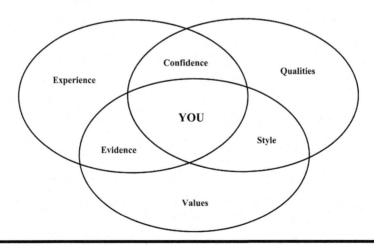

Figure 16.1.4   Elements of Who You Are Being.

Source: Copyright 2021 by Behnam Bakhshandeh.

- your authenticity
- your stand in and about life

Your Experiences

- from upbringing and your family
- from working, career, and profession
- from your relationships
- from your formal or unconventional education
- from upsetting, dramatic, or exciting life events
- from your successes and failures

Your Values

- on honesty and integrity
- on responsibilities and accountabilities
- on personal and professional growth
- on respecting others regardless of their status
- on having balance in life
- on others' experiences of yourself

Your Qualities + Your Experiences = Confidence

The combination of your qualities with your experiences will assist you in developing your *Confidence*:

- in yourself
- in what you are doing
- in establishing rapport
- in building relationships
- in what you are presenting
- in your leading and managing skills
- in your ability to use your tools and materials

Your Experiences + Your Values = Evidence

The combination of your experiences with your personal values will be *Evidence*:

- of your expertise
- of your managerial decisions

- of your leadership qualities
- of your abilities to deliver the intended outcomes
- of your preparation and credibility

Your Qualities + Your Values = Style

The combination of your qualities with your personal values will make up your *style*:

- of taking a firm stand for your values and principles
- of focusing on fulfillment of your vision
- of not compromising your integrity
- of practicing responsibility and accountability
- of communicating and listening
- of being true to yourself and your ideals
- of being a standout for greatness for your clients and teams

Your Qualities + Your Experiences + Your Values = You

The combination of your qualities, experiences, and values is the representation and display of *You* and:

- the way you live
- the way you think
- the way you operate
- the way you lead
- the way you relate
- the way you present yourself
- the way you are

Set of Coaching Questions for Your Future Activities and Maintaining What You Learned

- On what aspects of *Your Qualities* do you need to work, plan, or need support?
- What aspects of *Your Experiences* do you need to have more empowerment or forgiveness?
- What aspects or part of *Your Values* do you need to have, prepare, or provide for yourself and your life?

- What do you realize or notice about your qualities, experiences, and values that make you who you are?
- What are you willing to do, add, change, or alter to solve problems or issues on becoming yourself authentically?
- What are you willing to do, add, change, or alter to utilize in learning more about yourself and your life?
- What are you willing to do, add, change, or alter to apply what you learned into your business and life to generate value for yourself and others around you?
- What are you promising to yourself?
- What are you willing to do to keep your promise?
- Who will you discuss this with?

The Process of Self-Management and Maintenance of Learning

We are now at a place where we can create and invent practices that will assist us in reaching our potentials and greatness. If we do not manage and maintain what we learned to protect and support our vision, we cannot move forward in a productive manner. In this section, we will work on inventing new practices that will support our getting rid of any old and ineffective practices. This is where the rubber hits the road, the real black and white.

At this point, we will begin to understand how to fully support this new learning process so it can become a reality which will support us and help us to move forward and achieve our goals and accomplish our intentions in our high-performance coaching practice. First, I want to look at one of the biggest obstacles in our way to do that, and that is to avoid *failing*. We do not like to fail, and we will do anything not to face it. I am sure you can recognize the emotions and feelings that arise after the experience of failing.

Consider this. You never know whether you will fail unless you try. The way you will fail is if you are being negative about what you say to yourself and what you are about to do! One of the greatest quotes I have read on this topic is from Sir Winston Churchill, the British Prime Minister during World War II, who said, "[s]uccess is moving from failure to failure with no loss of enthusiasm."

Failure Is a Part of Life and Business

The one point that is hard to explain but simple to say is that failure is a part of the process to achieve success. While failure is difficult, it is part of the game of life and business and one of the things that, if used correctly, will make us stronger. We have personally failed in life more than we have succeeded, but we are absolutely certain of who is at the source of our successes and failures—us and us only. The problem starts when we do not see that the task that we failed at does not define who we are at the core. Why? Because we are not the project or the goal, but we are someone who is a *source* of the project or goal. When we look at a failure, it is how we choose to define it. By simply looking at only the failure and not how we failed, we are surrounded by the 'conspiracy for smallness' and are the source of our own suffering.

The other side of the coin is when we look at and relate to the project or goal as fulfilling our life vision; the idea becomes that nothing is wrong, but we have work in front of us. We must have an 'I can do it' attitude because we can accomplish anything with the abilities, intelligence, and resources needed. This is true even in our relationships. We must stand up, dust ourselves off, and get back in the saddle, so to speak. This is what I call 'conspiracy for greatness' and 'mastery of love within.'

We totally understand and can feel the pain of failure. We have been there, so we have compassion and understanding. But look at any goal or project we take on from this view. Am I worth fighting for? Yes, You Are! There is no doubt! We must be patient and committed to new practices, projects, or goals that we choose to do. This is how we will have our vision fulfilled. Remember, nothing will happen overnight. Patience and belief in the vision are very important to this process.

The following short story "The Miracle of the Chinese Bamboo Tree" shows us what we mean by patience:

> *The Chinese Bamboo tree is planted after the earth is prepared. For the first four years, all the growth is underground. The only thing visible above the ground is a little bulb and a small shoot growing out of it. Leaders know what it means to pay the price to prepare the ground, to plant the seed, and to fertilize and cultivate, water and weed, even when they can't see immediate results. They have faith, that ultimately, they will reap the fruits in the harvest. And what wonderful fruits they are—because in the fifth year, the Bamboo tree grows up to eighty feet!*

> *(Author unknown)*

You are as powerful as that little Chinese bamboo bulb, even if you are small outside, feel scared, even terrified to take on life and bring home the vision you dream about! However, you are strong inside, both powerful and determined! We hope that you can see we are relating to you as a coach. We can do anything we put our mind, heart, and soul into. Failure is not a negative until you say so. As a matter of fact, it is *nothing* until you say so!

First, start with inventing practices and actions that will guarantee the alteration of your life and business experiences. Go back and briefly review each of the previous chapters. Write down your primary realization and insights about yourself concerning the topics of each chapter. It might be something about yourself, the way you think or operate or something about others and the way they conduct their businesses or something about your style of coaching. Check yourself on what recognitions you have had and what changes you want to make to move forward in a positive light. Make the things you write as a promise to yourself and then keep that promise.

If you have not yet created a promise for yourself, it is time to do it. You are *being* responsible and accountable to what you say you want in your life and business. No more wishing, hoping, and dreaming! Now is the time to move forward! Unfortunately, the world is full of people with great potential, never realized. These sitting dormant people have kept their genius within and never recognized their inner power because the inner chatter said the task was too hard, or it would take too long. You might be one of them, but not anymore. You are learning *new* information, and now you *know* that greatness comes from within, like a garage filled with useful items that are left undiscovered because nobody ever opens the garage!

Fill yourself with integrity and relate to the relationships we are now forming with responsibility and most importantly, accountability. Be sure that you have taken the time to write your realizations and insights by briefly reviewing each chapter so your ideas will be fresh, and you will take them more seriously; otherwise, it will be hard to work on your true needs.

This segment will introduce you to some practices for maintaining and self-managing what you learned about high-performance coaching. They are as follows:

- the self-managing and maintaining list (SMML)
- weekly value practice
- visual structure
- monthly discipline of coaching self-rating

Knowing this will help you to maintain what you have learned so far and continue producing results out of what you have learned.

The Self-Managing and Maintaining List

The Self-Managing and Maintaining List, or SMML for short is designed to be a place to review what you learned, promises you made, and how you are making your promises a reality. Compile a three-section accounting of the actions you have promised to put into place:

Part One: Insights and Realizations

As we covered in the "Explanations. Descriptions and Directions for Answering Some of Above Questions" segment in the beginning of this chapter, go back in the chapters you have completed, pick out the insights or realizations you had after completing these chapters, reading the key factors of each chapter and coaching questions at the ends of each chapter.

It is vital that you have at least *one* insight or realization per chapter. It will be manageable. Try to keep it no more than one so the task is doable.

While the nature of the insight is usually bad news, it can be used in a positive way. This is to know and learn about yourself so you have the opportunity to do something about it. Tell the truth without holding back and allow yourself to feel and experience the impact and pain of the past negativity. This is very important because you can tend to avoid reality and not face the truth of a situation. That is why we said the nature of the insight could be bad news. For example, in Chapter 4, about rapport and how to build and establish rapport, you might have insight and realization that *I am lazy in building rapport and just want people to do their jobs.*

In the following SMML format (Figure 16.2.1), the first part of the three-part combination, we have provided you with just fifteen spaces (one space for each of fifteen chapters), but you are more than welcome to recreate that format on your own device and keep adding to it if it is necessary.

Right now, write your insights and realizations in the first part of the SMML before going on to part two. What are your insights and realizations about yourself, what are you avoiding, and where do you think you need further development?

Part Two: Operational Promises

Operational promises are those promises you make to yourself. These will impact the aforementioned insights and realizations that you have listed. In other words, if you keep the promises you made based on the insights you wrote, then you have altered and transformed the nature of your insights.

Part One Insights and Realizations		

CH.1 _____

CH.2 _____

CH.3 _____

CH.4 _____

CH.5 _____

CH.6 _____

CH.7 _____

CH.8 _____

CH.9 _____

CH.10 _____

CH.11 _____

CH.12 _____

CH.13 _____

CH.14 _____

CH.15 _____

Figure 16.2.1 Part One of SMML: Collection of Insights and Realizations.

Source: Adapted from Bakhshandeh (2009).

Operational means the promises must have worked before them. You must *do* something about them. They are not just conceptual like a pie in the sky! They are real and manageable, which is why these promises are categorized as operational.

Your answers to the following questions are examples of an operational promise:

■ What are you promising to yourself?
■ What are you going to do about this issue?
■ What do you see you need to handle or complete?

For example, if your insights in Chapter 4 about rapport that you mentioned in part one of SMML was:

I am lazy in building rapport and just want people to do their jobs.

Your Operational Promises related to that insight about rapport in Chapter 4 might be something as follows:

I promise to become responsible, take the necessary time and efforts for establishing rapport with my team members.

One important note is to start each sentence with "I promise" because, in that way, you are holding yourself accountable. These are *very* important promises because they are promises you have given to *yourself*, the most important person you will ever make a promise to.

If you choose not to keep these promises, your insights and realizations will not ever see the light of day! Make a note to yourself: What you *know* makes no difference in the quality of your life, it is what you *do* with your knowledge that will ultimately make a difference.

"Knowledge is not power; implementation of knowledge is power!"
(Bakhshandeh 2009, n.p.)

Look at how Part One of SMML notes on each insight and realization are relevant and make a promise. Now write it in Part Two. The number of your insights and realizations should match and correlate with the number of your promises.

Right now, write your operational promises in the second part of the SMML before going on to Part Three.

Part Three: Operational Practices

Operational practices are those practices that you put in place, the nature of which will fulfill the previously made promises. As you move further down the SMML, you should have one operational practice for each operational promise for each insight.

These are operational, which means they are something you *do*, both specific and measurable. This is a measurement of accountability to show the practice was completed, which means a promise is closer to being fulfilled.

Part Two Operational Promises
CH.1_____
CH.2_____
CH.3_____
CH.4_____
CH.5_____
CH.6_____
CH.7_____
CH.8_____
CH.9_____
CH.10_____
CH.11_____
CH.12_____
CH.13_____
CH.14_____
CH.15_____

Figure 16.2.2   Part Two of SMML: Collection of Operational Promises.

Source: Adapted from Bakhshandeh (2009).

These practice answers can be found at the end of the chapters where I ask:

■ What are you willing to do to keep your promise?
■ What actions are you taking to alter that behavior?
■ What is your plan for the changes you want to implement?

Here is an example based on what we already used if your insights were as follows:

I am lazy in building rapport and just want people to do their jobs.

And your Operational Promise was:

> *I promise to become responsible, take the necessary time and efforts for establishing rapport with my team members.*

Your Operational Practices could be something like:

> *I will use available exercises, practices, resources and tools to develop myself as someone who is capable of easily and authentically establishing rapport with others.*

Now, look at Part Two notes. Based on each operational promise, do an operational practice and write it in Part Three, the operational promises. The insights' numbers should correlate with the number of operational promises, and operational promises' numbers should correlate with the number of your practices. For example, Insight #1, Promise #1, and Practice #1 from Chapter 1 correlate. Continue in the same way for Chapter 2—Insight #2 and Promise #2, and Practice #2 Chapter, and so forth up to Chapter 15.

Right now, write your operational practices in the third part of the SMML.

Weekly Values and Practices

Every week, choose a value you care about and invent new practices to have that value experience be present for you during that particular week. Doing this will add more happiness, fulfillment, and self-expression to your daily life and career. They are your values, but they are the ones that you are good at and love to have present for you. So, we will manage that together.

- The best thing you can do is to reproduce the format of Figure 16.3 on your device so you can have access to it whenever you need to change, and alter it weekly.
- The first thing to do is to write your life or business vision and mission right on the top of the form because everything generates from your relating to that vision and mission.
- Once you do all these, complete the starting and ending date of the week, starting on Monday and ending on Sunday, and that will be the week you are targeting.
- Then you select a value that you care about and want to work on in that week. It could be communication, productivity, respect, health, and/or any other value.

Part Three
Operational Practices

CH.1 _____

CH.2 _____

CH.3 _____

CH.4 _____

CH.5 _____

CH.6 _____

CH.7 _____

CH.8 _____

CH.9 _____

CH.10 _____

CH.11 _____

CH.12 _____

CH.13 _____

CH.14 _____

CH.15 _____

Figure 16.2.3 Part Three of SMML: Collection of Operational Practices.

Source: Adapted from Bakhshandeh (2009).

- After that, invent just two new practices. Just two is enough, not more than that because we do not want you to feel as if you have a lot to do! Have fun with it, and keep it simple and real. These are practices that you have never done before or have not practiced for a very long time, maybe due to resignation and despair!
- When you do that, then do the other side and select old practices that you will eliminate and get rid of, so the experience of that value is present for you during that week. You know exactly what you need to stop doing, so just do it! Again, keep it simple and real. Removing what is not working is as essential as inventing new practices.

■ These two sides (inventing new practices and, at the same time, eliminating the old practices) will work hand in hand by empowering you to have the experience and the presence of your opportunities in your personal and professional aspects of your life and career and help in your growth as a professional coach.

■ You can also repeat the same process by altering the format for use by your team or when you are coaching an individual or a team on their high-performance coaching or any other type of coaching.

■ Going through this weekly process with your team (yours or your client's) and brainstorm about all the practices you and your team can invent for what you are doing about your performance, productivity, responsibilities, processes, and accountabilities. Doing this together will provide more cohesiveness, and create stronger bonds and effective communication along with anything else you all desire.

Here is an example of this simple but effective process:

The selected value of this week is communication.
New practices I am inventing based on the selected value are:

(1) I will pay attention to the speakers because what they are saying is very important.
(2) I will not interrupt the speakers until they finish their sentences.

Old practices we are eliminating based on the selected value are:

(1) Water down the speaker's issue immediately by saying: "That is not true," or "It was not like that."
(2) Acting as I am so busy and do not have time for complaints.

What Do I Have to Give Up for This Value to Be Present for Me?

Question "C" is very important to the effective implementation and workability of this process. Without giving up something in your life or profession, such as an old practice or old behavior or old belief, you cannot bring something new in its place. Replace the old with something simple but very elegant and powerful.

Remember the law of physics? No object can exist in the same place at the same time. We cannot say we want health, but we will not give up smoking. It just will not work. We cannot say we are valuing productivity but continue coming in late to work and then leaving early. It is just not a match. We cannot say we are valuing relationships but withholding our communications.

I highly recommend that you look at what your inner chatter is saying about the presence of that value in your life, or how hard it is to work on, or how frustrating it is to maintain, then you will know what you need to give up for that value to be present for you. For example, give up the righteousness of "it doesn't work" or "I can't do it" or "It doesn't matter" or any other negative, heavy barriers you are bringing into this process. Give them up for the possibility of having that value be present for you. I know it will not be easy, but considering your alternatives, why not?

Figure 16.3 represents the format for this process.

Self-evaluation is known as a method for methodically and thoroughly observing, examining, analyzing, and evaluating one's own behaviors, attitudes, approaches, actions, performances, and its related outcomes and results, personally and professionally. Self-evaluation will aid the evaluator in enhancing, improving, or alleviating their activities and performances. It also helps those who have conducted the self-evaluation to underline their strengths, adjust their performance weaknesses and develop new competencies, skills, and abilities. In order to do this powerful undertaking, they must be wanting and willing to acknowledge areas that need enhancement, improvement, alteration, or development. Self-evaluations can be conducted on individuals, teams, groups, departments, or on an organizational level (Hertzberg 2020; Rothwell 2013; Camp 2001).

Some of the benefits of self-evaluating your coaching performance are as follows:

(1) It helps you distinguish your own coaching performance strengths and weaknesses.
(2) It underlines areas of performance coaching that need enhancement or improvement.
(3) It gives you an opportunity to monitor and track your coaching performance competencies.
(4) It is rewarding to observe your own development.
(5) It increases your reputation as a self-devoted professional.
(6) It could be a cause for self-motivation and more interest for further development.
(7) It can be used as an instrument for guiding and planning your performance coaching sessions with individuals and teams.
(8) It builds up your self-awareness.

Weekly Values and Practices

Participant: _____   Date: _____

Team: _____   Manager/Supervisor: _____

Week starting _____   and ending:_____

Our Vision: _____

_____

Our Mission: _____

_____

The value I chose for this week is:_____

A. New practices invented for this value this week are:

1._____

2._____

B. Old practices eliminated about this value this week are:

1._____

2._____

C. What I have to let go of and give up for this value to be present for me are:

1._____

2._____

Figure 16.3   Inventing Weekly Practices Based on Weekly Values.

Source: Adapted from Bakhshandeh (2009).

Note: The content of this segment (the SMML) is from the book "Conspiracy for Greatness; Mastery of Love Within (Bakhshandeh 2009, 329–37) and used with express permission from Behnam Bakhshandeh and Primeco Education, Inc.

Self-Evaluating

Table 16.1 High-performance Coaches Self-Evaluating of Competencies/Skills and Importance of Competencies/Skills on Their Career Success.

High-Performance Coach's Self-Evaluation

Performance Coach: | *Month/Year:*

Manager/Supervisor: | *Department:*

Instructions:
Self-evaluate by rating your own a) ability to perform general coaching competencies and skills, and b) the importance of such skill on the success of your coaching career.

#	Evaluating Scale — General Competencies & Skills	My ability to perform this skill at my work					How important is this skill to my career success				
	Ratings from 1(lowest) to 5 (highest)	1	2	3	4	5	1	2	3	4	5
1	Using and presenting current models, concepts, methods and ideas.										
2	Tailoring coaching sessions based on individuals or teams' needed areas of development.										
3	Using effective communication and active listening for understanding coachees' perspectives and needs.										
4	Establishing clear and precise expectations for the coaching relationship.										
5	Adapting and implementing a coaching style for serving the coachees' unique needs.										
6	Providing constructive and empowering feedback to build coachees' confidence in their performance.										
7	Recognizing, acknowledging and rewarding coachees' attempt to perform in the highest possible potentials.										
8	Giving coachees enough responsibilities before they feel overloaded.										
9	Articulating, sharing and empowering the organization's vision, mission and principal values.										
10	Distinguishing possible reasons for individuals or teams' low performance and lack of resources.										

(Continued)

Table 16.1 (Continued)

	High-Performance Coach's Self-Evaluation		
	Performance Coach:	*Month/Year:*	
	Manager/Supervisor:	*Department:*	
	Instructions: *Self-evaluate by rating your own a) ability to perform general coaching competencies and skills, and b) the importance of such skill on the success of your coaching career.*	*My ability to perform this skill at my work*	*How important is this skill to my career success*
11	Recognizing team dysfunctions and sources of conflicts among individuals and their direct managers or supervisors.		
12	Understanding organization's compensation, incentives, and reward systems.		
13	Understanding source of personal and team's motivation for higher productivity and performance.		
14	Translating the concept of bigger picture into smaller objectives and desired outcomes for easier achievements.		
15	Describing and explaining individuals' and teams' contributions to the organization's success.		
16	Clearly explaining the chain of command, accountabilities and management among individuals, teams, departments, and the organization.		
17	Understanding and distinguishing performance and objectives' potential calculated risks.		
18	Assisting coachees to set their goals, priorities and importance of their intentions and desired outcomes.		
19	Creating safe environment and encouraging learning and development.		

	My ability to perform this skill at my work	How important is this skill to my career success
High-Performance Coach's Self-Evaluation		
Performance Coach:	Month/Year:	
Manager/Supervisor:	Department:	
Instructions: Self-evaluate by rating your own a) ability to perform general coaching competencies and skills, and b) the importance of such skill on the success of your coaching career.		
20. Holding myself accountable for quality of my performance and delivery of goods.		
Individual Totals		
Total of Above Individual Totals		
Final Average (Above totals divided by 20)		
Two actions for this month that will bring up my two lowest evaluation rates by at least 2 points:		
Action 1:		
Action 2:		

Source: Copyright 2021 by Behnam Bakhshandeh.

Table 16.2 Top Ten Coaching Processes Self-Rating for a Manger-as-Coach.

Description:
Use the following ten categories to conduct a self-rating process on your level of abilities, competencies, and skills as a manager-as-coach to deliver and conduct elements of each category. Authenticity, honesty, integrity, and accountability are the keys to conducting a useful and productive self-rating undertaking. Conduct this self-rating quarterly and adjust accordingly.

Date:	Manager-as-Coach:	Team:
Quarter:	Report to Manager/Supervisor:	Department:

Rating Scale: Rating Scale: 1 =Poor, 2 =Marginal, 3 =Acceptable, 4 =Good, 5 =Excellent

#	Categories	Declaration Statement	Rating				
			1	2	3	4	5
1	**Outcome**	My coaching approach assists my employees to be effective.					
		As a result of coaching, my employees' job performance has improved.					
		As a result of coaching, my team has demonstrated an increase in their performance.					
		My employees look forward to our coaching conversation.					
		My employees have expressed gratitude and appreciation for our coaching conversations.					
2	**Collaboration**	I display respect and courtesy during our coaching conversations with my employees.					
		I use encouraging and empowering language during our coaching sessions with my employees.					
		I do not pressure or compel my employees to join me in a coaching conversation.					
		I create a safe and positive environment for my employees to discuss their issues or ideas.					

Date:		Manager-as-Coach:	Team:				
Quarter:		Report to Manager/Supervisor:	Department:				
		During the coaching sessions, I ask my employees for their contribution, an input to the coaching process improvement.					
3	**Empathy**	During our coaching conversation, I make sure my employees notice that I understand their perspectives and positions.					
		I acknowledge and display understanding of my employees' feelings and emotions during coaching on sensitive issues.					
		I show patience during coaching by providing enough time for my employees to express themselves fully.					
		I do not interrupt their dialogues or invalidate my employees expressing their issues.					
		During our coaching conversation, I stay present to what it takes for my employees to express their issues without fear.					
4	**Awareness**	Before any coaching session with my employees, I make sure my mindset is positive and compassionate.					
		During coaching sessions, I ask questions that assist my employees in discovering other options to problems.					
		During coaching conversations with my employees, I make sure to provide relevant examples.					
		I make sure to provide positive and relevant feedback to my employees for them to continue productive conversations.					

(Continued)

Table 16.2   (Continued)

Date:	Manager-as-Coach:		Team:				
Quarter:	Report to Manager/Supervisor:		Department:				
Rating Scale: Rating Scale: 1 =Poor, 2 =Marginal, 3 =Acceptable, 4 =Good, 5 =Excellent							
		By the end of a coaching conversation, my staff has greater clarity about the issues they face					
5	**Goal Setting**	I make sure to set relevant and important goals for my employees' work and job performance.					
		During our coaching conversations, I do not push my agenda or goals as a manager to my employees.					
		I make sure to set realistic and attainable goals during my coaching sessions with my employees.					
		I ensure that all goals set during the coaching sessions are measurable.					
		Every quarter I encourage my employees to review and adjust their goals for increasing their performances.					
6	**Action Planning**	I always encourage my employees to develop a simple, clear, and attainable action plan.					
		I make myself available to assist my employees in designing and set their action plans.					
		During coaching sessions, I assist my employees in focusing on the concept of achieving success through planning.					
		During the coaching session, I keep notes and record my employees' action plans and deadlines.					
		I ensure to plan a review with my employees to check on their action plan and its progress every month.					

Date:		Manager-as-Coach:	Team:				
Quarter:		Report to Manager/Supervisor:	Department:				
7	**Processes**	During a regular coaching session, I ask my employees to provide a brief report on the progress of their goals.					
		During coaching conversations, I make sure to address any performance deficits directly with my employees.					
		I make sure to acknowledge my employees' progress and positive efforts in every coaching conversation.					
		I make sure my employees know the wisdom of "planning their work" and "working their plan."					
		Regularly I ask my top high performers to conduct a team coaching session on some related topics.					
8	**Accountability**	I hold myself accountable for maintaining my knowledge, abilities, and skills in performance coaching.					
		I keep my employees accountable for their actions, behavior, and attitude during our coaching sessions.					
		I keep my employees accountable for delivering their action plans and their related details.					
		During our coaching conversation, I always emphasize my employees' personal and professional responsibilities.					
		I ensure my employees are aware that accountability is being responsible before the fact, not after the fact.					
9	**Feedback**	During each coaching conversation with my employees, I provide feedback on using their productive conversation.					

(Continued)

Table 16.2   (Continued)

Date:		Manager-as-Coach:	Team:				
Quarter:		Report to Manager/Supervisor:	Department:				
Rating Scale: Rating Scale: 1 =Poor, 2 =Marginal, 3 =Acceptable, 4 =Good, 5 =Excellent							
		I ask my employees to complete a "coaching session evaluation form" when conducting a team coaching session.					
		I make sure the positive feedbacks are in a public forum when an opportunity is available.					
		I make sure potential negative feedbacks are in a private setting and in a constructive fashion.					
		I make sure to explain my feedback content and context to my employees for their education and development.					
10	Ethics	I make sure I follow all company's HR roles and policies during my coaching sessions with my employees.					
		During our coaching sessions, I do not ask my employees about the personal aspects of their lives.					
		I ensure my employees that anything they say in our coaching conversations will be kept confidential.					
		I keep all my employees' personal information that we talk about during coaching conversations confidential.					
		I am applying all professional, ethical policies related to our profession and industry.					
A. Quarterly Total Per Rating Scale							
B. Quarterly Total Per Rating Scale (total of all above rating scales)							

Date:	Manager-as-Coach:	Team:
Quarter:	Report to Manager/Supervisor:	Department:
C.Quarterly Final Rating Average *(above total of all rating scales divide by 10)*		
Three actions for this quarter that would bring up my three lowest manager-as-coach coaching processes ratings by at least one scale on the next quarter rating:		
Action 1:		
Action 2:		
Action 3:		
Note:		

Source: Copyright 2021 by Behnam Bakhshandeh.

Table 16.3   Monthly High-Performance Coach or Manager-as-Coach Discipline of Coaching Self-Rating Process Format.

Monthly Discipline of Coaching Self-Rating						
Performance Coach:		Month/Year:				
Supervisor:		Department:				
Rating Scale		1	2	3	4	5
#	Disciplines	Ratings from 1(lowest) to 5 (highest)				
1	Learning new, present or updated concepts, models, techniques and ideas in the industry.					
2	Continue learning about effective communication and active listening.					
3	Clarifying clear current and desired states.					
4	Displaying professional behavior and attitude.					
5	Displaying responsibility and accountability.					
6	Establishing rapport with others with ease.					
7	Monitoring and practicing what works.					
8	Maintaining relationships with individuals and teams.					

(Continued)

Table 16.3 (Continued)

Monthly Discipline of Coaching Self-Rating						
Performance Coach:		Month/Year:				
Supervisor:		Department:				
Rating Scale		*1*	*2*	*3*	*4*	*5*
#	Disciplines	Ratings from 1(lowest) to 5 (highest)				
9	Learning from their successes and failures and implementing correction actions.					
10	Asking questions and conducting inquires for uncovering what is happening.					
11	Empowering their individual and team clients.					
12	Continue learning from best coaches in their industry.					
13	Practicing professionalism and being approachable.					
14	Displaying humility, patience, and compassion.					
15	Displaying elements of Emotional Intelligence.					
Monthly Total per Scale						
Monthly Total (Total of above monthly totals per scale)						
Monthly Average (Above monthly total divided by15)						
Two actions for this month that would bring up my two lowest rating disciplines by at least two points:						
Action 1:						
Action 2:						

Source: Copyright 2021 by Behnam Bakhshandeh.

(9) It gives you more self-confidence as a professional high-performance coach.

(10) It opens new windows to understand and adjust your mindset, attitude, and behavior.

High-Performance Coach's Self-Evaluating

Table 16.1 represents the high-performance coach's self-evaluating form. High-performance coaches can use this form to self-evaluate their own

Coaching Session Evaluation Form

I would like to take this opportunity to say *Thank You* for participating in our Performance Coaching session on the topic of _____ on _____

To keep serving our clients, teams and employees with the highest quality, I would like your feedback on the form below:

Please circle one number based on a scale of 1 to 10 below on the following items:

1-2 = Poor   3-4 = Fair   5-6 = Good   7-8 = Very good   9-10 = Excellent

The Coach

o ………………………….   1 2 3 4 5 6 7 8 9 10
o Professionalism   1 2 3 4 5 6 7 8 9 10
o Attitude & Behavior   1 2 3 4 5 6 7 8 9 10
o Patience & Understanding   1 2 3 4 5 6 7 8 9 10
o Friendliness & Helpfulness   1 2 3 4 5 6 7 8 9 10

The Coaching

o Coaching Method   1 2 3 4 5 6 7 8 9 10
o Coaching Style   1 2 3 4 5 6 7 8 9 10
o Opportunity to Participate   1 2 3 4 5 6 7 8 9 10

The Content

o Content & Topics   1 2 3 4 5 6 7 8 9 10
o Handout & Material   1 2 3 4 5 6 7 8 9 10
o Clarity & Examples   1 2 3 4 5 6 7 8 9 10

Location & Event

o Appearance & Location   1 2 3 4 5 6 7 8 9 10
o Presentation & Organization   1 2 3 4 5 6 7 8 9 10
o Hospitality   1 2 3 4 5 6 7 8 9 10

Questions

o Did you receive value from this coaching session?   Yes   No
o Did your coach answer all of your questions, if you asked any?   Yes   No
o Would you be interested to more coaching in your department?   Yes   No
o What type of coaching would you be interested to receive in your team or department?
   ☐ Performance Coaching on the areas of: …………………………………………………………
   ☐ Management Coaching for myself or my manager/supervisor
   ☐ Mentorship for yourself or others in my team
   ☐ Team Training & Team Building for our team (Conflict Resolution & Team Building)
   ☐ Personal Development Workshops for our team or department

Comments

_____

_____

Today's Date: _____   Your name: _____

Your Team or Department: _____   Your Manager/Supervisor: _____

Your Direct phone #: _____   Your Email: _____

Figure 16.4   Coaching Session Evaluation Form.

Source: Adapted from Bakhshandeh (2008).

coaching performance by rating (1) their ability to perform general coaching competencies and skills and (2) the importance of such skill on the success of their coaching career.

Top Ten Coaching Processes Self-Rating for a Manger-as-Coach

Your knowledge, abilities, and skills as a manager-as-coach are also essential to your performance as a high-performance coach. You can use the following ten categories to conduct a self-rating process on your levels of abilities, competencies, and skills as a manager-as-coach to deliver and perform elements of each category.

Authenticity, honesty, integrity, and accountability are the keys to conducting a valuable and productive self-rating undertaking. Therefore, run this self-rating quarterly and adjust coordinately.

Monthly Discipline of Coaching Self-Rating

In this part of the self-evaluation segment, we introduce the "Monthly Discipline of Coaching Self-Rating" displayed in Table 16.3. As we have mentioned, the concept of self-rating and self-evaluation is a dignified act of self-awareness and self-regulation by professional high-performance coaches who are interested in their personal and professional growth and devotion to their clients and their careers. Table 16.3 displays some of the core disciplines of high-performance coaches.

Coaching Session Evaluation Form

One of the ways to conduct self-evaluation is providing an opportunity for your coaching clients, teams or coachees to rate you on your coaching presentation. This attempt could be for one-on-one individual presentation coaching, or teams' presentation coaching in a team seminar, workshop, or developmental training.

Figure 16.4 is an example of a coaching session evaluation form that you will give participants to evaluate your coaching session, using (1) rating systems, (2) close-ended questions, (3) invitations to further participation, and (4) open-ended questions:

Helpful Review of What Works for Self-Evaluation

At this point, besides the self-evaluating tools in this chapter, we are recommending that you to reviewing and use the following some self-evaluating elements and disciplines from previous chapters in this book:

■ Chapter 2
  – Table 2.2: Quarterly Performance Conversation and Reflection Check List for Employees/Coachees.
  – Table 2.3: High-Performance Coaching Tool. Inspired and adapted from Rothwell (2015).

■ Chapter 3
  – Table 3.3: Presence and Use of Emotional Intelligence at Work by a Manger-as-Coach Rating System.
  – Table 3.4: Leadership Qualities of Effective Manager-as-Coach Rating System.

■ Chapter 4
  – Table 4.1: Fundamental State of Being and Competencies for Establishing Relatedness and Rapport.

■ Chapter 5
  – Table 5.2: How to Determine Your Values.

■ Chapter 6
  – Table 6.1: Assessing the Current Vision Clarity of an Individual or a Team.
  – Table 6.4: Assessing the Job Performance Standards of an Individual or a Team.

■ Chapter 7
  – Table 7.4: Analyst's Competencies and Skills, and their Facilitating Outputs.
  – Table 7.6: Needed Abilities for a High-Performance Gap Analyst for Comparing "What Is Happening" and "What Should Be Happening."
  – Table 7.7: Needed Core Competencies for a High-Performance Gap Analyst for Comparing "What Is Happening" and "What Should Be Happening."

References

Bakhshandeh, Behnam. 2008. "Bravehearts; Leadership Development Training, 2nd Edition." Unpublished Training and Developmental Course on Coaching Executives and Managers. San Diego, CA: Primeco Education, Inc.

Bakhshandeh, Behnam. 2009. *Conspiracy for Greatness: Mastery of Love Within*. San Diego, CA: Primeco Education, Inc.

Camp, William G. 2001. "Formulating and Evaluating Theoretical Frameworks for Career and Technical Education Research." *Journal of Vocational Educational Research* 26, no. 1: 4–21.

Hertzberg, Karen. 2020. "How to Write a Self-evaluation." *Grammarly Blog Website*. www.grammarly.com/blog/how-to-write-a-self-evaluation/.

Rothwell, William J. 2013. *Performance Consulting: Applying Performance Improvement in Human Resource Development.* San Francisco, CA: John Wiley & Sons.

Rothwell, William J. 2015. *Beyond Training & Development, 3rd Edition: Enhancing Human Performance Through a Measurable Focus on Business Impact.* Amherst, MA: HRD Press, Inc.

Appendix A: Sources for Education and Implementations

Chapter 1

The General Concept of Coaching

Books

Chambers, Dave. 2013. *Coaching: The Art and the Science—The Complete Guide to Self Management, Team Management, and Physical and Psychological Preparation*. Illustrated edition. Richmond Hill, Ont. ; Buffalo, NY: Firefly Books.

Gallwey, W. Timothy, Zach Kleiman, and Pete Carroll. 1997. *The Inner Game of Tennis: The Classic Guide to the Mental Side of Peak Performance*. Revised ed. edition. New York: Random House Trade Paperbacks.

Martens, Rainer. 2012. *Successful Coaching*. Fourth edition. Champaign, IL: Human Kinetics.

Martin, G. L. 1987. *Coaching: An Effective Behavioral Approach*. LA: Times Mirror/ Mosby.

Sabock, Ralph J., and Michael D. Sabock. 2008. *Coaching: A Realistic Perspective*. 9th ed. Lanham, Md: Rowman & Littlefield Pub.

Articles

Brell, Carolin, Jens Rowold, Jürgen Weibler, and Martina Moenninghoff. 2011. "Evaluation of a Long-Term Transformational Leadership Development Program." *Zeitschrift Fuer Personalforschung. German Journal of Research in Human Resource Management* 25 (August): 205–24. https://doi. org/10.2307/23279289.

Harwell-Kee, Kathryn. 2019. Coaching. The Learning Professional, 40 (4), 66–67.

Kampa-Kokesch, Sheila, and Mary Z. Anderson. 2001. "Executive Coaching: A Comprehensive Review of the Literature." *Consulting Psychology Journal: Practice and Research* 53 (4): 205–28. https://doi.org/10.1037/1061-4087.53.4.205.

Mukherjee, Sraban. 2012. "Does Coaching Transform Coaches? A Case Study of Internal Coaching." *International Journal of Evidence Based Coaching and Mentoring* 10 (2): 76–87.

Segers, Jesse, Daniël Vloeberghs, Erik Henderickx, and Ilke Inceoglu. 2011. "Structuring and Understanding the Coaching Industry: The Coaching Cube." *Academy of Management Learning & Education* 10 (2): 204–21. https://doi.org/10.5465/AMLE.2011.62798930.

Stern, Lewis R. 2004. "Executive Coaching: A Working Definition." *Consulting Psychology Journal: Practice and Research* 56 (3): 154–62. https://doi.org/10.1037/1065-9293.56.3.154.

Witherspoon, Robert, and Randall P. White. 1996. "Executive Coaching: A Continuum of Roles." *Consulting Psychology Journal: Practice and Research* 48 (2): 124–33. https://doi.org/10.1037/1061-4087.48.2.124.

Videos

Center for Positiv Psykologi. 2014. *Margaret Moore on Positive Psychology and Coaching.* www.youtube.com/watch?v=segLzIJlW_Q.

Coaching: Introducing Annie Boate. n.d. Accessed October 15, 2021. https://video.alexanderstreet.com/watch/coaching-introducing-annie-boate.

Evercoach by Mindvalley. 2019. *Deep Coaching Techniques In A Live Coaching Session | Rich Litvin.* www.youtube.com/watch?v=rUTAh4gFGaQ.

Smith Leadership LLC. 2012. *What Is Coaching?* www.youtube.com/watch?v=nFx6yKZrzco.

TED. 2018. *Want to Get Great at Something? Get a Coach | Atul Gawande.* www.youtube.com/watch?v=oHDq1PcYkT4.

Webpages

Goldsmith, Wayne. 2019. "The Five Stages of Coaching: Going from Beginner to the Best Coach You Can Be." WG COACHING. March 27, 2019. https://wgcoaching.com/the-five-stages-of-coaching-going-from-beginner-to-the-best-coach-you-can-be/.

Schultz, Joshua. 2021. "*What is Coaching in the Workplace and Why is it Important?*" September 29, 2021. PositivePsychology.Com. https://positivepsychology.com/workplace-coaching/

Toneatto, Meriflor. 2021. "3 Ways to Capitalize on the Next Wave in Positive Psychology." International Coaching Federation. August 30, 2021. https://coachingfederation.org/blog/capitalize-on-positive-psychology.

Report

International Coaching Federation. 2020. 2020 ICF global coaching study executive summary. https://coachingfederation.org/app/uploads/2020/09/FINAL_ICF_GCS2020_ExecutiveSummary.pdf

Blogs

Martin, Carolyn. 2021. "Fempower Coaching: Together We Move Forward." *ICF Foundation* (blog). August 30, 2021. https://foundationoficf.org/fempower-coaching-together-we-move-forward/.

Martin, Carolyn. 2021. "Three Takeaways on the Coaching Industry's Recovery from the Pandemic." *ICF Foundation* (blog). July 30, 2021. https://foundationoficf.org/three-takeaways-on-the-coaching-industrys-recovery-from-the-pandemic/.

Morrison, Mike. 2010. "History of Coaching—A True Insight into Coaching." *RapidBI* (blog). November 29, 2010. https://rapidbi.com/history-of-coaching-a-true-insight-into-coaching/.

Tools

Coach/Coachee's agreement template by ICF foundation (direct download) https://foundationoficf.org/wp-content/uploads/2021/02/Ignite_Coaching-Agreement.docx

Matching coaches and coaches template by ICF foundation (direct download) https://foundationoficf.org/wp-content/uploads/2021/02/Ignite_TipsforMatching.docx

Chapter 2

Performance Coaching

Books

Angus, McLeod, and Thomas Will. 2010. *Performance Coaching Toolkit*. McGraw-Hill Education (UK).

Cook, Sarah. 2009. *Coaching for High Performance*. Electronic resource. 1st edition. IT Governance Publishing. https://go.oreilly.com/pennsylvania-state-university/library/view/-/9781849281041/?ar.

Holroyd, Jane, and Richard Field. 2012. *Performance Coaching Skills for Social Work*. London; Thousand Oaks, Calif.: Learning Matters : Imprint of SAGE Publications.

Payne, Vivette. 2006. *Coaching for High Performance*. Electronic resource. 1st edition. AMA Self-Study. https://go.oreilly.com/pennsylvania-state-university/library/view/-/9780761214618/?ar.

Ramsay, Jack, and Jim Lynch. 2004. *Coaching for Performance Improvement*. Dallas: University Press of America.

Review, M. I. T. 2018. *Coaching for High Performance*. Electronic resource. 1st edition. MIT Sloan Management Review. https://go.oreilly.com/pennsylvania-state-university/library/view/-/53863MIT60147/?ar.

Russell, Jeff, and Linda Russell. 2013. *Fearless Performance Reviews: Coaching Conversations That Turn Every Employee into a Star Player*. 1st edition. New York: McGraw-Hill Education.

Whitmore, John. 2002. *Coaching for Performance: GROWing People, Performance and Purpose*. Electronic resource. 3rd ed. People Skills for Professionals. London ; Naperville, IL: Nicholas Brealey. http://ezaccess.libraries.psu.edu/login?url=www.netLibrary.com/urlapi.asp?action=summary&v=1&bookid=75074.

Wilson, Carol. 2011. *Best Practice in Performance Coaching: A Handbook for Leaders, Coaches, HR Professionals and Organizations*. Reprint edition. London: Kogan Page.

Wilson, Carol. 2011. *Best Practice in Performance Coaching: A Handbook for Leaders, Coaches, HR Professionals and Organizations*. Reprint edition. London: Kogan Page.

Articles

Blackett, A. D., A. B. Evans, and D. Piggott. 2021. "Negotiating a Coach Identity: A Theoretical Critique of Elite Athletes' Transitions into Post-Athletic High-Performance Coaching Roles." *Sport, Education and Society* 26 (6): 663–75. https://doi.org/10.1080/13573322.2020.1787371.

Blackett, Alexander David, Adam B. Evans, and David Piggott. 2018. "'Active' and 'Passive' Coach Pathways: Elite Athletes' Entry Routes Into High-Performance Coaching Roles." *International Sport Coaching Journal* 5 (3): 213–26. https://doi.org/10.1123/iscj.2017-0053.

Chan, Jonathan T., and Clifford J. Mallett. 2011. "The Value of Emotional Intelligence for High Performance Coaching." *International Journal of Sports Science & Coaching* 6 (3): 315–28. https://doi.org/10.1260/1747-9541.6.3.315.

Dunn, Winnie, Lauren M. Little, Ellen Pope, and Anna Wallisch. 2018. "Establishing Fidelity of Occupational Performance Coaching." *OTJR: Occupation, Participation and Health* 38 (2): 96–104. https://doi.org/10.1177/1539449217724755.

Harvard Business Review. 2021. "Leaders Need Professional Coaching Now More Than Ever. March 2, 2021. https://hbr.org/sponsored/2021/03/leaders-need-professional-coaching-now-more-than-ever.

Kahjoogh, Mina Ahmadi, Mehdi Rassafiani, Winnie Dunn, Seyed Ali Hosseini, and Nazila Akbarfahimi. 2016. "Occupational Performance Coaching: A Descriptive Review of Literature." *New Zealand Journal of Occupational Therapy* 63 (2): 45–49.

Videos

Nice. 2016. *Performance Coaching: The Definition.* www.youtube.com/watch?v= HONNR6sZQ18.

NLP Times. 2017. *NLP Coaching: What It Is High Performance Coaching?* www. youtube.com/watch?v=3J3-SKp9Cos.

Performance Coaching: Definition & Overview—Video & Lesson Transcript. n.d. Accessed October 15, 2021. https://study.com/academy/lesson/performance-coaching-definition-overview.html.

Ruth Kudzi. 2020. *What Does A Performance Coach Actually Do?* www.youtube. com/watch?v=qBVTjS3AzxE.

Steve Long. 2017. *What Is Performance Coaching?* www.youtube.com/watch?v= VX9FKhevhMU.

The Performance Thinking Network. 2020. *Performance Coaching Part 1 | What Is Performance Coaching?* www.youtube.com/watch?v=PCPQFjlq95w.

Report

Human Capital Institute. 2016. Building a coaching culture with managers and leaders. www.hci.org/system/files/research//files/field_content_file/2016%2520ICF.pdf

Blogs to Follow

"Coaching Statistics: The ROI of Coaching in 2021." Luisa Zhou. January 12, 2021. www.luisazhou.com/blog/coaching-statistics/.

Anubha Kathuria Bellani. "Feedspot—A Fast, Free, Modern RSS Reader. It's a Simple Way to Track All Your Favorite Websites in One Place." Accessed October 15, 2021. www.feedspot.com.

Tools

Free Employee Coaching Template: Improve Employee Performance www.viamaven.com/s/Employee-coaching-template-viaMaven.docx

Chapter 3

Mindset, Attitude, Behavior and Performance

Book

Cannon, Fiona. 2017. "The Agility Mindset: How Reframing Flexible Working Delivers Competitive Advantage." Electronic resource. *Springer EBooks*. https://doi.org/10.1007/978-3-319-45519-8.

Long, Weldon. 2013. *The Power of Consistency: Prosperity Mindset Training for Sales and Business Professionals*. Electronic resource. 1st edition. Wiley. https://go.oreilly.com/pennsylvania-state-university/library/view/-/9781118526538/?ar.

McDonald, Kent. 2015. *Beyond Requirements: Analysis with an Agile Mindset*. Electronic resource. 1st edition. Addison-Wesley Professional. https://go.oreilly.com/pennsylvania-state-university/library/view/-/9780133039863/?ar.

Sheehan, Kevin, and Jessica Ryan. 2017. *Growing a Growth Mindset: Unlocking Character Strengths through Children's Literature*. Lanham, Maryland: Rowman & Littlefield Education.

Sweeney, John, and Elena Imaretska. 2015. *The Innovative Mindset*. Electronic resource. 1st edition. Wiley. https://go.oreilly.com/pennsylvania-state-university/library/view/-/9781119161288/?ar.

Article

"Seven Steps to Developing a High-Performance Mindset; Your Work ; Gina London The Communicator." n.d. Accessed September 6, 2021. https://advance-lexis-com.ezaccess.libraries.psu.edu/document/?pdmfid=1516831&crid=4ee014c4-6cd6-458a-b163-20e757ec7361&pddocfullpath=%2Fshared%2Fdocument%2Fnews%2Furn%3AcontentItem%3A5VNF-H8N1-DYTY-C2T8–00000–00&pdcontentcomponentid=333993&pdteaserkey=sr0&pditab=allpods&ecomp=qzvnk&earg=sr0&prid=7e5a2c79-d7b8–4f7d-a0ab-dc9ddccc8498.

Battistelli, Adalgisa, Maura Galletta, Igor Portoghese, and Christian Vandenberghe. 2013. "Mindsets of Commitment and Motivation: Interrelationships and Contribution to Work Outcomes." *The Journal of Psychology* 147 (1): 17–48. https://doi.org/10.1080/00223980.2012.668146.

Burgoyne, Alexander P., David Z. Hambrick, Jason S. Moser, and S. Alexandra Burt. 2018. "Analysis of a Mindset Intervention." *Journal of Research in Personality* 77 (December): 21–30. https://doi.org/10.1016/j.jrp.2018.09.004.

Business Wire. 2015. "Survey: Executives Say Mindset Most Important Factor in Business Performance and Career Success," May 11, 2015. www.proquest.com/docview/1679874600/abstract/3846F98E9C0C43F5PQ/1.

Ng, Betsy. 2018. "The Neuroscience of Growth Mindset and Intrinsic Motivation." *Brain Sciences* 8 (2): 20. https://doi.org/10.3390/brainsci8020020.

Nolder, Christine J., and Kathryn Kadous. 2018. "Grounding the Professional Skepticism Construct in Mindset and Attitude Theory: A Way Forward." *Accounting, Organizations and Society* 67 (May): 1–14. https://doi.org/10.1016/j.aos.2018.03.010.

Wright, P. C., & Geroy, G. D. (2001). Changing the mindset: The training myth and the need for world-class performance. *The International Journal of Human Resource Management, 12* (4), 586–600. https://doi.org/10.1080/09585190122342

Video

"EMPATHY—BEST SPEECH OF ALL TIME By Simon Sinek | Inspiritory—YouTube." n.d. Accessed September 6, 2021. www.youtube.com/watch?v=IJyNoJCAuzA.

Carol Dweck. 2014. *The Power of Believing That You Can Improve | TED*. www.youtube.com/watch?v=_X0mgOOSpLU.

Roger, D., & Petrie, N. (2016). *Work Without Stress: Building a Resilient Mindset for Lasting Success (Audio Book)* (1st edition). McGraw-Hill.

Simon Sinek. 2020. *What Makes the Highest Performing Teams in the World | Simon Sinek*. www.youtube.com/watch?v=zP9jpxitfb4.

Webpages

Goodridge, Clare Sarah. 2020. "How to Develop a High-Performance Mindset." The Flow Research Collective. November 5, 2020. www.flowresearchcollective.com/blog/high-performance-mindset.

Mackay, Anna-Lucia. 2015. "The Four Mindsets: How to Influence, Motivate and Lead High Performance Teams | Wiley." Wiley.Com. November 2015. www.wiley.com/en-us/The+Four+Mindsets%3A+How+to+Influence%2C+Motivate+and+Lead+High+Performance+Teams-p-9780730324782.

Blogs to Follow

Guise, Stephen. 2014. "Growth Mindset Vs. Performance Mindset." Stephen Guise. November 3, 2014. https://stephenguise.com/growth-mindset-vs-performance-mindset/.

Julie, Tiffany. n.d. "Blog." *Tiffany Julie* (blog). Accessed October 15, 2021. www.tiffanyjulie.com/blog/.

Laurie, Andrea. n.d. "The Blog | Andrea Laurie International." Andrea Laurie. Accessed October 15, 2021. www.andrealaurie.com/blog.

Peak Performance Mindset—21 Secrets How To Achieve More In Life. (2020, June 13). *The Athlete Blog*. https://theathleteblog.com/peak-performance-mindset/

Stillman, Jessica. n.d. "The Mindset Shift That Will Improve Your Performance at Everything." Accessed October 15, 2021. www.themuse.com/advice/the-mindset-shift-that-will-improve-your-performance-at-everything.

Chapter 4—Step 1

How to Establish Relatedness and Building Rapport?

Books

King, Serge Kahili. 1985. *Mastering Your Hidden Self: A Guide to the Huna Way*. 1st edition. Wheaton, Ill., USA: Quest Books.

Liska, Cathy, Meg Hanrahan, Marie Snidow, Brian McReynolds, Julie Binter, Amy Gamblin, Laurissa Heller, Margi Bush, Clinton Ages, and Ellen Zebrun. 2015. *Coaching Perspectives V*. CreateSpace Independent Publishing Platform.

O'Connor, Joseph, and John Seymour. 1993. *Introducing NLP: Psychological Skills for Understanding and Influencing People*. Rev ed. edition. Thorsons.

Starr, Julie. 2008. *Coaching Manual: The Definitive Guide to the Process, Principles & Skills of Personal Coaching*. 2nd edition. Harlow, England ; New York: Prentice Hall.

Whitworth, Laura, Karen Kimsey-House, Henry Kimsey-House, and Phillip Sandahl. 2007. *Co-Active Coaching: New Skills for Coaching People Toward Success in Work and, Life*. 2nd edition. Mountain View, Calif: UNKNO.

Article

Baker, Zachary, Emily Watlington, and C. Knee. 2020. "The Role of Rapport in Satisfying One's Basic Psychological Needs." *Motivation and Emotion* 44 (April). https://doi.org/10.1007/s11031-020-09819-5.

Boyle, Alysoun. 2020. "Self-Determination, Empowerment and Empathy in Mediation: Rehumanising Mediation's Effectiveness." *Newcastle Law Review, The*, January. https://search.informit.org/doi/abs/10.3316/informit.591932249556950.

Campbell, Rankyn M. 2016. "Does Enhancing Relatedness Amongst Varsity-Level Athletes Improve Team Performance?" 1–121.

Hadden, Benjamin W., C. Veronica Smith, and C. Raymond Knee. 2014. "The Way I Make You Feel: How Relatedness and Compassionate Goals Promote Partner's Relationship Satisfaction." *The Journal of Positive Psychology* 9 (2): 155–62. https://doi.org/10.1080/17439760.2013.858272.

Norfolk, Tim, Kamal Birdi, and Deirdre Walsh. 2007. "The Role of Empathy in Establishing Rapport in the Consultation: A New Model." *Medical Education* 41 (7): 690–97. https://doi.org/10.1111/j.1365-2923.2007.02789.x.

Tickle-Degnen, Linda, and Robert Rosenthal. 1990. "The Nature of Rapport and Its Nonverbal Correlates." *Psychological Inquiry* 1 (4): 285–93.

Video

Gutman, Mike. 2018. *Building Rapport with Remote Colleagues*. Accessed September 6, 2021. www.linkedin.com/learning/remote-work-foundations/building-rapport-with-remote-colleagues.

The Coaching Institute. 2020. *3 Steps to Building Rapport Online as a Coach | The Coaching Institute*. www.youtube.com/watch?v=XeLothGaOwg.

Tony Robbins. 2016. *How to Build Rapport | Tony Robbins*. www.youtube.com/watch?v=-9uHBEGpJm4.

WISE Workplace. 2013. *Professor Ray Bull: The Importance of Building Rapport*. www.youtube.com/watch?v=OIti6BY1XQs.

Webpages

"82 Ways How to Build Rapport With Anyone You Work With." 2019. Get Lighthouse. July 4, 2019. https://getlighthouse.com/blog/how-to-build-rapport/.

"Employer Factsheet: Coaching Skills—Building Rapport | Croner-i." May 31, 2019. Accessed October 15, 2021. https://app.croneri.co.uk/topics/coaching-and-mentoring/employer-factsheet-coaching-skills-building-rapport.

"Preparing For Coaching And Creating Inner Space." n.d. Accessed October 15, 2021. www.personal-coaching-information.com/preparing-for-coaching.html.

"Why Rapport Is Everything In Coaching." 2016. *Holistic Health and Wellness Training | Health Coach Institute* (blog). May 17, 2016. www.healthcoachinstitute.com/coaching/why-rapport-is-everything-in-coaching/.

Blogs

Ab-intus. 2019. "Building Client Rapport in Coaching." *Abintus* (blog). July 24, 2019. www.abintus.co.uk/building-client-rapport-in-coaching/.

Building Rapport: Establishing Strong Two-Way Connections. (n.d.). Retrieved September 6, 2021, from www.mindtools.com/pages/article/building-rapport.htm

Chandrasekaran, Sridhar. n.d. "Life Coach Bloggers: Rapport Building Statements and Questions in Coaching with Examples List." *Life Coach Bloggers* (blog). Accessed October 15, 2021. http://lifecoachbloggers.blogspot.com/2020/11/Rapport-Building-statement-Questions-life-Coaching-Examples-List.html.

Chapter 5—Step 2

What Is the Issue at Hand?

Articles

Bakhtiyari, Mehrsa. n.d. "Work Environment and Employee Performance: A Brief Literature Review." Authorea, Inc. Accessed September 6, 2021. https://doi.org/10.22541/au.156881614.48075353.

Barros Ahrens, Rudy de, Luciana da Silva Lirani, and Antonio Carlos de Francisco. 2020. "Construct Validity and Reliability of the Work Environment Assessment

Instrument WE-10." *International Journal of Environmental Research and Public Health* 17 (20): 7364. https://doi.org/10.3390/ijerph17207364.

Belk, William. 2017. "58% of High-Performance Employees Say They Need More Quiet Work Spaces." CNBC. March 15, 2017. www.cnbc.com/2017/03/15/58-of-high-performance-employees-say-they-need-more-quiet-work-spaces.html.

Björk, Lars E. 1975. "Work Organization and the Improvement of the Work Environment." *Ambio* 4 (1): 55–59.

Lenz, R. T. 1980. "Environment, Strategy, Organization Structure and Performance: Patterns in One Industry." *Strategic Management Journal* 1 (3): 209–26. https://doi.org/10.1002/smj.4250010303.

Vischer, Jacqueline C. 2008. "Towards an Environmental Psychology of Workspace: How People Are Affected by Environments for Work." *Architectural Science Review* 51 (2): 97–108. https://doi.org/10.3763/asre.2008.5114.

Video

O.C. Tanner Company. 2014. *Create a Culture of Happiness.* www.youtube.com/watch?v=c7ilDOzonrQ.

O.C. Tanner Company. 2020. *How Taco Bell Uses O.C. Tanner's Employee Recognition Platform to Celebrate Employees.* www.youtube.com/watch?v=RdTQg0xeTwc.

Webpages

"How to Use Coaching to Support Diversity and Inclusion." n.d. *Training Industry* (blog). Accessed October 15, 2021. https://trainingindustry.com/articles/diversity-equity-and-inclusion/how-to-use-coaching-to-support-diversity-and-inclusion/.

Fine, Alan. 2020. "How Coaching Helps Overcome the Most Common Hurdle to Diversity, Equity, and Inclusion." October 22, 2020. www.td.org/insights/how-coaching-helps-overcome-the-most-common-hurdle-to-diversity-equity-and-inclusion.

Marr, Lucy. 2020. "Top 10 Trending Diversity, Equity, and Inclusion Training Experts." *AAE Speaks: Blog | AAE Speakers Bureau* (blog). October 12, 2020. www.allamericanspeakers.com/blog/top-10-trending-diversity-equity-and-inclusion-training-experts/.

Blog

"Managing Diversity in the Workplace | CoachDiversity." September 13, 2021. *CoachDiversity Institute* (blog). Accessed October 15, 2021. https://coachdiversity.com/blog/managing-diversity-in-the-workplace/.

Blackbyrn, Sai. 2019. "30 Coaching Trends That You Must Know (2021 Edition)." June 30, 2019. https://coachfoundation.com/blog/30-coaching-trends/.

LaMark, Dottie. 2019. "How to Conduct a Skills Gap Analysis: A Step-by-Step Guide." The Predictive Index. December 6, 2019. www.predictiveindex.com/blog/how-to-conduct-a-skills-gap-analysis/.

Satyendra. 2020. "Organizational Environment and Its Impact on the Performance—IspatGuru." August 17, 2020. www.ispatguru.com/organizational-environment-and-its-impact-on-the-performance/.

Report

Agrawal, Sapana, Aaron De Smet, Pawel Poplawski, and Angelika Reich. 2020. "How Companies Are Reskilling to Address Skill Gaps | McKinsey." February 12, 2020. www.mckinsey.com/business-functions/people-and-organizational-performance/our-insights/beyond-hiring-how-companies-are-reskilling-to-address-talent-gaps.

Chapter 6—Step 3

What Should Be Happening?

Books

Andrei, Peter. 2020. *How Highly Effective People Speak: How High Performers Use Psychology to Influence With Ease*. Independently published.

Bornancin, Brandon. 2021. *Whatever It Takes: Master the Habits to Transform Your Business, Relationships, and Life*. Brandon Bornancin.

Burningham, Tim. 2019. *Be An Awesome Boss!: The Four C's Model to Leadership Success*. Independently published.

Frankl, Viktor E., William J. Winslade, and Harold S. Kushner. 2006. *Man's Search for Meaning*. 1st edition. Boston: Beacon Press.

O'Neill, Mary Beth A. 2007. *Executive Coaching with Backbone and Heart: A Systems Approach to Engaging Leaders with Their Challenges*. 2nd edition. San Francisco: Jossey-Bass.

Steven J. Stowell, Cherissa S. Newton M. Ed, and Eric D. Mead. 2019. *Coaching for Results: The 5 TIPS That Drive Performance*. Edited by Emily Hodgson-Soule. First edition. CMOE Press.

Stoltzfus, Tony. 2008. *Coaching Questions: A Coach's Guide to Powerful Asking Skills*. 1st edition. Virginia Beach, VA: Coach22 Bookstore LLC.

Trenton, Nick. 2021. *Stop Overthinking: 23 Techniques to Relieve Stress, Stop Negative Spirals, Declutter Your Mind, and Focus on the Present*. Independently published.

Articles

Katzenbach, Jon R., and Douglas K. Smith. 2015. *The Wisdom of Teams: Creating the High-Performance Organization*. Harvard Business Review Press.

Ng, Betsy. 2018. "The Neuroscience of Growth Mindset and Intrinsic Motivation." *Brain Sciences* 8 (2): 20. https://doi.org/10.3390/brainsci8020020.

Waal, André A. de. 2007. "The Characteristics of a High Performance Organization." *Business Strategy Series* 8 (3): 179–85. https://doi.org/10.1108/17515630710684178.

Webpages

"The Ultimate Guide To High Performance Coaching." 2021. Evercoach—By Mindvalley. Accessed October 15, 2021. www.evercoach.com/ultimate-guide-to-high-performance-coaching/become-a-high-performance-coach.

Boyatzis, Richard, Melvin Smith, and Ellen Van Oosten. n.d. "Coaching for Change." *Harvard Business Review*. Accessed September 7, 2021. https://hbr.org/2019/09/coaching-for-change.

Smith, Amanda. May 17,2020. "Hiring a Performance Coach: The 5 Things You Should Know." Accessed October 15, 2021. www.cxeinc.com/blog/bid/243052/Hiring-a-Performance-Coach-The-5-Things-You-Should-Know.

Video

Life Coach Hub. 2014. *Vision Coaching: What's Your Vision?* www.youtube.com/watch?v=Cg_vsTocQqs.

MindToolsVideos. 2018. *The GROW Model.* www.youtube.com/watch?v=K3iJwoydBbg.

Pranjic, John. 2021. "Why 'Vision' Is Important For Coaches and A Personal Story About Developing My Own [Coaching 01]." 3four3. 2021. https://343coaching.com/podcast/soccer-by-3four3/vision-important-coaches-personal-story-developing-coaching-01/.

Ruth Kudzi. 2020. *What Does A Performance Coach Actually Do?* www.youtube.com/watch?v=qBVTjS3AzxE.

Chapter 7—Step 4

What Is the Measurable Gap?

Articles

Buckingham, Marcus, and Ashley Goodall. 2015. "Reinventing Performance Management." *Harvard Business Review*, April 2015. https://hbr.org/2015/04/reinventing-performance-management.

Deshler, Donald D. 2005. "A Closer Look: Closing the Performance Gap | Adlit." *Stratenotes* 13 (4). www.adlit.org/topics/curriculum-instruction/closer-look-closing-performance-gap.

Meier, Kenneth J., Nathan Favero, and Ling Zhu. 2015. "Performance Gaps and Managerial Decisions: A Bayesian Decision Theory of Managerial Action." *Journal of Public Administration Research and Theory* 25 (4): 1221–46. https://doi.org/10.1093/jopart/muu054.

Morris, Donna. n.d. "Death to the Performance Review: How Adobe Reinvented Performance Management and Transformed Its Business." *WorldatWork Journal*, 10.

Pidun, Tim, and Carsten Felden. 2012. "On Improving the Visibility of Hard-Measurable Process Performance." *International Journal of Intelligent Information Technologies (IJIIT)* 8 (2): 59–74. https://doi.org/10.4018/jiit.2012040104.

Zhu, Ling, and Amanda Rutherford. 2019. "Managing the Gaps: How Performance Gaps Shape Managerial Decision Making." *Public Performance & Management Review* 42 (5): 1029–61. https://doi.org/10.1080/15309576.2019.1568886.

Webpages

"3 Steps to Closing the Performance Gap—KPMG Belgium." 2019. KPMG. September 30, 2019. https://home.kpmg/be/en/home/insights/2017/10/3-steps-to-closing-the-performance-gap.html.

"Guide to Gap Analysis with Examples | Smartsheet." n.d. Accessed September 15, 2021. www.smartsheet.com/gap-analysis-method-examples.

Guerra-López, Ingrid, and Alisa Hutchinson. 2013. "Measurable and Continuous Performance Improvement: The Development of a Performance Measurement, Management, and Improvement System." *Performance Improvement Quarterly* 26 (2): 159–73. https://doi.org/10.1002/piq.21151.

Jaenke, Richard. 2013. "Identify the Real Reasons Behind Performance Gaps." ATD. August 8, 2013. www.td.org/magazines/td-magazine/identify-the-real-reasons-behind-performance-gaps.

Moody, Kathryn. 2016. "Why Facebook Still Uses Traditional Performance Reviews." HR Dive. October 13, 2016. www.hrdive.com/news/why-facebook-still-uses-traditional-performance-reviews/428175/.

Peterson, Oliver. 2019. "Gap Analysis: How to Bridge the Gap between Performance and Potential | Process Street | Checklist, Workflow and Sop Software." July 19, 2019. www.process.st/gap-analysis/.

Tregear, Roger. n.d. "Define, Measure & Close Process Performance Gaps at Your Organization." Accessed September 14, 2021. https://blog.leonardo.com.au/define-measure-close-process-performance-gaps-at-your-organization.

Video

Center for Coaching Certification. 2019. *The Performance Gap Indicator*. www.youtube.com/watch?v=OZZsClZRqZ4.

GarryPlatt. 2010. *From Performance Gap to Needs Analysis*. www.youtube.com/watch?v=bJKowt50a0Y.

GarryPlatt. 2010. *When Is a Performance Gap a Developmental Need?* www.you-tube.com/watch?v=aNLWK0p22y4.

Integrity Solutions. 2018. *What's the Performance Gap When Coaching Doesn't Happen?* www.youtube.com/watch?v=_P1S6saf7IY.

Blogs to Follow

Guthrie, Gerorgina. 2019. "These Gap Analysis Tools Will Help You Identify Every Opportunity." Cacoo. January 10, 2019. https://cacoo.com/blog/gap-analysis-tools-will-help-identify-every-opportunity/.

Solutions, Lambda. 2019. "Why Your Organization Needs Skill Gap Analysis." January 23, 2019. www.lambdasolutions.net/blog/why-your-organization-needs-skill-gap-analysis.

Tools

"10 Performance Management Tools Every Hr pro Should Know." 2021. People Managing People. January 4, 2021. https://peoplemanagingpeople.com/tools/performance-management-tools/.

Doe, Jane. 2018. "John Doe Jr. Xyz Corporation," 11. www.edgetrainingsystems.com/wp-content/uploads/2019/07/EdgeGAP_Analysis_SampleReport.pdf

Chapter 8—Step 5

How Important Is the Gap?

Books

Fusch, Gene, and Richard C. Gillespie. 2012. *A Practical Approach to Performance Interventions and Analysis: 50 Models for Building a High-Performance Culture.* Upper Saddle River, N.J: FT Press.

Articles

Anyim, Wisdom Okereke. n.d. "Identifying Gaps and Opportunities to Improve Performance in University Libraries Using Benchmarking and Performance Appraisal System," 17.

Johnston, David, Dominic Miles-Shenton, and David Farmer. 2015. "Quantifying the Domestic Building Fabric 'Performance Gap.'" *Building Services Engineering Research and Technology* 36 (5): 614–27. https://doi.org/10.1177/0143624415570344.

Min, Byung Hee, and Youngmin Oh. 2020. "How Do Performance Gaps Affect Improvement in Organizational Performance? Exploring the Mediating Roles of Proactive Activities." *Public Performance & Management Review* 43 (4): 766–89. https://doi.org/10.1080/15309576.2020.1713826.

Wren, Carla. n.d. "Employee Perceptions of Leadership Styles That Influence Workplace Performance." Ph.D., United States—Minnesota: Walden University. Accessed September 15, 2021. www.proquest.com/docview/2013763038/abstract/77EE253520924813PQ/1.

Webpages

"What Is a Key Performance Indicator (KPI)? Guide & Examples." n.d. Qlik. Accessed October 15, 2021. www.qlik.com/us/kpi.

Pavlou, Christina. 2021. "Skills Gap Analysis Template: How to Identify Training Needs (Free, Downloadable Sample)." TalentLMS Blog. January 15, 2021. www.talentlms.com/blog/skills-gap-analysis-template/.

Votaw, Kathleen Quinn. 2017. "Address Talent Issues with a Gap Analysis." Vistage Research Center. August 14, 2017. www.vistage.com/research-center/talent-management/20170815-address-talent-issues-with-a-gap-analysis/.

Wright, Tom. 2021. "How to Implement the Balanced Scorecard (Strategy Framework)." 2021. www.cascade.app/blog/how-to-implement-the-balanced-scorecard.

Video

GarryPlatt. 2010. *When Is a Performance Gap a Developmental Need?* www.youtube.com/watch?v=aNLWK0p22y4.

ISO Training Institute. 2020. *Balanced Scorecard | Strategy Maps | Performance Management | Performance Evaluation | Kpi.* www.youtube.com/watch?v=I1xO7_KktSE.

OpenTuition. 2019. *SWOT, Objectives, Critical Success Factors and Benchmarking—CIMA E3.* www.youtube.com/watch?v=YIG_qVwfpPg.

Webinar:

Wilsey, D. (2019, November 14). *Webinar—Balanced Scorecard Basics.* Balanced Scorecard Institute. https://balancedscorecard.org/balanced-scorecard-basics-webinar/

Blogs

Assessing performance needs. www.ifc.org/wps/wcm/connect/c64343d0-f3ec-4ed4-ad5c-049f80d24180/GuideToTraining_p26-43_Assesing+Performance+Needs.pdf?MOD=AJPERES&CVID=ndeLnca

www.washoecounty.us/repository/files/13/Performance%20Gap%20Analysis%20
  web.pdf
Performance gap analysis: A tool to assist managers/supervisors.
Performance Gap to Needs Analysis. (2015, November 17). *Cerius Executives.*
  https://ceriusexecutives.com/performance-gap-needs-analysis/

Tools

Personal assessment coaching guide by Center for Army Profession and
  Leadership, October 2020. https://caccapl.blob.core.usgovcloudapi.net/web/
  repository/pdf-files/Personal-Assessment-Coaching-Guide.pdf

Chapter 9—Step 6

What Are the Root Causes of the Gap?

Books

Planitz, Mark A. 2008. "Handbook of Human Performance Technology: Principles,
  Practices, Potential (3rd Ed.) Edited by James A. Pershing." *Performance
  Improvement* 47 (8): 52–54. https://doi.org/10.1002/pfi.20023.
Prakacita, Rian. n.d. "The Quality Toolbox Second Edition." Accessed September
  15, 2021. www.academia.edu/32325558/The_Quality_Toolbox_Second_Edition.

Articles

Olsen, Jason. 2019. "The Nominal Group Technique (NGT) as a Tool for Facilitating
  Pan-Disability Focus Groups and as a New Method for Quantifying Changes in
  Qualitative Data." *International Journal of Qualitative Methods* 18 (January):
  1609406919866049. https://doi.org/10.1177/1609406919866049.

Webpages

Delbecq, Andre L., Andrew Van de, and David H. Gustafson. n.d. "Nominal Group
  Technique." Accessed September 15, 2021. https://chess.wisc.edu/niatx/con-
  tent/contentpage.aspx?NID=147.
Hessing, Ted. 2015. "Nominal Group Technique." *Six Sigma Study
  Guide* (blog). November 21, 2015. https://sixsigmastudyguide.com/
  nominal-group-technique/.
MindTools. n.d. "Cause and Effect Analysis: Identifying the Likely Causes of
  Problems." Accessed September 15, 2021. www.mindtools.com/pages/article/
  newTMC_03.htm.

Video

HarvardX. 2017. *How to Create Cause-and-Effect Diagrams.* www.youtube.com/watch?v=mLvizyDFLQ4.

Nathan Orme. 2017. *Root Cause Analysis.* www.youtube.com/watch?v=TKv4Mw7qQbI.

System Improvement. 2020. "Seven Secrets of Root Cause Analysis—YouTube." 2020. www.youtube.com/watch?v=-3KacrTlZJg.

TapRooT®. 2021. *Seven Secrets of Root Cause Analysis.* www.youtube.com/watch?v=-3KacrTlZJg.

Blogs to Follow

Directpoint. 2018. "Comparing Delphi and NGT Decision Techniques." *Directorpoint* (blog). December 5, 2018. https://landing.directorpoint.com/blog/delphi-and-ngt-decision-techniques/.

Goodrich, Belinda. 2011. "Brainstorming vs Nominal Group Technique—PMP Exam Concepts." *PM Learning Solutions* (blog). May 30, 2011. www.pmlearningsolutions.com/blog/brainstorming-versus-nominal-group-technique-pmp-concept-13.

Treu, Jason. 2019. "Employee Performance Issues: How Root Cause Analysis Can Move Employees Forward." *Executive Coach, Culture Change and Employee Engagement in Dallas* (blog). November 11, 2019. https://jasontreu.com/2019/11/11/employee-performance-issues-how-root-cause-analysis-can-move-employees-forward/.

Tools

Kane, Robert, and Rosalie Kane. n.d. "How to Use the Fishbone Tool for Root Cause Analysis," 3. www.cms.gov/medicare/provider-enrollment-and-certification/qapi/downloads/fishbonerevised.pdf

Chapter 10—Step 7

How Many Ways Can the Gap Be Closed?

Books

BCC, Dr David Neal. 2019. *Bridging The Gap: How to Connect, Coach, and Create with Millennials, Gen Z and Beyond.* Aletheia Press.

Douglas, Christina A., and William H. Morley. 2000. *Executive Coaching: An Annotated Bibliography.* Greensboro, N.C: Center for Creative Leadership.

Franklin, Maren. 2006. *Performance Gap Analysis: Tips, Tools, and Intelligence for Trainers.* American Society for Training and Development.

Gilbert, Thomas. 2013. *Human Competence: Engineering Worthy Performance.* Pfeiffer.

Stanier, Michael Bungay, Lolly Daskal, Daniel H. Pink, Robin Sharma. 2019. The Coaching Habit by Michael Bungay Stanier, Leadership Gap. *The Coaching Habit, Leadership Gap [Hardcover], Drive Daniel Pink, The Leader Who Had No Title 4 Books Collection Set.* Stockholm: Simon & Schuster UK.

Articles

Bush, Mary Wayne, and John Lazar. n.d. "International Journal of Coaching in Organizations," 67.

Chevalier, Roger. "Updating the Behavior Engineering Model." Performance Improvement, 42, 5, 8–14.

Webpages

Fisher, Ossa. 2015. "8 Proven Ways to Help Close the Achievement Gap—EdSurge News." EdSurge. October 27, 2015. www.edsurge.com/news/2015-10-27-8-proven-ways-to-help-close-the-achievement-gap.

Mackay, Anna-Lucia. 2015. "The Four Mindsets: How to Influence, Motivate and Lead High Performance Teams | Wiley." Wiley.Com. November 2015. www.wiley.com/en-us/The+Four+Mindsets%3A+How+to+Influence%2C+Motivate+and+Lead+High+Performance+Teams-p-9780730324782.

Mankins, Michael C., and Richard Steele. 2005. "Closing the Strategy-to-Performance Gap: Techniques for Turning Great Strategy Into Great Performance—Strategy—United States." 2005. www.mondaq.com/unitedstates/operational-performance-management/34286/closing-the-strategy-to-performance-gap-techniques-for-turning-great-strategy-into-great-performance.

Narum, Claire. n.d. "Uncovering Performance Gaps With Front End Analysis." Accessed October 15, 2021. www.dashe.com/blog/instructional-design/front-end-analysis-improving-performance/.

Rose, Robertson. 2020. "The 4 Steps To Conduct An Effective Training Needs Analysis." *Roundtable Learning* (blog). October 15, 2020. https://roundtablelearning.com/the-4-steps-to-conduct-an-effective-training-needs-analysis/.

Taylor, Johnny C. 2021. "How to Address the Skills Gap." SHRM. October 12, 2021. www.shrm.org/resourcesandtools/tools-and-samples/how-to-guides/pages/how-to-address-the-skills-gap.aspx.

Video

Claudia, F. n.d. "Identifying Competency Gaps in the Workplace—Video & Lesson Transcript." Study.Com. Accessed September 15, 2021. https://study.com/academy/lesson/identifying-competency-gaps-in-the-workplace.html.

Blog

"No Gap No Coaching | ICF Credentialing Coach | Mentor Coach | Carly Anderson, MCC." 2018. Anderson, Carly. 2018. "No Gap No Coaching." June 15, 2018. https://carlyanderson.com/no-gap-no-coaching.

"The 4 Steps To Conduct An Effective Training Needs Analysis." 2020. *Roundtable Learning* (blog). October 15, 2020. https://roundtablelearning.com/the-4-steps-to-conduct-an-effective-training-needs-analysis/.

Anderson, Carly. 2019. "The What Who and How of Coaching." September 14, 2019. https://carlyanderson.com/the-what-who-and-how-of-coaching.

Moran, Joanna. 2017. "Closing an Employee Performance Gap." February 8, 2017. http://mysite-d94745a2.dudaone.com/closing-an-employee-performance-gap.

Moran, Joanna. 2017. "How to Lead a Huge Performance Leap Forward." February 8, 2017. http://mysite-d94745a2.dudaone.com/how-to-lead-a-huge-performance-leap-forward.

Chapter 11—Step 8

What Is the Most Effective Way to Close the Gap?

Books

Franklin, Maren. 2006. *Performance Gap Analysis: Tips, Tools, and Intelligence for Trainers*. American Society for Training and Development.

Marr, Bernard, and James Creelman. 2011. "Selecting Strategic Initiatives." In *More with Less: Maximizing Value in the Public Sector*, edited by Bernard Marr and James Creelman, 112–33. London: Palgrave Macmillan UK. https://doi.org/10.1057/9780230300408_6.

Surface, Eric A. 2012. "Training Needs Assessment: Aligning Learning and Capability with Performance Requirements and Organizational Objectives." In *The Handbook of Work Analysis: Methods, Systems, Applications and Science of Work Measurement in Organizations*, 437–62. Series in Applied Psychology. New York, NY, US: Routledge/Taylor & Francis Group.

Articles

Chevalier, Roger. 2010. "Gap Analysis Revisited." *Performance Improvement* 49 (7): 5–7. https://doi.org/10.1002/pfi.20160.

Evans, Bill. 2004. "Closing the Performance Gap: Five Simple Tools Can Help." *Handbook of Business Strategy* 5 (1): 191–94. https://doi.org/10.1108/10775730410493496.

Henri, Jean-François. 2004. "Performance Measurement and Organizational Effectiveness: Bridging the Gap." *Managerial Finance* 30 (6): 93–123. https://doi.org/10.1108/03074350410769137.

Kellogg, Marion S. 1967. "Closing the Performance Gap; Results-Centered Employee Development."

Middlebrook, Rebecca Helminen, and Angela Palchesko. 2004. "Turning Research Into Results: A Guide to Selecting the Right Performance Solutions: [1]." *Performance Improvement* 43 (1): 44–46.

Smith, Ken G, Edwin A Locke, and David Barry. 1990. "Goal Setting, Planning, and Organizational Performance: An Experimental Simulation." *Organizational Behavior and Human Decision Processes* 46 (1): 118–34. https://doi.org/10.1016/0749-5978(90)90025-5.

Zairi, Mohamed. 1992. "The Art of Benchmarking: Using Customer Feedback to Establish a Performance Gap." *Total Quality Management* 3 (2): 177–88. https://doi.org/10.1080/09544129200000019.

Webpages

"Aligning Employee Performance to Organization Performance and MVVs | Kent State University." n.d. Accessed September 15, 2021. www.kent.edu/yourtrainingpartner/aligning-employee-performance-organization-performance-and-mvvs.

"Coaching Training for Managers." n.d. Performance Consultants. Accessed September 15, 2021. www.performanceconsultants.com/coaching-training-managers.

"Conducting a Gap Analysis to Improve Team Performance." 2018. Ready Training Online. April 4, 2018. https://readytrainingonline.com/articles/gap-analysis/.

"Dealing With Poor Performance: Is It Lack of Ability or Low Motivation?" n.d. Accessed September 15, 2021. www.mindtools.com/pages/article/newTMM_80.htm.

F., Claudia. n.d. "Aligning Group Goals With Individual Performance Goals— Video & Lesson Transcript." Study.Com. Accessed September 15, 2021. https://study.com/academy/lesson/aligning-group-goals-with-individual-performance-goals.html.

Heathfield, Susan M. n.d. "Use 6 Steps to Coach Employees to Help Improve Their Work Performance." The Balance Careers. Accessed September 15, 2021. www.thebalancecareers.com/use-coaching-to-improve-employee-performance-1918083.

Nebes, Bill. 2016. "The Eight-Step Approach To Closing Performance Gaps." Nebes Consulting. November 21, 2016. http://nebesconsulting.com/uncategorized-en/eight-step-approach-closing-performance-gaps/

SHRM. 2021. "How to Address the Skills Gap." SHRM. July 2, 2021. www.shrm.org/resourcesandtools/tools-and-samples/how-to-guides/pages/how-to-address-the-skills-gap.aspx.

Verlinden, Neelie. 2021. "10 Tips for Effective Employee Performance Coaching." *AIHR* (blog). May 14, 2021. www.aihr.com/blog/performance-coaching/.

Video

Babson College. 2014. *Managing Poor Performers: What You Need To Know Before Taking Action*. www.youtube.com/watch?v=bBBdx_oVcs4.

Cmoeinc. 2014. *Performance Coach: The One Minute Employee Coaching Session*. www.youtube.com/watch?v=7loZQmqL1AI.

Leadership and Talent Development. 2019. *2020 Performance Management: Feedback and Coaching*. www.youtube.com/watch?v=IjFppQL4fiQ.

TEDx Talks. 2013. *Cleverly Connected: Sir John Whitmore at TEDxCheltenham*. www.youtube.com/watch?v=6fld90L6Hkw.

Blogs to follow

"Problem Solving Critical Thinking Reasoning Decision Making Planning." n.d. Accessed September 16, 2021. www.basicknowledge101.com/subjects/problemsolving.html.

Cherry, Kendra. n.d. "Effective Problem-Solving Strategies and Common Obstacles." Verywell Mind. Accessed September 16, 2021. www.verywellmind.com/problem-solving-2795008.

Githens, Greg. 2012. "Identify Performance Gaps and Get Out of the Rut of Solutioneering." *Leading Strategic Initiatives* (blog). July 17, 2012. https://leadingstrategicinitiatives.com/2012/07/17/identify-performance-gaps-and-get-out-of-the-rut-of-solutioneering/.

Problem Solving—3 Basic Steps. (n.d.). Retrieved September 16, 2021, from https://blog.thinkreliability.com/problem-solving-three-basic-steps

Webinars

Nickols, F. (2020). *Thirteen problem-solving models*. 1–28. www.uapb.edu/sites/www/Uploads/Assessment/webinar/session%203/13%20Problem%20Solving%20Models.pdf

Chapter 12—Step 9

What Are the Consequences of Closing the Gap?

Books

Cook, Marshall. 1998. *Effective Coaching*. McGraw Hill Professional.

Fournies, Ferdinand, and Ferdinand F. Fournies. 1999. *Coaching for Improved Work Performance, Revised Edition*. 3rd edition. New York: McGraw-Hill Education.

Hargrove, Robert. 1999. *Masterful Coaching Fieldbook*. San Francisco: Pfeiffer.

Articles

Bachkirova, Tatiana, and Carmelina Lawton Smith. n.d. "From Competencies to Capabilities in the Assessment and Accreditation of Coaches." *International Journal of Evidence Based Coaching and Mentoring* 13 (2): 123–40. https://doi.org/10.3316/informit.386228358655701.

Chase, Melissa A., Cathy D. Lirgg, and Deborah L. Feltz. n.d. "The Sporr Psychologist, 1997,11,8–23 O 1997 Human Kinetics Publishers, Inc. Do Coaches' Efficacy Expectations for Their Teams Predict Team Performance?"

Funke, Joachim, Andreas Fischer, and Daniel V. Holt. 2018. "Competencies for Complexity: Problem Solving in the Twenty-First Century." In *Assessment and Teaching of 21st Century Skills*, edited by Esther Care, Patrick Griffin, and Mark Wilson, 41–53. Educational Assessment in an Information Age. Cham: Springer International Publishing. https://doi.org/10.1007/978-3-319-65368-6_3.

Hagemann, Norbert, Bernd Strauss, and Dirk Büsch. 2008. "The Complex Problem-Solving Competence of Team Coaches." *Psychology of Sport and Exercise* 9 (3): 301–17. https://doi.org/10.1016/j.psychsport.2007.04.003.

Jones, Rebecca J., Stephen A. Woods, and Yves R. F. Guillaume. 2016. "The Effectiveness of Workplace Coaching: A Meta-Analysis of Learning and Performance Outcomes from Coaching." *Journal of Occupational and Organizational Psychology* 89 (2): 249–77. https://doi.org/10.1111/joop.12119.

Webpages

"Finally, We Are Shifting from Performance Management, to Coaching for Performance." 2017. *Mark Hocknell | Customer Value. Business Results* (blog). October 10, 2017. www.markhocknell.com/finally-shifting-performance-management-c4p/.

Lawson, Karen. n.d. "How to Coach for Improved Performance | Edward Lowe Foundation." Accessed September 15, 2021. http://edwardlowe.org/how-to-coach-for-improved-performance-2/.

McNamara, Carter. n.d. "Problem Solving and Decision Making (Solving Problems and Making Decisions)." Accessed September 16, 2021. https://managemen-thelp.org/personalproductivity/problem-solving.htm.

Blogs

Dumitrascu, Sorin. 2021. "Skills and Competencies for Problem Solving." Medium. August 29, 2021. https://medium.datadriveninvestor.com/skills-and-competencies-for-problem-solving-419fe3db7876.

Harris, Robert. 2002. "Problem Solving Techniques." January 5, 2002. www.virtualsalt.com/problem-solving-techniques/.

Malouff, John. 2018. "Over Fifty Problem-Solving Strategies Explained." Using Psychology. October 15, 2018. https://blog.une.edu.au/usingpsychology/2018/10/15/over-fifty-problem-solving-strategies-explained/.

Chapter 13—Step 10

What Are the Damages of Inaction?

Books

Argyris, Chris, David A. Schon, Donald A. Schön, and David Schon. 1996.
Organizational Learning II: Theory, Method, and Practice. Addison-Wesley
Publishing Company.

Dattner, Ben. 2011. *Credit and Blame at Work.* www.simonandschuster.com/
books/Credit-and-Blame-at-Work/Ben-Dattner/9781439169575.

Weick, Karl, and Kathleen Sutcliffe. 2007. "Managing the Unexpected Resilient
Performance in an Age of Uncertainty" 8 (January).

Weiss, Antonio E. 2012. *Key Business Solutions: Essential Problem-Solving Tools and
Techniques That Every Manager Needs to Know.* Pearson UK.

Articles

Metcalfe, Mike, and Elizabeth Hobson. 2001. "Concern Solving Not Problem
Solving," 9.

Webpages

Berglas, Steven. 2002. "The Very Real Dangers of Executive Coaching." *Harvard
Business Review*, June 1, 2002. https://hbr.org/2002/06/the-very-real-dangers-
of-executive-coaching.

Sandahl, Phillip. 2021. "How To Turn Team Conflict Into Trust, Resilience &
Results." 2021. https://teamcoachinginternational.com/team-conflict-trust-
resilience-results/.

Weick, Karl, and Kathleen Sutcliffe. 2007. "Managing the Unexpected Resilient
Performance in an Age of Uncertainty" 8 (January).

Video

Debbie Narver. 2016. *Lesson 1: Strategic Problem Solving and Decision Making for
Managers.* www.youtube.com/watch?v=JsWrrfqgIBc.

Life Coach Training Institute. 2021. *Overthinking & Inaction —Week 3: How to Get
out of Your OWN Way.* www.youtube.com/watch?v=1EfndfdiZw4.

TED-Ed. 2016. *5 Tips to Improve Your Critical Thinking—Samantha Agoos.* www.
youtube.com/watch?v=dItUGF8GdTw.

Blogs to Follow

Lipovski, Terry. 2020. "The Problem with Problem Solving Managers | LinkedIn."
2020. www.linkedin.com/pulse/problem-solving-managers-terry-lipovski/.

"Why Is Problem Solving Important for Leaders." 2018. Florida Tech Online. December 28, 2018. www.floridatechonline.com/blog/business/problem-solving-a-critical-leadership-skill/.

Problem solving. (n.d.). Retrieved September 16, 2021, from www.icaew.com/learning-and-development/job-essential-skills/employability-skills/problem-solving

Tools

Miller, Kelly. 2021. "12 Essential Coaching Skills for Managers and Leaders." 2021. https://positivepsychology.com/coaching-skills-managers-leaders/.

Chapter 14—Step 11

How to Implement the Solution?

Books

Clutterbuck, David, and David Megginson. 2005. *Making Coaching Work: Creating a Coaching Culture*. CIPD Publishing.

King, Serge Kahili. 1985. *Mastering Your Hidden Self: A Guide to the Huna Way*. 1st edition. Wheaton, Ill., U.S.A: Quest Books.

Nieuwerburgh, Christian van. 2015. *Coaching in Professional Contexts*. SAGE.

Articles

Pulakos, Elaine D., Rose A. Mueller-Hanson, Ryan S. O'Leary, and Michael Meyrowitz M. n.d. "Building a High Performance Culture: A Fresh Look at Performance Management," 44. www.shrm.org/hr-today/trends-and-forecasting/special-reports-and-expert-views/Documents/High-Performance-Culture.pdf

Webpages

"Creating A Coaching Culture, Transformational Leadership Culture—Performance Consultants." n.d. Accessed October 15, 2021. www.performanceconsultants.com/coaching-culture.

"How to Instill a Coaching Culture." n.d. CCL. Accessed September 16, 2021. www.ccl.org/articles/leading-effectively-articles/instill-coaching-culture/.

Video

"What Is a Coaching Leadership Style?" 2020. Performance Consultants. November 10, 2020. www.performanceconsultants.com/what-is-a-coaching-leadership-style.

GreggU. 2020. *Performance Management Leadership.* www.youtube.com/watch?v=EFcCEYj9c80.

Webinar/Podcast

"How HR Can Establish a Successful Coaching Culture." 2020. *AIHR* (blog). September 16, 2020. www.aihr.com/blog/coaching-culture/.
Jody Holland Training & Speaking. 2017. *Employee Performance Coaching Tips!* www.youtube.com/watch?v=p7cp6heXUlU.

Blogs

Reid, Joanne, and Victoria Hubbell. n.d. "Creating A Performance Culture." *Ivey Business Journal* (blog). Accessed October 15, 2021. https://iveybusinessjournal.com/publication/creating-a-performance-culture/.

Tools

Assess Your Leadership, Coaching, and Culture Status: www.clemmergroup.com/online-quizzes/assess-leadership-coaching-culture/
Building a coaching culture: https://cdn2.hubspot.net/hubfs/3064731/Building%20a%20Coaching%20Culture%20-%20Building%20Champions.pdf?__hssc=32416289.1.1580855845385&__hstc=32416289.5e6021c8a77d31870025897a4bfe7c69.1556636235610.1580756487443.1580855845385.476&__hsfp=1312878196&hsCtaTracking=7514023f-d272–4bf8-b274–8e36e27c60ba%7C1d1d0424-ec7b-40ff-9bb9–962f87b8842a&utm_content=115228995&utm_medium=social&utm_source=facebook&hss_channel=fbp-157493064283
Coaching Culture Assessment. Developing 7 Core Competencies that Create a Sustainable Competitive Advantage: https://craneconsulting.com/docs/crane_sample_report.pdf
Supervisor's Guide to Performance Management, Coaching & Corrective Action: www.depts.ttu.edu/hr/documents/CorrectiveActionWebsiteResources.pdf

Chapter 15—Step 12

How to Evaluate the Successful Implementation?

Books

Hernez-Broome, Gina, and Lisa A. Boyce. 2010. *Advancing Executive Coaching: Setting the Course for Successful Leadership Coaching.* John Wiley & Sons.
Killion, Joellen, Chris Bryan, and Heather Clifton. 2020. *Coaching Matters, 2nd Edition. Learning Forward.* Learning Forward.

Rynne, Steven B., Clifford J. Mallett, and Martin W. O. Rabjohns. 2016. "High Performance Coaching: Demands and Development." In *The Psychology of Sports Coaching*. Routledge.

Articles

Ely, Katherine, Lisa A. Boyce, Johnathan K. Nelson, Stephen J. Zaccaro, Gina Hernez-Broome, and Wynne Whyman. 2010. "Evaluating Leadership Coaching: A Review and Integrated Framework." *The Leadership Quarterly*, Leadership Development Evaluation, 21 (4): 585–99. https://doi.org/10.1016/j.leaqua.2010.06.003.
Ibarra, Herminia, and Anne Scoular. 2019. "The Leader as Coach." *Harvard Business Review*, November 1, 2019. https://hbr.org/2019/11/the-leader-as-coach.
MacLean, Joanne C., and Packianathan Chelladurai. 1995. "Dimensions of Coaching Performance: Development of a Scale." *Journal of Sport Management* 9 (2): 194–207. https://doi.org/10.1123/jsm.9.2.194.

Webpages

"Managing and Evaluating Performance | Supervisory Development Program." n.d. Accessed September 16, 2021. https://supervising.umn.edu/managing-and-evaluating-performance.
Inc, Gallup. 2020. "Get Progress Reviews Right during Covid-19 (and After)." Gallup.Com. May 6, 2020. www.gallup.com/workplace/309965/progress-reviews-right-during-covid.aspx.
Performance Consultants Sir John Whitmore. 2018. *Sir John Interview Reflections-GROW #9*. www.youtube.com/watch?v=n2JAApll2X0.

Video

LearningFromWOeRK. 2011. *Evaluating Coaching Sessions*. www.youtube.com/watch?v=X5ii4kJa4zw.

Blogs

"Coach | Conducting an Effective Performance Review." n.d. *Performance Culture* (blog). Accessed September 16, 2021. https://performanceculture.com/conducting-effective-performance-review-part-ii-coach/.

Tools

Coaching Performance Evaluation Form. Human Resources & Academic Personnel Services: https://forms.humboldt.edu/sites/default/files/coaching_performance_evaluation_updated_9-5-17_pdf.pdf

Performance Management—Coaching as Conversation: https://hr.fas.harvard.edu/files/fas-hr/files/pm_conversations_2.26.18.pdf

Chapter 16

How Effective Are You?

Books

Evered, Roger D., and James C. Selman. 1989. "Coaching and the Art of Management." *Organizational Dynamics* 18 (2): 16–32. https://doi.org/10.1016/0090-2616(89)90040-5.

Peterson, David B., and Kurt Kraiger. 2003. "A Practical Guide to Evaluating Coaching: Translating State-of-the-Art Techniques to the Real World." In *The Human Resources Program-Evaluation Handbook*, by Jack Edwards, John Scott, and Nambury Raju, 262–82. 2455 Teller Road, Thousand Oaks California 91320 United States of America: SAGE Publications, Inc. https://doi.org/10.4135/9781412986199.n13.

Article

Berg, Morten Emil, and Jan Terje Karlsen. 2016. "A Study of Coaching Leadership Style Practice in Projects." *Management Research Review* 39 (9): 1122–42. https://doi.org/10.1108/MRR-07-2015-0157.

Cannon, Mark, Susan Douglas, and Deborah Butler. 2021. "Developing Coaching Mindset and Skills." *Management Teaching Review*, April, 23792981211006876. https://doi.org/10.1177/23792981211006877.

De Meuse, Kenneth P., Guangrong Dai, and Robert J. Lee. 2009. "Evaluating the Effectiveness of Executive Coaching: Beyond ROI?" *Coaching: An International Journal of Theory, Research and Practice* 2 (2): 117–34. https://doi.org/10.1080/17521880902882413.

Emil Berg, Morten, and Jan Terje Karlsen. 2012. "An Evaluation of Management Training and Coaching." *Journal of Workplace Learning* 24 (3): 177–99. https://doi.org/10.1108/13665621211209267.

Murphy, Mandy. 2020. "A Coaching Mindset within OH—Release Your Inner 'Enabler.'" *Occupational Health & Wellbeing* 72 (6): 22–25.

Stenzel, Beth K. n.d. "Correlation between Teacher Mindset and Perceptions Regarding Coaching, Feedback, and Improved Instructional Practice." Ed.D., United States—Nebraska: University of Nebraska at Omaha. Accessed October 15, 2021. www.proquest.com/docview/1750083416/abstract/F7FE7847622344C8PQ/1.

Webpage

"38 Best Coaching Tools and Assessments To Apply With Clients." 2019. PositivePsychology.Com. June 26, 2019. https://positivepsychology.com/coaching-tools-examples-assessments/.

"How to See If Your Employee Coaching Is Having a Positive Effect." n.d. Accessed October 15, 2021. www.goalplan.com/blog/how-to-see-if-your-employee-coaching-is-having-a-positive-effect.

kpetkovic. 2019. "Six Fundamentals to Adopt a Coaching Mindset." Assured Strategy. May 7, 2019. www.assuredstrategy.com/six-fundamentals-to-adopt-a-coaching-mindset/.

Schuy, Marcel. 2018. "Coaching Evaluation—Deliver Highly Effective Coaching with These 2 Steps." *CleverMemo—The Best Coaching Software for Sustainable Results and a Thriving Business* (blog). January 27, 2018. https://clevermemo.com/blog/en/effective-coaching-evaluation/.

Stange, Jocelyn. n.d. "Coaching to Engage: 12 Rules to Effective, Ongoing Employee Coaching." Accessed October 15, 2021. www.quantumworkplace.com/future-of-work/12-rules-for-effective-employee-coaching.

Wilson, Graham. n.d. "What Are Coaching Styles and How Do They Work?" Accessed October 15, 2021. www.thesuccessfactory.co.uk/blog/coaching-styles-and-how-they-work.

Video

Leadership Lessons. 2019. *A Practical Method to Effective Coaching.* www.youtube.com/watch?v=628AGudM17s.

LearningFromWOeRK. 2011. *Evaluating Coaching Sessions.* www.youtube.com/watch?v=X5ii4kJa4zw.

Proctor Gallagher Institute. 2015. *What Is Effective Success Coaching?* www.youtube.com/watch?v=DUrBSpImifo.

TEDx Talks. 2014. *Building Your Inner Coach | Brett Ledbetter | TEDxGatewayArch.* www.youtube.com/watch?v=q7a5TIzOmeQ.

TEDx Talks. 2018. *Leaders Who Coach Are Creating Better Workplaces, and so Can You. | Saba Imru-Mathieu | TEDxLausanne.* www.youtube.com/watch?v=ypKRJ0IPP-k.

The Coaching Institute. 2021. *Foundations Of Coaching Success | TCI Courses.* www.youtube.com/watch?v=iHLFauEK1_U.

The Coaching Institute. 2021. *What Leadership Looks Like In The New Norm | The Coaching Institute.* www.youtube.com/watch?v=bAysORfwy8k.

Blogs

"How to Coach Teammates: A Key Responsibility of Effective Leaders." 2018. Wavelength by Asana. January 23, 2018. https://wavelength.asana.com/coaching-workplace-why-examples/.

"Planning with Solution-Focused Coaching." 2021. Erickson Coaching International. July 30, 2021. https://erickson.edu/planning-solution-focused-coaching.

"What It Takes to Coach Your People." n.d. CCL. Accessed October 15, 2021. www.ccl.org/articles/leading-effectively-articles/what-it-takes-to-coach-your-people/.

"Why Workplace Coaching and Why Now?" n.d. Integral. Accessed October 15, 2021. www.integral.global/blog/why-workplace-coaching-and-why-now.

LLC, Julia Stewart Coaching & Training. n.d. "Coaching Blog." Accessed October 15, 2021. www.schoolofcoachingmastery.com/coaching-blog.

Tools

"Practical Methods for Evaluating Coaching | Institute for Employment Studies (IES)." n.d. Practical Methods for Evaluating Coaching | Institute for Employment Studies (IES). Accessed October 15, 2021. www.employment-studies.co.uk/resource/practical-methods-evaluating-coaching.

Index

Note: Page numbers in *italics* indicate a figure and page numbers in **bold** indicate a table.

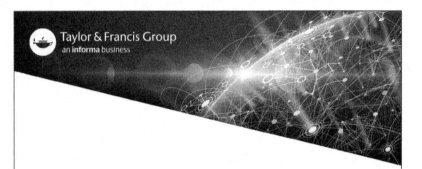

Printed in the United States
by Baker & Taylor Publisher Services